THE IN\

The Invisible Hand offers a radical departure from the conventional wisdom of economists and economic historians, by showing that 'factor markets' and the economies dominated by them—the market economies—are not modern, but have existed at various times in the past. They rise, stagnate, and decline; and consist of very different combinations of institutions embedded in very different societies. These market economies create flexibility and high mobility in the exchange of land, labour, and capital, and initially they generate economic growth, although they also build on existing social structures, as well as existing exchange and allocation systems. The dynamism that results from the rise of factor markets leads to the rise of new market elites who accumulate land and capital, and use wage labour extensively to make their wealth profitable. In the long term, this creates social polarization and a decline of average welfare. As these new elites gradually translate their economic wealth into political leverage, it also creates institutional sclerosis, and finally makes these markets stagnate or decline again.

This process is analysed across the three major, pre-industrial examples of successful market economies in western Eurasia: Iraq in the early Middle Ages, Italy in the high Middle Ages, and the Low Countries in the late Middle Ages and the early modern period, and then parallels drawn to England and the United States in the modern period. These areas successively saw a rapid rise of factor markets and the associated dynamism, followed by stagnation, which enables an in-depth investigation of the causes and results of this process.

Bas van Bavel is distinguished professor of Transitions of Economy and Society at Utrecht University. He acts as the academic director of the Utrecht University interdisciplinary priority area—Institutions for Open Societies—and he is a member of the Royal Dutch Academy of Sciences. His research activities focus on reconstructing, analysing, and explaining economic development and social change, emphasizing long-term transitions and regional diversity, and using comparative analysis—both over time and across regions—as the main tool. More specifically, he aims to find out why some societal arrangements are successful in generating wealth, equity and resilience, and others not, and what drives the formation of these arrangements.

The Invisible Hand?

*How Market Economies have Emerged
and Declined since AD 500*

BAS VAN BAVEL

OXFORD

UNIVERSITY PRESS

OXFORD
UNIVERSITY PRESS

Great Clarendon Street, Oxford, OX2 6DP,
United Kingdom

Oxford University Press is a department of the University of Oxford.
It furthers the University's objective of excellence in research, scholarship,
and education by publishing worldwide. Oxford is a registered trade mark of
Oxford University Press in the UK and in certain other countries

Published in the United States of America by Oxford University Press
198 Madison Avenue, New York, NY 10016, United States of America

British Library Cataloguing in Publication Data
Data available

Library of Congress Cataloging in Publication Data
Data available

ISBN 978–0–19–960813–3 (Hbk.)
ISBN 978–0–19–882045–1 (Pbk.)

Preface

There are very many people to thank. In writing this book, I greatly enjoyed the company of a host of young scholars who have worked with me at Utrecht University in recent years: Michele Campopiano, Daniel Curtis, Jessica Dijkman, Erika Kuijpers, Auke Rijpma, and Jaco Zuijderduijn. They made possible great progress in this field, by way of their empirical research and skilful analyses of early market economies. Their research, and my own, was financed through a grant by the Netherlands Organisation for Scientific Research (NWO) for the project 'Economic growth and stagnation in the pre-industrial era: Iraq, Italy and the Low Countries, 600–1700', undertaken in Utrecht in the period 2007–12. The results of the project also inspired me to formulate the hypotheses to be tested in the European Research Council (ERC)-sponsored project 'Coordinating for life' (ERC advanced grant no. 339647). I gratefully acknowledge the financial support offered by the NWO and ERC.

Bram van Besouw, Rutger Claassen, Oscar Gelderblom, Maarten Prak, and Jan Luiten van Zanden read and extensively commented on a first draft of the manuscript. The comments of these Utrecht colleagues greatly helped me to improve the book. Through his careful and critical reading of an early version of the text, Maarten Prak forced me to rephrase and clarify many passages of the book. A more mature version of the book was read by Sheilagh Ogilvie (Cambridge) who shared her thoughts on many of these issues with me, in part through critical comments, and thus stimulated me to do another round of revisions. Clearly, writing this book was only possible thanks to their help.

Other colleagues, too, have read parts of the book. Michael Morony (University of California, Los Angeles), Jessica Dijkman (Utrecht University), and Maaike van Berkel (University of Amsterdam) helped me with their comments on Chapter 2, Daniel Curtis (Utrecht University) and Guido Alfani (Bocconi) with their comments on Chapter 3, Michele Campopiano (York) with his suggestions for Chapters 2 and 3, Geoff Hodgson (Hertfordshire) with his comments on the introduction and conclusion, and Lewis Evans, with his MA thesis (Utrecht University), and Ann Coenen (Utrecht University) through finding complementary information, especially for Chapter 5. Also, I thank Jedidja Inkelaar and Ilona Luijsterburg for their technical editing of the references, Auke Rijpma for helping with the graph, and Annelies Tukker for her help with the maps and references. I should also very much like to thank Eileen Power, who corrected the English of the manuscript and shielded me from evil sins against the rules of the English language.

Parts of this book were tried out as papers, presented at the Royal Dutch Academy of Sciences workshop on Ancient Markets (Amsterdam, 2011), the Histomat reading group (Amsterdam, 2011), and the Economic History core seminar in Cambridge (2011), and at meetings at Hong Kong University of Science and Technology (2012), at CASS Economics in Beijing (2012), at Ghent University (2013), and at University of California, Los Angeles (2014), at the WINIR conference in Greenwich (2014) and the Economic and Social History seminar at Utrecht University (2014). I would like to thank all participants of these meetings for their comments. More indirectly, I benefited from, and greatly enjoyed, the discussions and brainstorms with my colleagues involved in the interdisciplinary research programme 'Institutions for Open Societies', at Utrecht University. Together with the department of Economic and Social History, this research programme has offered me the lively and high-quality setting that has helped me to write this book.

This academic community forms a main part of my life. At times, but not often, I hope, this is to the detriment of my own little community, at home. This is a good moment to let you know, Astrid, Sarah, and Noortje, that I consider being with you the most precious thing in my life.

Contents

List of Figures, Maps, and Tables

1

Introduction
Markets in Economics and History

1.1. MARKETS, THEIR HISTORIOGRAPHY, AND SOME MAJOR ASSUMPTIONS

Everything that is necessary for human life is made by combining the three factors of production: land, labour, and capital. Whether and how people have access to resources, to a livelihood, to food, and to wealth is thus critically determined by the way a society organizes the exchange and allocation of land, labour, and capital. This organization of allocation and exchange also shapes social relations, and it provides the main building blocks of social structures. Moreover, the ways in which mankind copes with ecological or climatologic challenges or threats, handles demographic shocks, or develops and employs technological means and thus generates economic growth and wealth are strongly linked to the organization of exchange and allocation. Resilient response to shocks, capacity for innovation, and the maintenance or increase of welfare levels demand a flexible and efficient exchange, and an equally efficient allocation of resources associated with this exchange. The organization of the exchange and allocation of land, labour, and capital thus forms the bedrock of any society.

Exchange can be organized in many ways. These include centralized or state redistribution and allocation; ritual exchange; decentralized forms of coercion; quasi-voluntary or mutual exchange within associations, families or kin; exchange by way of the market; and combinations of these systems. Among these exchange systems, the market stands out, on account of the fast mobilization of production factors and flexibility of exchange it enables, and also because of its dominant position in many parts of the present-day world.[1] Especially over the past decades, the role of the market worldwide has expanded prodigiously. The resulting, current dominance of markets is striking not so much with respect to the exchange of output—which in many historical periods and places was carried out through the market—as with respect to the exchange of land, labour, and capital, which in most societies was organized through the other allocation systems mentioned above, including the state and family systems, rather than through the market. Societies that use the market as the dominant system of exchange and allocation,

---

[1] See section 5.3, 239–43.

not only for output, but also for land, labour, and capital—labelled market economies here—are quite rare in history.

This book focuses on these market economies and their institutional arrangement. By investigating selected historical cases of the most thriving market economies, it aims to find patterns in the interaction of market institutions, economic development, and social structures in the very long run. It doing so, it wants to identify and explain the feedback mechanisms between these three elements. The resulting analysis leads to the proposition that the rise and dominance of markets for land, labour, and capital are self-undermining, as these feedback mechanisms result in welfare declining again and in markets losing their quality in facilitating successful and rapid exchange, and contracting again, with the relative or even absolute downfall of the market economy in question. Thus, the book departs radically from the conventional wisdom of economists and economic historians, with its more linear view on the development of market economies.

More specifically, the book will demonstrate that factor markets—the markets for land, lease, labour, and capital[2]—and the economies in which these markets form the dominant allocation system—the market economies—are not modern creations, but existed at various times in the past. It will also show that these market economies are not always rising, but after some time they stagnate and decline again, and that they are not uniform, but consist of very different combinations of institutions embedded in very different societies.[3] The book argues that factor markets create dynamism and flexibility in the exchange of land, labour, and capital, but perhaps less economic growth than assumed in economic literature; instead they also build on the growth already generated by these societies in the previous period, when the societies in question had used different exchange and allocation systems, including the state, kin, associations, and corporations, often in combination with output markets. The book will highlight how the subsequent rise of factor markets, and the economic opportunities and imperatives they bring, further pushes up economic growth, but also enables a few groups to privatize and accumulate financial assets, natural resources including land, and services. In the longer run this induces social polarization and a reduction in welfare for ordinary people. Also, the process engenders growing political inequality, as new market elites translate their economic wealth into political leverage, and it leads to institutional sclerosis. As the organization of factor markets thus becomes less favourable, and more skewed towards the interests of the market elites, economic growth stagnates or even turns into decline. Also, people start to retreat from the market, and factor markets shrivel again. The process thus ends in the decline of the market economy.

---

[2] Strictly speaking, these markets may concern stocks and flows. Transacted can be property rights vested in stocks, such as land, slaves (or labour power), and capital goods, and in the flows of 'services' from these stocks, as with labour that is hired, the use of land that is leased, and capital that is borrowed. Typically, when factor markets are discussed, and also in this book, this concerns the land market (sale of the stock), the lease market (the use of land for a specific period), the labour market (the hiring of labour for a specific period), and the credit market (the borrowing of capital for a specific period).

[3] For an inventory of these institutions, see section 1.3, 25–6.

This book reconstructs and analyses this process for the three major, pre-industrial examples of successful market economies in western Eurasia: Iraq in the early Middle Ages, Italy in the high Middle Ages, and the Low Countries in the late Middle Ages and the early modern period. These cases are pre-eminent examples of market economies and they each experienced a rapid rise of factor markets, more than anywhere else at their time, which allows for an in-depth investigation of the causes and results of this process.[4] Before turning to the three cases, I will look at prevailing academic ideas on the long-run development of markets, and see how they have become modified and refined, but also reinforced by recent studies. Despite a great deal of recent research, the historiography of markets, both in economics and history, remains dominated by much received wisdom. I will first discuss the major assumptions, of which I accept some—but not very many, as will become clear later on when questioning them in this book.

Some Assumptions and Received Wisdom

Generally, and also in this book, markets are defined as systems for exchanging and allocating resources by way of monetary transactions, with prices primarily determined by the forces of supply and demand, and with mulitiple, competing buyers and sellers who are mainly geared towards maximizing their own utility or profit. A major general assumption—mostly implicit—is that markets defined in this way are a modern phenomenon. This modernity would hold even more for market economies, that is, economies which use the market as their main coordination and allocation system, and not only for output, but also for the production factors: land, labour, and capital, with the owners of these factors of production being able to trade these in the market.

Markets for output are generally considered to have been present to some extent in many of the more advanced pre-industrial societies, from Antiquity onwards, with ancient Babylonia, Egypt, Italy, and China and their thriving commodity markets as examples.[5] Only much later in time, in the modern era, it is assumed, did some societies start to use the market as the *main* system for the exchange and allocation of goods. Economies which organize not only the exchange of output, but also that of land, labour, and capital through the market are much rarer and are even more explicitly deemed modern. The last economies are assumed to have grown out of older, more stagnant ones, which had more traditional mechanisms for the exchange and the allocation of land, labour, and capital, and this shift is thought to have helped these societies develop and become wealthy.

Surprisingly, economists have paid only little attention to the question of what markets actually are and how they are structured.[6] Many economists in the twentieth century have tended to see these markets as homogenous entities, a kind of abstract playing field where supply and demand meet. Assuming the homogeneity

---

[4] For the selection of these cases, see section 1.4, 35–7.

[5] Braudel, *Les jeux de l'échange*, 93–110. See for these ancient economies and their markets also section 1.4, 31–3.

[6] North, 'Markets and other allocation systems', 710.

of markets is perhaps partly stimulated by the desire to develop general economic laws that are not historically specific.[7] Scholars who have rather highlighted the institutional underpinnings of these markets, including the critical role of property rights, often also have essentialized the market. Removing obstructions, including monopolies, information asymmetries, and other elements that create market imperfections, would make the market conform more closely to this essence and allow it to continuously adapt to changing circumstances and to cater for changing needs. It is thus often assumed that markets, if unobstructed, offer flexibility, and a rapid mobilization and efficient allocation of production factors, and that they create ongoing economic growth and a rise of welfare.

The latter assumption has a long pedigree, and is often ascribed to Adam Smith in particular.[8] It has regained strength and respectability in the 1980s and 1990s, in an interaction of academic scholarship and trends in politics and society. In academia, alongside a growing interest in information asymmetries, moral hazard, principal-agent problems, externalities, and social networks, there was a strong current of economists who saw unfettered, or unobstructed markets as the most secure way to rising welfare, a view found with Robert Barro, Thomas Sowell, and many other influential scholars. Also, there was the prominent role of the Chicago School of Economics and its outstanding (neo-classical) scholars, including Milton Friedman and several other Nobel Prize laureates, with their work that breathes a firm belief in the welfare-enhancing role of free markets.[9] In politics and society, this belief gained perhaps even more prominence, with the rise of Thatcherism and the adoption and propagation of laissez-faire policies by the World Trade Organization, the International Monetary Fund, and the World Bank. Economic developments seemed to endorse this belief. It was widely assumed that deregulation and the opening up of markets enabled the Western economies to escape from the economic stagnation of the 1970s.[10] Alternative views did exist, of course, but the idea of free, perfect markets, deregulation and privatization as the most secure road to growth and welfare was perhaps shared more widely than ever before.

Equally widely accepted, again perhaps more in politics and general discourse than in academic economics, became the link between markets and political and individual freedom. The underlying assumption is that the economic freedom to act within free markets on the one hand and political and legal freedom on the other hand will, or should, mutually reinforce each other. This idea was pioneered by Friedrich Hayek and his influential *The Road to Serfdom* (1944), where he argues how state planning and government coercion, and the associated reduction of free markets, go hand in hand with tyranny and lack of personal freedom.[11] These ideas were elaborated by Milton Friedman, who states that in the nineteenth and early

---

[7] Hodgson, 'Markets', 252 and 258–60.

[8] Friedman, *Capitalism and freedom*, 133. For the nuances on this assumption made by Adam Smith himself, see section 1.3, 21–2.

[9] Van Horn and Mirowski, 'The rise of the Chicago School'.

[10] Cohen, ' "Economic freedom" ', 2–6. See for these economic developments, and how this assumption can be questioned, also section 5.3, 240–5.

[11] Hayek, *The road to serfdom*.

twentieth centuries 'political freedom clearly came along with the free market and the development of capitalist institutions' and that—although it is not a sufficient condition—'capitalism is a necessary condition for political freedom'.[12] According to Friedman, the market is able to offer coordination without coercion, it provides economic freedom, permits a wide diversity and prevents the concentration of power. In the 1980s, these ideas were enthusiastically embraced by neo-liberal thinkers and policy makers.

Since the 1990s some of these assumptions have come to be criticized, however, or at least refined. There has been a growing trend in the field of economic sociology, sparked off by Mark Granovetter, which stresses that there are no 'free', abstract markets where rational, atomized actors with perfect information operate, contrary to the assumption of many neo-classical economists. Rather, he argues, any market is embedded in society and there are always social relations, rules, and hence power disparities at play.[13] Further, there was the revival of institutionalist thinking in economics, as expressed most clearly in the growing influence of the New Institutional Economics, and the works by Douglass North in particular, which made an impact in the field of economics and subsequently in economic history.[14] The resulting studies have highlighted how markets are a web of formal institutions (e.g. property rights, contracting rules) and informal institutions (norms, customs), that is, as a complex and varying set of rules of the game of exchange, and not a uniform, almost abstract playing field where supply and demand directly meet.[15] Thus, there is not a single, universal type of market but many different types of markets, depending on their institutional make-up. The specific arrangement of their particular institutions lends each market its own individual characteristics and its effects, which can be either positive or negative.

The idea that markets are intrinsically flexible and adaptive has also been qualified more strongly in recent years. It is clear that market institutions can become frozen and sometimes do not adapt to changing economic, technological, or ecological circumstances and requirements, even in cases where their inflexibility damages growth, or where changing trade flows, waning success in international competition, or ecological challenges would require institutional adaptation. The concept of institutional sclerosis, as put forward by, for instance, Mancur Olson, who stressed the role of specific interest groups in paralysing institutional change,[16] or more generally the notion that institutional adaptability can be lacking, has found fairly broad acceptance in academia, also in relation to market institutions.

---

[12] Friedman, *Capitalism and freedom*, 9–10 (where these citations are taken from) and 13–15. For the possibility that the spread of markets contributed to the emergence of representative states and liberal culture: Bowles, 'Liberal society', 72.

[13] Granovetter, 'Economic action and social structure'; Fligstein and Dauter, 'The sociology of markets'.

[14] Hodgson, 'Markets', 260–1, for the institutionalist revival.

[15] North, *Institutions*; Williamson, 'The new institutional economics'. See for a discussion of the formal institutions, section 1.3, 25–6.

[16] Olson, *The rise and decline*, 36–74, esp. 53–8 and 69–73. North, Wallis, and Weingast, *Violence and social orders*, 140–2, are much more positive about interest groups, as these can counterbalance each other and thus uphold open access markets.

Further, the popular but problematic notion that institutions develop more or less spontaneously because they provide a good answer to economic or ecological needs, is questioned now. This notion suggests that efficient institutions—'efficient' being defined as contributing most, in a given set of circumstances, to the welfare of society—will gradually, more or less automatically prevail over less efficient alternatives or, as a result of competition between societies, weed out the inefficient ones.[17] Unfortunately, as has become clearer over the past years, the reality is different. Many societies see institutions that had been beneficial in the past, but that are now becoming suboptimal, being protected by the social groups that benefit from them. Or societies end up with obviously inefficient institutions, as with privileges or monopolies, simply because powerful groups or individuals create and sustain institutional arrangements that support their own interests, or protect their own investments, if necessary at the expense of aggregate welfare. A more credible way to account for the development of institutions thus is the 'social conflict view': the notion that institutions are the effect of a confrontation of various social groups.[18] This view implies that the institutions in place are not automatically the most efficient ones for society at large, and are not easily adapted when economic, technological, or ecological circumstances change; they instead best suit the interests of the group or groups in power.

Also, in recent years more people—both inside and outside academia—have come to question the welfare-enhancing effect of markets again. One argument they bring forward is the seeming inability of markets to benefit all parties involved in market exchange, as can be seen most conspicuously in many developing countries. Although it is clear that market exchange is not a zero-sum game, and it will drive up economic growth through specialization, division of labour, and the necessity of ongoing investments, the fruits of growth can be distributed very unevenly and may even make one of the parties involved worse off than before this exchange started.[19] An example of the detrimental effect of market exchange is the production, purchase, and export of food crops from countries whose own people are desperately in need of food but unable to pay for it with the wages they receive in the labour market. In some cases, these food crops are bought and transported over great distances in order to be used as fodder for cattle in the wealthy importing countries. When peasants in developing countries lose their direct access to land and the means of production, and become reliant on markets for food, land, and wage labour, they can actually become more dependent and even more vulnerable than they would have been in a peasant society with limited market influence, and markets can well result in draining food from areas where it is most needed.[20] Other critics of the market point to the economic crises and problems in financial

---

[17] As in the tradition of Demsetz, 'Toward a theory', a notion also found in the earliest works by Douglass North.

[18] This point is made more generally in the literature on political economy, and was forcefully made again by Ogilvie, '"Whatever is, is right"?'. See also Ogilvie and Carus, 'Institutions and economic growth', 470–3.

[19] Essentially one of the points made by Marx. See Clarke, 'Marx and the market'.

[20] Vanhaute, 'From famine to food crisis'. For the negative role markets may play in famine, using the example of the Bengal famine of 1943: Sen, *Poverty and famines*.

markets—and hold that these are at least in part the result of the fact that such markets have been allowed to operate more freely in recent decades and their functioning has been permitted to become isolated from democratic control and regulation. Again other critics, including welfare economists such as Robin Hahnel, development economists and ecological economists, but also established economists such as Joseph Stiglitz and Paul Krugman, point us to the negative social and ecological effects associated with market competition.[21]

These criticisms are not shared by all, however. The latter one is especially contentious, since many neo-classical and other economists would hold that the ecological and social problems are not the intrinsic result of markets but rather of their malfunctioning because of obstructions, interference by governments, influence exerted by special interest groups, or flaws in the current market frameworks. Correcting these flaws, and having markets function more freely, would solve these problems; a position held by Douglass North, and also by Deirdre McCloskey, who argues that problems are not the result of having too much market but rather of insufficient access of people to markets.[22] More generally, despite the growing interest in the institutional organization of markets and the possible problems associated with market competition, the assumptions that factor markets are modern, help dynamism, and stimulate economic growth still stand and are widely held; not only by neo-classical and neo-institutional economists but also by many neo-Marxists,[23] who see them as at least instrumental or perhaps crucial in helping traditional, feudal societies to escape from stagnation and to develop their productive forces.

Their ideas go back to the founding fathers of these intellectual and ideological currents: Karl Marx and Adam Smith. Marx offered the first comprehensive analysis of capitalism, which could be defined as a society in which there is a pronounced division between property-less wage earners and entrepreneurs who privately own the means of production, and thus have a way to appropriate the surplus, and in which both producers and entrepreneurs are dependent on the market.[24] Through the market, in the words of Marx, each of them became subjected to the anonymous power of capital.[25] At the same time, and despite its negative social effects, under capitalism—and enabled by the dynamism of capitalism and the effects of competitive markets that force capital owners to keep on investing—productive forces would grow and help to pave the way for the transition to a socialist and later communist society. Although Marx later suggested that alternative paths to communism might also exist, such as a direct step from peasant communal ownership in Russia to a communist society, he mostly saw capitalism as a necessary stage,

---

[21] See for instance Stiglitz, *Freefall*.

[22] North, Wallis, and Weingast, *Violence and social orders*, 129–33; McCloskey, *The bourgeois virtues*, 14 and 32.

[23] See Rigby, *Marxism and history*, 9, 41, and 44–8; below, 7–8.

[24] This is the definition suggested by Hilton, 'Capitalism'; and van Bavel, 'The transition in the Low Countries'. In order to avoid the connotations the term 'capitalism' carries—either positive or negative ones—the term will not be often used in this book. See for this also section 6.2, 270–4.

[25] Clarke, 'Marx and the market'.

following upon earlier stages in history, most notably the stage of feudalism.[26] Also, he expected other countries to follow in the footsteps of the capitalist ones.

In this respect, Karl Marx's ideas were akin to those of Adam Smith, who used a four-stage framework (which comprises hunting, pastoralist, agricultural, and commercial societies) with each society having its own form of justice, property, and social and political organization, growing in size and complexity.[27] Although Smith did not sketch history as a fully unilinear development towards commercial society, and neither did he see commercial society and especially its most developed form—labelled by him as natural liberty—as an inevitable end stage, most later commentators have interpreted his story as one of progression, with commercial society forming the peak.[28] Willingly or not, both thinkers have thus imbued us with a unilinear view of history and the development of markets.

Although Marx was less interested in the market per se than in the system of social relations as a whole, he and Smith also shared their positive appraisal of the opportunities offered by markets and market economies to enhance productivity greatly. Market competition, and the associated necessity of innovation and enlargement of scale, was exactly the reason that Marx attributed to capitalism the unique ability to develop a society's productive power.[29] His ideas, and those of Adam Smith, continue to influence our thinking about markets, if only through the many who have been inspired by them. As we will see in the following section, their assumptions about the modernity and positive effects of factor markets on development and economic growth at first sight seem to be endorsed by much of the historical research of recent years. On closer inspection, however, and based on a more profound reading of today's research, those assumptions may turn out not to be warranted, as the remainder of this book will show.

1.2. ON THE MODERNITY OF MARKETS: THE VERDICT OF RECENT HISTORICAL RESEARCH

Most research into the history of markets, some of it conducted by sociologists, archaeologists, and economists but mainly by economic and social historians, essentially treats markets for land, labour, and capital as a modern phenomenon. The main result of recent, empirical studies is that the dating of the rise of factor markets is pushed somewhat further back in time. Polanyi in the 1940s and 1950s, in his influential works, had still asserted that comprehensive factor markets were a revolutionary innovation of the nineteenth-century English economy. Profit-maximizing behaviour, and the supply and demand price mechanism in fully open

---

[26] This led to teleological reasoning, found with many marxist thinkers, including Cohen, *Karl Marx's theory*. See Rigby, *Marxism and history*, 106.

[27] Smith, *Wealth of nations*, 689–94, also 606–7 and 687–8. See also Kim, 'Adam Smith's theory of economic development'.

[28] The nuances made by Adam Smith are highlighted by Alvey, 'Adam Smith's three strikes'.

[29] Marx and Engels, *Economic and philosophic manuscripts*, 210–16 (the communist manifesto); Clarke, 'Marx and the market'.

markets for land and labour, were not found earlier, according to him, and neither did they occur later, as in the twentieth century redistribution became more important again, now by way of the growing welfare state.[30]

In stating this, and proposing a very strict definition of the market, Polanyi offered a very useful warning against those who would too easily project our present ideas about modern, open, and free-functioning markets onto the markets of the past. In doing so, however, Polanyi seems to have overestimated the extent to which nineteenth-century markets and those of the present-day market economies conform to abstract ideas about freely functioning markets. It is clear, for instance, that no land market, past or present, is ever fully open and free, since land markets are always heavily influenced by tradition, familial relations, and personal attachment, and also by state legislation.[31] Even the United States, as the champion of free markets, has its factor markets at present clearly influenced and regulated by the public authorities, by way of legislation, agricultural subsidies, monetary regimes, zoning laws, and government regulation of financial markets, for instance.

Douglass North, in grappling with Polanyi's ideas, has done a lot to break the supposed dichotomy between market and non-market elements in the organization of exchange, and show how they interact, complement each other, and often are integrated within the market framework, with a crucial role for the state, especially in enforcement.[32] As North observes, if we followed the strict definition of Polanyi, we would find markets nowhere at all, not even at present. Not only do non-market elements play a fundamental role in the functioning of all markets, but market economies are also capable of accommodating and integrating non-market forms of exchange and allocation, and even turn elements seemingly inimical to the market into a vital part of their functioning, as was the case in eighteenth- and early nineteenth-century Britain and the United States with its slave labour and forms of indentured labour, used for instance on plantations, which were developed by entrepreneurs who used land markets and financial markets, and used complementary wage labour, and which produced for the commodity market.[33]

Moreover, market exchange often presupposes social relations between the exchanging parties. Human actions within markets are seldom atomized and solely driven by the pursuit of self-interest, in contrast to what is assumed by some economists, but mostly they are embedded in social relations, if only by way of implicit trust or morality, or in order to overcome agency problems and information asymmetries.[34] This is an insight elaborated by a number of historians, especially for

---

[30] Polanyi, *The Great Transformation*, 81–9, 106–7, and passim; Polanyi and Pearson, *The livelihood of man*, 6–11, 43, and 276 (on ancient Greece). Finley, *The ancient economy*, 22–4, 33–4, and 158–60 equally argued against the existence of factor markets and market forces in antiquity.

[31] Van Bavel and Hoppenbrouwers, 'Landholding and land transfer'.

[32] North, *Institutions*. See also North, 'Markets and other allocation systems'; Didry and Vincensini, 'Beyond the market-institutions dichotomy'.

[33] See Steinfeld, *The invention of free labor*, passim. For the integration of slaves in a capitalist market system Bhandari, 'Slavery and wage labor', and for the Roman era Temin, 'The labor market'.

[34] Classical statement: Granovetter, 'Economic action and social structure'. See also Fligstein and Dauter, 'The sociology of markets'.

markets characterized by insecurity, agency problems, or multiple-part transactions, as in long-distance trade or the credit market.[35] Ethnic ties or common beliefs and normative systems can be vital in this, as argued by Avner Greif for the Maghribi traders, the group of Jewish merchants that held a firm position in the Mediterranean trade in the tenth to twelfth century.[36] Likewise, associations and guilds can provide a framework for, and generate, social networks that sustain transactions. And even if exchange is sometimes virtually impersonal, as in some modern markets, still notions of fairness, honesty, reputation, and trust play a role, bargaining between people may take place, and all kinds of social mechanisms are at work. Formal and informal institutions complement each other within the market, and informal constraints that stem from personal and social relationships play a crucial role in guaranteeing the quality of market exchange and buttress the more formal rules.[37]

These formal rules are often formed and upheld by a government, public authority, or third party, especially where they concern the protection of property rights, the enforcement of contracts, and the reduction of insecurity in markets. To a large extent, state enforcement and formal institutions can form an alternative for social constraints, enabling exchange to become more impersonal. Although social networks and social control, or guilds and trade associations, can also offer some of this oversight, protection, and third-party enforcement of contract, the role of government and public authorities in market systems is often crucial, or even inevitable.[38] Also, in labour and capital markets, some internal control and surveillance of one party over another party involved remain necessary.[39] Through this role of public authorities, and likewise through the role of guilds, associations, and networks, and through the necessity of internal control, the social context comes in, that is, the role and the weight of the social groups that are able (or unable) to influence or dominate governments, associations, and networks.

Even in the modern period, (factor) markets thus are socially and politically embedded, and markets and market economies are never fully free and ruled by the forces of open market competition alone. Instead of assuming that markets are open, this book will question and problematize their openness and investigate how the degree of their inclusiveness and accessibility changed over time and why. The preceding does not mean markets cannot be identified as such. Even though the market—in the approach adopted in this book—may always contain some non-market influences, stemming from state intervention, family relations, or associative arrangements, it is different from other allocation systems because the exchange and allocation of resources is predominantly carried out by way of

[35] Muldrew, 'Interpreting the market'.
[36] Greif, 'Contract enforceability'. Compare, however, the critical notes by Edwards and Ogilvie, 'Contract enforcement'; Ogilvie and Carus, 'Institutions and economic growth', who rather stress formal, legal rules and the role of public authorities.
[37] Nee and Ingram, 'Embeddedness and beyond'.
[38] Fligstein and Dauter, 'The sociology of markets', 113–16.
[39] Bowles and Gintis, 'Contested exchange', 167–9 and 187–8. See more extensively section 1.3, 28–9.

monetary transactions, the prices are primarily determined by the forces of supply and demand, and the competing actors are mainly geared towards their own economic profit or utility. As such, market economies can be fairly clearly demarcated from economies dominated by other exchange and allocation systems. This book will do so, particularly by investigating how the market in some historical societies became the dominant system of exchange and allocation of land, labour, capital, and goods, and how it superseded in these cases the non-market allocation systems, including those offered by the state, kin, associations, or the manorial system.

Recent Studies on the Rise of Factor Markets

Investigations into early market economies have been scarce in the past decades, in part owing to Polanyi's legacy. Not only did he *over*estimate the openness of 'free' markets, but at the same time, and exactly because of his too strict definition of markets, he *under*estimated the role of factor markets in the past, their volume and the mobility in the exchange of production factors they brought.[40] Polanyi's ideas on the absence of 'real' markets for land, labour, and capital in the past were highly influential over the past decades, but they have been nuanced in recent years. Recent economic historical research has highlighted the fact that factor markets actually did exist before the nineteenth century, and has analysed the ways in which they functioned. This attention to the history of factor markets was long overdue. Apart from scattered investigations, especially into the English land market,[41] the rise and development of factor markets has hardly ever been systematically studied and was for a long time a rather neglected topic. Even though all kinds of assumptions were made in the literature, actual empirical research for the earlier periods was scarce.

This changed from the late 1990s onwards, as a stream of studies was published on the rise of markets for land, lease, labour, and capital in late medieval and early modern Western Europe. Again the land market historiographically led the way, with four large volumes containing about a hundred studies on the pre-industrial land markets in Europe appearing within only one decade.[42] In contrast, the pre-industrial lease markets remain relatively underinvestigated, but still saw the publication of one volume on leasing in the pre-industrial North Sea area.[43] Similarly underrepresented remain the labour markets, apart from individual studies on England and the Low Countries.[44] The pre-industrial financial markets have become much better investigated, with an influential monograph on credit in early modern Paris, various studies on markets for public and private debts in the late

[40] McCloskey, 'Other things equal'. For ancient economies: Feinman and Garraty, 'Preindustrial markets'; Silver, 'Karl Polanyi and markets'.
[41] See for instance Harvey, *The peasant land market*.
[42] Feller and Wickham, *Marché de la terre*; Cavaciocchi, *Il mercato*; van Bavel and Hoppenbrouwers, *Landholding and land transfer*; Béaur and Schofield, *Property rights*.
[43] Van Bavel and Schofield, *The development of leasehold*.
[44] For instance van Bavel, 'Rural wage labour'; van Bavel, 'The transition in the Low Countries'. See also Whittle, *The development of agrarian capitalism*, 225–304.

medieval and early modern period and a volume with papers on credit in the rural economy,[45] all published in recent years.

These recent studies, with their focus on (north)western Europe in the late medieval and early modern period, have yielded a number of insights. First, it is now clear that factor markets in many regions at this time were already large, not only in the towns but also in the countryside. These studies have broken, for instance, the pre-existing idea that private capital markets were an innovation of the eighteenth century; their rise started in the late Middle Ages.[46] Also, it is clear now that most of the agricultural land already in the late Middle Ages was regularly exchanged in the land market, with annual turnover rates at 1–3 per cent, which are not dissimilar to modern rates.[47] Moreover, large shares of the land were also leased out in competitive lease markets. In many regions, and especially along the southern shores of the North Sea, in the sixteenth century half to three-quarters of the land was leased out. Also, in the Low Countries a substantial proportion of rural labour was performed for wages; in the sixteenth century this was between a quarter and half of all labour, with peaks of up to 60 per cent.[48] The towns probably had similar shares of wage labour—defined as economically dependent but legally free contractual labour performed for an employer for payment of a wage. At that point, in several parts of the Low Countries, most of the land, labour, capital, and commodities in these economies was exchanged and allocated through competitive markets. The market had become the dominant allocation system there.

Second, recent studies show that these markets were dynamic, fairly flexible, and responded to changes in supply or demand. The functioning of the price mechanism had long been investigated for late medieval and early modern grain markets, and these studies have yielded important insights into the growing correlation of prices and integration of these markets especially in northwestern Europe.[49] The price mechanism is now also shown to have worked in markets for land, lease, labour, and capital. An example is the lease market in sixteenth-century Holland, which quickly responded to the population growth and increasing demand for land by massive rises of lease prices, with nominal prices rising fourfold between 1520 and 1570.[50] The labour market all over Western Europe showed a sharp rise in wages in the late fourteenth century, as a result of the Black Death and the resulting scarcity of labourers. Nominal wages in Flanders doubled between 1349 and 1390, while they rose by half in England and Italy.[51] Likewise, wages declined

---

[45] Hoffman, Postel-Vinay, and Rosenthal, *Priceless markets*; Schofield and Lambrecht, *Credit and the rural economy*. For a short historiographic discussion Zuijderduijn, *Medieval capital markets*, 5–13 and 249–68. For early modern Germany Ogilvie, Küpker, and Maegraith, 'Household debt'.

[46] Zuijderduijn, *Medieval capital markets*, 183–99 and 227–41.

[47] Van Bavel and Hoppenbrouwers, 'Landholding and land transfer', 28–31. For leasing: van Bavel, 'The emergence and growth', esp. 189–95.

[48] Van Bavel, 'Rural wage labour'.

[49] Tits-Dieuaide, *La formation*; Persson, *Grain markets in Europe*; Jacks, 'Market integration'.

[50] Kuys and Schoenmakers, *Landpachten in Holland*.

[51] Malanima, 'Wages, productivity', 158 and 165; Munro, 'Wage-stickiness', 211–12, 243, and 255, who stresses the roles of inflation and institutional factors.

in the sixteenth century as a result of the population growth. Equally sensitive was the capital market, exemplified by the robust decline in interest rates following the Black Death and the associated changes in the ratio between people and capital.[52]

Compared to the output markets, however, the integration of these factor markets was generally less, and responses to shifts in supply or demand slower, especially owing to differences in the institutional layout of these markets and the greater influence of non-market elements and non-economic considerations within them. This is observed especially in the land market, with familial relations, customary rules, community regulation, government legislation, and lordly influence forming major elements in the exchange of land and the functioning of this market.[53] The same applies to the labour market, which was often interspersed with forms of dependency or customary rules, resulting in 'wage-stickiness', for instance.[54] To repeat, however, this is not fundamentally different from factor markets today, since these likewise contain all kinds of non-market elements that stem from non-market considerations, as most notably those installed by the state.

The insight that the formal and informal rules of exchange and behaviour—the institutions—shape markets, has led to many of these recent studies stressing the importance of the exact institutional arrangement of these markets for their functioning, and highlighting the changes in this arrangement over time. This emphasis links up with the rising popularity of the New Institutional Economics, providing a lot of the theoretical background against which the same studies were framed. Also linking up with the New Institutional Economics and its generally optimistic outlook on the progress of historical development, many of these studies show how non-market elements were reduced over time and allowed factor markets to function more openly. Most researchers would stress that this was not a uniform and unilinear development, but rather one with regional nuances and temporal ups and downs. Still, the same researchers often focus more on the rise of these markets than on their stagnation or decline, and generally suggest that in northwestern Europe this protracted process led to secure and open markets there at an early stage, that is, in the late medieval and early modern period, thus still contributing to a unilinear picture, with northwestern Europe leading the way.

These studies have even further sharpened the contrast with the picture sketched for other parts of the world. Studies of the exchange of land, labour, and capital outside Europe are much scarcer, and they stress instead the absence of factor markets in the late medieval and early modern period. They argue that the markets for labour and land remained especially weak and small almost all over the globe, up to the nineteenth century. This applies to areas such as India and Southeast Asia, Africa and the Ottoman empire, but also to highly developed societies such as

[52] Epstein, *Freedom and growth*, 55–62.
[53] Van Bavel, 'The land market in the North Sea area'.
[54] Munro, 'Wage-stickiness', 195–204.

China and Japan.[55] In China, and perhaps even more in Japan, exchange by way of the market grew in importance in the early modern period. Kenneth Pomeranz stresses the favourable institutional framework of factor markets in early modern China.[56] Japan in the eighteenth and nineteenth centuries even possessed well-developed, secure markets for land and capital.[57] However, the pace of this development in East Asia was much slower than in the North Sea area and the size of these factor markets remained modest.

Another observation is that the recent historiography on the topic shows a numerical dominance of English and Dutch researchers, and of studies focusing on these areas surrounding the North Sea. These are also among the few countries for which studies have attempted to assemble the newly gained insights into an overview of all factor markets. Bruce Campbell for England and the present author for the Low Countries, for instance, have done this for the medieval period.[58] These syntheses confirm that a number of areas of England saw the emergence of factor markets in the twelfth and thirteenth centuries, and after some stagnation these developed further in the early modern period. In the northern parts of the Low Countries the rise of factor markets was even more potent. These areas did not possess real factor markets in the early and high Middle Ages, but saw their rise in the thirteenth and fourteenth centuries, and had most of the land and a very substantial share of labour and capital exchanged by way of the market by the six-teenth century.

Recent Historical Literature on the Relation between Markets, Wealth, and Freedom

Although this recent literature pushes back the rise of the prominence of markets and the development of market economies several centuries from the date widely accepted some years ago, the resulting chronology still suggests that factor markets are a relatively modern phenomenon—with other parts of the world bound to follow the leading example of northwest Europe at some point later in history. It also suggests that the rise of factor markets—which as a result of this recent research is now located even more clearly in northwest Europe—must have stimulated development and created wealth, since we are much wealthier now than in the past and also much wealthier than parts of the world where factor markets remained weak and restricted longer, or are still weak and restricted.

The latter impression, that is, the relationship between the rise of markets and growing wealth, seems to be underpinned by the reconstructions of GDP per capita,

---

[55] Pamuk, 'Changes in factor markets'; van Bavel, De Moor, and van Zanden, 'Factor markets', and the contributions to this issue by Tirthankar Roy (on India), Gareth Austin (Africa), and Osamu Saito (Japan).

[56] Pomeranz, *The great divergence*, 69–82; Pomeranz, 'Land markets'. More negative is Huang, *The peasant family*, 202–11 and 214–16.

[57] Saito, 'Land, labour and market forces'.

[58] Campbell, 'Factor markets'; van Bavel, 'The organization and rise'; van Bavel, 'The transition in the Low Countries'. See also sections 4.2, 154–70, and 5.1, 209–11.

most obviously those by Angus Maddison.[59] Even though Maddison discredited the old, Malthusian view, which had assumed that before the modern period societies were unable to generate economic growth and were stuck just above subsistence level, in a Malthusian trap, his survey for the different parts of the globe over the period from the first millennium to the present still shows low levels and a modest growth of GDP per capita before the modern era. Maddison thus offers a powerful, compelling picture of how wealth growth took place especially in the last two centuries and how this was concentrated in the Western world, where it was unilinear.

More specifically, Maddison's figures show how societies in the pre-industrial period experienced low levels of income per capita, just above subsistence level, that is at $400 per annum, where the bare subsistence level is typically set. Around 1300, GDP per capita in Western Europe, according to Maddison's estimates, was still barely above this level, at about $600, slowly rising further to $800 around 1500, $1,000 around 1700, and $1,200 around 1820, in a unilinear process of growth.[60] At that point, still according to Maddison, GDP per capita there was already twice as high as the levels reached in Eastern Europe, Latin America, and Asia, and three times as high as those in Africa. Within Western Europe, by far the highest levels were reached in the United Kingdom and the Netherlands, the cores of market development. Growth in Western Europe further accelerated from 1820 onwards, from about $1,200 to about $3,500 on the eve of the First World War, with the differences with the other parts of the globe having become even larger. The per capita income rise in Western Europe would thus have taken place in exactly the same period as factor markets in the traditional literature were thought to have developed.

In recent years, however, not only has the dating of the growth of factor markets in Western Europe been revised, locating it a few centuries earlier, but also Maddison's chronology of wealth growth has come under revision. The start of this process, too, is now located earlier in time. The latest reconstructions of GDP per capita in the pre-industrial period show much higher levels for the late Middle Ages than assumed by Angus Maddison. Around 1300, most Western European economies according to these latest estimates would seem instead to have been at GDP per capita levels of $800, and many of them witnessed quite substantial growth in the following centuries, to levels of $1,000–1,500 in the sixteenth century.[61] The centre and north of Italy, the part of Western Europe where commodity and factor markets developed first and foremost, had reached this high level earliest, by around 1300.[62] Growth took place later, but was even more pronounced, in Holland, the western part of the Netherlands, with its late medieval development

---

[59] Maddison, *The world economy*. For a general critique on using GDP per capita as the sole benchmark of economic success, see section 1.3, 20 and 24–5.

[60] Maddison, *The world economy*, 244–65, esp. 264. The dollars used here, and used throughout this book, are 1990 international dollars.

[61] Broadberry et al., *British economic growth*, table 10.02.

[62] Lo Cascio and Malanima, 'GDP in pre-modern agrarian economies'; Malanima, 'The long decline', esp. 186–8. Note that the estimates are sometimes labeled 'Italy' but in fact mostly relate to the centre and north of Italy only.

Table 1.1. Estimates of GDP per capita in Western Europe and in Holland (1300–1700, in 1990 $), by Angus Maddison ('traditional') and by recent investigators ('revised', by the authors mentioned in notes 61–3)

	1300	1500	1700
Traditional Western Europe (average)	600	800	1,000
Revised Western Europe (average)	800	1,000–1,500	1,200–1,600
Revised Holland	850	1,400	2,600

of thriving markets. Here, the growth of GDP per capita started around 1300, rising from about $800–900 to $1,400–500 around 1500 and no less than $2,400–2,600 around 1600 (see Table 1.1).[63]

These recent calculations push back the start of economic growth in Western Europe by several centuries. They form a welcome revision of earlier estimates, and they result in a fuller and more correct picture of developments. As the development of factor markets in the recent economic historical investigations is now also dated several centuries earlier than assumed before, the new GDP per capita estimates still point to the same causality as the older studies did, and thus the rise of markets and the start of economic growth still seem to coincide.

It seems hard to argue against the logic which links the rise of open and dynamic markets to wealth and productivity. And this is roughly the teleological story which is explicitly told, or at least implicitly suggested, by most of the few economists who discuss long-term economic developments, including David Landes and Douglass North. Actually, in their pioneering book Douglass North and Robert Thomas as long ago as 1973 pointed to the Dutch case and the precocious development of markets there in the period 1500–1700 to demonstrate the value of their institutional approach.[64] They argued that the removal of restrictions imposed by the guilds and the manorial lords, the growing protection of private property, and the emergence of open, efficient markets for commodities, finance, and labour formed the key explanation of the economic success of the Netherlands, the first country to achieve sustained economic growth. A similar story is told in 1997 in the study by Jan de Vries and Ad van der Woude on the economy of the Netherlands in the early modern era.[65] They posited that as early as the sixteenth century its western part, Holland, in particular possessed a highly developed market economy, characterized by a large degree of market freedom, efficient markets, and low transaction costs, resulting in 'modern' economic growth.

Even more optimistic about the effect of dynamic markets, probably overly optimistic, is Graeme Snooks, who claims that in twelfth-century England, and even under the mounting population pressure of the thirteenth century, the growing size and the efficiency of factor markets promoted a more effective allocation of

[63] See broadly van Zanden and van Leeuwen, 'Persistent but not consistent'. The underlying figures were kindly provided by Bas van Leeuwen, 4 February 2013.

[64] North and Thomas, *The rise of the western world*, 132–45. See also North, *Structure and change*, 152–4; Landes, *The wealth and poverty*, 42–4, 59, and 442–58.

[65] De Vries and van der Woude, *The first modern economy*, 159–65.

resources, which in its turn enabled a simultaneous growth of population numbers, technological innovation, and real GDP per capita.[66] A not dissimilar story, but for the early modern period instead, is told by the neo-Marxist Robert Brenner, who links the transition of the English rural economy, the rise of agrarian capitalism, and the working of competitive lease markets to the subsequent growth of agrarian surpluses, the Industrial Revolution, and the associated rises in labour productivity.[67] According to Brenner, loss of the means of subsistence and direct access to surpluses, which makes all actors fully dependent on commodity and factor markets, is necessary to have markets perform their favourable work and generate sustained economic growth. On this point, despite differences in other fields, neo-Marxists and neo-Smithians are in broad agreement.

Recent empirical research also seems to confirm the idea that favourable market development and political and personal freedom reinforce each other. This is a point suggested by Jan de Vries and Ad van der Woude, who hinted at the absence of a genuinely feudal past and the weak position of the nobility as the main underlying cause of the rapid growth of open markets in late medieval and early modern Holland. Similarly, the present author has associated the late medieval rise of dynamic land, lease and labour markets around the North Sea, and the varying chronology in this development, to the dissolution of manorialism and other forms of non-economic coercion, and has shown how these reinforced each other in a positive feedback cycle.[68] Market development, increasing freedom, and economic growth seem to have reinforced each other, in a process starting as far back as the Middle Ages.[69]

The idea that open polities and open markets strengthen each other in a positive feedback cycle, resulting in economic growth, is stated in its most general form, and by surveying the whole of history, by Acemoglu and Robinson, and even more clearly by North, Wallis, and Weingast,[70] who make the robust claim that thriving market economies facilitate and sustain the stability of 'open access societies', in several ways. Competitive markets provide for long-run economic prosperity and, therefore, promote the stability of the system, which in its turn provides for open markets. Further, the price mechanism promotes pluralism and civil society, since it signals disturbances and forces governments to act responsibly. Likewise, international competition in open markets removes the possibility that governments will resort to rent-seeking policies and it forces them to offer credible commitments and secure property rights.[71] This is a story that essentially is not very dissimilar from the one told by Friedman a few decades earlier.

---

[66] Snooks, 'The dynamic role of the market', 49–54 and 194–5. See for the criticisms on the work by Snooks section 5.1, 209.

[67] Brenner, 'The agrarian roots'; Brenner, 'Property and progress', 60–1.

[68] Van Bavel, 'The organization and rise'; van Bavel, 'The transition in the Low Countries'. For Holland: de Vries and van der Woude, *The first modern economy*, 159–65.

[69] Van Zanden, *The long road*, 294–9.

[70] Acemoglu and Robinson, *Why nations fail*, esp. 76–7; North, Wallis, and Weingast, *Violence and social orders*, esp. 129–33.

[71] North, Wallis, and Weingast, *Violence and social orders*, esp. 129–32. For the latter argument also: North and Weingast, 'Constitutions and commitment'.

North, Wallis, and Weingast date the rise of these open access societies with their open markets and open polities fairly late, in the nineteenth century, as first Britain and the United States made the decisive steps towards this type of society, but the first moves towards it, according to them, were made in the sixteenth to eighteenth century.[72] In view of the recent investigations cited above, including my own, the start of these developments towards open markets, freedom, and wealth can now be traced even further back in time, to the late Middle Ages. Some of the authors involved warn us that this was not an inevitable movement towards more efficient arrangements. Still, they all have contributed to sketching out a teleological process in which open polities and open markets reinforced each other, a process which is supposed to have started in northwest Europe in the late medieval and early modern period and from there spread across the world. This seems to have become the new orthodoxy in economic history.

1.3. A NEW APPROACH TO MARKETS: THIS BOOK

Summarizing the preceding overview of the historiography, we can see how between the 1940s and the 1970s many influential scholars tended to situate both the rise of markets—especially factor markets—and sustained economic growth in the nineteenth and twentieth centuries, suggesting a strong link between the two. The research of the following, most recent decades has pushed back the rise of factor markets in Western Europe to the late Middle Ages, and at the same time this research has now also located the start of 'modern' economic growth in the late Middle Ages, in Western Europe. As a result, the advent of the two phenomena has been pushed back several centuries. This is to a large extent a justified and necessary correction of the older historiography, but still the notion remains that factor markets are a relatively modern phenomenon and part of a modernization process, with other parts of the world bound to follow the leading example of northwest Europe at some point in history, as optimists would say, or unable to do so because of the obstacles posed by non-European-derived beliefs and values, as pessimists would hold. Whether people adhere to the optimistic or the pessimistic view, they share two deeper, underlying notions. These are: that the rise of factor markets must have stimulated growth and made us—in the West—wealthy, and that the rise of these markets in an interactive process was intimately linked to political and personal freedom.

These notions, which emanate from more abstract, theoretical works and also from recent historical, empirical research, will probably keep their influence in the economic and historical literature for the moment. The field of economics is not likely to change this conception in the coming years, since it deals mainly or even almost exclusively with the modern period, and more specifically with its contemporary part, and can hardly be expected to develop a new view on the pre-modern period. Mainstream economists, when doing empirical research, mostly focus on

---

[72] North, Wallis, and Weingast, *Violence and social orders*, 27 and 69 ff.

short-run analyses. When dealing with long-term economic changes, most economists, apart from a few notable exceptions, resort to abstract, mathematical modelling, with their approach to these long-term changes often being highly abstract and based on theoretical concepts, and much less on their knowledge of historical reality.[73] Also, the drive in economics, and in the social sciences more generally, to find general laws, seems to scare off economists to deal with historical specificity and empirical testing by way of concrete historical cases rather than using history as an illustration of these general laws.[74]

The discipline of history will not be of much help either. At present, most historians choose a descriptive approach to history, often oriented to major military or political events, cultural highlights, or prominent individuals. The more structural approaches to history, which were dominant in the decades after the Second World War, have waned. Social analysis at the macro level has become rare in historical studies, and the will to analyse or reconstruct patterns and to identify underlying causes has also been abandoned, while post-modernism and post-structuralism have become popular.[75] In many respects, history has moved away from the social sciences.

We, therefore, run the risk of ending up for a long time with a picture of markets rising and economies growing, and of these phenomena starting earlier and more intensively than we thought before. Also, there is the risk that we know a lot about crashes and temporary crises, thanks to an extensive literature on contemporary cases, but much less about the possibility that these markets can structurally decline, and these economies enter into long-run stagnation or decline, after these periods of growth. This requires us to ask whether the rise of markets and economic growth are indeed connected, and what the exact chronology and causality are. And is this a one-way development or can market economies and their markets decline again, and how? This book, by looking afresh at historical developments, and analysing them in the very long run, aims to offer new insights on these issues.

The book does not dispute that markets are now more dominant worldwide than ever before, nor that the markets in the past were often influenced more by non-economic elements than nowadays, but it seeks to break with the one-sided or even teleological view which associates dynamic markets—and especially factor markets—with modernity and with modern welfare. Using and combining the insights from recent, empirical research on early market economies,[76] research that was not available to great scholars like Fernand Braudel who worked earlier on these topics, the book will show that factor markets are not exclusively modern, but rather existed in a number of periods throughout history. The same even

---

[73] Hodgson, 'The great crash', 1209–12 and 1217–18, a criticism earlier voiced by diverse scholars such as Milton Friedman (Hodgson, 'The great crash', 1210); Thomas Piketty, *Capital*, 32–3.

[74] Hodgson, 'Markets', 258–9.   [75] Van Bavel, 'History as a laboratory'.

[76] Here, I am indebted to many colleagues, in Utrecht, the Low Countries, and elsewhere in the world, but I would like especially to mention the young scholars who worked with me at Utrecht University in recent years, including Michele Campopiano, Daniel Curtis, Jessica Dijkman, Erika Kuijpers, Auke Rijpma, and Jaco Zuijderduijn. See also the acknowledgements in the Preface.

applies to market economies, that is, economies which to a large extent, or even predominantly used markets to exchange not only goods but also land and labour. Likewise based on the latest empirical research, the book will also show that these markets are not always rising, but after some time they stagnate and decline again. These elements sever the assumed link between markets and modern wealth, and they may form a powerful antidote to teleological assumptions on markets and their beneficial effects.

The book goes a step further by probing an alternative explanation of the formation, functioning, and development of market economies in the long run. This explanation, which again will be tested empirically, combines a number of elements found in the more critical works on markets discussed in the first section. I hypothesize, firstly, that markets create flexibility and mobility in the exchange of land, labour, and capital, but little real growth, apart from the first phase in the rise of these markets. The economic growth they initially bring is mainly the result of the increased flexibility they offer in the exchange of production factors, which enlarges the scope for specialization and division of labour. To some extent, however, the economic growth these markets generate may be merely the result of the commodification of social wealth (such as services produced outside the market, leisure time, social security) that had been created by these societies in the period preceding that of market dynamism, in which they had used other exchange and allocation systems, including communities, associations, and kinship systems. This commodification appears to push up economic growth, because formerly unpriced assets now crop up in calculations of GDP per capita, but this may be at the expense of social welfare and equity.[77] In the longer run, and combined with the effects of market competition, it is hypothesized, this process creates social polarization, especially reflected in a skewed distribution of property. Next, the new market elites, that use the market to accumulate resources and make them profitable, start to convert their economic wealth into political influence or even outright power.

The book further tests the hypothesis that the growing role of the market and the associated social polarization, in wealth and especially in political leverage, subsequently create sclerosis of the institutional organization of exchange and allocation, or even the deterioration of these institutions. This is largely the result of the interference of the ever more dominant social groups which have benefited from the growing market exchange. They tend, it is hypothesized, to freeze and preserve the market institutions which had exerted their beneficial effect on them and had helped them to come to the fore, or even distort these institutions to better suit their interests. Next, the sclerosis and deterioration of market institutions block any necessary adaptations, and this reduces the quality of markets, and finally causes them to stagnate or decline again. Contrary to North and his co-authors, I hypothesize that this process is not a result of the detrimental effect of non-market

---

[77] For this possibility: Stiglitz, Sen, and Fitoussi, *Report*, 12–13, 21, and 85–91. This discrepancy between economic growth and declining social welfare can be observed through the analysis of real wages or average heights. For this and a related criticism on the use of GDP per capita as a yardstick, see this section, 27–8.

forces, but rather the endogenous effect of the forces called forward by the dominant markets themselves and the market elites they created. It is hypothesized that this forms a self-reinforcing process: holders of economic power consolidate their economic and later political domination and acquire formal, legal power as well, which they use to sustain the market institutions that benefit them or develop new institutions that consolidate their dominant position in the markets.[78] Because the now dominant groups increasingly use their revenues to acquire status and political leverage and to obtain means of coercion, and less to make productive investments—for instance in new technology—and they also leave other groups fewer opportunities and means to make these investments themselves, the economy stagnates or even declines. Combined with the social polarization and the negative externalities of market competition, it is hypothesized, this leads to a decrease in average welfare.

An important element in this hypothesis is the link between markets and the social distribution of property and power, an element missing in most neo-classical and neo-institutional analyses of the formation, functioning, and effects of markets. This absence of the social dimension is remarkable, when viewed in the light of the legacy of both Karl Marx and Adam Smith, the two great thinkers who inspired, and still inspire—albeit often indirectly or implicitly, two of the main currents in the interpretation of economic and social change. Obviously, Karl Marx stressed the political economy of markets and their resulting accumulation of capital and social polarization, but the same applies to Adam Smith. The latter is held aloft as the champion of neo-liberal thought by many present-day commentators, but perhaps they would not have done so if they had read his works. His ideas about the functioning and the effects of markets can only be understood when taking into account the social context and the social distribution of property in which he envisaged these markets to function.

Adam Smith argued that accumulation of capital is necessary for production to improve, but he saw this as the result of the accumulation of smaller, individual savings, and he reasoned from a situation typical of the early-modern, pre-industrial world, which was characterized by relatively small-scale, owner-managed production.[79] Even though in his time, the late eighteenth century, the then dominant factor markets in England were already giving rise to new market elites and accumulation, and they would do so even more clearly in the following decades,[80] Adam Smith still envisaged that these markets would be used by independent actors who owned the means of production. Markets, according to him, exerted a positive influence and allowed for specialization and division of labour, but they worked best with individual, small-scale buyers and sellers, who had symmetrical exchange relations and could not individually influence the market, in a situation of atomistic competition.[81] This social context is crucial in understanding his ideas.

---

[78] See Acemoglu, Johnson, and Robinson, 'Institutions as a fundamental cause', 388–96.
[79] Smith, *Wealth of nations*, 14–30.   [80] See section 5.2, 215–18 and 22–3.
[81] For exactly this idea, Adam Smith was criticized by Brenner, 'Property and progress', who sees the growth of productivity only occur if producers are fully market-dependent. See also Clarke, 'Marx and the market', 9 and 11.

Also, Adam Smith, although mostly optimistic about commercial society, discussed the greed and selfishness that might be associated with the growth of commerce and with the increase in the number of merchants and manufacturers, despite their useful role in the economy, and he was concerned about the poverty and inequality that would remain even in a well-functioning, free market economy, which would require the state to step in.[82] This contrasts with the ease with which many of his later adherents exclude any considerations of power and property, and believe that these markets will reinforce a situation of equity, since the effect of the market system in the long run would be relatively egalitarian compared to other systems with their alleged, much higher inequality in income and wealth, while they also assume that monopolies would be negligible in a free market economy, if only individuals are freely allowed to pursue their own interests.[83] These are assumptions which can be questioned, and will be questioned in this book, by looking more closely at the long-term effect of market exchange on the distribution of property and power, and at the effect of changes in the distribution of property and power on the organization of market exchange.

This book is therefore not primarily aimed at investigating the relationship between institutions and economic growth, since this is a much-told story. Especially since the rise of the New Institutional Economics this relationship has been at the forefront of scholarly attention, albeit often more through descriptive stories than explanatory ones. Nor is the book solely aimed at understanding how the social context shapes institutions, since this is also a more familiar topic and perhaps even a fairly self-evident one, albeit less so in conventional economics.[84] This book is about the interaction of institutions, economic development, and social structure—with social structure understood here more specifically as the relation between social groups as based on their ownership of production factors and access to political influence—and it analyses the feedback cycle between these three elements at the macro level. It hypothesizes that this cycle by way of the rise and dominance of dynamic factor markets changes the social fabric and, in its turn, this results in a new, negative institutional framework in which markets and welfare decline again. This is where the book diverges from earlier studies in the sense that where these discuss this interaction, they do so mostly as part of a chain of development leading to a certain final destination, generally of a positive nature, as found with those writers inspired by Adam Smith or Karl Marx, or, more recently, Douglass North and Francis Fukuyama.[85] Perhaps as a result of the Christian, eschatological legacy with which Western thinking is imbued,[86] and strengthened by the solid trust in infinite progress brought by the Enlightenment,

---

[82] Smith, *Wealth of nations*, 668–70, 781–2, and passim. See also Sen, 'Uses and abuses', esp. 262 and 266.

[83] Friedman, *Capitalism and freedom*, 121–36, especially 133, where he invokes Adam Smith's invisible hand, and 161–76.

[84] Ogilvie, '"Whatever is, is right"?' and more generally in political economy.

[85] Fukuyama, *The end of history*; also North, Wallis, and Weingast, *Violence and social orders*, despite their assertion that they do not want to tell a teleological story.

[86] Löwith, *Weltgeschichte und Heilsgeschehen*, 211–22. For notions of a cyclical development: section 6.2, 274–5.

the French Revolution, and the Industrial Revolution, we apparently tend to envisage human development in terms more of linear developments and progression than of cycles. This notion is also firmly embedded in historiography, up to now, by the late nineteenth century school of linear historical thinking.

The tendency to think in terms of unilinear progress is reinforced by technological changes, which seem to pick up ever more speed. Even if we have become more aware of the dangers of new technology and the fact that it cannot be assumed to solve all problems, the growing technology still seems to change and shape human developments, on a progressive path with no return, and making the present fundamentally different from the past. Average wealth in the world, and even more so in the West, has risen dramatically over the past two centuries. GDP per capita and real wages have risen more than tenfold over this period, a rise which is associated with technological innovation, the adoption of new techniques, and the rise of labour productivity resulting from this. At first sight all this reinforces a linear view of history and the notion that technology drives history. Karl Marx, for instance, although his concept of forces of production includes more than technology alone, largely subscribed to this idea, as epitomized by his saying: 'the hand-mill gives you society with the feudal lord...'.[87]

This view of technology as the driver of historical change has been a powerful one, but it has been largely discredited by empirical research. Most researchers in the field would say technology is important, and a vital field of study in itself, but that it does not shape or determine history and the path of human societies. Technologies are not autonomous, but rather are products of society.[88] Moreover, even if the pool of technology available within societies is similar, these societies can be characterized by economic growth or decline, by labour intensification or extensification of production, by social inequality or equality, by different social relations, and by differing levels of welfare, even between neighbouring societies.[89] Technology in itself is not determinative. Rather the reverse holds, that is, the development, choice, and application of technology is to a large extent determined by other, more structural factors embedded in society, as perhaps most clearly by the social and political context and by the formal and informal rules of the game created by people.[90] These factors decide what technology will be developed, how much will be invested in it, and to what ends.

The developmental path of societies is, therefore, not shaped by technology, but rather by human actions, and especially by the rules formed by people and which guide their actions, for instance in developing and employing certain technology, or not, and in making investments, or not, but also in promoting equality, or not, etcetera. This requires us to look more closely at these rules, or institutional arrangements, and the social context in which they are formed. It also requires us to accept the possibility that these social and institutional arrangements do not

---

[87] Bimber, 'Three faces'.
[88] Heilbroner, 'Technological determinism revisited; Mokyr, *The lever of riches*, 151–6.
[89] A demonstration for the medieval Low Countries: van Bavel, *Manors and markets*.
[90] Mokyr, *The lever of riches*, 151–5 and 167–83.

conform to a unilinear development but rather display a cyclical one, even if the form of economic developments and levels of wealth change over time because of technological innovation. This social-institutional cycle may thus play out at ever higher levels of GDP per capita, which in turn may remain at fairly high levels or even slowly increase further during the last, negative phases of the cycle. Economic decline in these last phases thus becomes relative instead of absolute.[91] Still, the underlying social-institutional framework—which is central to this book—may display a cyclical process.

The cyclical nature of the social and institutional development of market economies may also have become obscured by technological innovation in another way. Declining transport costs, more rapid transmission of information, more advanced technology, and growing economic and political connectedness make the relevant areas ever larger and cause a higher degree of interaction between them in their different stages of this cycle. This, too, may buffer decline in one area or obstruct the rise in another, and it may lead to developments becoming more synchronous. Again, this should not distract us from trying to identify the cyclical development underlying these more complex patterns, and especially the interaction between the rise and organization of factor markets, the social distribution of wealth and political influence, and the development of the economy, the interaction that is central to this book.

Elements Investigated in the Book

Following from the preceding, and in order to test the hypotheses formulated above, there are a number of elements to be investigated in the present book, preferably by analysing them for a few relevant cases, that is, for selected market economies that can be tracked and followed in their development over the very long run. What is required for this analysis is, firstly, a quantitative reconstruction of the rise, stagnation, and decline of factor markets for each of these cases. Where possible, we will reconstruct what shares of land, labour, and capital were transferred and allocated through the market compared to other allocation systems and how these shares developed over time. For the Low Countries in the sixteenth century, for instance, it is possible to assess the share of the land leased out in competitive lease markets and the share of labour performed for wages.[92] Annual turnover rates of land in the market may, likewise, form an indicator of the size of the land market. The reaction of prices of land, labour, and capital to changes in supply or demand, and the integration of prices, may also form an indicator of the functioning of factor markets. The number of coins in circulation is a more problematic indicator, since coins can also be used for other purposes, including hoarding, tax payments, and other non-market transfers. Still, the wide availability of small or medium currency denominations, as the petty coins made out of copper or silver, does form an indicator, since these are often used for market transactions

---

[91] I will return to these issues in the conclusion, section 6.3, 284–7.
[92] Sections 4.2, 157–8; and 4.3, 174–5.

and wage and rent payments.[93] They may be taken as an indicator of monetization, and of the importance of output and factor markets, and will be used as such.

Physical market places were less important in factor markets than in output markets, although they did exist. An example is Awn Street in Al-Karkh, the commercial district of Baghdad, where the bankers and money changers in the tenth century assembled around their own markets and bankers' bazaars.[94] Another one is the Amsterdam Bourse, housed in a new, grand building, erected in 1611, where the first stock exchange in permanent session was held. In the labour market, in seventeenth-century England, the hiring fairs formed a main occasion for masters and prospective servants to meet.

Much more important to understand factor markets, however, are the non-physical, institutional underpinnings of these markets. Before discussing these institutions, it is important to note that factor markets also require the absence of constraining institutions connected to other, alternative systems of exchange and allocation. An example is the disappearance of serfdom or other forms of coercion of labour, which would prevent people from being able to enter the labour market. One can also think of the disappearance or weakening of the influence of family, lords, and communities on the transfer of property rights on land, for instance through inheritance laws, systems of periodic redistribution, or restrictions on alienation, which would prevent people from selling their land in the land market.[95] The absence or disappearance of these competing institutions can be taken as an indicator for the opportunities for the rise of factor markets or at least as a necessary precondition for the rise of these markets.

Even more central to the book are the formal institutions that underlie exchange in factor markets themselves. This book will devote ample attention to analysing these institutional arrangements, their quality, and their changes over time. Opportunities to do so are large, since the formal institutions have left many written traces. Only some transactions, where the exchange is very direct and clear without involving agency problems or effects later in time, can be made orally, as most notably sales of products or goods, or labour agreements for a day or a week, paid after the performance of the work. Most transactions or agreements in factor markets, however, require written evidence, or at least the security of the agreement is enhanced by this evidence.

More than output markets, where the transaction can exist of a single exchange of goods for a sum of money, factor markets required written contracts and administration: to prove property rights and transactions, and to administer future obligations, especially because the obligation to make payments or deliver services may stretch far into the future. In the lease market, this gave rise to an extensive body of administrative types: lease contracts for the two parties involved, lease agreements recorded by courts in protocols, lease books in which the landholder administered

---

[93] Lucassen, 'Deep monetisation', 74 and 80–3.
[94] See section 2.3, 75–6. For the following examples section 4.4, 191–2, and 5.1, 216, respectively.
[95] See for an extensive discussion of the weakening of these contraints in the Low Countries section 4.2, 154–6.

the land leased out, and lease accounts or account books which noted the lease sums and payments. Likewise, financial markets gave rise to rent contracts, public or notarial registers with rent transactions, procedures for summary execution, legal arrangements for mortgages and securities, etc.[96] All this generated enormous amounts of written material, produced by the parties involved in the transaction, by notaries, judicial courts, or other public or semi-public bodies. It is no coincidence, therefore, that periods of extensive factor markets are often also the ones that have left most written sources behind, much more so than periods or societies where markets were weak or restricted, and this even applies to market economies very early in history.[97]

These formal institutions, and their changes over time, are central to this book. It is exactly the changes and the different organization of these institutions that are crucial to our analysis. Lease contracts, for instance, can have very different arrangements regarding the length of the lease (one year to decades or lifelong), the termination of the lease (at the end of the contract or with the possibility of premature notice by the landlord), the rules for investment (by the tenant or reimbursed by the landlord), etc. The exact arrangement may be more beneficial for the tenant or for the landlord, and it thus reflects the relationship, or power balance, between the two parties entering into the agreement. This is where, again, the social context enters the analysis.

In the book, for each of the cases, the various institutions underpinning market exchange will be reconstructed and discussed. These more descriptive, qualitative assessments will be complemented, where possible, with more concrete, quantitative indicators of the accessibility, mobility, and flexibility these market arrangements offered. We shall also investigate the economic and social effects of the functioning of these markets on society at large.

In view of the suggested link with the social distribution of power and property, there is also a need for a reconstruction of the distribution of land and capital, and the changes in this distribution over time, and of the control that various social groups were able to exert over offices, legislative bodies, and other forms of authority, both at the time of the emergence of factor markets and during their functioning. We need some idea of which people made up the ruling groups, and whether they benefited from growing factor markets, or even had come to the fore as a result of the growing market exchange, or rather were the old, 'feudal' elites, who had simply retained their position and would have done so irrespective of factor markets emerging or not.

Another requirement for testing the hypotheses formulated above is a precise reconstruction of the chronology of economic growth and decline. This may be done by making use of the most up-to-date estimates of GDP per capita, where available. Even though GDP per capita cannot be considered the sole benchmark of economic performance, let alone of social well-being,[98] it is a clear and widely

---

[96] An overview for late medieval Holland: Zuijderduijn, *Medieval capital markets*, 199–225.

[97] Van Bavel, 'New perspectives on factor markets', 156–7 and 163.

[98] See the comments by Stiglitz, Sen, and Fitoussi, *Report*, 8 and 85–91.

used yardstick for measuring levels of economic activity. When available, which is not always the case for early economies, it will be used here as such. Where possible we will attempt to complement, or contrast, these figures on GDP per capita with indicators of living standards, most notably data on real wages. Future research can perhaps also make use of data on human stature. These are not easy to interpret, and hardly systematically analysed for early periods as yet, but may be used as another proxy for welfare, since average height is determined mainly by the quality of food, housing, health, environmental quality, and leisure time, that is, the main elements of welfare.[99] Especially for periods early in history, for which quantitative, written data needed for calculating GDP per capita or reconstructing real wages are scarce if present at all, they may become useful.

These measures will be used in order to allow for a quantitative assessment of the effects of the rise of factor markets in each of these cases. Clearly, other elements than market developments also affected levels of growth and welfare, including climatic changes and demographic shocks. These will be treated cursorily throughout the book, and only in order to isolate the effect of factor markets, that is, to see how their organization and functioning enabled, or failed to enable, societies to cope better with these demographic and climatic changes and challenges. This requires a sharp chronology, in order to identify causality, and some comparison,[100] and in order to separate the effects of 'exogenous' natural events from the endogenous effects of markets.

This investigation will be undertaken for the macro level. An alternative approach would be to look at the micro level, where the choices and dealings of individuals can be observed and analysed. I do not deny that the 'real' decisions of people with regard to transactions are taken at this micro level, but the analysis of these separate decisions will often be unable to account for their joint effects at the macro level, also because conventional micro economic theory generally does not take issues of power and collective action into account.[101] Moreover, the actions taken by individual actors are influenced, or even determined, by the rules and structures that are developed at the meso and macro levels, and these are mostly treated as a given when focusing on the micro level, while the changes therein are central to the analysis of this book. Accounting for the developments at the macro level by focusing on the micro level would be particularly difficult, or even misleading, when it is assumed that the accumulated effects of all individual decisions on society at large will be as rational and efficient as these individual decisions are for each of the individual actors separately. This is a problem even within the thriving field of the New Institutional Economics, where in recent decades enormous progress has been made in microanalysis and in understanding partial mechanisms, as Oliver Williamson observed, but much less so in the formulation of overarching

[99] Steckel, 'Strategic ideas'. See, however, for critical remarks about selection bias in most samples used Bodenhorn, Guinnane, and Mroz, 'Problems'.

[100] Although the main focus of the book will be more on empirical testing by way of individual cases of market economies than on comparison. See also section 1.4, 29–38.

[101] Bowles, 'Liberal society', 77. See also Bowles and Gintis, 'Contested exchange', 166, where they try to include these issues.

theories on long-run developments at the macro level.[102] For these reasons, I would like to start here by reconstructing and analysing what is actually happening at the macro level, and I will leave the micro level for researchers more versed in microanalysis.[103]

Although at times this book will go into more detail and look at separate trans-actions as an illustration of the larger picture, it focuses on the macro level of societies at large, and it looks at developments in the very long run, leaving out the effects of events or short-run fluctuations. The hypotheses developed here will be tested by investigating the elements mentioned above, and especially the long-run chronology of developments regarding these elements. This chronology will be based not only on intuitive or qualitative assessments, since it would run the risk of being subjective, arbitrary, or even self-fulfilling, but when possible on quantitative indicators. Therefore, I will make full use of the recent reconstruc-tions of long-run developments in the shares of land or labour transacted through market exchange, the levels of wealth inequality, levels of GDP per capita, nominal and real wages, human stature, and urbanization rates,[104] or try to estimate these myself for the cases investigated. In all these issues, reconstruction of the chronology is crucial, since this will enable us to find out how causality worked. The causal links assumed to be present in the hypothesis can be falsified, for instance, when a development assumed to be the cause is found after the explanandum, instead of before.

This test is performed by looking not so much at output markets—as was often done in earlier studies on markets and their effects in the very long run[105]—but especially at *factor* markets. Whereas output markets are almost universal in his-tory, and thrived in many places and times,[106] factor markets were rarer, since many other, feasible ways of exchanging and allocating land, labour, and capital exist, including those offered by the state, family and kin, and horizontal associations. Also, factor markets arguably are much more intriguing than output markets. They do not deal with inanimate goods, but directly affect each person's labour power and their most valuable assets, their land and capital. Land is not just a commodity but, especially in agrarian societies, the main source of status, power, continuity, and subsistence, a role in part taken over in industrial societies by capital and cap-ital goods. As a result, the rules regarding the exchange of land, labour, and capital are often much more elaborate and influenced or even dictated by values, norms, and traditions than those regarding goods.

But there are more reasons that make factor markets more relevant than output markets in order to understand the economic and social changes in market economies. The market exchange of labour and capital possesses complexities and information

---

[102] Williamson, 'The new institutional economics', 595–6 and 611.

[103] A framework for such a microanalysis could be Bowles and Gintis, 'Contested exchange'.

[104] For reasons of comparison, I will calculate urbanization rates not by looking at the settlements legally defined as towns (since these definitions vary hugely per society and era), but at settlements with more than 10,000 inhabitants (or another minimum number when indicated) that fulfilled urban functions and predominantly had a non-agricultural population.

[105] An example: Persson, *Grain markets in Europe*.

[106] Braudel, *Les jeux de l'échange*, 93–110 ('Partout des marchés et des boutiques').

asymmetries that are less frequently found in market exchange of output, also because transactions involving labour or capital require an ongoing, repeated interaction of the parties involved that cannot be fully determined beforehand and will only be completed at some point in the future, in contrast to the sale of a commodity, which may be a one-time sale.[107] This interaction creates insecurity, and requires a more elaborate institutional arrangement, with a potentially large role for informal institutions or for a government or another third party to develop and uphold the relevant institutions. Also, some elements in the transaction of labour and capital cannot be enforced from the outside by a third party, or be precluded by a contract, because of the complexity and the difficulty of monitoring them, but need internal control by the parties involved by way of surveillance, sanctions, forms or control or incentives.[108] This brings power relations into the equation, while transactions in the output market can be anonymous and independent of personal relations. In combination, factor markets differ far more in their institutional arrangement, and in the roles played by their social and political context, than output markets do.

The latter brings me to another reason to focus on factor markets, that is, they vary more in their effects than output markets. This is, first, because of their larger variety in institutional make-up and the bigger effect of their varying social and political context, just discussed. Moreover, factor markets allow for much more fundamental changes in society than output markets do. While output markets may allow for some degree of wealth accumulation, especially in the hands of those who are successful in large-scale or long-distance trade, the presence of land (sale and lease), labour and capital markets is required to make accumulated wealth really profitable and to allow for higher degrees of wealth accumulation. This is because the rise of these factor markets is intrinsically linked up with the erosion or abolition of non-market restrictions on the accumulation of land and capital, and also because these markets enable the owners to profitably exploit their accumulated wealth, through leasing land out, hiring wage labourers, or lending capital out for interest.[109] Factor markets, therefore, may enable monumental changes, including changes in the distribution of resources and power over social groups, especially when markets become dominant as systems of allocation and exchange. These cases of market economies, and the differences in arrangements, their changes over time, and their long-run effects are central to this book.

1.4. CASES OF MARKET ECONOMIES

Most existing research on market economies focuses on the modern period and on those cases where markets are clearly dominant at present, that is, on Western Europe and the Western offshoots. This easily leads to teleological reasoning and to

---

[107] Bowles and Gintis, 'Contested exchange', 202.
[108] Bowles and Gintis, 'Contested exchange', 167–9 and 187–8.
[109] See more extensively the conclusion in section 6.2, 260–5.

the dominance of a view that history is slowly progressing, despite occasional setbacks, towards an ideal type of market economy. Views like these favour more descriptive approaches and preclude a more systematic analysis of the factors that make market economies rise and decline. This is exactly the analysis I want to make here, by employing the full range of opportunities that history has to offer. To this end, I will start by using the newest literature and the insights it generated in recent years in order to make an inventory of those societies in history in which markets have at some point become the dominant mechanism for the allocation and exchange of land, labour, and capital. In compiling this inventory, I include economies with factor markets that are not fully open, competitive, impersonal, and free, since if we ruled them out, we would find market economies nowhere at all, not even at present, as observed above.[110] Nor do the market economies in this inventory have the market as the sole system of exchange and allocation. Other systems co-exist with the market in all cases, including the modern ones, but the market is the dominant one.

Another caution that is necessary before making this compilation relates to the geographical delimitation of the cases discussed. This book looks at fairly large areas, somewhat similar to present-day countries, which mostly overlap with a single political organization, be it the core of an empire, a set of principalities, or a nation-state. Within these societies, regional differences can exist, in geography, economy, or social organization. These regional differences are highly relevant as a historical phenomenon, and their analysis casts light on the determining factors in the long-run development of economy and society,[111] but here they will be mostly left out of consideration. I will concentrate instead on a larger geographical scale, where these regions interact with each other—often through markets for output, land, labour, and capital—and where they interact with political power, especially at the level of the state. It is exactly at the state level that many of the market institutions are formed and upheld and where, as we will see, the market elites establish their political influence most clearly. Focusing on this geographical scale will thus make it more possible to capture the feedback cycle between market organization, economic development, social structure, and political power that I want to analyse.

Possible Cases of Market Economies

When we want to compile an inventory of early market economies, that is, economies in which the market was the main system of exchange and allocation, we are hampered by the scarcity of sources, especially for periods far back in history. In a number of cases, we can only rely on indications and we can in any case not assess the importance of markets in a quantitative way. Still, the number of qualitative indications we can rely on has grown considerably in recent years, thanks to the progress made

---

[110] See the remarks on Polanyi's approach, which is too strict and—in a way perhaps surprising to Polanyi himself—anachronistic: section 1.2, 8–10.

[111] As such they were the subject of my book, *Manors and markets*.

in this field. Additional research was done for this book and will be extensively presented in the chapters below. Even though the following survey still cannot claim to be exhaustive, we know much more now than only a few decades ago.

A first case to consider as a possible market economy is Iraq, or Babylonia, in the first centuries of the second millennium BC. Babylonia in this period possessed thriving markets for output, but also for land purchases, land rentals, and labour. From at least the middle of the third millennium BC, temples and notables leased out their land for a share of the crop—usually one-seventh or one-eighth—or a fixed amount of silver. In the nineteenth century BC written lease contracts start to appear, with the numbers rising in the eighteenth and seventeenth centuries BC.[112] Also, loans with interest in silver and grain between private parties, or with their involvement, existed in the late third millennium BC, with interest rates of 50 per cent or 33.3 per cent per year, although the volume and competitiveness involved are perhaps not sufficient to label this a real market.[113] Wage labour had become important around the year 2000 BC, and gained further importance in the centuries that followed.[114] In later periods, references to wage labour dwindled again, and hiring labour was often alternated, or became mixed, with corvée labour, dependent labour, or even outright coerced labour. Likewise, the markets in land, lease land, and capital declined again.

The next case is perhaps Iraq in the neo-Babylonian period. The long sixth century BC, which is relatively well documented by thousands of surviving tablets and became well investigated thanks to the recent work by Michael Jursa in particular, showed a strong demographic growth and urbanization, monetization of exchange, and the growth of land and especially labour markets, with an associated rise in cash crop production, regional specialization, and occupational specialization.[115] Another candidate for consideration as an early market economy is the northern part of China during the fourth to second century BC, as the society became market-oriented, combined with first the introduction and later an enormous boom in the production of copper, bronze, and other coins used in market transactions.[116] This part of China became highly monetized, as indicated by an extensive administration of salaries paid in the private sector and by the state, and by evidence of buying and selling on credit.

Another possible case of a market economy is Classical Athens in the fourth century BC. Some scholars have argued that Athens, or the region of Attica as a whole, in this period was characterized by a predominance of monetary transactions in fairly anonymous markets, which had gradually replaced an economy based on social and familial relationships.[117] These markets had developed from the

---

[112] Mauer, *Das Formular der altbabylonischen Bodenpachtverträge*; Leemans, 'The rôle of landlease in Mesopotamia'.

[113] Steinkeller, 'The renting of fields', 141–3.

[114] Silver, 'Karl Polanyi and markets'; van Bavel, 'New perspectives on factor markets'.

[115] Jursa, *Aspects of the economic history*; Jursa, 'Factor markets in Babylonia'.

[116] Scheidel, 'The monetary systems'; Wang, 'Official salaries'.

[117] Cohen, *Athenian economy and society*, 3–8 and 87–90. For the following on bankers: Cohen, *Athenian economy and society*, 14–18, although others have contested this interpretation of the material.

sixth century BC, a process gaining momentum in the subsequent century, as property rights became more defined and written contracts increased in number and were assigned supreme validity, thus offering an institutional framework geared towards facilitating market exchange.[118] Labour markets, especially in the towns, enabled a strong division of labour, while the countryside had its land and lease markets, with the large, institutional landholders mostly leasing out the land in small parcels, with the lease sums paid in coins.[119] Also, owners of smallholdings often hired themselves out for wages to complement their income. More generally, the economy became highly monetized and characterized by specialization. The services sector (trade, transport, and financial services) expanded hugely, with the financial services including business loans, mortgages, financial partnerships, and credit for long-distance trade. As a result of market developments, in the fourth century a new elite of entrepreneurs, bankers, and shipowners had risen, in part replacing the old landowning aristocracy.

Italy from the second century BC to the second century AD may also be considered a market economy. It saw the rise of output and also factor markets. Even though there was widespread use of slavery, Rome had a well-functioning labour market, with the wages of free labour fluctuating, influenced by supply and demand, and organized through clear labour contracts.[120] This period was characterized by rising urbanization and economic growth, with GDP per capita in Roman Italy reaching levels of $1,400, that is, similar to seventeenth-century England.[121]

The next case is Iraq in the early Islamic period, the seventh to tenth century AD.[122] Land sales in this period became easier than before and were widespread, as all kinds of indicators show. Further, leasing and later sharecropping leasing became more important. Most labour was performed within forms of tenancy and through free or semi-free independent labour, while wage labour was also employed. The rural economy in this period was highly monetized and market-oriented, within a system of private landownership. Moreover, and in contrast to common ideas about Muslim restrictions, credit and capital markets started to blossom. Iraq developed highly advanced financial markets and had large numbers of money changers, pawnbrokers, and merchant financiers. The latter employed sophisticated instruments including convertible bills and promissory notes as early as the mid-eighth century. This period of dynamic factor markets lasted to around the turn of the millennium.

It may be that the Lower Yangtse delta in China in the period between c. 1000 and 1400 forms a similar case. Especially in the eleventh and twelfth centuries, during the Song dynasty, as all kinds of restrictions on market activities were

---

[118] Halkos and Kyriazis, 'The Athenian economy', 262–3 and 265–71.

[119] Bresson, *L'économie*, 113–15 and 160–2.

[120] Temin, 'The labor market'. We will eagerly await the results of current research at Ghent University and the VUB in Brussels, by Arjan Zuiderhoek, Koen Verboven, and Paul Erdkamp.

[121] Lo Cascio and Malanima, 'GDP in pre-modern agrarian economies', revising earlier estimates, including those by Angus Maddison. They also use international 1990 dollars.

[122] Extensively discussed in Chapter 2, where the relevant references can be found.

removed, markets flourished, including markets for land.[123] The output of copper coins, used for wage payments and small transactions, and indicating the prevalence of labour and output markets, was larger than in any earlier or later period, at 800 to 1,300 million coins a year.[124] This major coin production—and especially the issue of small coins used in small-scale transactions in labour and output markets—may be regarded as an indicator of deep monetization and the large volume of markets.[125] Also, in the eleventh century, paper money made its appearance, alongside an increasing use of bills and promissory notes, and a proliferation of credit. The Song period was also one of remarkable urban growth, including the rise of smaller market towns, or perhaps even an urban revolution, associated with growing trade and specialization of the economy.[126]

The next case is the first one in which the sources—much more plentiful here than for the earlier cases—enable us to assess the importance of factor markets somewhat more quantitatively. This is the centre and north of Italy in the late Middle Ages.[127] Here, besides the already existing output markets, markets for land, lease, labour, and capital also grew, from the eleventh century. They developed further and grew to dominance in the twelfth and thirteenth centuries. By 1300, for instance, short-term leasing here had become highly important; up to three-quarters of the agricultural land was leased out on fixed or sharecropping leases.

Shortly afterwards, in the thirteenth and fourteenth centuries, a similar rise of factor markets took place in the Low Countries.[128] By the sixteenth century, these markets had become dominant and most of the land and very substantial shares of labour and capital were exchanged by way of the market, especially in the regions along the North Sea. Half to three-quarters of the land there was leased out for short terms in competitive lease markets and between a quarter and half of all labour, with peaks up to 60 per cent, was performed for wages. Also, the great majority of output was produced for the market, and was allocated through the market.

The next, even more familiar case of a market economy is early modern England.[129] After the growth of factor markets in the fifteenth and sixteenth centuries, up to three-quarters of all agricultural land in England around 1600 was leased, while the proportion of wage workers in the total rural population amounted to between a quarter and a third. At that point, large shares or even the majority of the land sales, land tenancies, and labour were allocated through the market, even though many customary and non-market determined elements continued to play a role in these markets. In the seventeenth century, many of the remaining non-economic considerations were removed and replaced by the cash nexus, and England became a full market economy, with very substantial and dynamic markets for land, lease, and labour. Last to emerge was the financial market, in the late seventeenth

[123] Liu, *The Chinese market economy*, chapter 3; Kishimoto, 'Property rights, land, and law'.
[124] Liu, *The Chinese market economy*, section 2.1.
[125] As argued by Lucassen, 'Deep monetisation'.
[126] Elvin, *The pattern*, 117–18, 128–30, 146–50, and 167–78.
[127] Extensively discussed in Chapter 3.
[128] Extensively discussed in Chapter 4.   [129] See section 5.1.

century. At that point, investment capital had become abundant and financial services more advanced, while newly established joint-stock companies offered fresh opportunities for investment and speculation.

Surprisingly, the number of potential market economies does not grow exponentially now we have entered the (early) modern period. Several parts of Western Europe, including France and western Germany, of course, had developed dynamic output markets, where agricultural and industrial products were intensively traded. In factor markets, however, the picture for the early modern period is much more mixed. The share of land leased out through the lease market forms an indication of the importance of factor markets in these two areas, where by far the majority of the population lived in the countryside. For the period around 1900 a comprehensive overview of the importance of leasing is made and this shows that even at the time in Germany only some 10 per cent of the area was held in lease and in France about 40 per cent, while in the coastal areas of the Low Countries and in England these shares were 50–90 per cent.[130] In contrast to the small and weak lease markets, the land markets in some parts of France and western Germany became more open and dynamic, especially in the eighteenth century, as indicated by the annual turnover of land in the market. Figures for regions such as the Beauce in France and Swabia in Germany show turnover rates that are not dissimilar to those found in England and the Low Countries, although other parts (such as the German region around Braunschweig) show very low rates, close to zero, indicating the near-absence of a land market there.[131]

In the early modern period, there were thus many Western European countries that possessed markets in land, lease land, labour, and capital, especially in some pockets of market development. However, outside the Low Countries and England the market clearly was not the *dominant* system for the allocation of land, labour, and capital. We have to wait another century or two to find the next society where factor markets became dominant—the United States. Here, the growth of factor markets can be located particularly in the eighteenth century, with their breakthrough to dominance in the opening decades of the nineteenth century.[132] From then on, the number of market economies starts to grow and multiply, especially in Western Europe, with their proliferation accelerating again in the final decades of the twentieth century and including other parts of the globe too (Table 1.2).

Some of these cases have been identified earlier as examples of pre-industrial 'golden ages', for example by Jack Goldstone, who singled out some of them as economies which witnessed an efflorescence or significant upturn.[133] Indeed, all of the cases listed in Table 1.2 were also the economic leaders of their periods. As we have seen in the succinct overview above, each of these cases reached a level of

---

[130] Van Bavel, 'The emergence and growth', 189–90, using the material collected by Barthel Huppertz in 1939.
[131] Van Bavel and Hoppenbrouwers, 'Landholding and land transfer', table 1 and the references there.
[132] See section 5.2.   [133] Goldstone, 'Efflorescences and economic growth'.

Table 1.2. Certain and possible cases of market economies, with approximate dates of their rise and decline (possible cases indicated with ? or ??)

??Babylonia	Ur III / old-Babylonian period	c. 2100–1600 BC
?Babylonia	neo-Babylonian period	c. 700–300 BC
??Athens	Classical period	c. 600–300 BC
?Italy	Roman period	c. 200 BC–200 AD
Iraq	early Islamic period	c. 600–1000 AD
?Lower Yangtse	Song period	c. 1000–1400 AD
Italy		c. 1100–1500 AD
Low Countries		c. 1300–1800 AD
England		c. 1500–
United States		c. 1800–

GDP per capita that was much higher than that of other societies of the period.[134] This book, however, does not primarily focus on economic rise and decline, but on an aspect of these economies that seems not to be noted by Goldstone, that is, that all were market economies and particularly used the market to allocate and exchange land, labour, and capital. Nor is this book primarily concerned with the rise and fall of empires or political regimes, let alone with types of moral decadence as a cause of the downfall of empires, as in some of the more traditional literature.[135] The feedback cycle investigated in this book, and the associated hypotheses, are located in the institutional framework of factor markets, the socio-political context in which these function and their effects, primarily on the social distribution of wealth and power, and the processes of economic growth or decline, with which they interact.

The Cases Investigated in this Book

In this book, the development and role of factor markets will be analysed, and the elements of the feedback cycle will be tested, for three of the preceding cases. Chosen to this end are the three major, pre-industrial examples of successful market economies in western Eurasia: Iraq in the early Middle Ages, Italy in the high Middle Ages, and the Low Countries in the late Middle Ages and the early modern period. These three cases were selected because of their specific characteristics with respect to the role of factor markets.

Firstly, they are the main examples of market economies in this part of the globe during these successive periods. These societies used the market as a major or even the main system of exchange and allocation, not only for output but also for land, labour, and capital. In this sense, Iraq was exceptional in the early medieval period, and to a large extent this also applies to Italy in the high Middle Ages and the Low

---

[134] Above, 31–3, and also section 1.2, 14–17.

[135] See for assumed moral decadence and its relationship to market development section 6.3, 278–9.

Countries in the late Middle Ages. These cases thus stand out because of the importance of their factor markets and the dynamic exchange of land, labour, and capital they created.

Secondly, in contrast to some of the earlier possible cases, most notably Babylonia and Athens, these three cases have left us sufficient source material to thoroughly investigate all relevant aspects of their development. For Iraq, we have to rely mainly on qualitative sources, including literary sources, legal treatises, and geographical descriptions,[136] while for Italy and the Low Countries there is much more quantitative material available, including fiscal sources, accounts, lease books, etcetera. Also, they have long been the subject of investigation, and this has generated the literature on which this study can largely build, even though the scope and volume of this literature varies per case. The Low Countries have been thoroughly investigated for these issues in recent years, inspired particularly by the New Institutional Economics, whereas the literature for Italy is mainly from earlier decades and more embedded in social history. Studies on markets and economic development in early medieval Iraq are more scarce, although the pace of research has been picking up in recent years.[137] Also, the present author has tried to supplement this literature on Italy and Iraq by launching research projects on which this book is partly built.[138]

Thirdly, in contrast to the later examples in the nineteenth and twentieth centuries, these three cases all operated more or less in isolation, vis-à-vis possible market economies in other parts of the world. Either no other market economies existed at the time or they did exist in other parts of the world but further away and interaction among them was very weak. Even Italy and the Low Countries, while situated on the same continent, hardly influenced each other's development as market economies.[139] This contrasts with the later cases, whose development interacted much more, as with England and the United States in the eighteenth and nineteenth centuries, making the socio-economic processes of each case harder to isolate.[140]

Each of the three cases selected here in its period reached the highest level of economic development and wealth in western Eurasia, or even in the world as a whole: Iraq in the eighth and ninth centuries, Italy in the thirteenth and fourteenth, and the Low Countries in the sixteenth and seventeenth. Each reached levels of GDP per capita higher than anywhere else at that time. If positive effects of market development can be expected anywhere, it would be in these three cases that operated at the extreme margin of economic development and growth. Despite this dynamism and growth, however, they all three witnessed stagnation or even

---

[136] See for a more extensive discussion of the Iraqi source material section 2.1, 41–2.

[137] See the references to the work by Maya Shatzmiller, Michele Campopiano, and Michael Morony and others in Chapter 2.

[138] More specifically the project 'Economic growth and stagnation in the pre-industrial era: Iraq, Italy and the Low Countries, 600–1700', undertaken in Utrecht in the period 2007–12, and sponsored by the Organisation for Scientific Research (NWO) in the Netherlands. See for the scholars involved in this project also the acknowledgements in the Preface, v–vi.

[139] See more extensively section 6.3, 285–6.

[140] This is an issue addressed in sections 5.3, 249–50, and 6.3, 284–7.

decline after some time and they lost their leadership to another area. This enables us to investigate the mechanisms at play during all stages of development.

This investigation will be undertaken by empirically testing the hypotheses formulated above for each of the three cases. The book thus does not entail a direct, detailed historical comparison between the cases, except for the general overview and the reconstruction of the various chronologies in the conclusion. Neither is the book aimed at comparing the cases of market economies with cases of non-market economies, for instance in order to better understand why these market economies emerged at all. Its purpose, instead, is to trace out recurrent structures and patterns in the development of market economies, to assess the validity of the conceptual framework on the development of market economies presented above and to test the related hypotheses by way of the empirical findings for each of these cases.

These three cases are all pre-industrial ones. They are not chosen because I want to investigate the specific characteristics of *pre-industrial* societies, most notably their agrarian character, but because this book aims at a *very long-run* analysis, which is needed to arrive at meaningful insights on this cycle which is hypothesized to cover several centuries. The pre-industrial period offers the opportunity to carry out such an analysis, whereas the modern, industrial period does not: the nineteenth and twentieth centuries are too short a period to span the full cycle investigated here. In Chapter 5, however, we will try to see whether in modern cases, including England and the United States, this feedback cycle can at least in part be observed and the same causal links hold, or whether the modern democratic, parliamentary systems or other elements preclude the occurrence of these links. The latter is argued by Douglass North and his co-writers, who claim that early markets developed within 'natural states', and repeatedly fell back into the default position of the natural states, while modern markets are within open access societies, which enables them to retain their qualities.[141] We will see, in an explorative way, whether this holds. Going over the modern cases also allows us to assess the extent to which the unprecedented technological innovation, the increase in scale, and the growing number of market economies, and their growing interaction, affect the process.

The three pre-industrial areas investigated here are labelled as Iraq, Italy, and the Low Countries. More specifically, they are the fertile lands between Euphrates and Tigris in present-day Iraq (Iraq), the centre and north of Italy (Italy) and the present-day countries of the Netherlands and Belgium (the Low Countries). These areas are of approximately equal size, each measuring some 100,000–200,000 km². As noted, they are not fully homogeneous, but consist of different regions, each possessing their own geographical and social characteristics, and sometimes displaying different chronologies in their socio-economic development, although these are clearly related within each of the cases, because of the interaction through the market but also that through the political sphere. These regional differences within each of the cases will be indicated throughout the book where relevant, and

---

[141] North, Wallis, and Weingast, *Violence and social orders*, 13 and passim.

they will be discussed more fundamentally in the conclusion, but the main focus here is on the regions that figure most prominently in the development of factor markets and also on the higher geographical level, where they interact with the political organization of the area as a whole.[142]

The three cases investigated differ greatly in their political organization. One of them was the centre of an empire, one consisted of a host of city-states, and another was an amalgam of principalities. But in economic terms, there are many similarities. Each of these areas, as remarked, was the economic frontrunner of its era and had flourishing, dynamic markets, not only in output, but also in land, labour, and capital. The market became the main system for exchange and allocation of land, labour, and capital there. If a positive effect of the rise of market exchange is assumed, one would expect to find it especially in these three cases. Hence, these three economic leaders allow for a test at the extreme margin of success, and the same applies to the cases of England and the United States, which are glanced at in Chapter 5. The following reconstructions will show, however, that after a century or two all three of the areas examined in the case studies started to experience stagnation, and found themselves overtaken by others. It will also be shown that external shocks, of a climatologic, epidemic, or military nature for instance, cannot be blamed for this decline; it will be demonstrated that, instead, the causes are mainly endogenous. The hypothesis of the book is that the rise, organization, and functioning of factor markets—and the negative feedback cycle resulting from their rise and dominance—form the key elements in this. The three cases will be used to reconstruct and analyse the causal links in this process and—more generally—to better explain the causes and effects of the rise of factor markets, especially in cases in which they have become dominant, in order to enable us to go beyond what an oversimplistic and one-sided reading of Adam Smith would seem to tell us.

---

[142] See for the importance of the political sphere at the state level also section 6.2, 265–71.

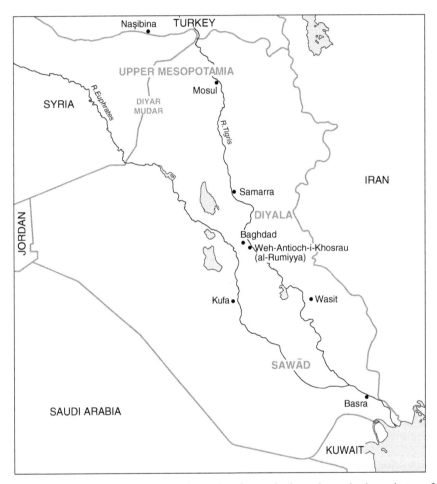

Map 2.1. Towns and regions in early medieval Iraq (indicated are the boundaries of present-day countries).

2

Markets in an Early Medieval Empire
Iraq, 500–1100

2.1. THE ROUGH CONTOURS OF ECONOMIC DEVELOPMENT

In the early Middle Ages, Iraq was probably the most economically advanced part of western Eurasia, while it was characterized by highly dynamic markets, not only for goods but also for land, labour, and capital. This chapter seeks to reconstruct the development of these factor markets and the way they interacted with economic and social developments.

The chronological contours of Iraq's economic development are roughly clear. It is common knowledge that Iraq rose to witness a period of florescence in the eighth and ninth centuries, and experienced a splendid period under caliph Harun al-Rashid in particular, while it subsequently underwent decline or even a downfall. However familiar this picture of rise and decline may be, the sources needed to make this reconstruction more precise and quantitatively better supported are scarce compared to those available for modern economies. Accounts, property registers, and detailed fiscal lists from this period are virtually absent. The absence of a firm quantitative base has allowed the discussion on the long-run development of the Iraqi economy at times to become tainted by ideology-ridden speculations, either in a positive or in a negative sense. The positive approach is found with some scholars of Middle Eastern history who highlight the blossoming of early Islamic Iraq but do not deal with its decline or just blame it on exogenous events. The negative one is found with David Landes, for example, who suggests that Middle Eastern economies were set on a path of stagnation and decline almost from the outset, because of despotism and rigidities of religion, while he ignores the periods of florescence.[1] Both accounts are too one-dimensional and, therefore, cannot explain the alternation of growth, florescence, and decline.

Opportunities for a thorough investigation of the Iraqi economy and society of this period are not abundant, but they are available, and they are increasingly being used. Even though quantitative material is scarce, there are numerous chronicles,

---

[1] Landes, *The wealth and poverty*, 392–418. For the exogenous events highlighted in the positive accounts: this section, 45–6, and section 2.4, 82–94.

geographical descriptions, jurisdictional and legal treatises, administrative manuals, historical and biographical works, and literary sources from this period.[2] These contain qualitative information on economic and social issues, and sometimes also quantitative data—which have not yet been fully employed. The same applies to all kinds of archaeological finds, including coin hoards.[3] This material has allowed further progress in the social, political, and economic history of this period, as made by a number of scholars of Middle Eastern history in recent years, and also for research inspired by the New Institutional Economics.[4] Even though the discussion here will remain more patchy and tentative than for the other, later cases discussed in this book, these and other investigations will make it possible to delve deeper into this process in Iraq and to try to uncover the underlying mechanisms. I will do this by concentrating on the role factor markets played in this development. First, I will be looking at the social context in which factor markets developed, and the role played by social revolts in the genesis of this social context. Next, I will look at the organization and functioning of factor markets and at their social and economic effects.[5] Before doing so, I will recapitulate some of the main lines of economic development in early medieval Iraq.

This recapitulation must begin with one of the clearest indicators of the florescence of this area in the eighth and ninth centuries, that is, the presence of a number of huge cities. Baghdad, with an estimated 300,000 to 400,000 inhabitants around the year 800 was larger than any other city in the Near East or Europe, and the towns of Kufa, Basra, and Wasit also counted among the largest of their time, with about 100,000 inhabitants each.[6] Even though these estimates are rough, and vary by author, they reflect the power of the Iraqi society to generate agrarian surpluses and develop non-agricultural sectors.

Urbanization rates are more difficult to calculate, since the size of the rural population can only be estimated very roughly. If we define Iraq here as the core area of the present-day country of that name, consisting of the fertile valleys, plains, and marshes of the rivers Tigris and Euphrates, some 200,000 km^2 in size, the estimates of its total population around the year 800 vary between 2.5 million and 4 million.[7] The latter, higher estimate is based on archaeological research. Similar archaeological research has yielded even higher figures for the late antique period, and the population decline in between may be attributed in part to the Justinian plague and the later epidemics from the mid-sixth to the mid-eighth century that

---

[2] A succinct overview: Lewis, 'Sources', esp. 86–92.

[3] Shatzmiller, 'Economic performance', 140–9.

[4] An example of the latter is the project undertaken at Utrecht University in the period 2007–12, with Michele Campopiano as the main researcher of Iraq (see his publications, infra).

[5] In reconstructing the development of factor markets, I benefited from the work together with Michele Campopiano and Jessica Dijkman, resulting in our joint publication: van Bavel, Campopiano, and Dijkman, 'Factor markets'.

[6] Micheau, 'Baghdad in the Abbasid Era', esp. 232–5; Bosker, Buringh, and van Zanden, 'From Baghdad to London'. The high figures are given by Ashtor, *A social and economic history*, 88–90. See also Table 2.3.

[7] The high estimate is found in Ashtor, *A social and economic history*, 87–9, but is often considered too high. See also van Bavel, 'New perspectives on factor markets'.

afflicted this area.[8] Although the numbers are debated, it is clear that these epidemics took a serious toll and at least retarded population growth in Iraq at the beginning of the early Middle Ages. Also, in some regions villages appear to have been deserted in the period of the Arab conquest, that started around the year 634, due to the political-military turmoil and the later shift of populations to the cities newly founded by the new Muslim regime, although in other regions population numbers and rural settlement remained more intact.[9] When taking the two population estimates for the year 800 as lower and upper bounds, and putting the population of the large towns at 650,000, it is clear that the urbanization rate in Iraq at that time must have been very substantial, that is, in the range between a sixth and a quarter, being the highest share in contemporary Western Eurasia.

These high urbanization levels point to the ample availability of economic surpluses. Partly these were a result of the flows of tribute to the caliph—tribute that also came from other parts of the Abbasid empire—but mostly of the endogenous development of Iraq. The latter can be inferred from various indicators of economic development, such as the advanced technology employed in agriculture, industries, and hydrology, the high level of occupational specialization, and the importance of non-agricultural activities.[10] The high quality of irrigation works was especially crucial, as most of the agricultural activity in the arid area was dependent on the water from the rivers Tigris and Euphrates and their tributaries.

This period was also one of increasing market exchange. Output markets had always been important here, and the use of coins had been growing already from the third century,[11] but now further increased in importance, in association with the processes of urbanization and specialization for the market, both in industries and in agriculture. Agricultural specialization is evidenced, for instance, by the rise of cash crop production; a rise which also helped to spread the agricultural labour input more evenly over the year and allowed for the introduction of more intensive rotation systems.[12] A major example is the production of sugar cane, which was limited in Iraq up to the sixth century, but quickly spread in the seventh century and afterwards, in combination with the perfection of refining techniques and the growth of the sugar industry and the sugar trade. By the tenth century, as described by the contemporary geographer al-Muqaddasi, this process had given rise to regional specializations in certain crops, produced for the market and to be processed further in industries, such as silk and wool, but also cash crops newly introduced to Iraq, such as sugar cane and cotton. A few areas around Baghdad specialized in the production of lettuce, taking some 300 hectares of land there, and all of its produce

[8] Aperghis, *The Seleukid royal economy*, 35–40, based on the research by Adams, *Heartland of cities*, but also criticized for being too high. For the Justinian plague: Dols, 'Plague in early Islamic history'.

[9] Settlement decline was established especially in the countryside around ancient Uruk, between Baghdad and Basra: Adams and Nissen, *The Uruk countryside*, 63–5 and 93. See also section 2.4, 79–81.

[10] A very favourable picture of the advances made in the early Islamic period is sketched by al-Hassan and Hill, *Islamic technology*,18–28 and passim; Shatzmiller, *Labour*, 180–2 and passim.

[11] Rezakhani and Morony, 'Markets for land, labour and capital', 243–4.

[12] Watson, 'The Arab agricultural revolution', 8–35. For the following: Ouerfelli, *Le sucre*, 20–3.

was sold in Baghdad, yielding some 50,000 dinars per year in revenues, or the equivalent of some 1,500 times the yearly wages of a skilled labourer.[13] Similarly, in industries, some towns became noted for certain products, such as Kufa for its silk turbans and Naṣibina in the north for an extremely specialized product such as inkstands.[14] In the eighth and ninth centuries also markets for wage labour, land (sharecropping), and capital expanded, as will be elaborated below.

Connected to this, the money supply in the eighth and ninth centuries was abundant, after a rise in the coin supply that had started in the Sasanian period and accelerated in the seventh and eighth centuries, as can be inferred from the growing activities in mining and minting, and also by the number of coins from this period found in hoards all over the Islamic empire, including its heartland Iraq. The Islamic empire inherited a sophisticated monetary system and millions of Sasanian coins, which would remain in use up to the ninth century.[15] At the end of the seventh century a standardized bi-metallic system was introduced, with the *dinar* as a stable gold currency, that was mainly used for long-distance trade, hoarding, and fiscal transfers, and a large number of silver coins, *dirhams*, that were used in larger wage payments and market transactions.[16] Dirhams with a low silver content, and the numerous small copper and billon coins minted by regional authorities, were used for smaller payments and daily transactions. The largest numbers of coins, as various indicators show, were found in the eighth and early ninth centuries. This was a high point in the monetization of the Iraqi economy,[17] surpassing all earlier levels of monetization reached in the Middle East. In the same period, and continuing in the ninth and tenth centuries, there was also the rise of credit systems.[18] Letters of credit came widely into use, further enabling and stimulating financial transactions and market exchange.

It seems only logical to see this period of the eighth to tenth century as the economic high point of Iraq and to link this to the rise of commercialization and markets.[19] Still, on closer inspection, this must be qualified in two respects. First, archaeological research indicates that earlier, in the sixth century, under the Sasanians, Iraq had already experienced the start of growth, as evidenced by the carrying out of large-scale irrigation works and the extension of agricultural land. In the Diyala region, situated east of later Baghdad, for instance, at that time the maximum level of cultivation was reached and all available agricultural land was put to use, which was realized by way of huge, state-organized irrigation schemes.[20] The eighth- and ninth-century monetary upsurge, too, rather seems to be a continuation or acceleration of a development which started as early as the sixth

---

[13] Margoliouth, *The table-talk*, 70. For the conversion to yearly wages, see Table 2.2, 73.

[14] Al-Muqaddasi, *The best divisions*, 32, 116–17 and 132–3.

[15] Rezakhani and Morony, 'Markets for land, labour and capital', 243–5; Morony, *Iraq after the Muslim conquest*, 38–51.

[16] Ehrenkreutz, 'Studies'; Heidemann, 'Numismatics', 649–50 and 657–61.

[17] Heidemann, *Die Renaissance*, 362. More extensively on numbers of coins and monetization: section 2.3, 60–1.

[18] See for credit section 2.3, 74–6.

[19] As is done by Shatzmiller, 'Economic performance'.

[20] Adams, *Land behind Baghdad*, 69–83.

century, in the Sasanian era.[21] The period of florescence of the eighth and ninth centuries thus seems to have its roots, or its start, before the Islamic period, in the sixth century.

Second, the eighth- and ninth-century increase of market exchange, monetization and the growing mobility of land, labour, and capital in the market, to be reconstructed in later sections of this chapter, did not lead to further growth. Instead, as early as the ninth century, there were the first signs of stagnation, and these became more apparent in the tenth century. Irrigation works fell into disrepair, the cultivated area shrank, output declined, and the urbanization rate fell.[22] In the ninth century, most large towns already experienced demographic decline, and this was counterbalanced only by a further growth of the capital, Baghdad. In the tenth century, Baghdad joined the decline of the other towns, a decline proceeding in the next century, and resulting in the urban population being reduced by more than half in absolute numbers.[23] In this period, Iraq lost its dominant economic position and went into a sharp downfall.

Various explanations have been put forward for this decline, often in a tentative or intuitive way. We will return to these possible explanations more extensively in the last section of this chapter,[24] but it may be noted here that none of them seems fully convincing. Explanations stressing an inherent weakness of Islamic institutions, or hostility to innovation, cannot cover either the earlier florescence or why exactly the critical transition leading to decline occurred after the ninth century. Another type of explanation is that focused on the effect of great external shocks, of a climatologic, epidemic, or military nature. Indeed, such shocks did hit Iraq, but their chronology makes it difficult to link them conclusively to the economic decline which started in the ninth century and gained pace in the tenth and eleventh centuries.

The available data on climate, for instance, suggest that a climatic deterioration had occurred much earlier, at the turn of the late antique period to the early Middle Ages. The subsequent period of the seventh to ninth century was much drier than the preceding centuries,[25] which must have hurt agriculture especially in dry, marginal areas where rainfall was already insufficient. Apparently, however, this had not prevented the florescence of Iraq in exactly these centuries. After the ninth century, there were more wet winters and a colder period set in, but there was no radical climatic shock. Similarly, epidemics are hard to blame for Iraq's decline. A massive wave of epidemics, including the terrible Justinian plague, had struck Iraq and adjacent areas, but this was in the mid-sixth century with later outbreaks in the seventh and early eighth century, that is, long before the economic decline of Iraq.[26] Later epidemics were more limited in scope. Another type of shock

---

[21] Morony, *Iraq after the Muslim conquest*, 38–51.

[22] On agricultural output: Campopiano, 'State, land tax and agriculture'. See for these indicators of decline more extensively section 2.4.

[23] Data kindly provided by Eltjo Buringh, Utrecht University, 3 May 2011. See also Table 2.3, 91.

[24] Section 2.4, 82–94.   [25] Izdebski, 'Why did agriculture flourish'.

[26] Dols, 'Plague in early Islamic society'.

traditionally blamed for Iraq's downfall is the Mongol invasion and the sack of Baghdad.[27] This was indeed a terrible episode, causing massive destruction and loss of lives, but it took place only in 1258, that is, long after the decline had set in. Between the seventh and thirteenth centuries, that is, in the time frame in which the process of rise and decline unfolded, no big external shocks seem to have taken place.

When we recapitulate what we know about the economic developments in Iraq in this period, we can see a gradual rise from the sixth century onwards, that is, starting before the advent of Islam, but proceeding and accelerating in the early Islamic period. This is also a period of dynamic markets and high levels of monetization. Stagnation starts in the ninth century, and is followed by rapid decline. Explanations which can account for both the rise and the decline are scarce. This probably contributed to the predilection for evoking external factors for the decline of the Iraqi economy.

Here, we will probe an alternative explanation. The present chapter investigates the extent to which the process of economic decline, which took place mainly in the tenth and eleventh centuries, was not the result of external factors but linked to developments occurring *within* Iraqi society. I will argue that these developments were associated with the organization and the functioning of factor markets in Iraq. The large volume of these markets, the mobility and flexibility they brought in the transfer and allocation of land, labour, and capital, and the opportunities for accumulation this offered, resulted in a growing social polarization, especially in the ninth century, and gave rise to new and ever more powerful elites who exerted an ever greater influence on the institutional framework of exchange, which in its turn to a large extent caused the economic decline. A few centuries before, in the sixth to eight century, a reverse, positive development had taken place, as the rise of Iraq was connected to a large extent with the development of relatively open and dynamic factor markets. These markets, I will argue, were organized within a relatively balanced society, characterized by a host of different social groups that each could exercise some economic and political power, and thus kept each other in check. We will start by taking a closer look at this period.

2.2. SOCIAL REVOLTS AND THE GROWTH OF FACTOR MARKETS FROM THE FIFTH TO THE MID-EIGHTH CENTURY

When we look at Iraq in the seventh and eighth centuries the first thing that strikes us is the fact that it was the core of a large, centrally ruled empire which had a highly developed system of taxation—the major part inherited from the preceding, Sasanian empire—which paid for a strong bureaucracy and army. Still, this society was not dominated either by bureaucrats and military officers or by a powerful senior nobility, but rather had a balanced distribution of property and power,

---

[27] Especially in the older and more general overviews, as noted and discussed, for instance, by Lewis, *The Middle East*, 97–9.

thanks to the presence of a host of influential social groups. This balance was formed and consolidated in the previous period, and originated in the various social revolts which had occurred within a relatively short span of time and had broken the power of the old upper aristocracy.

Social Revolts and Societal Balance

The first of these revolts took place at the beginning of the sixth century, before the Arab conquest. This was the Mazdakite social revolt, a radical, anti-aristocratic movement, mainly supported by peasants and the poor, but also by artisans and some noblemen. The Mazdakites strove for an egalitarian society, which would be achieved by taking land, slaves, and other property from the rich and redistributing it to the poor, and by having this wealth owned in common, with its possession being equally distributed.[28] Their communal ideas perhaps drew inspiration from the common management of pastures practised by village communities and families. The initial success of this revolt, which was probably largely based in Iraq, undermined the power of the upper aristocracy and the old noble houses. After the suppression of the revolt, the senior aristocrats regained much of the wealth that had been taken from them, but more permanent was the damage done to their legitimacy, after they had been humiliated during the revolt.[29] The ensuing land redistribution and tax reforms initiated by the Sasanian king Kawadh I (488–531, see Table 2.1 for the main dynasties and rulers in this period), and later partly revoked but also partly extended by Khosrow I, had a similar effect in breaking the power of these aristocrats and made room for the rise of new groups in society, including a petty aristocracy, the *dahāqīn*.[30] In the process, the position of ordinary people was also improved, although evidence for this is more patchy.

The Arab conquest and the advent of Islam in the seventh century also enabled social dynamism and the rise of new groups.[31] Old elites, including urban elites, the *dahāqīn*, and the Christian church authorities, retained much of their position, while leaders of Arab tribes, military leaders, and new urban administrators now came further to the fore. The mixture of elites became ever more diverse with each outbreak of social revolt. Moreover, the Quranic ideals of equity, justice, and mutual assistance, mixed with the fairly egalitarian outlook of the Bedouins and the Arab tribes, and their resistance to hierarchy,[32] may have had an effect after the conquest of Iraq. The egalitarian tendencies generated with the Islamic conquest need to be qualified, however, in view of the huge revenues, spoils, and booty amassed by the early conquerors and their adaptation to local practices, and also in

---

[28] Crone, 'Zoroastrian communism'; Pigulevskaja, *Les villes*, 205–11.

[29] Altheim and Stiehl, *Ein asiatischer Staat*, 131–4 and 169–72; Daryaee, *Sasanian Persia*, 26–30.

[30] Campopiano, 'Land tenure'; Rezakhani and Morony, 'Markets for land, labour and capital', 249–51. See more extensively on these reforms and the *dahāqīn* below, 50–1.

[31] Robinson, *Empire and elites*, 30–2, 58–9, and 87–93 (for the north of Iraq); Morony, *Iraq after the Muslim conquest*, 191–214 and 236–58.

[32] Marlow, *Hierarchy and egalitarianism*, extensively discusses the tension between this egalitarianism and the actual existence of inequality in wealth and power.

Table 2.1. Main dynasties and rulers (kings and caliphs) in early medieval Iraq

Dynasty	Ruler	Years
Sasanian		
	Kawadh I	488–531
	Khosrow I	531–79
Islamic		
	Abu Bakr	632–4
	Umar I	634–44
Umayyad		661–750
Abbasid		750–940s
	al-Mahdi	775–85
	Harun al-Rashid	786–809
	al-Mu'tadid	892–902
	al-Muqtadir	908–32
Buyid		940s–1055
Seljuq		1055–

view of the social stratification immediately established in the new garrison towns, Kufa and Basra.[33] Likewise, the effect of Islamic norms of poverty alleviation and the introduction of a charity tax (the *zakāt*) must be nuanced,[34] if only because Christianity had possessed similar norms with possibly a similar effect. Wealth did actually become more equally distributed, however, as a result of the introduction of Islamic inheritance laws, which promoted partible inheritance over a wide group of kin, and the fact that wealthy men were allowed to have more than one wife and therefore had more children. This will have resulted in an increased division of wealth compared to societies with other inheritance and marriage rules.

The late seventh century again saw a series of religious and political revolts, often with social undertones, for instance directed against the caliph and his governors. Some of these revolts remained localized, but others were large, lasted for many years, and spread over extensive areas. Kufa saw a local revolt in 684, as people especially from the lower classes were inspired by a revolutionary leader who called for a transformation of society. Further, there was the revolt against the authoritarian governor of Iraq, al-Hajjaj, in 699–701, around Basra and Kufa, as the rebels seized the crown lands and burnt the central tax and property registers in Kufa.[35] The movement of the Kharijites, who strove for a more democratic and egalitarian society, was more lasting, and they revolted several times between 661 and 680, especially around Kufa and Basra, and again in Upper Mesopotamia in 736 and 744.[36]

[33] Kennedy, *The armies*, 7, 37–42, and 59–71; Ashtor, *A social and economic history*, 23–7.

[34] Kuran, 'Islamic redistribution', esp. 276–81, who qualifies the extent of redistribution. See section 2.4, 86–7, for the weakening of these norms in the tenth century.

[35] Duri, *Arabische wirtschaftsgeschichte*, 32 and 40, and notes 22 and 28; Campopiano, 'State, land tax and agriculture', 18. For the egalitarian tendencies of these revolts: Marlow, *Hierarchy and egalitarianism*, 95–6.

[36] Ashtor, *A social and economic history*, 31–2 and 76; Tucker, *Mahdis and Millenarians*, passim (focusing on the religious ideas of these and other sects).

Revolts such as these paved the way for the successful and victorious Abbasid revolution in the mid-eighth century, which in part built on these revolts, although the Abbasid coalition was broader and more moderate. The Abbasid revolution which overthrew the Umayyad dynasty was not a simple *coup d'état* at the top governmental level only, but a social movement aimed at reforming society. In this process, the Abbasids cleverly used popular unrest and discontent, felt especially in Iraq and Khurasan, and included some disaffected groups such as Kharijites, dependent peasants, and non-Arab Muslims in their coalition.[37] The revolution was directed against the remaining old elites, against the Umayyad dynasty and the Arab families who had acquired massive fortunes during the conquest, and it aimed at bringing closer the Islamic ideals of justice and equality. Although some of their radical supporters later felt betrayed by the lack of reformist zeal of the new rulers, the revolution still produced some reforms and again brought new groups to the fore, including non-Arab groups and recent converts, and thus further con- tributed to the diversity of the social fabric in Iraq. At the same time, the Abbasid revolution seems to have closed off the possibility of further large social upheaval, by paving the way for a now dominant coalition between the Arab and non-Arab large landholders, as we will see below.

Within the relatively short time span of barely two centuries, Iraq had therefore witnessed four major social revolts, some of them supported, and others even driven and led, by broad layers of society, including peasants and the poor. In marked contrast to any ideas about the immobile, indifferent masses in Asiatic societies and the absence of clear opposition between social classes,[38] each of these revolts profoundly shook up society, broke the ancient power elite of top noble- men and brought new groups to the fore. Together these revolts created a balanced social fabric, beginning before the Muslim conquest and developing further after the conquest, with the caliphal relatives, Muslim elites, government bureaucrats, courtiers, Arab generals, other military officers, townsmen, merchants, higher Christian clergy, Muslim religious leaders, judges (*qadis*), legal scholars (*'ulamā*), petty landlords, and village notables all holding secure positions in society, and also in the distribution of landed property and political leverage.

Within this relatively balanced social context, factor markets in early medieval Iraq grew in volume and dynamism. These markets were building to a considerable extent on pre-existing institutions, developed during earlier phases of market dynamism in the preceding centuries or even millennia. The old Babylonian period, at the beginning of the second millennium BC, and the neo-Babylonian period, especially the long sixth century BC, for instance, had seen thriving output markets but also markets for land and labour.[39] The extent and volume of these

---

[37] Kennedy, *The early Abbasid caliphate*, 35–7, 40–1, and 58; Robinson, *Empire and elites*, 110 ff., for a detailed account of the process in Mosul. See also Daniel, 'Arabs, Persians, and the advent of the Abbasids'.

[38] Ideas as found with Karl Marx and some Marxists. See Krader, *The Asiatic mode*, 144 and 288–9.

[39] Van Bavel, 'New perspectives on factor markets'; Jursa, 'Factor markets in Babylonia'. See also section 1.4, 31.

factor markets are difficult to ascertain, but we do know that their importance in Iraq rose and declined over time. The high point in market activity during the neo-Babylonian period, for instance, was followed by just such a decline, as in the fifth century BC power networks and coercion became more important than market allocation.[40] But in the early Islamic period, or possibly starting already in the late Sasanian period, the importance of factor markets rose again. This went along with the development of new institutions and organizational configurations, while at the same time these markets made use of pre-existing institutions. The institutional arrangement of the land market in particular showed continuity over the centuries. In Iraq, absolute, exclusive property rights to land had never existed, in the sense that the state always held an important element of the bundle of property rights, more specifically the fiscal right to a substantial share of the output. In contrast to the situation in Western Europe in the high Middle Ages, however, in Iraq the other elements of the bundle of property rights, that is to use, inherit, enjoy access to, and sell the land could well be united into the hands of one person.[41]

The important role of taxation, and the stake the state thus permanently had in the bundle of property rights to the land, were a continuation of the situation before the Islamic conquest, under the later Sasanian empire. Up to the reign of Khosrow I (531–79), taxation seems to have been based on a system that assessed the land tax on the basis of a share of the crops.[42] The noblemen had to collect the tax in the area under their control and hand in a share of it to the central authorities.[43] Apart from the crown lands which were under the direct control of the king, the central authorities were thus mainly dependent on the cooperation of the noblemen who remitted the taxes to them.

The administrative reforms accomplished under Khosrow I fundamentally changed this system and reduced the role of the old nobility. Tax assessment now became based on a cadastral survey of the land and the fiscal system became much more centralized, thus making the bureaucracy more closely involved in the collection of taxes and reducing insecurity and arbitrariness. Taxes were now collected on the basis of a fixed amount of money per unit of surface area, varying according to the nature of the cultivation or crops sown.[44] The increasing involvement of the state in this system is also witnessed by the important role of the 'judge' (*dādwar*). These judges were made responsible for the adjudication and registration of property rights to the land and other matters pertaining to land administration, thus covering similar competences to those of a modern day cadastral bureau.[45]

Land tenure relations also seem to have changed, in some areas of the empire, as a result of the reforms in the sixth century. A consequence of Khosrow's policies

---

[40] Jursa, 'Factor markets in Babylonia', 191–2 and 196–8.
[41] See this section, 51–2. See for the situation in the high medieval West: van Bavel, 'The land market in the North Sea area'.
[42] Morony, *Iraq after the Muslim conquest*, 99–106.
[43] This and the following is largely based on Campopiano, 'Land tax alā l-misāa'.
[44] Mårtensson, '"It's the economy, stupid!"', 221–3.
[45] Campopiano, 'Land tax alā l-misāa'.

was that landholding was increasingly seen as a simple grant from the sovereign. Together with the development of a cadaster and the more efficient legal system, this probably increased the opportunities for land transfer.[46] Also, this evolution, combined with the breaking of the position of the old, senior nobility, changed the balance of power within Sasanian society. The petty aristocrats, or *dahāqīn* as they are called in Arabic sources, came to the fore and became the backbone of the Sasanian military organization, owing their position in part to royal land grants and the administrative role they fulfilled in the new fiscal system.[47] Villages under the administration of *dahāqīn* were the main taxation units at the time of the Arab conquest. The *dahāqīn*, together with fiscal agents who helped them collect taxes and mediated between the peasantry and the central bureaucracy, played a major role in the collection of rural surpluses and their transmission to the state in the form of taxes.[48]

The land tax assessment in Iraq after the Arab conquest generally followed the outlines of the reformed Sasanian system. The main land tax or *kharaj* was imposed on the land of conquered populations who had not accepted Islam and had not signed a special agreement with the new regime but were left in possession of the land.[49] Taxes levied on *kharaj* land, that is, most of the land in Iraq, largely consisted of a fixed amount of money, crops, or both, per unit area.[50] The Muslim rulers, after some initial discontinuity—especially in the north—also tried to further strengthen their administrative control over people and land, for instance through the carrying out of extensive land surveys, which were indispensable in this type of fiscal system.[51] The tax burden on land was probably substantial—although information on the exact level is very scarce—while taxes on cattle, precious metals, and commodities were much lower. Another kind of land tax assessment, which was assessed on the land owned by Muslims, was the tithe (*ushr*), which was lower than the land taxes levied on non-Muslim landed property. Besides these, there were the farmers residing on state lands, who were bound to pay tax or rent proportionate to the yield, it seems, as in the Sasanian period.[52]

Land and Lease Markets

The strong presence of central authority by way of the fiscal structure in no way meant that land could not be sold or exchanged.[53] On the contrary, fiscal claims

---

[46] Rezakhani and Morony, 'Markets for land, labour and capital', 237–9.

[47] Campopiano, 'Land tax alā l-misāa'; Daryaee, *Sasanian Persia*, 29–32 and 147; Altheim and Stiehl, *Ein asiatischer Staat*, 134–8; Rezakhani and Morony, 'Markets for land, labour and capital', 249–51.

[48] Morony, 'Landholding in seventh-century Iraq', 139 and 147; Cahen, 'Fiscalité, propriété'.

[49] Campopiano, 'Land tenure'; Donner, *The early Islamic conquests*, 239–41.

[50] Morony, *Iraq after the Muslim conquest*, 101–6.

[51] Al-Qādī, 'Population census'. For the less-ordered collection of taxes in the north: Robinson, *Empire and elites*, 44–50 and 82–3.

[52] Morony, *Iraq after the Muslim conquest*, 99–106; Campopiano, 'State, land tax and agriculture', 7–8 and 18–19.

[53] Morony, 'Grundeigentum', 135.

were now clearly registered and not subjected to arbitrariness, and property rights to land were clear and secure. As a result, land was regularly bought and sold, both before and after the conquest. In the late Sasanian period, land in Iraq was bought, sold, leased, and mortgaged by Zoroastrians, Christians, and Jews, with its sale usually being recorded in writing, and registered by royal or communal officials.[54] After the Muslim conquest, in the seventh and eighth centuries, registered contracts of land sales were also common, although perhaps not obligatory, and land sales were frequent.

In fact, the number of land sales probably increased in the early Islamic period, as it became even easier to buy and sell land. Islamic law had a clear concept of private property, a concept already well established in the Arabian Peninsula.[55] Moreover, the ideas developed within the Hanafi school, one of the most important schools of legal thinking in the Muslim world, originating in Kufa in the eighth century, helped to transform land into a commodity. Also, starting from the fiscal reforms, the payment of a land tax offered a clear proof of private property rights to that land, which in its turn allowed for easy transaction.[56] As a result, sales of land were widespread, as is suggested by much (albeit fragmentary) evidence.

The landowners held their holdings in private, individual ownership, at least in the case of arable land. Grazing grounds and springs were held in common, to be used by the Bedouins and tribes or clans for grazing and watering their cattle. Some villages or towns also had commons (*hima*), consisting of meadows and bogs or fens situated near or around the village, which provided grazing, water, and firewood and were probably used more or less collectively.[57] There was also some state land, the crown domains, most of which had already belonged to the crown in Sasanian times, and to which now the wastelands and the confiscated lands were added.[58] Much the greater part of the arable land in Iraq, however, was held privately and was bought and sold between private parties. Smaller holdings and individual plots of a hectare or so were often bought and sold. Law books dating from the eighth century extensively discuss the widespread practice of land purchases, by Christians but mainly by Muslims.[59] As well as the land held and exchanged by peasants and petty noblemen, land was also acquired by the new Arab Muslim elites, in part through sale. An example is the sale of land by a petty nobleman to Abdullah ibn Masud, a companion of the prophet Muhammed.[60] Wealthy Arabs were increasingly converting the precious metals, jewels, coins, and other movables they obtained as booty during the conquests, and also their monetary pensions, into landholdings.

---

[54] Perikhanian, 'Iranian society', 672. For the Islamic period: Shemesh, *Taxation in Islam* I, 50.

[55] Løkkegaard, *Islamic taxation*, 32.

[56] Johansen, *The Islamic law*, 7–19. See, however, the nuances on this positive story by Morony, 'Landholding in seventh-century Iraq', 139; Banaji, 'Aristocracies, peasantries', 79.

[57] Løkkegaard, *Islamic taxation*, 20–4 and 36–7.

[58] Morony, 'Landholding in seventh-century Iraq', 153–5.

[59] For instance, by Yahya ben Adam: Shemesh, *Taxation in Islam* I, 27, 28, 30, 33, and 47–50.

[60] Campopiano, 'State, land tax and agriculture', 23–4.

The mobility of land in the market gradually resulted in the accumulation of holdings, especially in the hands of the emerging Muslim elites. These also extended their landownership by way of another mechanism, that is, land grants by the new rulers. The caliphs granted land to the new Arab leaders, including wastelands and swamps to be reclaimed, as in the case of large tracts of land around Basra, but also parcels of fertile agricultural land. The first caliph, Abu Bakr, and his son, immediately after the conquest of Iraq in the 630s, had already made a number of these grants to their relatives, friends, and political supporters, each grant consisting of some 15–100 hectares of land, while the third caliph, Uthman, even granted whole estates.[61] Another example is the land grant to Maslama ibn Abd al-Malik, the son of the former caliph Abd al-Malik ibn Marwan, at the beginning of the eighth century. A marshy area in the south of Iraq was granted to him, on the condition that he invest 3 million silver dirhams in the reclamation. After the acquisition of the de facto ownership of this land and its successful reclamation, also by constructing some new canals, Maslama brought in semi-dependent peasants and also substantial sharecropping tenants to work the land.[62] Added to these grants were the many land purchases by the new magnates in the market, causing the emergence of extensive estates around Basra, some of them up to hundreds of hectares in size.

This all led to growing polarization in landownership. The fragmentary evidence suggests that around the Arab conquest much of the land had initially remained in the hands of the petty noblemen, the *dahāqīn*, and some probably with the substantial peasants, the *tuna*. Perhaps, although this is more speculative, there was even an increase in the number of middle-sized peasant holdings immediately after the Arab conquest, because these peasants were able to benefit from the confusion among the elites during this turbulent period,[63] although most of the rural population remained tenants or landless. Now, however, small and medium-sized landed property gave way to large landed property. Especially from the beginning of the eighth century, this accumulation process led to the downfall of the petty landlords, as these lost out to the new Muslim elites and their acquisitive power.[64] Land purchase by Muslim elites, in combination with the land they acquired through grants, tenure, and forms of confiscation, was apparently so widespread in this period that it caused concern on the part of the authorities, since the heavy *kharaj* tax was in theory levied on the land of non-Muslims, while the lower *ushr* was originally levied on Muslim-owned land.[65] The fear of loss of tax revenues, and the desire to protect the fiscal grip of the state over the most fertile lands, caused the Umayyad caliphs to prohibit the sale of land in the fertile area between the rivers, the Sawād, to Muslims,[66] but accumulation seems to have proceeded.

---

[61] Morony, 'Landholding in seventh-century Iraq', 157–61; Donner, *The early Islamic conquests*, 242–3.

[62] Ashtor, *A social and economic history*, 61–2.

[63] As argued by Watson, 'The Arab agricultural revolution', 29; Morony, 'Landholding in seventh-century Iraq', 152 and 165. Banaji, 'Aristocracies, peasantries', 79–82, stresses the dependency and landlessness of the rural population.

[64] Morony, 'Grundeigentum', 137; Duri, *Arabische wirtschaftsgeschichte*, 41 and 47.

[65] Campopiano, 'State, land tax and agriculture'.

[66] A nuanced discussion by Morony, 'Landholding in seventh-century Iraq', 139–41. See also section 2.3, 62.

Larger landholdings were often leased out. Leasing was not an innovation of the period, but a practice which had existed already for millennia in this area, albeit with clear ups and downs in its importance. From the middle of the third millennium BC, many countrymen tilled the land in exchange for part of the crop or a fixed amount of silver, and in the nineteenth century BC written lease contracts start to appear.[67] In the neo-Babylonian period, especially in the sixth century BC, there was again a spell of intense leasing activity. The fairly rich source material shows tenants of smaller, family-sized plots of land (mostly less than 5 hectares), but also agricultural entrepreneurs leasing larger holdings from temples or crown land.[68] These entrepreneurs, often also acting as money lenders to the estate holders, could manage these large holdings themselves, but they could also decide to sublet the land, which gave rise to hierarchies of tenants. After the sixth century BC, the importance of leasing seems to have decreased again.

In the Sasanian period, as documented for Jewish tenants in the Talmud, the main form of tenancy was sharecropping for one-quarter to one-third of the crop.[69] The sharecroppers held permanent rights, and they could even sublet the land, thus offering them a strong position in relation to the land. In the late Sasanian period, we see the emergence of substantial tenants, later called *muzara'un*, who are supplied with land and seed by the landowner and in return have to deliver a share of the crops.[70] They were made jointly responsible with the landowner for the payment of taxes, and therefore more or less bound to the land, but at the same time had fairly strong rights to the land. The large landowners, who leased the land out, lived mainly in the towns. At a lower social level there were the workers on the land (*hoker, akkār*), in part labourers, landless peasants or (semi-)bound people, and in part free tenants who held their own land or leased it for a fixed annual payment of money or crop, without any permanent rights to the land.[71] All in all, the late Sasanian period showed a diversity of people working the land, with different degrees of freedom and grip or tenancy rights to the land, although dependence on the lords in some form seems to have prevailed.

After the Muslim conquest, this situation did not drastically alter, but Muslim ideas about leasing may have enhanced the position of the tenants. The prophet Muhammed in principle was not in favour of leasing and said to his followers that if a person was not able to use the land himself, he should have it used by his brethren for free, without rent.[72] More specifically, however, Muhammed was against leasing for a share of the crop, which he explicitly prohibited, while he stated that it was allowed to lease land for a fixed quantity of gold or silver coins. In part, this aversion to sharecropping had to do with the element of uncertainty

[67] Leemans, 'The role of land lease in Mesopotamia', 134–45. See also van Bavel, 'New perspectives on factor markets'.

[68] Jursa, *Aspects of the economic history*, 184–206; van Driel, 'Agricultural entrepreneurs'.

[69] Morony, 'Landholding in seventh-century Iraq', 162–5.

[70] Altheim and Stiehl, *Ein asiatischer Staat*, 170–1; Wiesehöfer, *Ancient Persia*, 176–7.

[71] Rezakhani and Morony, 'Markets for land, labour and capital', 254.

[72] Hadith, chapter 17, book 10, nrs. 3716–41 (leasing out land), 3742–6 (renting out land for food), 3751–2 (sharecropping), and 3747–50 (renting of land by gold or silver). See also Johansen, *The Islamic law*, 27–8.

about the size of the crop, making it a kind of gambling, but also because the sharecropping system could be interpreted as a type of *riba al-fadl*, or undeserved income from unequal exchange of land, leading to the exploitation of weaker groups in society, as tenants.[73] Even though Islamic jurists in line with Muhammed were in principle opposed to sharecropping, in practice their opposition had little observable effect in Iraq. Leases for fixed, monetary rents may have become somewhat more important, but sharecropping leases also remained widespread, although with a somewhat improved position of the tenants, who had more contractual freedom and security than before.[74] In the eighth century, the opposition to sharecropping in Iraq declined even further, connected with an expansion of sharecropping leases.[75]

Perhaps the sources will eventually tell us more about the exact organization of leasing, but information on Iraq is scarce. Scattered sources suggest that most of the leases were for only one or two years, or for indefinite, unspecified terms at the will of the landlord, but direct information on this for Iraq is very scarce.[76] It seems that sharecroppers leasing grain land, *muzaraʿah*, mostly held leases for one or two years only. The type of crops was decided by the landowner, and the tenants were left with a third or a quarter of the output.[77] This is close to a labour-renting contract, with labour paid for by a share of the crops.[78] Sharecroppers leasing plots with fruit or olive trees were usually better off and had longer contracts, which is not surprising in view of the long-term investments needed before these trees became profitable. A further type of tenant held plots of land for a fixed rent only valid for one year. If these short lease terms were indeed predominant, this would have created insecurity for the tenant and reduced his incentives to invest in the land. A positive element, on the other hand, is that Islamic jurists stressed the importance of contractual consent and the fact that the actual rent should never exceed the contractually determined rent,[79] which—if respected—enhanced the tenant's position. His position was also strengthened by the development by Islamic jurists of the notion of 'fair rent', an amount considered fair when compared with the average market price for plots of a similar soil quality and size. According to these jurists, valid lease contracts needed to state the size, quality, and location of the leaseholding, the use to which the holding was going to be put, the duration of the contract and the amount of rent. Rent only needed to be paid if the owner and the tenant had made a valid contract and the tenant received the 'property of use' without interference by the owner; a legal position which reduced the insecurity for the tenants. This also enabled the tenant to sublease the land. In general, we can conclude that the position of the tenants and the security of their leases improved during the early Islamic period.

[73] Campopiano, 'Land tax alā l-misāa'. For *riba* also: Johansen, 'Le contrat salam', 870.
[74] See this section, 57–8.   [75] See section 2.3, 64–6.
[76] Banaji, 'Aristocracies, peasantries'. See for a similar lease terms in early medieval Egypt: Banaji, *Agrarian change*, 199 and 237–8.
[77] Løkkegaard, *Islamic taxation*, 174–5, also for the following.
[78] See this section, 58.
[79] Johansen, *The Islamic law*, 32–9, also for the following, although perhaps somewhat too optimistic thoughts.

The share of the cultivated area let out on short-term lease and its development over time are very difficult to reconstruct. The sources available for the Sasanian and early Islamic periods (chronicles, juridical manuals, and geographical treatises) do not allow us to give precise figures on the diffusion of short-term leases. The mentions in the works of the jurists, and the few scattered pieces of information we have from the chronicles, however, lead us to surmise that leasing and later, in the eighth century, sharecropping leasing became more important.[80]

Labourers and Labour Markets

Besides the tenants, many rural inhabitants after the Arab conquest were *akara*, peasants, a major portion of them consisting of poor segments of the Nabataeans, the indigenous sedentary population of Iraq.[81] They were the main type of workers on the larger estates, either as labourers, lessees with leases at-will, or peasants. They often lived in a semi-dependent position, more or less tied to the land. Their position was usually weak. If they rented a plot of land they could often be dismissed at will, making their position hardly different from wage labourers, since they brought in only their labour and were remunerated with a small share of the crop.[82] Using the labour power of these semi-dependent *akara* was one of the constellations applied in early medieval Iraq for using or making profitable one's landed property. Other possible scenarios were large landowners leasing out their land to sharecropping tenants, middling peasants working their own land, or landlords having dependent peasants, using slaves, or employing landless wage labourers, with all kinds of intermediate forms in between.

Even though types of (semi-)dependence persisted, coercion with regard to the allocation of labour seems to have diminished in the early Islamic period. In the preceding, late Sasanian period, slavery had been more important, with slaves being owned by the kings, elites, and Zoroastrian temples, and used in the mines and in massive numbers in agriculture, construction work, and manufacturing. Greek and Syrian captives were also used on the estates of the petty lords, the *dahāqīn*, and in large-scale irrigation works.[83] In the towns, too, labour was often coerced in the Sasanian period. Many towns were founded by the Sasanian kings and settled by captives or deported people, such as the inhabitants of Antioch in Syria, who were deported and resettled in Weh-Antiokh-i-Khosrau by king Khosrow I in 541, probably in order to work mainly in manufacturing. There was also corvée labour, which had to be performed for the king or elites. Although some organization of artisans seems to have existed in the Sasanian towns, with these artisan corporations or crafts having their own deans or heads,[84] the scope for self-organization was probably limited, especially among the coerced people.

---

[80] See Beg, 'Agricultural and irrigation labourers'.

[81] Morony, *Iraq after the Muslim conquest*, 169–81.

[82] Banaji, 'Aristocracies, peasantries', 81–3; and section 2.3, 64–7.

[83] Morony, *Iraq after the Muslim conquest*, 266–70; Adams, *Land behind Baghdad*, 70. For slaves in Sasanian Iran: Perikhanian, 'Iranian society', 634–41. Rezakhani and Morony, 'Markets for land, labour and capital', 251–5.

[84] Pigulevskaja, *Les villes*, 159–61.

In the countryside, substantial proportions of the population were bound to the land or in a state of (semi-)dependency, and some were even slaves.[85] The traditional picture, found in descriptions of the so-called Asiatic mode of production, is of self-sufficient, autarkic villages with property held in common, which largely produced the same, subsistence-oriented crops, and with the main share of the small surpluses being extracted from an undifferentiated mass of servile villagers, in the form of compulsory levies, taxes in kind or parts of labour in the form of corvée labour. This portrayal is now generally found to be inaccurate, especially for the early Islamic period.[86] The rural economy was highly market-oriented, communal agriculture was relatively unimportant, social differentiation highly developed, and corvée labour was scarce, since most labour was performed within forms of tenancy or as free or semi-free independent labour, while wage labour was also used. Just as with leasing, in the realm of wage labour as well, Iraqi society could build on some of the institutions which had developed in the earlier phases of dynamic labour markets in the area of the Euphrates and Tigris, starting in the fourth quarter of the third millennium BC and again in the first half of the second millennium and the neo-Babylonian period, in the sixth century BC.[87] During these periods of dynamic labour markets, which alternated with long periods in which these dwindled again, it was usual to hire labourers during periods of peak agricultural activity, such as harvest, but also for labour-intensive tasks such as digging canals and transport. They were hired mostly by the month but also by the day or the year, and paid in silver or rations of grain.

After the neo-Babylonian period the importance of wage labour had declined, as it was replaced by corvée labour and the compulsion of dependent labourers,[88] but it gained in strength again in the early Islamic period, when the freedom of labour probably increased, especially in the towns but also in the countryside. It is even claimed in eighth-century sources that after the Muslim conquest of Iraq caliph Umar I had freed the people of the fertile, alluvial river plain, the Sawād, which probably refers to the freeing of slaves and enslaved tenants on the crown lands.[89] The importance of free wage labour is also apparent from the three options that were envisaged for using the confiscated lands of the defeated opponents who fled or were killed. Aside from granting land out or selling it, hiring people to cultivate it for money wages was seen as a main option.[90] Apparently, hiring wage labourers was common. This attitude was enforced by the Quran and its normative interpretations, in which wage labour was presented as a natural, common feature, not at all to be objected to, and hiring one's labour power was considered as normal as hiring a house or hiring capital goods.[91]

---

[85] Morony, 'Landholding in seventh-century Iraq', 165.

[86] A picture found with Marx and some Marxist literature. See Krader, *The Asiatic mode*, 286–96.

[87] Silver, 'Karl Polanyi and markets', 808–9. For the neo-Babylonian period: Jursa, *Aspects of the economic history*, 660–700; also section 1.4, 31.

[88] Jursa, 'Factor markets in Babylonia', 179–85.

[89] 'Morony, 'Landholding in seventh-century Iraq', hesitates about this and suggests that this claim may just be part of eighth-century legal discourse.

[90] Shemesh, *Taxation in Islam* I, 27.   [91] Rodinson, *Islam and capitalism*, 14 and 16.

In the seventh century, wages for labourers and seasonal workers in the countryside were paid partly in kind, but more and more in cash,[92] proving the monetization of the economy and the freedom of some people to hire themselves out. Some wage labour in the cultivation of land was rewarded with a share of the crops in lieu of cash. In this case, a plot of land was allotted to a cultivator, who brought in his labour power, while the landowner supplied the seed for sowing, the oxen, and the implements, and also paid the taxes. After the harvest, the cultivator received a share of the crop, varying from one-third to one-seventh.[93] The validity of this type of labour contract, which was akin to a sharecropping contract, was debated among late eighth- and ninth-century jurists. Most concluded that it would be fairer if the landowner in these cases hired a labourer for a fixed wage, because in the contract under discussion a crop failure would mean that the labour of the cultivator would remain completely unrewarded. Still, this system seems to have been widely used in the period, although other cultivators, ploughmen, and especially seasonal workers such as sowers and harvesters were paid money wages.

Free wage labour was frequently employed in irrigation works. In the seventh century, in the Umayyad period, forced labour and peasants owing labour rents were still used in the large irrigation projects, alongside free labourers, but from the mid-eighth century this practice ceased. Among the many wage labourers now employed were skilled workers who built and repaired irrigation machines, operators of these machines and engineers, but of course also large numbers of diggers, reed binders, and other unskilled labourers, who were mostly hired via contractors.[94] The contractor, the 'arīf, received a fee per labourer, a practice also found with weavers, sweepers, and other workers hired via contractors in larger numbers. These groups were geographically mobile. Most of the tenants and peasants, however, remained more or less bound to the land. In the Umayyad and early Abbasid periods it was not unusual for country dwellers who left their land and migrated to the cities to be sent back to their villages, especially when they were countrymen who were supposed to perform corvée labour.[95] So, although on the one hand most of the peasants were free, and could work independently or hire themselves out for wages, at the same time many peasants were to some extent bound to the land or subjected to restrictions.

In the towns there was clearly much more free labour in the early Islamic period than under the Sasanians, no limitations on free movement existed, and the growth of wage labour was even more conspicuous than in the countryside. The large numbers of soldiers garrisoned in or near the Iraqi towns were mainly paid cash wages, as well as some rations in kind, and the same applied to most civil servants. Around the year 700, there were some 100,000 professional soldiers in Iraq, mainly concentrated in the garrison cities of Kufa and Basra,[96] pushing up

[92] Beg, 'Agricultural and irrigation labourers', 19–20.
[93] Van Bavel, Campopiano, and Dijkman, 'Factor markets', 272; Banaji, 'Aristocracies, peasantries', 82–3.
[94] Beg, 'Agricultural and irrigation labourers', 23–7.
[95] Forand, 'The status of the land'; Løkkegaard, *Islamic taxation*, 176–8.
[96] Kennedy, *The armies*, 19–20 and 67–74.

the proportion of labour performed for wages in Iraq by several percentage points. These soldiers received a minimum wage of some 200 dirhams a year, and their cash expenditures must have had a profound effect on the commercialization of goods and services, especially in these two towns. More generally, the towns in early medieval Iraq were bustling with trade, traders, and markets, varying from small street vendors to retailers in the bazaars and the large open air markets, and the big merchants in long-distance trade, meeting each other in caravanserais or khans, where merchants could stay overnight and commodities could be stored or exchanged.

Credit and Financial Markets

In general, Islam looked very favourably on trade and profit making, which some have attributed to the fact that Muhammed himself was a merchant and Mecca was a dynamic centre of trade.[97] Further, the Quran supports private ownership of property and considers property rights to be fairly absolute.[98] Also, the Quran is not negative about personal enrichment, especially by way of commodity trade, thus helping to legitimize profit-driven trade. About credit and interest Islam is more reserved, although not to the extent sometimes assumed. The notion that a presumed Islamic prohibition of interest would have obstructed the rise of any credit market in the Middle East is incorrect. What is condemned in the Quran is *Riba*, an Arab or Meccan practice whereby the debt would double if the borrower did not pay it back in time, which could lead to confiscation of his goods or even enslavement.[99] It is especially this usurious practice, and the immiseration and enslavement as a result of credit—and consumptive credit in particular—which is condemned in Islamic law.

A major effect of the Quranic exhortations was therefore the limitation of the level of interest and an emphasis on leniency towards the borrower, not the prohibition of credit. Muslims in the seventh century had already found ways to circumvent restrictions on interest, or were not disturbed by them, especially in the sphere of trade, where the risk of enslavement or immiseration was lower.[100] This rather flexible attitude is illustrated by Abbas, uncle of Muhammed and a very wealthy man. He was a usurer himself, and despite the fact that Muhammed denounced his activities, he did not stop them. More generally, although at least some religious leaders continued to be opposed to interest, and some restrictions remained,[101] credit and capital markets grew. Starting in this period, but gaining much more pace in the ninth and tenth centuries, Iraq developed highly advanced financial markets, compared to surrounding areas or contemporary Europe. As early as the mid-eighth century Iraq had numerous money changers and pawnbrokers, as well

---

[97] Rodinson, *Islam and capitalism*, 12–19 and 28–9; Kuran, *The long divergence*, 46–7.
[98] Wichart, *Zwischen Markt und Moschee*, 89–94.
[99] Rahman, 'Ribā and interest'; Kuran, *The long divergence*, 143–7; Rubin, 'Institutions', 1315–16.
[100] Kuran, *The long divergence*, 143–50. For the eighth century and onwards: Udovitch, 'Credit as a means of investment'.
[101] Wichart, *Zwischen Markt und Moschee*, 180–221.

as merchant financiers who employed sophisticated instruments including bills of exchange and letters of credit.[102]

When taking stock of developments in factor markets in the seventh and eighth centuries, we can thus see a clear growth in freedom and mobility of production factors, especially from the Islamic conquest onwards. This applies especially to the freedom of labour, both in town and countryside. Further, the leasing system became more open and offered a better balance between landowner and tenant. Changes in the land market are less conspicuous, but nevertheless markets in land were fairly open and extensive in this period. Most striking perhaps is the start of the development of financial markets.

2.3. DYNAMIC FACTOR MARKETS AND GROWING SOCIAL INEQUALITY FROM THE LATE EIGHTH TO THE TENTH CENTURY

Factor markets in Iraq had thus become large and dynamic by the mid-eighth century, after a steady rise from the late Sasanian period and a further acceleration in the early Islamic period. Later, in the late eighth and the ninth centuries, they grew even further in importance. This is the period in which many more coins came into use and that added to the large numbers of late Sasanian and Arab-Sasanian coins that remained in use until the ninth century.[103] Gold coins from the Umayyad and early Abbasid period, the dinars, which were used in long-distance trade and fiscal transfers, and for hoarding, were very consistent in fineness and weight.[104] Much more striking than the gold coins, however, is the increase in the number of smaller, silver coins in the eighth and ninth centuries, with Basra and Kufa being among the main mints.[105] These dirhams are the coins used in actual market exchange, and also for larger wage payments in the labour market.[106] The number of these dirhams, which in this period generally were of high-quality silver, rose dramatically, as evidenced by the increasing numbers of coins found in hoards. The numbers found in the Middle East rise from virtually none from the seventh century to 15,000 dirhams from the eighth century, to 23,000 from the ninth century.[107] The dirhams with a low silver content, and the numerous small copper coins minted by regional authorities in this period, were used for smaller payments and daily transactions, and they indicate a growing monetization of the economy.[108]

This period of high monetization ended, however, in the tenth and eleventh centuries, as the number of coins struck declined dramatically, in Iraq even more than in other parts of the empire. The number of dirhams seriously declined after

---

[102] General: Udovitch, 'Reflections'. See for the later florescence of financial markets: section 2.3.

[103] Rezakhani and Morony, 'Markets for land, labour and capital', 243–5.

[104] Ehrenkreutz, 'Studies', 130–45.   [105] Heidemann, 'Numismatics', 649–50 and 657–61.

[106] Heidemann, *Die Renaissance*, 361.

[107] Kovalev and Kaelin, 'Circulation of Arab silver', 565–6 (recalculated into totals per century). For the dirhams found in hoards in the north of Europe and their interpretation, see section 2.4, 91.

[108] Heidemann, 'Numismatics', 649–50 and 657–61; Heidemann, 'Der Kleingeldumlauf' (copper coin emissions from Kufa, second half of the eighth century).

the ninth century, as evidenced by the coin finds mentioned above, for instance. While 23,000 dirhams from the ninth century are found, there are only 6,000 from the tenth century and fewer than 1,000 from the eleventh. At the same time, especially towards the end of the tenth century, the quality of the gold dinars greatly decreased.[109] The production of copper coins even ceased entirely in Iraq at the end of the ninth century. From then onwards, fragments of silver and gold coins were used for small daily transactions, but these coins also became more rare.[110] One specialist, Stefan Heidemann, asserts that monetization in the eleventh century had shrunk to a low level not seen since the Hellenistic period, a millennium before.

In the period of high monetization and dynamic factor markets, that is, the eighth and ninth centuries, Iraq underwent striking social changes. It started to lose the social balance so characteristic of the previous period. This loss was largely the result of the rise of an elite of large landholding families from the Sawād, the fertile, alluvial lands between the Tigris and Euphrates, who also acted as tax farmers and merchant bankers. In addition, they dominated the grain trade, acquired trade monopolies, and further extended their market-oriented large landholdings, as we will see in this section.

Accumulation and Effects in Land and Lease Markets

In accumulating land, these elites were able to use the land market. Some of the sales in the market were small-scale, as exemplified by the story from Basra in the first half of the ninth century, about a pedlar who sold peppers and other vegetables, but was able to save some money and thus buy a piece of arable land of 100 *jarib* (16 hectares).[111] The emphasis in the story is on the thrift of this pedlar of modest origins, but not on his land purchase itself, suggesting how usual and general this practice was. Besides these small-scale transactions, larger landholdings also changed hands and seem to have been accumulated by the new Muslim elites. Property lists are not available, but anecdotal evidence gives some idea of the properties built up by these elites, which consisted of rural estates, real estate in the towns, and hard cash. The supreme judge Ibn Daoud in the mid-ninth century, for instance, possessed more than 1 million dinars worth of property, consisting mainly of landed estates, whose value was equivalent to 30,000 times the yearly wage of a skilled labourer.[112] Sometimes, large rural properties entered the market, as in 862. The new caliph first 'bought' the properties of two rival pretenders, worth more than 10 million dinars—in a process which was more of a disguised confiscation—and in the following months had these properties sold in the market.[113]

---

[109] Ehrenkreutz, 'Studies', 147.
[110] Heidemann, 'The agricultural hinterland', 55; Heidemann, 'Numismatics', 657–61.
[111] Pellat, *Le livre*, 44.
[112] Sabari, *Mouvements populaires*, 35 and 37, with other examples; Cahen, 'Fiscalité, propriété', 138 ff.
[113] Forstner, *Das Kalifat*, 23–4.

Attempts of the state to prohibit land sales in the Sawād occurred from the Umayyad period onwards and intensified in the following centuries.[114] The rationale behind this policy may initially have been to prevent the loss of revenue through the sale of land by non-Muslims to Muslims, and the resulting loss of the heavy *kharaj* tax which the state levied on the landed property of non-Muslims.[115] As a reaction to this, from the beginning of the eighth century, the idea that the fiscal status of the land was linked to the land itself and independent from the status or religion of the landowner seems to have prevailed, as can be seen in the writings of the influential scholar Yahya ben Adam, who worked in Kufa around 800.[116] The attempts to enforce a prohibition of land sales in the Sawād and the need to make the status of *kharaj* land independent from the religious beliefs of the owners thus both point to the emergence of a Muslim landed elite and a concentration of landed property in its hands which had started by the beginning of the eighth century.[117] However, in practice the attempts to stop this did not work at all and accumulation proceeded.

As well as land sales, grants from the caliphs especially to members or clients of the ruling dynasty, and often aimed at land reclamation, also encouraged the formation of an elite of landlords. In the ninth century, again, parts of the state lands in the Sawād were granted to the caliphal favourites, but also to military officers, civil servants, and merchants, to be held as a kind of non-military land grant. These elite landholders were usually obliged to pay the tithe instead of the heavy *kharaj*, or they avoided paying taxes at all.[118] This also enabled them to appropriate even more of the surplus, by having their tenants pay the *kharaj* and remitting to the state only the lower *ushr*, keeping the difference for themselves.

The state's access to agricultural surpluses was, from the end of the ninth century onwards, limited not just by the power of these large landlords but also by the multiplication of the intermediaries because of the rise of tax farming.[119] Tax farming, or the leasing out of the right to levy certain packages of taxes, offered a temporary solution to the state's lack of hard cash. After an absence of several centuries, it made its (re)appearance in Iraq in the late ninth century under caliph al-Mu'tadid, who welcomed this 'innovation' as a way to help him to acquire cash, and who in the following years increased ever further the number of fiscal districts to be farmed out. These districts could be identified at the central or regional level, or within smaller districts, and were sometimes farmed out by auction, although increasingly tax farms were sold outside the public market for a cash sum or sold through brokers, with the profit of a tax-farming contract sometimes amounting

---

[114] Campopiano, 'State, land tax and agriculture', 10.

[115] Morony, 'Landholding in seventh-century Iraq', 140–1; Campopiano, 'State, land tax and agriculture', 15–16. See also section 2.2, 50–1.

[116] Shemesh, *Taxation in Islam* I, 15 and 48, and III, 83.

[117] Campopiano, 'Land tax alā l-misāa', 253–4.

[118] Campopiano, 'State, land tax and agriculture', 17–20. Morony, *Iraq after the Muslim conquest*, 211–13. See for the earlier land grants also section 2.2, 50–1.

[119] For the decline of tax revenues in this period, partly connected to the emergence of tax farming, see section 2.4, 79–81.

to hundreds of thousands of dinars.[120] To offer the necessary cash or financial guarantees to the state, the tax farmers had to be chosen from the upper classes of
Abbasid society. The highest state official, the vizier, around 900 stated that only
wealthy merchants, chief officials, and large landholders qualified as tax farmers.[121]
This thus strengthened the power of the already existing commercial and landholding elites, which often overlapped, leading to a weakening of the rights of the state
on land and rural surpluses. More generally, the tax farmers could directly influence state policies, for instance by withholding sums from the government, or even
build up their own ·rule in the provinces they taxed, as shown by a number of
examples from the early tenth century on.

One effect associated with this development was that the elites lost their interest
in getting access to the rural surpluses by way of state offices, but instead focused
on tax farming in combination with a more direct access to the surplus through the
ownership of the land and build-up of large estates. This is also reflected by changes
in the legal discourse of the eighth century, most clearly in Kufa—but also in
Mosul, for instance, where the study of law and the legal scholars detached themselves from public authority and became patronized more by the landowning
elites, whose interests they increasingly voiced.[122] This is, again, an indication
that the social balance was shifting, perhaps decisively, in the second half of the
eighth century.

In the same period, smallholding was declining. In the Umayyad period there
had still been peasant and medium-sized freeholders, but in the course of the seventh to ninth century land became concentrated into the hands of Muslim elites,
as we have seen in the previous section. The last phase in this process took place in
the tenth century, as ever more large estates were built up, swallowing the last
remaining smallholdings and leading to the disappearance of the smallholding
peasantry—a development which was enabled by the freedom of buying and
selling land.[123] Buying land was considered the safest investment of wealth. Ibn
al-Jassas, a jeweller from Baghdad, around 960 possessed land in the Baghdad
commercial quarter of al-Karkh worth 50,000 dinars, land near one of the city
gates worth 30,000, property in Basra worth 100,000, and several rural estates, in
all totalling 900,000 dinars, as well as 100,000 dinars in cash and 300,000 dinars
in slaves, jewels, and other valuables, and this was only what was left after most of
his property had been confiscated by the caliph.[124] Properties such as these, worth
equivalent to 30,000 times the yearly wage of a skilled labourer, do not seem to
have been unusual at the time. The merchant Abu Hassan al-Talibi, who was born
in Kufa and moved to Baghdad, in the second half of the tenth century possessed

---

[120] Mez, *Die renaissance*, 124–5; Ashtor, *A social and economic history*, 136–9. See also Løkkegaard,
Islamic taxation, 98–9, for auctioning, referring to the work by Hilal as-Sabi from the beginning of the
eleventh century.

[121] Shimizu, 'Les finances publiques', 15–16.

[122] Campopiano, 'Land tax alā l-misāa', 256. See also the paragraphs on the introduction of *muqasama* land tax below.

[123] Johansen, *The Islamic law*, 81.

[124] Margoliouth, *The table-talk*, 16–18. For the following example: Sabari, *Mouvements populaires*, 38.

some 40,000 hectares of land, which produced 20 million dirhams in crops per year. He paid 2.5 million dirhams per year as *kharaj* tax, that is, one-eighth of the crop, which is a fairly small share in the context of the larger tax shares we encountered earlier. The profits he made he invested in buying new land in the south of Iraq and having it worked by labourers, thus further pushing up his profits.

These large profits from real estate were not unusual in the period. Some other merchants and officials, too, had yearly revenues of 1 million dinars from their estates alone, some 30,000 times the yearly wage of a skilled labourer.[125] Part of these large estates was devoted to cash crop production, as with rice, cotton, and sugar plantations, and these were probably mainly worked by wage labourers and slaves, but the rising dominance of large landownership also pushed up the importance of short-term leasing.

Information on the exact organization of leasing in Iraq in the eighth to tenth century is scarce. From mentions in narrative sources we know that leasing and subleasing of small plots of land took place,[126] but larger holdings were also leased out. Just as in the earlier, Umayyad period, most of the leases were for only one or two years, or for indefinite, unspecified terms at the will of the landlord, it seems. Longer lease terms did exist, as shown by the exhortations of jurists to limit the lease contract of the land of religious and charitable foundations to a maximum of three years, in order to avoid having the tenant pay less than the fair rent.[127] If these short terms were indeed predominant, this would have created insecurity for the tenant and reduced his incentives to invest in the land. Also, even though the tenant still had full use rights during the lease term, the legal discussions about leasing from the tenth century reflect the increasingly more unequal and hierarchical relationship between landowner and tenants, which may be contrasted with the emphasis on contractual consent and equity between the contracting parties in the earlier centuries.[128]

We know more about the payment of the lease: in money, kind, or as a share of the crop. In the period after the conquest, sharecropping seems to have been very important in Iraq. This is reflected in the legal discourse. Islamic jurists initially were in principle against sharecropping, but in the course of the eighth century more jurists in Iraq tried to legitimize its use.[129] The works of the chief Muslim jurist Abu Yusuf (†798), and others, who increasingly supported sharecropping and other forms of short-term leases from the second half of the eighth century onwards, can be taken as a reflection of the further diffusion or even dominance of sharecropping in Iraq. In discussing sharecropping contracts in which the lessor receives half, a third, or a quarter of the yield, Abu Yusuf even explicitly mentions that his colleagues in Arabia are against this practice, but his colleagues in the Iraqi town of Kufa are more open to it and he himself thinks sharecropping leases are

[125] Ashtor, *A social and economic history*, 140–1 and 155–7. For labour on these estates: below, 68–70.
[126] E.g., from a Basra narrative from the first half of the ninth century: Pellat, *Le livre*, 173.
[127] Johansen, *The Islamic law*, 34. See for lease terms also section 2.2, 55.
[128] Johansen, *The Islamic law*, 38–43.
[129] Campopiano, 'Land tax alā l-misāa', 259–61. See also section 2.2, 54–5.

allowed and valid.[130] The criticism of sharecropping as an unjust instrument of exploitation remained a topic only among a few jurists, as with the scholar Abu Bakr Ahmad ibn Ali al-Bayhaqi, who was not a native of Iraq but came from Khurasan, in the first half of the eleventh century. It is striking, however, that the initial opposition of Islamic jurists to sharecropping, and the attention to its exploitative nature, had already weakened in the course of the eighth century, and especially among jurists working in Iraq, probably because sharecropping was so dominant there and it was impossible to ban its use.

The share of the agricultural output paid as lease sum in early medieval Iraq was generally about equal to the tax share, although the exact share varied according to the legal status of the land. Tax rates probably increased somewhat after the Muslim conquest, as the Umayyads increased the state's grip on taxation, but afterwards tax rates did not change radically over time.[131] A main shift in the tax assessment, however, took place in the late eighth century, with the introduction of the *muqasama* land tax, a tax assessed on the basis of a share of the crops and not a fixed amount of money or crop output per area. This new tax system became more widespread under caliph al-Mahdi (775–85) and replaced the earlier system of fixed tax payments. According to the sources, the shift to this new taxation system was made at the request of 'the people'.[132] These people, as suggested by the sources, included the tax-paying peasants, who requested this change because the previous system of fixed payments had led to an unjust distribution of the taxes and oppression of the weak by the strong. Their complaints were boosted by the brutal methods of tax collection. The new system would make the peasants and tenants less dependent on tax farmers and merchants, especially since the need to convert the crops into coins before the tax payment, and sometimes to sell these crops at a bargain price, was now removed.[133] Producers thus improved their position vis-à-vis the fiscal apparatus, making a positive contribution to the social balance in Iraq.

There was, however, also a more powerful group which benefited from this change and probably belonged to the 'people' who asked for the change in the tax assessment: the new Muslim elite of large landowners. In the case of the land they leased out, they had to pay a large share of the taxes themselves, and they were often responsible for the tax payments more generally. Since they derived most of their rural revenues from sharecropping leases, they would be squeezed between low revenues and high fixed monetary taxes in periods of crop failures, as found in the late eighth century.[134] The new taxation system enabled them to escape this situation and created a much more agreeable fiscal arrangement for them, which also strengthened their position vis-à-vis the state and left them ample scope to

---

[130] Shemesh, *Taxation in Islam* III, 114–16; Yanagihashi, *A history*, 253–75.
[131] Morony, *Iraq after the Muslim conquest*, 103.
[132] Campopiano, 'Land tax alā l-misāa', 257–63, also for the following; Shemesh, *Taxation in Islam* III, 101, also for the level of taxes.
[133] Shimizu, 'Les finances publiques', 20–2.
[134] Campopiano, 'Land tax alā l-misāa', 257–63; Campopiano, 'State, land tax and agriculture', 33–7.

extract large portions of the rural surpluses, by way of the high shares levied through sharecropping contracts.

For this period it is possible to observe what share of the harvest was due as *muqasama* tax and which as rent, and also how high the total level of levies was. Different rates are given for the new land tax, with a maximum rate of 50 per cent and minimum rate of 10 per cent, which depended on factors such as the irrigation of the land, the type of crops cultivated, and the location of the plots. Most data in the sources point to rates of 30–40 per cent paid as taxes. An impression of the distribution of the surplus between taxation and rent in a sharecropping contract can be gained by looking at a late eighth-century text by Abu Yusuf, who discusses the case of a landlord who hires a peasant to cultivate the land, or leases the land to a tenant, for the payment of 5/6 or 6/7 of the produce, whilst the owner provides the seed and animals and meets all the other expenses, including the payment of the new *muqasama* land tax.[135] If we assume a tax rate of 50 per cent of the crop, the leasing rent would have been about one-third of the yield. In this case the landlord must have paid for the seed. With lower tax rates, the rent may have been as high as three-quarters of the yield. In both cases, the levies were very high, and often they were combined with all kinds of other levies. This situation induced the peasants to try to evade payment of taxes and rents, or to leave the land, for instance for the booming Iraqi towns, as evidenced by the mentions of peasants fleeing the land in this period.[136]

A big question is how all this promoted—or blocked—investments in agriculture, either by the landlord or by the tenant farmer. This is not easy to assess. In the early period after the Muslim conquest, investments were stimulated by the legislation on bringing wastelands and 'dead' land into cultivation again. This land, which required heavy investments in the construction of drainage or irrigation canals, digging wells, enclosure, and the construction of farm buildings, was granted to the investor, who received the ownership rights, received tax exemption for three years and thereafter had to pay only the low *ushr* tax on his 'revived' lands.[137] The policy was explicitly aimed at extending the cultivated area and increasing the tax revenues from formerly unused lands, and it must have encouraged agrarian entrepreneurship enormously in the seventh and eighth centuries. After this initial effect, the availability of suitable land dried up and this effect waned. Much more important now became the general incentive structure for investments by landowners and tenants.

Opportunities to assess their incentives are offered by the descriptions of how the investments in sharecropping contracts were organized and how the jurists describe different combinations of labour and capital inputs (seed, animals, buildings, etc.). These show that there was little security for the tenant, an issue we also encountered above when discussing the shortness of lease terms. The tenant was not certain to

---

[135] Shemesh, *Taxation in Islam* I, 116. For the link of this arrangement to the labour market and the renting of labour: section 2.2, 58.

[136] Cahen, 'Fiscalité, propriété', 145; Ashtor, *A social and economic history*, 67–8.

[137] Shemesh, *Taxation in Islam* II, 31–5, and III, 73–5.

reap the benefits of his investments and in practice in most cases only brought in his labour. So, investments should be made by landlords, but they had little incentive to invest either, because the lease sum was only a relatively small part, since the share taken as tax was often equally big. Moreover, investment in commodity trade, speculation in bullion and cattle trade was more lucrative than investment in land or in an increase of land productivity, because the taxation levels were much lower. Taxation rates again varied, but on commodities generally only the low *zakāt* tax had to be paid and taxes were mainly levied at the borders only. The late eighth-century fiscal handbooks mention taxation levels of 2.5 per cent on internationally traded commodities for Muslim merchants and 5 per cent for Christians and Jews, 2.5–3 per cent on sheep, a similarly low tax on camels and horses, the *zakāt* tax of 10 per cent on silver and gold, and a 20 per cent tax on minerals.[138] These levels are much lower than those levied on land and arable produce, which varied between 20 per cent and 50 per cent of the output.

Taxes were to a considerable extent paid in cash or at least delivered to the central administration in cash. The list of tax revenues from 785 shows that the Iraqi Sawād, the Tigris basin, the southern Iraqi region around Kufa, the northern region around Mosul, and the upper Euphrates region together yielded 133 million silver dirhams in cash in tax revenues and virtually nothing in kind, although in other years more was delivered in kind.[139] This indicates that producers, middlemen, or tax collectors had access to markets in order to convert agricultural produce into cash. From the moment the system of tax farming was reintroduced, in the late ninth century,[140] this conversion of payments in kind to money was mainly done by tax farmers, who themselves received most of the taxes in kind and thus were offered an opportunity to make an additional profit. More generally, the system of tax farming enabled the tax farmers and their agents to make additional profits through the market. One example of this is the manipulation of prices which hurt the fruit producers in the Kufa region in 932–4.[141] Here, an agent had sold their fruit to the tax farmers at far below market price, and the producers subsequently had to pay the remaining amounts when settling their tax accounts, which were based on a fixed monetary sum. Although cases such as these were widespread, judging from the numerous mentions in the narrative sources, tax payers were not totally abandoned to the cruelty and greed of officials and tax farmers. They could complain and file petitions against government officials at the *mazalim* court, which was mostly supervised by the vizier and mainly dealt with complaints regarding fiscal issues.[142] The aim and effects of this procedure were the dismissal of the offending officials, and perhaps the mulcting of their wealth, but it did not give rise to structural improvements in the fiscal system or the negative consequences it invited.

---

[138] Shemesh, *Taxation in Islam* I, 33–4 and 56–7, II, 45–50 and 54–5, and III, 91.

[139] Shatzmiller, 'Economic performance', 146–8; Campopiano, 'State, land tax and agriculture, 13–15.

[140] See above, 62–3.

[141] Van Berkel, *Accountants*, 23; Løkkegaard, *Islamic taxation*, 123–4.

[142] Van Berkel, 'Embezzlement and reimbursement'.

Even more difficult to tackle were cases in which favourites of the caliphs and viziers exploited their position between the producers, the market, and the state to make huge profits. One of these was Abu Abdallah Ibn Abi Auf around 900, who acted in concert with the vizier. First, state clerks on the order of the vizier negotiated a market price with some corn mongers for 100,000 *kurr* of corn (equal to 300 million kg, with a value of some 6 million dinars) from the Sawād, levied by the caliph, next the vizier allowed Abu Abdallah to buy the same produce for 1 dinar per kurr less, in order to give him the opportunity to resell it to the corn mongers for the agreed price and make a profit of 100,000 dinars.[143] The profit he made in this single transaction, with hardly any risk involved, was some 4,000 times the yearly wage of a skilled labourer. In the following years, the vizier and Abu Abdallah, and other viziers with their favourites, would repeat this lucrative chain of transactions many times. These practices made litigation and good connections more important than productive investments. Since these tax farmers also operated as main financiers of the caliphs, their political influence was big. This type of influence was new, as tax farming had not been practised in Iraq before the late ninth century.

Clear, direct links also developed between the newly introduced system of tax farming and the grain trade, especially when tax farmers themselves became involved in grain trading. Around 895, Ahmad Ibn Muhammed al-Ta'i made this type of link, and he used his strategic position in the grain market and the control he held over vast amounts of grain in order to speculate on grain prices. Not surprisingly, people held him responsible for the subsequent rise of prices in Baghdad.[144] This link was even more clear in 919, as the vizier himself leased the fiscal revenues in Iraq and next pushed grain prices up. This produced a revolt in Baghdad, and even though the vizier remained in office, the caliph felt compelled to dissolve the lease.

Free Labourers and Growing Number of Slaves

When looking at developments in the labour market in the eighth to tenth century, we can observe differences between town and countryside. Especially in the towns, labour was generally free and legal instruments were used to shape labour relations for wages. In Islamic law, the most common legal interpretation of labour in return for payment was to envisage it as a contract of usufruct (*ijara*).[145] The concept of *ijara* can be divided into the rent of objects such as land, houses, animals (and slaves, who also belong to this category), and labour services. In the latter case a person cedes his labour to another man, either for a specified period or for carrying out a certain task, in return for payment. Jurists distinguished between

---

[143] Margoliouth, *The table-talk*, 49–50. For another example (involving 30,000 kurr of corn and a profit of 2 dinars per kurr): Margoliouth, *The table-talk*, 184–5.

[144] Campopiano, 'State, land tax and agriculture', 39–40; Shimizu, 'Les finances', 16. For the following example: Mez, *Die Renaissance*, 124–5; and Ben Abdallah, *De l'iqta' étatique*, 143–5. See also more extensively, section 2.4, 81–2.

[145] Van Bavel, Campopiano, and Dijkman, 'Factor markets', 276–7.

'employees working for the public' (self-employed craftsmen who were paid for the products commissioned by their customers) and 'employees working for a particular person', who were paid a monthly or daily wage: both types of agreement were referred to as *ijara*.[146] Contracts of this kind were probably not often put in writing, and as far as we know none have been preserved for Abbasid Iraq.

In the countryside, however, we instead observe a decline in freedom. Most striking is the spread of slave labour. Slaves were imported from abroad and used in cash-crop production, as in the sugar plantations, and in the harsh work of salt production and land reclamation, most notably in the marshes around Basra, where thick layers of soda had to be removed in order to use the land. The Basra elites here combined their property rights to large tracts of land in their hands, their wealth, the availability of credit opportunities, as Basra was a major centre of banking and finance, and the availability of slaves, as the same town also was a main port of transfer in the slave trade.[147] Besides the peasantry, slaves were used by large landowner entrepreneurs in order to reclaim the land and prepare it for the lucrative cultivation of cash crops such as cotton and especially sugar cane, a crop that could be cultivated on salty soils, reclaimed from these brackish and salinated marshlands.[148] The slaves, numbering some 15,000 in this area, forming perhaps a quarter of the labour force, performed this hard work in large gangs, overseen by the agents of the large entrepreneurs, and were lodged in large work camps owned by these entrepreneurs, many of the latter belonging to the Hashimite, Barmakid, and Abbasid families, the most powerful ones in the Muslim world. These slaves, often suffering from malaria in these brackish marshlands, were not allowed to marry and did not have children;[149] they were no more than capital goods procured by the wealthy Basra elite.

Over the centuries, hundreds of thousands or even millions of black Africans, Berbers, Turks, and Slavs from northeastern Europe were brought to the Middle East.[150] Slaves had already been brought to Iraq in some numbers during the Umayyad period, in the seventh and eighth centuries, but most of them were obtained as prisoners during military campaigns or levied as tax. In the ninth century, the numbers of slaves increased and now most of them were obtained through the market, resulting in a climax of the slave trade in Iraq. Some contemporany writers in the second half of the ninth century estimated that at that point no fewer than 300,000 slaves were employed in Iraq,[151] which seems exaggerated but still points to their widespread use. Many slaves were brought in from Africa, especially by merchants from Basra and Kufa, who had settled in Berber villages near the supply routes of black slaves. In Iraq, the slaves were sold in the big slave markets

---

[146] Wichard, *Zwischen Markt und Moschee*, 242; Yanagihashi, *A history*, 73–4; Hallaq, *Sharī'a*, 256–8.

[147] Popovic, *The revolt*, 13–25. For banking in Basra: below, 75–6.

[148] Ouerfelli, *Le sucre*, 22–4; Waines, 'The third century', 301–2. Talhami, 'The Zanj rebellion reconsidered', 453 and 458–60, nuances the emphasis on the assumed east African origin of most slaves.

[149] Beg, 'The "serfs" of Islamic society', esp. 114–15.

[150] Shatzmiller, 'Economic performance', 151–5; Beg, 'The "serfs" of Islamic society'.

[151] Ben Abdallah, *De l'iqta' étatique*, 111.

in Baghdad, Basra, or Samarra, with each of these markets being huge complexes, with rooms, shops, and alleys.[152]

Slaves were used not only in agriculture, but also as household servants and in craft production. The weaver Abdallah al-Nassaj in the early tenth century, for instance, worked his silk-weaving workshop near Bab-al-Kufa with a number of slaves.[153] Slaves could also be rented out. The attention paid in legal treatises to the complications regarding liability for damages in situations such as this suggests that this was common practice.[154] Most striking, however, is the use of slaves in systems of cash crop production, as on the sugar plantations mentioned above, or in salt production or textile industries. This slave labour on the one hand may be interpreted as akin to capitalist wage labour, especially in view of the market orientation of production and the fact that many slaves did receive some monetary remuneration.[155] On the other hand, slave labour is fundamentally different because of the coercion applied, and it did replace labour performed by legally free wage labourers. This also applied to the slaves who were used as soldiers; a practice introduced in the ninth century and forming a social watershed. Tens of thousands of Turks were imported as slaves to serve in the army, and they gradually replaced the earlier waged soldiers. In the early ninth century, the first Turkish slave troops were bought and imported—a few thousand in number—to form a Turkish guard and to serve alongside regiments of free professional soldiers, also used in order to repress popular revolts.[156] Besides some money payments, the rewards for the Turkish soldiers and their commanders consisted mainly of land grants.[157]

In the towns, the labour force continued to have greater freedom, even though labourers probably became more dependent on large entrepreneurs. One instrument used by urban craftsmen in order to pool resources and skills was the partnership. Partnerships in general were a core element of Islamic law as it emerged in the first centuries after the conquest. Since jurists living and working in the cities of Iraq had an important role in the formation of early Islamic law, we can be fairly sure that it does indeed reflect economic conditions in Baghdad, Kufa, or Basra. Labour partnerships could be formed between artisans with the same profession, but, at least according to the jurists of the important Hanafi law school, also between artisans with different but complementary skills, such as a weaver and a dyer, or between an artisan and a tradesman who owned a market stall. Juridical treatises explicitly state that these arrangements responded to economic needs.[158] Some of these needs no doubt referred to scale: some ventures required a greater amount of capital or a greater variety of skills than an individual could muster. However, it is important to note that partnerships also lent legal legitimacy to subcontracting and thus to entrepreneurship on a larger scale.

---

[152] Savage, *A gateway to hell*, 67–89 (description for Samarra is from al-Yakubi, late ninth century).
[153] Sabari, *Mouvements populaires*, 25–6.   [154] Yanagihashi, *A history*, 61, 67–9.
[155] Bhandari, 'Slavery and wage labor', 404–6.
[156] Gordon, *The breaking*, 15–23. For their role in repressing revolts: section 2.4, 85–9.
[157] Kennedy, *The armies*, 118–24 and 126–31.
[158] Udovitch, 'Labour Partnerships'; Udovitch, *Partnership and profit*, 65–77. See also Dijkman, 'The fabric'.

The latter enhanced the position of the large entrepreneurs, who increasingly also acquired non-economic sources of influence and power. An example is the wealthy and influential entrepreneur al-Rasbi around 900, who owned some 80 textile workshops in Baghdad, southeastern Iraq, and adjacent Khuzistan, but at the same time was one of the major tax farmers and practically ruled these districts through his financial power.[159] Still, besides these large entrepreneurs in this period many small-scale, independent producers also remained in urban industries, as indicated by the revolt of numerous cotton and silk weavers in Baghdad in 984 and again in 998, against a new tax on weaving workshops.[160] However, many of these producers, too, became more dependent, for instance on large merchants for the marketing of their produce, or on merchant entrepreneurs within putting-out systems, as they gradually became reduced to the position of wage labourers. Next, there were casual labourers to be hired for cash wages. Sources from this period show how these labourers, whether hodmen, diggers, and dockhands, or more skilled labourers including carpenters, house painters, and masons, gathered in each quarter in a kind of labour exchange or physical market. Entrepreneurs and private individuals came there early in the morning to hire them, for a price fixed on the spot. In Mosul, for instance, one of the *suqs* called the Wednesday Market had 'an expansive area where hired people and harvesters congregate',[161] as observed by geographer al-Muqaddasi in the second half of the tenth century. Apparently, rural labourers could also be hired in this urban market.

The wages of these labourers came under pressure. Between the early eighth and the late tenth centuries, and particularly around 900, food prices rose sharply and they were not matched by rising wages. As a result real wages of labourers, and especially the unskilled among them, declined, sometimes even substantially.[162] More generally, real wages of unskilled labourers in the towns were substantially reduced. In order to get access to labour power and solve possible labour shortages, landowners and entrepreneurs applied coercion instead of raising wages, as exemplified in the growing use of slave labour. Wages for highly skilled labourers in the large towns probably remained more robust, because their skills were greatly in demand by the wealthy elites and their bargaining power was quite considerable. Indicative of this is perhaps that one of the few strikes known to us is that of the Baghdad calligraphers in the mid-eleventh century who demanded a higher rate per page.[163] In general, wages became highly skewed towards the upper end, especially when non-wage revenues from landed property and capital are included in the picture, as shown by the scattered data and estimates from the early tenth century (see Table 2.2[164]). The table also shows that wages for foot soldiers and cavalry were relatively high, and probably higher than for skilled labourers and

---

[159] Ben Abdallah, *De l'iqta' étatique*, 74; van Bavel, Campopiano, and Dijkman, 'Factor markets', 267.
[160] Dijkman, 'The fabric'; Duri, *Arabische wirtschaftsgeschichte*, 85–6.
[161] Al-Muqaddasi, *The best divisions*, 125–7.   [162] See also section 2.4.
[163] Sabari, *Mouvements populaires*, 23.
[164] For their help in making the estimates in Table 2.2, I would like to thank Bas van Leeuwen (communications of 25 August 2011 and 4 October 2011) and Jessica Dijkman (4 October 2011).

other non-military. Still, military wages were equally skewed when comparing the salaries of foot soldiers with the huge revenues of officers and military leaders. Another wealthy group in Iraqi society was formed by the wholesale merchants and traders in luxuries, who were often also involved in financial transactions and possessed large rural properties. Much wealthier than these groups, however, was the senior market elite, who combined large landholdings with tax farms, high offices, and financial dealings.

For the early tenth century, as the sources are relatively numerous, we can try to reconstruct income and wealth inequality. Since for Iraq no such estimates are available in the literature, in contrast to the later cases discussed in this book, we will make this reconstruction here. If we assume that Iraq at that time had some 2.5 million inhabitants, and we use the standard assumption that the active labour force comprised 40 per cent of the total population, this means that some 1 million people in total had some type of revenue.[165] These were mostly men, but also women and older children who worked part time, mostly in non-wage earning activities. Although the figures listed in Table 2.2 are mainly rough estimates, and they derive from data which are not easy to interpret, because the monetary system in this period disintegrated and became more regionalized,[166] they give at least some idea of income and wealth inequalities.

More specifically, by roughly estimating, or guesstimating, the numbers of people in each of these professional categories, we can calculate a Gini coefficient of income inequality. With the tentative estimates made in Table 2.2, this figure is somewhere around 0.6, making Iraq in this period one of the most unequal societies recorded in history, with a level of income inequality comparable to the most notoriously unequal countries in world history.[167] Wealth inequality, with a Gini of 0.99, had even reached the highest level for all historical and contemporary cases where estimates are available.

Much of the wealth accumulated found an outlet in the financial markets. In the ninth and tenth centuries, land, lease, and labour markets became distorted, restricted, and less free, as a result of the dominance of the new elite that combined market operations with political leverage, but the financial markets further developed and flourished. The rise of these financial markets, being the last of the factor markets to develop, was closely linked to the high degree of commercialization of the economy, but also to the fiscal system and state power, and it formed an outlet for accumulated private wealth. At the local village level, the link between credit, taxation, and wealth was evident in the practice of *qabala*, in which a rich man or village notable advanced the tax payment to the tax officer for the local community, in order to be reimbursed later by the community, with compensation. This practice could result in abuses, and as early as the late eighth century it was condemned

---

[165] For population numbers: section 2.1, 42–3.

[166] Heidemann, *Die Renaissance*, 369–72 and 377. This does not affect the following calculations of inequality too much, however, since the data used are at least from one area, Iraq.

[167] Compare Milanovic, Lindert, and Williamson, 'Measuring ancient inequality', 14–18 and 77.

Table 2.2. Estimates of monthly wages and wealth ownership in Iraq (early tenth century, in dinars) and a guesstimate of the number of people in these categories. Additional revenues from rural estates and other properties (next to wages, salaries, etc.) marked*. Guesstimates are between [ ]

	Monthly wage[168]	[Number]	Wealth[169]
Semi-unemployed, seasonal workers [vagrants, beggars, disabled]	0.5–1	100,000	[0]
Unskilled labourers [and lower peasants]	1–2	500,000	[0–2]
Skilled labourers [and middling peasants]	2–3	200,000	1–4
Ordinary soldiers, policemen [and slave soldiers]	2–3	25,000	1–4
Pedlars, junior clerks	up to 3	25,000	1–4
Small tradesmen, craftsmen	[2–7]	75,000	1–100
Highly skilled labourers	3–7	20,000	[4–20]
Minor officials, lower judges	6–7	5,000	[15–50]
Well-trained soldiers	7–10	15,000	[15–100]
Middle-ranking officals, cavalry men [and slave cavalry]	12–14	10,000	[200–500]
Managers of state offices, professors, doctors, judges, and market inspectors [and military officers]	20–100+5*	1,500	[2,000]
Merchants	100–500+20*	1,000	10,000
Senior judges and directors of state bureaux	100–500+40*	300	20,000
Bankers, large merchants	500+200*	1,000	100,000
Provincial governors [and military leaders]	3,000+2,000*	20	1 million
Close relatives of the caliph	4,000*	10	2 million
[Vizier] and directors of financial administrators	5,000–10,000+6,000*	3	3 million
[Caliph]	50–100,000+20,000*	1	0 million
Total revenue earners		**c. 1 million**	
Total revenues per year	**c. 41 million**		
Total wealth			**c. 187 million**
Inequality (Gini)	**0.59**		**0.99**

[168] Van Berkel, *Accountants*, 104–10; Ashtor, *A social and economic history*, 133, 139, and 154; Kennedy, *The armies*, 129–31; Ashtor, *A social and economic history*, 154 (unskilled labourer 1.5 dinar; skilled labourer 2 dinars, clerk 3, low official and low judge 4–7, cavalryman 12–14, middle official 8–20, high official >30, professor 50, judge 100 dinars); Dijkman, communication 7 September 2011 (unskilled labourers 1.1–2 dinars; skilled labourers 2.5–7 dinars); Sabari, *Mouvements populaires*, 34–5 (vizier 5,000 dinars plus property, provincial governors 2,500–3,000 dinars, head of state bureau 500 dinars, assistant of state bureau 20 dinars, official in state bureau 25 dinars, lower officials 10 dinars, market inspector 200 dinars), 36 (cavalry 40 dinars, infantry 6 dinars, lower guards 5–9 dinars, higher guards 10–14 dinars, high officers 800–1,000 dinars), 40 (glass engraver 1.33–1.5 dirham per day, day labourers 1–1.5 dirham per day).

[169] Margoliouth, *The table-talk*, 16–18 (jeweler: 1 million dinars), 42 (jug-manufacturer: 100 dirhams), 64 (confectioners and pedlars: 1–3 dinars), 176 (cloth-merchant: 400,000 dirhams); Ashtor,

by the chief Muslim jurist Abu Yusuf, in part because he feared that with this system the state would receive less than in the case of direct collection.[170] Peasants alternatively resorted to lending money from wealthy urbanites in order to pay their taxes, but lenders often used the plight of these peasants to ask very high, usurious interest rates.[171] Also, the inability to pay the interest or repay the debt made the peasants dependent on the lenders, who used this position to buy the peasants' produce below market price.

The link between credit, power, and markets also operated at the state level, as we will see, but at the same time the towns saw credit and financial markets develop in a more favourable way, linked to the functioning of the real economy. One example is the practice called *salam*, widespread in urban industries and crafts, where the buyer paid the producer in advance for a commodity, which was then produced and delivered, that is, an early example of a futures contract.[172] Even more crucial were financial markets in the realms of long-distance commodity trade and taxation. There was the proliferation of letters of credit (*suftaja*), to be cashed at a bank, and enabling safe transfer of amounts up to thousands of dinars (or a thousand times the yearly wage of a skilled labourer) over long distances of hundreds of kilometres or even more.[173] These letters of credit, which were widely used, were used also in fiscal administration, by officials and tax farmers from remote provinces for transfers to Baghdad, and in trade, showing the interaction of taxation and trade, as well as the relationship between state elites and merchant elites. The instrument was also used by depositing unpaid letters of credit with bankers, as a security for loans. Another financial instrument which had existed before but came into regular use in the tenth century was the *ṣakk*, a bill of exchange, used for sums up to thousands of dinars or even more.[174] Bankers charged a share in paying out, for instance a commission of 1 dirham per dinar (equivalent to 5–10 per cent, depending on the exchange rate in the period),[175] a practice which offered them a handsome profit, while at the same time the reasonable level of this commission indicates the smooth functioning and security of this system.

The ninth and tenth centuries were thus a period of booming financial markets and new financial instruments. In this period, all kinds of banking activities flourished, with money changers and merchant bankers (*jahbadh*) changing coins,

A social and economic history, 149 (small traders and retailers 100–200 dinars in wealth), 140–1 (high-ranking officials having 1 million dinars per year from their estates); Forstner, *Das Kalifat*, 23–4 (pretenders to the caliphat: 5,000, 20,000, and 80,000 dinars per year and 3 million dirhams respectively 10 million dinars in wealth); Sabari, *Mouvements populaires*, 33–4 (relatives of the caliph: 13 million dinars, 10 million dinars, 1 million dinar per year).

[170] Løkkegaard, *Islamic taxation*, 95–6, where he equates this practice with tax farming, whereas it may be closer to credit.

[171] Cahen, 'Fiscalité, propriété'.

[172] Johansen, 'Le contrat salam'; Heidemann, *Die Renaissance*, 360.

[173] Fischel, *Jews*, 17–21; Ray, 'The medieval Islamic system', 71–2. See, however, Heidemann, *Die Renaissance*, 359, who nuances the importance of this instrument in the tenth century.

[174] Mez, *Die Renaissance*, 447–8 (examples from the tenth century); Labib, 'Capitalism in medieval Islam', esp. 89–90.

[175] Margoliouth, *The table-talk*, 215–16.

verifying the value of different coins, collecting payments, and offering banking facilities, including to the government and its officials. The first of these exchanger bankers are mentioned in the second half of the eighth century, but they proliferated in the tenth century.[176] Among them were Muslim Arabs, but also Christians and many Jews. Some of the Jewish *jahbadh* became state bankers, and built close connections to the caliph and the viziers. Links between the exchanger bankers and the state were formalized around 910 with the establishment of a central bank, under the direction of two prominent bankers, an entity that was made responsible for the monthly payment of advancements of cash to the state, secured on future tax revenues. A further formalization took place with the establishment of the *diwan al-jahabidhah*, a kind of central banking agency, with branches in all major towns, under a governor, appointed by the state, mentioned for the first time in 928.[177] The exchanger bankers also became the private bankers of the wealthy, including senior officials and merchants, who deposited their money with them. In order to shield this money from taxation or confiscation, these sums were often not entered in the books of the bankers, even when the sums in question were as large as tens of thousands of dinars.

At the beginning of the tenth century, there were also financiers (*sarrafs*) who offered all kinds of credit facilities to a wide public.[178] Sums lent could be huge, such as the loan of 200,000 dinars extended by the Baridis, a family of tax farmers and generals, to vizier al-Kalwadhari in 931 through the financial intermediary Ibn Quraba, at an interest of 1 dirham per dinar, that is about 8 per cent per year.[179] As caliph Ibn Mutaz noted around 900, financiers could make the highest profits by extending loans to former members of the elite who had been ruined, with interest rates of up to 1,000 per cent per annum. Mostly, however, the interest rates were modest, that is, somewhere between 4 and 10 per cent per year,[180] rates which indicate a fairly well-functioning, secure capital market.

Both bankers and financiers combined their banking activities with trade and also with advancing money to the state, secured by future tax revenues, which they sometimes collected themselves. By way of their credit operations they thus relieved the state of cash shortages, which grew especially from the mid-ninth century, as a result of reduced coin supplies, declining tax revenues, and the accumulation of coins in the hands of a private, wealthy elite.[181] Credit thus formed an escape route for the state.

Banks as autonomous institutions did not develop, but banking activities were widespread and operated within a market, including physically. In the large towns, such as Basra or in al-Karkh, the commercial district of Baghdad, these bankers and money changers assembled around their own markets, bankers' bazaars, or

---

[176] Fischel, 'The origin of banking', also for the following. See also Sabari, *Mouvements populaires*, 29–30 and section 2.4, 89, for lending operations.

[177] Chaci, 'Origin and development'; Ben Abdallah, *De l'iqta étatique*, 87.

[178] Udovitch, 'Bankers without banks'; Fischel, 'The origin of banking'.

[179] Ray, 'The medieval Islamic system', esp. 68.

[180] Ashtor, *A social and economic history*, 86.

[181] See for the decline of tax revenues section 2.4, 79–81, and for the reduction of coin supplies section 2.4, 91.

streets, such as the Awn Street in al-Karkh.[182] In Basra around 1000, an observer noted that virtually every merchant had his own bank account and paid only in cheques on his bank in the banking bazaar there.

At that time, people from Basra had earned a reputation for their financial activities, and were sometimes ridiculed or despised for this, as shown in the ninth-century satirical book by al-Jahiz containing numerous anecdotes about the niggardly bankers from Basra.[183] Some of these acquired great wealth, such as Zubaida ibn Humaid, famous for his avarice, who owned wealth with a value of some 100,000 dinars, and Ahmad ibn Halaf al-Yazidi, whose father left him and his brother sums of 2.6 million dirhams and 140,000 dinars respectively. These sums are not even hugely large, but the fact that they possessed liquid means, which had become ever more scarce and much needed by a cash-poor state,[184] lent these families political leverage also. The same families were also linked to the religious elite, again undermining the idea of a supposed Muslim distrust of financial dealings. Of the religious scholars of the Arabian heartland, including many from Iraq, a substantial portion was involved in business, sometimes combined with tax farming, including some investors and moneylenders. The proportion of moneylenders and financial dealers among them grew in this period, from 3 per cent of the scholars before the ninth century to 5–8 per cent in the ninth to eleventh century.[185]

The high wealth inequality of the period, and the presence of large fortunes, also promoted the rise of wealth-storing devices outside the market. The Iraqi elites started to immobilize their wealth in *waqfs*, or religious and charitable foundations, partly in order to shield it from taxation by the state. The *waqf*, as an unincorporated and inalienable trust, appeared on the stage around the mid-eighth century and grew in importance in the ninth century, especially in Iraq.[186] The first treatises in the Islamic world which deal extensively with the *waqf* were produced by authors from late ninth-century Iraq, one from Basra and one by the chief judge of Baghdad, and they reflect how the *waqf* at that time had become an important and fully regular institution in Iraq.[187] A major motive for the foundation of a *waqf* was the wish to serve a religious, charitable, or public purpose, ranging from the provision of health care or education to the housing of orphans or the provision of drinking water. For the founder, some additional advantages of using this instrument were that he could appoint himself as an administrator of the *waqf*, he could set his own salary to be paid out of the *waqf*'s funds, he could nominate relatives to positions paid for by the *waqf*, and he could designate his children as his successors. This last advantage helped him to circumvent the Islamic inheritance laws and the partible inheritance these prescribed, while at the same time he could shield the family property from taxation by public authorities.[188] This instrument became even more attractive in the tenth century, as the economic decline that

[182] Ray, 'The medieval Islamic system', 72–3, also for the following.
[183] Pellat, *Le livre*. For the following examples: Pellat, *Le livre*, 49–51 and 59.
[184] For the lack of cash: section 2.4, 89–91.
[185] Cohen, 'The economic background', esp. 32–3 and 43–4.
[186] Kuran, 'Legal roots', 3–4 and 7–8.   [187] Cahen, 'Réflexions', 41.
[188] Kuran, 'Legal Roots', 4–5 and 8–10.

was then beginning made profitable investments of capital in the real economy less feasible, while wealth also became less secure as a result of the growing risk of confiscation by the authorities, and at the same time looting became an endemic problem.[189] The *waqf* formed an effective way to shield a family's property from these risks.

At the same time, besides the positive effects of the *waqf* for the founder and his descendants, and its contribution to the public good, there were also negative effects. The extensive use of the *waqf* led to a growing immobility of land and resources, which were frozen within the *waqf* and could no longer be alienated, and thus to a reduction in market exchange. Because of the inflexibility in the destination of *waqf* funds, a destination that could no longer be changed, it also led to growing difficulties in the adaptation of the economy to new social and economic requirements.[190] Also, since it protected big fortunes and helped to prevent the partition of inheritance, it led to a further accumulation of wealth. This instrument, moreover, also helped the rich to use their wealth to gain societal influence and get a hold on public services.

In the meantime, other opportunities to convert wealth into political power also sprang up. Around 900, the sale of public offices and the payment of fees in order to stay in office (*istithbat*), and the receipt of bribes by office holders, became institutionalized. In 917, the secret profits bureau was established by the vizir, in order to tax the bribes accepted by officials. In 961, for the first time the office of chief judge was sold, followed shortly afterwards by that of chief police officer of Baghdad.[191] Venality, bribery, and sale of offices had existed before, of course, but the early tenth century forms a watershed with regard to the extent, and especially the openness and institutionalization of these practices, as they now became enshrined in formal procedures.

In the tenth century, Iraq thus saw a number of related developments. First, more than previously, an interlinked, almost unitary elite in Iraqi society came to be formed, consisting of owners of large landholdings, tax farmers, senior officials, bankers, and merchants,[192] with the members of this elite mostly combining these roles, either in person or within their family. The build-up of large landholdings was facilitated by the freedom of buying and selling land, and it was often combined with tax farming and large-scale trade. This also enabled wholesale dealers in grain, tax farmers, and large landholders to dominate or even monopolize the market. Second, this elite was richer than ever before, with wealth and income being distributed very unequally, and with inequality reaching levels among the highest recorded in history, as we have seen. Land was accumulated through the market, slaves were bought, and coins and valuables were hoarded. In this society, the drive to become wealthy was paramount, a drive colouring the atmosphere of the period.

---

[189] For confiscation and looting, see section 2.4, 87–90.

[190] Kuran, 'The provision of public goods', stresses this point, even though it is not undisputed.

[191] Mez, *Abulkâsim*, XX.

[192] Ashtor, *A social and economic history*, 132–60; Fischel, *Neue Beiträge zur Geschichte*. This elite figures prominently in the tenth-century descriptions of Iraqi society, such as that by the 'Mesopotamian judge': Margoliouth, *The table-talk*.

The tenth-century sources from Iraq, much more than the earlier ones, reveal a prodigious desire to accumulate more and get rich, with the appetite for money being equalled only by the fear of its loss.[193] Third, the financial markets in this period were booming and they formed an outlet for the accumulated wealth. Fourth, the sale of offices became well established and the system of tax farming was introduced. Together with the growing use of the *waqf* these instruments enabled the wealthy to acquire social and political influence, and to combine the wealth they had acquired and made profitable through factor markets with their now acquired political leverage.

2.4. LONG-RUN EFFECTS ON ECONOMY, POLITICS, AND SOCIETY FROM THE NINTH TO THE ELEVENTH CENTURY

After its heyday in the eighth and early ninth centuries, the Iraqi economy started to decline. For this decline all kinds of possible causes are mentioned in the literature. Among them are diverse factors such as governmental mismanagement, warfare, invasions, inroads made by Bedouins, religious sectarianism, the inherent culture of Islamic hostility to innovation and climatic deterioration.[194] The effects of the dynamic factor markets in Iraq are not mentioned as a possible cause, but we have seen above that a major cause for the decline may be found here. This section delves more deeply into this possibility. To this end, it surveys the main economic, social, and political developments of the ninth to eleventh century, the period of decline. It assesses how these relate to the preceding discussion of the role and effects of factor markets or, alternatively, to the other factors traditionally mentioned as causes of decline. By way of shedding more light on the chronology of changes in all these domains, we will try to get a better idea of possible causal links.

The Chronology of Economic Decline

In our search for indicators of long-run changes in the period, needed in order to better establish the exact chronology of economic decline, we would be enormously helped by reliable estimates of GDP per capita. Although progress has been made in recent years, estimates are still virtually absent, and those available are highly tentative. For the second half of the first millennium BCE, blessed with relatively abundant source material, some estimates are available now. These show GDP per capita fluctuating between about $600 and 800, with the high point of $800 reached in the latter part of this period, around 100 BC.[195] Relevant material is scarcer for the early medieval period. The highly tentative estimates for southern

---

[193] As observed by Fischel, 'The origin of banking', 569.
[194] See also section 2.1, 45–6.
[195] Foldvari and van Leeuwen, 'Comparing per capita income', using 1990 international dollars.

Iraq show GDP per capita at about a similar level as the estimates for the earlier period: $890–990 around 720 AD, declining to $770–860 around 1060 and $640–720 around 1220.[196] If anything is suggested by these figures with their wide margins of error, it is, first, that changes in GDP per capita over the very long run were limited and, second, that Iraq after a period of economic florescence in the eighth century witnessed a decline in the following centuries. More important than these changes in GDP per capita in early medieval Iraq are, however, those that took place in the organization of the economy and in the distribution of wealth. What is clear is that even with broadly similar levels of GDP per capita, the high and growing inequality of the eighth to eleventh century discussed above must have resulted in a substantial deterioration of the welfare of average people. We will come back to this issue below.

Another way to get an idea of long-run changes in levels of welfare would be through archaeological research into human bones, which could enable us to reconstruct long-term trends in human stature, especially crucial for periods in which written material is scarce. This would also enable us to compare the early medieval figures to those obtained for the preceding centuries and those available for the modern period.[197] Some early medieval results are available, for instance for Tell Ashara on the Euphrates in present-day Syria, not far from Iraq,[198] but they are too scarce to allow any conclusions to be drawn. We must therefore eagerly await the progress of archaeologists.

Neither approach, therefore, offers reliable clues as yet. We will have to use other indicators of economic growth and decline, each of which is beset by interpretation problems but which, used in combination, enable us to obtain a clearer picture. One of these indicators is the development of land tax revenues over the centuries, on which a fair amount of data is available. These revenues at the beginning of the tenth century were much lower than at the end of the eighth century, while these in their turn were much lower than those from the sixth or early seventh centuries, as the peak level was reached under the Sasanian king, Khosrow II.[199] More specifically, the land tax revenues from the fertile river plains, the Sawād, had risen from 210–40 million dirhams in the sixth century to a peak of 340 million around 625, but then suddenly declined to 110–50 million around the mid-seventh century. This sharp decline is probably an artefact of changing taxation methods and the new delimitation of fiscal districts in this period of the Islamic conquest and the ensuing political transition; with similar boundaries the figure for the sixth century would probably have been around 120 million.[200] More relevant here are the later figures, which are not distorted by administrative changes and are thus indicative of more fundamental shifts. The figures show that revenues very gradually

---

[196] Pamuk and Shatzmiller, 'Plagues, wages', 220–1.

[197] For the modern period: Stegl and Baten, 'Tall and shrinking Muslims'.

[198] Sołtysiak, 'Preliminary report on human remains'. For data from the first millennium BC: Jursa, *Aspects of the economic history*, 805–6. For height also: van Bavel, 'New perspectives on factor markets'.

[199] Adams, *Land behind Baghdad*, 71 and 84–5.

[200] Morony, *Iraq after the Muslim conquest*, 119–23.

went down for two centuries, declining from about 125 million to 90 million dirhams between c. 640 and c. 850, but then rapidly falling to only about 25 million dirhams in the early tenth century.

When looking at the sharp decline in fiscal revenues from the first half of the ninth century on, which interests us most here, it is striking that Iraq stands out among the different parts of the empire, as it was the area where the decline was most pronounced.[201] Whereas the earlier, gradual decline in Iraq from c. 630 to the second half of the ninth century had been similar to that in all other areas within the empire, the further and sharp decline in Iraq and Upper Mesopotamia in the second half of the ninth century and later clearly contrasts with the stability of fiscal revenues in Egypt, Jordan, Palestine, Syria, Khuzistan, Fars, and other areas.

When trying to explain this sharp decline in fiscal revenues in Iraq, we have to consider two possible causes: the fall in agricultural production, and the fact that private elites through the market, the leasing system, and otherwise extracted a growing share of the surplus at the expense of fiscal state revenues.[202] The possibility is suggested by the fact that in the early tenth century national income, as calculated in Table 2.2, was some 600 million dirhams per year, of which at that point only some 4–7 per cent was received by the state in the form of tax revenues, as can be seen from a comparison with the figures assembled in Table 2.3.[203] The state and its fiscal system in this period, therefore, had become fairly unimportant as an allocation system; the market had become dominant. The rise of tax farming from the late ninth century also diminished the share of the state, with the extracted surpluses now partly ending up with the tax farmers instead of the state. However, even if the state had extracted a much higher share, the decline in revenues would still be pronounced. The decline thus also points to a more structural cause, that is, the total of rural surpluses to be extracted or allocated in any way had declined as a result of the problems in the agricultural sector.

These problems are most clearly apparent in the reduction of the cultivated area. Adams' research on early medieval Iraq has shown that the tilled surface area at the end of the tenth century had shrunk substantially since the seventh or eighth century. The exact chronology differed somewhat per region. In the countryside around ancient Uruk, roughly halfway between Baghdad and Basra, the chaotic years of the Muslim conquest and the foundation of the new, nearby towns of Kufa, Wasit, and Basra, had drawn people from the countryside as early as the seventh century. The greatest decline, however, took place afterwards. Of the twenty then remaining settlements no fewer than seventeen had been abandoned by the tenth century and all of them were deserted in the twelfth century.[204] In the Diyala region and around Baghdad this retreat accelerated later, especially around the mid-ninth century, with almost two-thirds of all recorded settlement outside Baghdad

---

[201] Mez, *Die Renaissance*, 122–3; Ashtor, *A social and economic history*, 63–5, 129, 172–5, 207–8, and 259–60.

[202] Campopiano, 'State, land tax and agriculture'; Waines, 'The third century', 287 and 291–5. For the rise of tax farming, see section 2.3, 62–3.

[203] With 23 and 40 million dirhams forming the lower and upper bounds of the tax revenues, producing the minimum and maximum percentage, while total national income is an estimate.

[204] Adams and Nissen, *The Uruk countryside*, 59–65 and 93.

Table 2.3. Tax revenues from the Sawād (in millions of dirhams), c. 500–1340, calculated and/or interpreted by various authors[205]

	Waines	Campopiano	Adams	Ashtor
c. 500	–	–	214	–
608	–	–	240	–
628	–	–	340	–
Islamic conquest				
634–44	–	116	128	128
661–80	–	150	100	100
680–6	–	–	–	135
694–714	–	–	–	118
717–20	–	112	124	120
738–44	–	–	–	100
788	88	124	–	134
800	88	–	–	–
819	112	115	108	108
845–73	94	113	87	78
893	75	–	75	c. 60
915	23	–	–	–
918–19	–	27	31	c. 40
968	–	–	42	42
c. 975	–	–	30	30
1180–225	–	–	–	30
1336–40	–	–	18	c. 16

being abandoned by the early tenth century.[206] At that latter date, even the last prosperous areas also started to decline. A similar picture is found for the Diyar Mudar, in northern Mesopotamia, along the river Euphrates. The rural economy here had flourished in the late Sasanian and early Islamic periods, and this florescence even increased in the mid-eighth century, as a result of growing urban demand. At that time, the rich agricultural landscape, with extensive systems of irrigation, was dotted with rural settlements.[207] But from the late ninth century decline set in, and in the eleventh century only a few settlements remained and the area had become home to nomads and their pastoral activities. Physical output must have dramatically declined.

This agricultural decline cannot be explained by a contraction in demand or by falling food prices. On the contrary, prices in the period were sky-rocketing. Nominal grain prices had risen tenfold between c. 800 and the beginning of the tenth century. This rise was only to a small extent the result of coinage debasements, since the fineness of the silver dirhams declined somewhat but remained at a fairly high level during this period.[208] The rising prices, which were not matched

[205] Waines, 'The third century', 286; Campopiano, 'State, land tax, agriculture'; Adams, *Land behind Baghdad*, 71 and 84–5; Ashtor, *A social and economic history*, 63 and 172.

[206] Adams, *Land behind Baghdad*, 97–105. See also Adams, *Heartland of cities*, 183–5.

[207] Heidemann, 'The agricultural hinterland'.

[208] Campopiano, 'State, land tax, agriculture', 16–17 and appendix 2. Heidemann, *Die Renaissance*, 369–72, shows that debasement and regional variety from the tenth century both increased, especially with silver coins.

by equally rising wages, soared especially in periods of harvest failure and political unrest, as they attained levels three to tenfold above the normal, already high levels. Problems were aggravated by the hoarding of food, practised by the urban wealthy, tax farmers and merchants, and the grip they had on grain markets enabling them to push up prices.[209] In the tenth century this situation became endemic. Whereas famine had been rare before, Baghdad was hit by famines in 934–5, 937, 940–4, and 948, with the chronicles describing how corpses were buried in common ditches and starving people ate dogs and excrement to stay alive, and again in 982–3 and 986–8, giving rise to despair, fury, and unrest. In his description of the Islamic world in the second half of the tenth century, the geographer al-Muqaddasi characterizes Iraq as 'the home of dissension and high prices, and every day it retrogresses'.[210]

Causes of the Economic Decline

That the food scarcity and high food prices did not stimulate a rise in food production in the countryside points to fundamental problems in the agricultural sector. One possible explanation could be climatic deterioration. By combining archival sources with analyses of tree ring data and pollen records, climate changes in the early and high medieval Middle East can now better be reconstructed, although many questions and interpretation problems remain, preventing us from drawing any firm conclusions yet. This is also because indications often apply to very large areas, such as 'the eastern Mediterranean', for instance, or to neighbouring areas such as Iran, and it is not always clear how they affected Iraq. What we do know, however, does not point to a great effect of climate. On the basis of our present knowledge, the period of sharpest agricultural decline, the ninth to eleventh century, does not stand out as a particularly unfavourable climatic period.

Actually, after a humid and favourable climatic spell in the fifth and sixth centuries, it was instead the seventh to ninth century in the Middle East that were characterized by severe desiccation and aridization, as evidenced by pollen curves, for instance.[211] This aridity damaged agriculture especially in dry, marginal areas where rainfall was already insufficient. However, this unfavourable climatic period coincided with the economic florescence of Iraq, as the agricultural sector does not yet seem to have been in severe decline. Around the year 1000, when the agricultural decline was underway, the climate improved instead, and the hot and dry phase gave way to a wetter and more favourable one. In this period, there was a higher frequency of wet winters, especially in the first half of the tenth century and most of the eleventh.[212] Further, some authors have suggested that the Middle East in the tenth to early twelfth century experienced a colder period, or even a climatic

---

[209] Section 2.3, 67–8.

[210] Al-Muqaddasi, *The best divisions*, 104. For these famines: Ben Abdallah, *de l'iqta' étatique*, 150–7 and 165–7.

[211] Issar and Zohar, *Climate change*, 215–22; Izdebski, 'Why did agriculture flourish'.

[212] Vogt et al., 'Assessing the medieval climate', 28–9. This impression is also gained from the investigation of chronicles by Grotzfeld, 'Klimageschichte des Vorderen Orients'.

cooling, which was also felt in Baghdad, where some instances of prolonged snow-fall are reported for the period.[213] These cold spells affected the crops, and especially damaged date palms, but compared to the highlands of Iran, for instance, the effects were limited in this area of more moderate climate. The wetter and colder climate may even have been favourable for agriculture here. This, however, was the phase during which tax revenues reached their all-time low and many agricultural regions were abandoned. In view of the chronology reconstructed here, admittedly on the basis of the disparate findings, climate does not seem to have played a substantial role in the decline.

Rather, the agricultural decline seems to be connected to falling investments in the agricultural sectors and related problems with the irrigation systems. Crop output may have declined mainly because of the salinization of the soil and the deterioration and breaches of the irrigation canals, due to lack of maintenance or destruction during the continuing unrest in the Iraqi countryside.[214] The climate in Iraq had always been harsh and people were constantly confronted with the risk of salinization, a risk many previous societies had successfully combated. However, in the ninth and tenth centuries the breaches of canals and the floods, and possibly also overirrigation, caused increased salinization, which especially damaged the vulnerable wheat crops. It is telling that in the south of Iraq, where salinization was most severe, wheat in this period was replaced by barley, which was less sensitive to salinization but also much less valuable as a crop.[215] Lack of maintainance of canals may have played a major part in this.

More generally, there was a decline in investments in the agricultural sector. The new fiscal *muqasama* system, gaining ground from the late eighth century and imposing taxes as a share of the crops, as we have seen, reduced the incentives of landowners to invest, since every increase in output had to be shared with the state. Also, access to land became more dependent on political favour and relationships than on clear property rights, resulting in landowners becoming focused on short-term gains and not geared to long-run investments.[216] Peasants, in their turn, lacked the resources to invest, squeezed as they were between substantial taxes and high lease shares, taking by far the largest part of their output. In cases where they had to pay their taxes in cash, their situation became even more difficult, as they had to sell their crops immediately to merchants in order to get the necessary coins. This drove down the prices for their crops, as contemporaries around 800 noted.[217] The profits went to the urban merchants, who later sold the crops for higher prices in the market, thus taking money out of the agricultural sector. Moreover, at the next stage, taxation was increasingly organized by way of tax farming, which was introduced in the late ninth century.[218] Tax farmers were made responsible for the investments in large irrigation works and other infrastructure, but were much more interested in short-term gains, again to the detriment of investments.[219] Moreover, tax farming was often combined

[213] Bulliet, *Cotton*, 69–72 and 77–8.   [214] For rural unrest: below 84–5.
[215] Waines, 'The third century', 294.
[216] Campopiano, 'State, land tax and agriculture', 33–41.
[217] Mårtensson, '"It's the economy"', 213–14.
[218] See section 2.3, 62–3.   [219] See on the *iqta'* system section 2.4, 89.

with coercion and violence in the levying of taxes, sometimes linked to coercive dealings in land and credit markets. One extreme but probably illustrative story from the
tenth century relates the experience of a man tortured by the tax collectors, who
forced him to sell them a piece of land and lent him the balance of the money he
needed to pay his taxes at an interest rate of 1,000 per cent.[220]

Nor did the rural population have much incentive to invest, even if they were
able to at all. The dismantling of small and medium-sized landholdings reduced
the number of potential investors and their opportunities to invest. Nor did the
organization of the lease system and labour-renting system offer much incentive,
as we have observed.[221] The large landowners, who were mostly urban-based, only
made substantial investments in cash-crop plantations and slaves. Apart from this,
they instead focused on the exploitation and squeezing of the rural population.
Because of the dominance of cities and urban elites in Iraq, and the resulting flows
of rural surpluses to the towns, through rents and taxes, the economic situation in
the countryside became worse sooner and to a more extreme degree than in the
towns, resulting in mounting hardship for the country dwellers. Both push and
pull factors thus led to a massive flight of these people to the towns, as evidenced
for Upper Mesopotamia in the second half of the eighth century, for instance.

In this period, the countryside also became the scene of unrest and recurrent
troubles, as a result of mounting inequality, poverty, and despair. There were a
number of peasant rebellions, but in contrast to the earlier ones, by now these had
become desperate acts of powerless people, without any chance of success. In 774,
in Upper Mesopotamia, there was a revolt of peasants, mainly of Christian background, who attacked and burned down the houses of wealthy landowners and
murdered caliphal officers. The chronicler Dionysius of Tel Mahre in the first half
of the ninth century tells about the immiseration and indebtedness of the peasantry in Upper Mesopotamia and how the peasants rebelled against this, attacking
especially the barns and warehouses of the townspeople. These were hated most,
because of their activities as merchants and money lenders, sucking the countryside dry with high interest rates.[222] These are just examples: poverty and discontent
in the countryside fuelled many more revolts by peasants and slaves, especially
from the mid-eighth century to the mid-tenth, but in contrast to the large successful revolts of the earlier period, these were all crushed, mainly by mercenary armies,
hired in the labour market, and later slave armies.

The most notable uprising was the Zanj revolt, in the south of Iraq, lasting for
more than a decade, from 869 to 883. This was led by the Arab Ali bin-Muhammad,
himself descended from slaves, who inspired and organized the black slaves used in
the harsh work in the marshes around Basra in order to fight the deprivation and
social abuses they suffered.[223] This was done on the basis of a programme aimed
at the improvement of the social position of the slaves and the assertion of their
right to own property, houses, and slaves [sic!]. Other people, including peasants,

[220] Mez, *Die Renaissance*, 126–7.   [221] Section 2.3, 64–7.
[222] Cahen, 'Fiscalité, propriété'; Ashtor, *A social and economic history*, 66–8.
[223] Talhami, 'The Zanj rebellion reconsidered', 453–5; Popovic, *The revolt*, 33–43. See for the slaves
also section 2.3, 69–70.

Bedouins, craftsmen, and day labourers, joined the revolt, and its aim was broadened, to fight social injustice more generally. Most rebels were motivated especially by their shared hatred of the large landowners and slaveholders from Basra. This city was taken and completely destroyed by the rebels. In their attempts to crush this revolt, the Abbasid caliphs initially relied on slave soldiers, who were introduced in the ninth century, supplemented by local levies, under Turkish command.[224] As the revolt continued, they had to bring in more reinforcements, with big armies of Turks, Berbers, Afghans, and Nubians, being slave soldiers, captives, marginal groups, and also some hired freemen.[225] The archers proved crucial in winning the battle, and they were also useful to put to death the captured and imprisoned Zanj rebels. These prisoners were lucky, since one of the Zanj leaders was first flogged 200 times, his arms and legs were amputated, his body slashed with swords, his throat slit, and finally he was burnt, all in the presence of the caliph. The revolt left no lasting results, after Basra had recovered, except for a destroyed countryside.

Only a few years later, a subsequent, major revolt broke out among the Qarmatians, a Shi'ite, millenarian movement led by Hamdān Qarmat, a carter from a village near Kufa. This movement, sparked by widespread desperation and anger over heavy taxes and tax-farming abuses, strove for equity, social justice, and welfare, and found many supporters among the Bedouins and the peasantry in the south of Iraq, especially the most wretched and distressed among them.[226] The revolt, and the assistance it provided to the poor, were financed by taxation levied among themselves and by robbing merchant caravans. In 898, the latter yielded 2 million dinars. After its initial success in Iraq and several decades of fighting, the revolt was finally put down. Its effects were entirely negative, including the destruction of agriculture and infrastructure, with irrigation canals being destroyed and breached, and the land becoming afflicted by salination, as had also happened during the Zanj revolt.

The enduring insecurity and the damage to the countryside caused by these revolts reduced even further the incentives to invest in agriculture. Combined with the negative effects of the changes in taxation, the introduction of tax farming, the lease and labour rent systems, massive peasant flight, and recurrent unrest, this reduced investments in the countryside and brought down agricultural output.

The negative changes of this period were not yet felt directly in the towns, at least not by the urban elites. The exchange and allocation of land, labour, and capital in the countryside, and the organization of the fiscal system, were subjected to the interests of the landowning elites and the tax-receiving state, mainly operating from the towns. Nor did these changes, or the urban interests, conflict with or block market exchange. On the contrary: the functioning of the factor markets, and the commercialization of the rural economy, suited the interests of these urban elites, and increasingly so, as they amassed more land and capital. The organization of land tenure and leasing seems to have been well suited to both squeezing the

---

[224] For the introduction of slave soldiers: section 2.3, 70. See also Kennedy, *The armies*, 118–24.
[225] Kennedy, *The armies*, 153–8.
[226] Waines, 'The third century', 303–5; Tucker, *Mahdis and Millenarians*, 115–17.

countryside and rural labour, and at the same time introducing new crops which generated market profits and increasing surpluses, which indirectly also promoted urbanization. The Iraqi towns were among the largest of their time, but within a socio-economic constellation which came at the expense of the countryside. In the long run, this resulted in declining investments in agriculture and heightened pressure on the rural population. It is therefore not surprising that signs of economic decline and social unrest had manifested themselves in the countryside first, that is, as early as the eighth century.

In the next phase, however, the effects also came to be felt ever more severely in the cities, and especially by the lower groups in urban society. An early example of social tensions as a result of the growing inequalities and the hardship of the urban poor was in 812–813, during the siege of Baghdad when the ordinary people were armed, in order to help defend the city. This led to unease and fear among the wealthy and the notables, expressed in derisive references to these people, such as 'vagabonds', 'riff-raff', or 'scum'.[227] Among them were also street vendors and 'people of the market', from whom the merchants from the commercial district of al-Karkh, who chose the opposite, victorious side during the siege, carefully sought to distance themselves. This social rift came to the fore even more conspicuously as the culture of the urban elite further developed in the ninth century, the period of the desperate revolts of impoverished countrymen. This elite culture was elaborated furthest with the rise of the *zarafā*, 'the stylish people', who cultivated an elegant, refined style of dining, dressing, consuming literature, and behaving developed in contrast to the habits of the common people.[228] These stylish people came from the new elite of merchants, financiers, and tax farmers and senior officers. Of all the Islamic world these *bon chic*, *bon gens* came most clearly to the fore in the Iraqi towns, such as Basra and Kufa, where they lived in their wealthy quarters in large houses filled with stylish luxuries.

At the same time, Iraq saw changes in poor relief, which were opposed to the ideas held earlier by the scholars in Medina. Instead of aiming for full integration of the poor into the Muslim community by way of alms and entitlements, and extending the right to these entitlements to all, as earlier Medina scholars had wanted, the Iraqi scholars and their school in Kufa wished to limit alms to the deserving poor, who were disabled and destitute, but accepted their position and did not beg.[229] This conservative view was not aimed at eliminating inequality, in contrast to many of the earlier social movements we encountered in the sixth to eighth century, both in the Mazdakite revolt and in early Islam, but rather at consolidating social cleavages while at the same time maintaining social peace and order. More radical currents within mainstream Islam, which had been important in the earliest period, had long been weakened or crushed. The *zakāt*, for instance, functioned more as an instrument to justify and make respectable the private

---

[227] Hoffmann, 'Al-Amin, al-Ma'mun und der "Pöbel" of Bagdad'; Bonner, 'Definitions of poverty', esp. 335–6.
[228] Ghazi, 'Un groupe social'. See also the illustrative examples in Mez (ed.), *Abulķâsim*.
[229] Bonner, 'Definitions of poverty'.

wealth of the rich, soothe their conscience, and dampen the resentment of the poor,[230] than as a way to eradicate poverty and reduce inequality.

The signs of growing social divergence and ensuing tensions became even more apparent in the next period, fuelled by the deterioration of the living standards of ordinary people and growing poverty. The declining agricultural output resulted in a rise in food prices between the eighth and tenth centuries, not only in nominal prices but also in real terms. This directly affected the position of wage labourers and town dwellers. As descriptions in the narrative sources show,[231] the decades around 800 had still been prosperous for the people of Baghdad, with a relatively high purchasing power, but especially from the late ninth century, inflation and rising prices hit the urban population. Meat, around 800 still widely consumed, largely disappeared from the menus of the ordinary people, and for many their diet became restricted to barley, oats, small fish, beans, dates, inferior rice bread with fat and garlic, and bread made out of cheaper millet with pulses and peas.[232]

Although economic circumstances in the towns had remained more favourable longer than in the countryside, and average income levels were higher, now there too inequality increased, particularly in the large cities of Basra and Baghdad, and the number of poor people rose. The fortunes of the rich, who benefited from the flows of surpluses from the countryside, their landed estates, the growth of financial markets, tax farming, and the flourishing trade in luxury items, contrasted sharply with the plight of the urban poor, who were hit by rising food prices. Abulqasim, the character created by the writer Mutahhar, around 1000, described Baghdad as a paradise for the rich and a place of suffering for the poor.[233] Sketches such as these are confirmed by the figures on income and wealth distribution, as discussed above and in Table 2.2. These figures, however tentative, show that social inequality in the tenth century had risen to great heights, with the Gini of income inequality being around 0.6, a historical high, and wealth inequality even hitting a staggering 0.99.

One riot after another erupted in the Iraqi towns, often sparked by high food prices, and popular anger was frequently directed against merchants. In 865, people in Samarra used the temporary weakening of caliphal power to attack the bazaars of jewellers, merchants, and money changers, and looted them.[234] In 919–920, in the towns, a series of riots broke out against rising prices and speculation on the market by large merchants and tax farmers, which caused a famine. Speculators were aided by the vizier, who deliberately delayed and blocked the shipment of corn from the provinces to Baghdad in order to generate price rises and profit from them. In response, people in Baghdad rioted, plundered the corn warehouses, broke open the prisons, and destroyed the mansion of the head of police. Repression was harsh, as the government used soldiers to attack and fight the masses, and had the captured rioters flogged or chopped off their hands. Increasingly, however, soldiers deserted and joined the rioters, which compelled the government to give

---

[230] Kuran, 'Islamic redistribution', 281–4.   [231] Ahsan, *Social life*, 135–49.
[232] Ahsan, *Social life*, 135–49; Waines, 'Cereals, bread and society', esp. 279–82.
[233] Mez, *Abulâsim*, 73.   [234] Forstner, *Das Kalifat*, 101–2.

in. The corn stocks of the vizier, his mother, the military officers, and senior officials, who had all apparently speculated on high prices, were now released, and corn prices were lowered.[235] In other instances, the introduction of new taxes ignited a riot, as in 985, as a tax on silk and cotton was introduced. The silk workers in Baghdad rose against this tax, which was abolished, but introduced again fourteen years later, with harsh repression of the unrest and crucifixion of the rebels.[236]

From the early tenth century, urban riots, rebellions, and disturbances were frequent and even became endemic, but without any lasting changes. A few rebellions achieved some limited, practical success, but did nothing to structurally alter the situation. Rather, they further exacerbated relations between elite and non-elite groups. One of the most conspicuous expressions of social tensions was the emergence of the *'ayyarun*. These poor day labourers, pedlars, and unemployed youngsters roamed the streets and looted shops, broke into houses of the wealthy and compelled them to flee the city or to organize night watches to protect their possessions.[237] Sometimes the looting *'ayyarun* are portrayed as hooligans, but they also had high moral principles and honour, they were hospitable and helped the poor, while their activities were mainly directed against the rich, the markets— where they levied their own tolls—and against the wealthy merchants and the police, showing some of their underlying motives, which exceeded mere hooliganism.[238] Fear of these activities and social revolts resulted in increasing reliance of the elites on armed force, and on hired soldiers, in order to protect their properties and positions in society. The police force of Baghdad (*shurta*) in the early tenth century was composed of 9,000 men. They guarded the prisons and gates, and acted as a security force, but mainly maintained public order, supported in performing these tasks by cavalry and foot soldiers.[239] Expenditure on the police and military grew enormously.

At the same time, the unrest, looting, and insecurity hurt the urban economy. Since the beginning of the tenth century, the al-Karkh quarter, the main commercial and financial district of Baghdad, had become a major target of rebels and looters, as shops, markets, and banks were hit regularly, perhaps almost yearly. In the year 972 this happened twice, as the quarter was first looted and next set on fire by a coalition of disgruntled groups, destroying some 300 shops and stores.[240] Wealthy merchants and bankers chose to leave this insecure place, as a group of Jewish and Zoroastrian merchants did in 942 and another a little later, leaving Baghdad for Syria.

All these uprisings and troubles in the towns and the countryside were desperate and unsuccessful, and they did not bring about any positive change. Rather, they indirectly strengthened the role and position of the military in Iraqi society. In the 920s,

---

[235] Sabari, *Mouvements populaires*, 62–3; Ben Abdallah, *De l'iqta' étatique*, 143–5.
[236] Dijkman, 'The fabric', 15.   [237] Sabari, *Mouvements populaires*, 64–5 and 77–100.
[238] Duri, 'Baghdad', 37–8; Sabari, *Mouvements populaires*, 91–6.
[239] Kennedy, *The armies*, 157–8 and 163. More generally for the growing role of professional soldiers in this and other cases: section 6.1, 257.
[240] Ben Abdallah, *De l'iqta' étatique*, 160–3 and 201. For merchants and bankers leaving Baghdad: Ben Abdallah, *De l'iqta' étatique*, 154 and 156.

as the Qarmatians had attacked Kufa and were threatening to march on Baghdad, the regime relied mainly on slave regiments.[241] One of these was the cavalry regiment called Hujariya, consisting of some 12,000 slaves (*mamluks*), normally stationed at the caliphal palace. As a result of growing tension, revolts, and waning central power, the caliph had to rely increasingly on them and on other slave and mercenary regiments, consisting mainly of Turks, but also Armenians, Berbers, and Nubians. Expenses on the military sky-rocketed. Something over 80 per cent of the state budget was spent on the army around 900,[242] which is an enormous share considering the fact that Middle Eastern governments traditionally funded many vital functions in administration and infrastructure, to which large shares of the budget had formerly been allocated. But even if large funds now were redirected to the military, this was still insufficient, and caliphs were unable to pay for the large numbers of troops, also because of the dwindling tax revenues of the state and the declining availability of coins in this period. The caliphs increasingly had to rely on financiers, tax farmers, and Jewish bankers to advance them the money to pay the troops, offering these financiers future tax revenues as security.[243] A minor example of this was the loan of 10,000 dinars the vizier Ali ben Isa contracted in 913 with two Jewish bankers, for sixteen years, and an interest payment of 2,500 dirhams per month (that is, an interest rate of some 15 per cent per year), with incoming letters of credit pertaining to future tax revenues from a designated province as security. Ingenious constructs such as these, and the more general reliance on credit and financiers, did not offer a structural solution, but only further weakened the state, also because in the process it had to compromise future income streams and concede its position of power to the financiers.

The next step in this process was the rise under the new Buyid dynasty—in the second half of the tenth century—of the so-called military *iqta'*, a system based on the concession of the fiscal rights of the state over land as a grant, in place of a salary.[244] This process had started under the Abbasid caliph al-Muqtadir in the early tenth century, but really gathered pace under the Buyids, from the mid-tenth century on. Confronted with widespread unrest and rebellions, declining trade, taxes which had to be farmed out or even granted away, and declining agricultural output, the caliphs saw themselves compelled to grant ever more tax farms and state properties to the Turkish and Iranian army leaders, on whom they depended for maintaining power and quelling unrest and opposition.[245] This process at times slowed down or was even in part reversed, but generally it proceeded ever further. The *iqta'*-holders were geared towards making short-term profits and had no interest in making investments in their district, which especially hit the areas dependent on expensive irrigation systems, as in central and southern Iraq.[246] Also, from the

---

[241] Kennedy, *The armies*, 160–4 and 196–8.   [242] Kennedy, *The armies*, 156.
[243] Fischel, 'The origin of banking', 578–83, also for the following example. See for the role of financiers section 2.3, 74–6.
[244] Cahen, 'L'évolution de l'iqta'; Ben Abdallah, *De l'iqta' étatique*.
[245] Kabir, *The Buwayhid dynasty*, 145–66.
[246] Heidemann, *Die Renaissance*, 306–12 and 351, and also 314–16, where he nuances the effects on Northern Mesopotamia, where irrigation was much less important.

beginning of the tenth century all kinds of legal and jurisdictional offices were sold in order to refill the empty caliphal coffers, as we have seen happening with the offices of supreme judge and head of police,[247] a practice which offered the wealthy elite even more political and jurisdictional leverage.

Another source of revenue that near-bankrupt rulers sought to tap was the confiscation of wealth. This can be interpreted as a rather desperate act in the search for state revenues, now the power of the market elites had become too strong to have their wealth taxed along regular lines within a generic tax system. The only option for rulers was to target individuals and to try and take part of their wealth, either under the cloak of death duties or so-called fines, or as outright arbitrary confiscation or extortion. This practice already existed in the eighth and ninth centuries, but only as a punishment for misbehaviour or fraud. Now, in the course of the tenth century, it became common, caused by the state's growing lack of cash, declining tax revenues, and the growing private wealth of the period.[248] The victims were individual bankers, officials, notaries, and merchants, and especially those who lacked or lost the protection of the ruling elite. This situation created insecurity and stimulated the wealthy to consume their wealth quickly, or shield it through the creation of *waqfs*, which appeared in the mid-eighth century but really gained importance in the late ninth century, as we have seen.[249] Also, wealth was concealed by hoarding precious metals, for instance in the form of silver and gold bowls and cups that could easily been hidden, so that bullion was no longer available for coining, contributing to the growing scarcity of coins.[250] All these elements limited the productive use and investment of capital.

Now also industries and trade started to get hit. In order to make up for declining tax revenues from the countryside, in the second half of the tenth century the state introduced new levies on trade and commodities; levies that originally had been considered illegal under the basic Islamic law.[251] These new levies were quite heavy, for instance 100 dirhams on a load of linen, and numerous.[252] Custom duties and imposts on cargo ships passing through Basra, which were introduced and multiplied in the tenth century, were strictly levied through rigorous searches and close supervision of trade. After a reform of these duties around the mid-tenth century, they yielded some 2 million dirhams per year. Also, new taxes were introduced on textile production, mills, flour, and foodstuffs. The introduction of all these levies must have created an obstacle to trade and industrial specialization.

As a result of declining tax revenues and rising food prices, caused by the desertion of villages, the deterioration of irrigation works and the decline of the agricultural area we observed, the basis for economic growth was eroded and towns, mainly relying on surplus extraction from the countryside, started to shrink. The tenth and following centuries saw a decline of industries in Iraq, which had become largely dependent on elite consumption.

---

[247] See section 2.3, 77.
[248] Kabir, *The Buwayhid dynasty*, 158–60; Mez, *Die Renaissance*, 108–11.
[249] Section 2.3, 76–7.   [250] Heidemann, *Die Renaissance*, 371–2 and 374–5.
[251] For the eleventh century: Heidemann, *Die Renaissance*, 324 and 339–42.
[252] Al-Muqaddasi, *The best divisions*, 121–2, where he observed how these levies were first introduced. See also Kabir, *The Buwayhid dynasty*, 153–5.

Coins now increasingly flowed out of the country, in order for the wealthy Iraqi elite to be able to pay for luxuries, such as slaves and furs, purchased in Scandinavia and the north of Russia. By far the greatest number of the dirhams found by archaeologists are from hoards deposited in northern Europe. The number of dirhams found within these hoards rises from virtually none from the seventh century, to 17,000 from the eighth and 67,000 from the ninth century, to reach a peak of 183,000 from the tenth century, declining to 62,000 dirhams from the eleventh century.[253] Most of these silver coins ended up and were deposited in silver-poor northern Europe, traded for goods imported to the Middle East, and they witnessed the trade deficits of Iraq. This is also evidenced by the fact that, at the same time, silver coins in Iraq became scarce.[254]

As a result of the combined effect of these factors, the urban economy was now also hit hard and the urban population rapidly declined. The current information on sizes of towns, although sketchy, confirms this outline. The absolute size of towns grew to a peak around 900, arguably as a result of the increasing success in the extraction of surpluses from the countryside, also by making use of the market, and increasingly drawn to the capital, Baghdad. This is shown by the share of Iraqi urbanites living in Baghdad, which reached its peak in the tenth and eleventh centuries, as almost three-quarters of the urbanites were living there. In the tenth century the erosion of the productive base of the countryside further proceeded and also hit the towns and eventually Baghdad itself, resulting in sharp urban decline in absolute numbers, as shown in Table 2.4.[255]

While the urbanization rate initially remained at a high level, of about a fifth of the population, in line with the preceding argument about the growing pressure on the countryside and the increasing extraction of rural surpluses by urban elites, this

Table 2.4. Population numbers of big towns in Iraq, 800–1400 (in thousands, only towns with more than 10,000 inhabitants)

City/year	800	900	1000	1100	1200	1300	1400
Mosul					10	20	20
Baghdad	350	450	300	250	200	95	90
Kufa	100	80	40	30	20	15	10
Basra	100	80	40	30	30	30	15
Wasit	100	80	40	30	30	30	15
Hilla					10	15	10
Total	**650**	**690**	**420**	**340**	**300**	**205**	**160**
% Baghdad	**54**	**65**	**71**	**74**	**67**	**46**	**56**

[253] Shatzmiller, 'Economic performance', esp. 144–9, using the data from Kovalev and Kaelin, 'Circulation of Arab silver'. Her interpretation of this chronology (that is, as a sign of monetization) is more positive, but incorrectly so, I think, in view of the other evidence.

[254] Heidemann, *Die Renaissance*, 369–72.

[255] Bosker, Buringh, and van Zanden, 'From Baghdad to London'; estimates kindly provided by Eltjo Buringh, 3 May 2011.

rate started to decline from the eleventh century on.[256] A final element in this urban decline was formed by the invasions by the Seljuqs, in the eleventh century, and the Mongols in the thirteenth century, culminating in the sack of Baghdad in 1258. Rather than seeing these invasions as a cause of decline, however, it would be better to say that they hit an already weakened, declining, and vulnerable society.

When we go back to the start of the period discussed, and try to summarize, we can see how the social and political changes and upheavals in the late Sasanian and early Islamic periods, in the sixth and seventh centuries in particular, helped bring into being a relatively balanced socio-political structure. This balance in turn allowed for a more open and favourable framework of market exchange, and thus aided a relatively unrestricted functioning of markets for goods, lease land, labour and capital, and the growth of market exchange. These developments were most conspicuously expressed in the increasing freedom of wage labour and (sharecropping) leasing in the seventh and eighth centuries, and later, in the eighth to tenth century, in the growth of financial markets. The development of the market economy is also reflected in the growing monetization of the economy and the growth of market-oriented agrarian production observed above, while the positive economic effects are also indicated by the high and rising urbanization rates of the period.

At the same time, the freeing up of land, labour, and capital for accumulation through the market, and the profits the owners of land and capital made by way of the market, also increased inequality and furthered the rise of new, ever more powerful elite groups. This process culminated in sharp social polarization, as witnessed by the inequality figures reconstructed for the early tenth century. One group became dominant in Iraq especially in the late eighth and ninth centuries, consisting of large landholding families from the Sawād, who increasingly also acted as tax farmers, financiers, and merchant bankers, and acquired high positions in the bureaucracy and thus translated their economic wealth into political leverage. In contrast to the earlier period, as civil servants were drawn from various parts of the empire and were often of diverse religious and social backgrounds, in the course of the ninth and early tenth centuries the higher offices were increasingly taken by this small group of families of large landholders and merchants from the Sawād.[257] The members of this group rewarded their friends and relatives with jobs and gifts, and increasingly pushed other social groups aside.

The same groups made huge profits, by combining their position in the markets with the acquisition of key positions in the fiscal regime, bureaucracy, and finance. These positons were acquired especially through their dominance in financial markets and their capacity to advance cash to a state increasingly starved of liquid means. When they entered the markets they thus had not only vast amounts of land and capital at their disposal, but now also the capability and

---

[256] Heidemann, *Die Renaissance*, 314–16, sketches a more positive picture for northern Mesopotamia, which was much less dependent on irrigated agriculture, and thus shows the regional differences in this process.

[257] Van Berkel, *Accountants*, 72–9.

political leverage to use and sometimes adapt the rules of market exchange, as we have seen with leasing, labour-renting contracts, and sharecropping leases, and in the development and use of financial instruments. The elites availed themselves of the market in order to squeeze the countryside and used the non-economic, coercive opportunities offered by and within the market, first to the detriment of the countryside, but later also to that of the urban populations. All these processes further fuelled social polarization, and reduced the incentives to make productive investments.

Further, in the next stage, the changes increasingly hampered the functioning of markets, and markets themselves started to decline, as non-market coercion became more attractive to the elites than market exchange. This happened especially in the late ninth and tenth centuries, with the growth of tax farming, the spread and formalization of the sale of offices, the growing use of slavery and the introduction of slave soldiers, and the growing use of the *waqf*, to highlight some of the major developments of the period. To be sure, the replacement of hired soldiers by slave soldiers and the freezing of land and capital within *waqfs* both entailed a reduction of market exchange and caused factor markets to decline again. Perhaps, but this is more speculative, the non-elite groups also increasingly avoided the markets, where they were confronted with ever more wealthy and powerful elite actors. Even leaving the latter possibility aside, the markets did indeed decline in this period, as is also reflected, for instance, by the sharp decline in the number of coins observed for the tenth and even more for the eleventh century.

During this latter phase, Iraq became confronted with economic decline. In the countryside this decline had started earlier than in the towns, as we have seen, but after the mid-ninth century it became a general phenomenon, in both countryside and towns. Among the main causes were the disappearance of the middling peasants who could potentially invest, the insecurity of the leasing system with regard to the reimbursement of investments, the lack of incentives for investment in agriculture more generally, the accumulation and freezing of capital in *waqfs*, and the expenditure on status and luxuries where demand was satisfied by foreign producers or in sectors where opportunities for 'modern' economic growth were weak. Irrigation works were no longer maintained or, if destroyed by fighting troops, not repaired anymore, and canals silted up. Arable farming from the tenth century receded to some last strips, as along the Tigris, and the land was gradually taken over by extensive, nomadic pastoralism.[258] Baghdad and other towns decayed. Visitors to Iraq found ruins where once large cities had been. As Yaqut-al-Hamawi wrote in his geographical encyclopaedia around 1224, some decades before the Mongol attack, about the area along the Nahrawan, the gigantic irrigation canal from the Tigris: 'it is now in ruins and all its cities and villages are mounds and can be seen with [only] walls standing'.[259] This was the result of a decline that had started in the tenth century, and earlier in the countryside.

---

[258] Adams, *Land behind Baghdad*, 102–6; also above, 80–1.
[259] Adams, *Land behind Baghdad*, 87.

The preceding discussion suggests that the organization and effects of factor markets have played a crucial role in these developments in Iraq. Their rise had pushed up economic dynamism and growth in the seventh and eighth centuries, from a level which was already fairly high. Next, their dynamism led to social polarization, especially as financial markets also expanded in the ninth century. In a further stage, the market elites used the economic wealth they had accumulated in order to acquire more social and political leverage, thus making the societal context in which markets functioned less equitable. Also, these elites used their leverage to adapt the rules of market exchange to better suit their interests. As these markets thus became distorted, and elements of extra-economic coercion became more important, this led to the retreat of ordinary people from the market, and it made economic investments less attractive, thus being at the root of the subsequent economic stagnation and decline. Their effects thus made Iraqi society more vulnerable, be it to natural disasters, erosion and salinization of irrigation works, to greed and dissension, or to military invasions and nomadic encroachments. They thus made this society more vulnerable to the events that are perhaps more apparent at first sight but would distract us from the major, deep cause of decline.

Map 3.1. Towns, villages, and regions in late medieval Italy (indicated are the boundaries of present-day countries).

3

Markets in Medieval City-States
The Centre and North of Italy, 1000–1500

3.1. THE EMERGENCE OF FACTOR MARKETS IN THE ELEVENTH TO THIRTEENTH CENTURY

The next case of an early market economy, which formed the successor to Iraq as the most advanced economy of western Eurasia, is Italy in the high and late Middle Ages. Italy had always been a relatively urbanized area, and had remained so even in the early Middle Ages, during the difficult centuries after the fall of the Western Roman Empire.[1] Despite the crises, the declining population numbers and the drop in prosperity, which occurred especially in the seventh and eighth centuries, towns and urban output markets had survived to some extent, and they started to grow again in the high Middle Ages. Alongside these output markets, from the eleventh century onwards markets for land, labour, and capital also developed, especially in the centre and north of Italy, and this was accompanied by rapid economic growth.

This chapter focuses on these northern and central parts of Italy, specifically the regions comprising present-day Lombardy, Liguria, Emilia Romagna, Tuscany, Umbria, the Marches, and the Veneto. This area of some 100,000 km² in total formed the heartland of economic development in this period, as shown, for instance, by the rapid rise of cities here. Towns had started to expand again in the tenth century, and already in the eleventh and twelfth centuries they had become prominent there, compared to other parts of Europe. It was the thirteenth century especially, however, which saw a rapid growth of urbanization. In particular, the giant cities of Florence, Venice, Genoa, and Milan saw the number of their inhabitants grow sharply. Genoa grew from 22,000 to 100,000 inhabitants and Florence from 45,000 to 95,000 in the relatively short time span between 1100 and 1300, while middle-sized towns such as Cremona also grew dramatically in this period, from 10,000 to 40,000 inhabitants. The urbanization rate in northern and central Italy peaked around 1300, with 21 per cent of the population living in cities,[2] a figure almost three times higher than in most

---

[1] Wickham, *Framing the early Middle Ages*, 212–14 and 644–56.
[2] Malanima, 'Urbanisation and the Italian economy', esp. 101–3. The population figures of towns are based on the dataset 'Baghdad to London'; access kindly provided by Eltjo Buringh, 7 June 2012.

other parts of Europe and comparable to levels in Iraq during its early medieval florescence.

Population densities became very high, in a process of population growth which probably also started in the tenth century, and reached a peak around 1300. At that point, the countryside around Pistoia had thirty-eight persons per km² and the whole territory including the city forty-eight persons.[3] For Florence and San Gimignano and their territories the latter figure was as high as sixty-five and eighty-five persons per km²; figures which were not reached again before the nineteenth century and were by far the highest in all of Europe. Despite the population growth and high population densities—and the associated pressure on resources—the real wages, GDP per capita, and agricultural output per worker around 1300 were far higher in Italy than in surrounding areas.[4] Ample surpluses were available and enabled urban patricians to spend huge amounts of money on the arts in order to enhance their prestige, social status, and indirectly their influence and power.[5] Florence and the other towns witnessed an unprecedented cultural peak as they entered the Renaissance, with a florescence of painting, architecture, and literature.

These developments took place in a context of increasing market exchange. Markets for goods, as observed, had always remained present to some extent in the centre and north of Italy even though evidence is meagre. Most *fora* survived in the early Middle Ages as market areas, and these grew again from the beginning of the eleventh century. Interregional trade in the Mediterranean had largely disappeared by the seventh and eighth centuries, but developed again, and by the eleventh and twelfth centuries there was a great deal of cargo traffic there once more. Venice from c. 800 onwards developed into a centre of this reviving international trade, especially in luxury goods. Also, there was the recovery of export industries in the north of Italy from the ninth century on, especially in ceramics, first marketed locally, but from c. 1000 increasingly also regionally and even between regions.[6] Alongside these product and commodity markets, markets for land, leases, labour, and capital, after their emergence in the eleventh century, also grew, especially in the twelfth and thirteenth centuries, as we will see.

A Context of Relative Equity

These factor markets were formed in a social context that, from the twelfth century, was characterized by a relatively wide participation in political decision making, especially in the towns. Towns were originally dominated by the nobility, who had remained more urban-based during the early Middle Ages in Italy than elsewhere in Western Europe. Each town in Italy had an elite composed of aristocratic families, who were also landowners and held secular and ecclesiastical offices, but

---

[3] Herlihy, 'Population, plague', 231–2.
[4] For real wages and other economic indicators around 1300, see below, 110–11.
[5] Goldthwaite, *Wealth and the demand for art*, passim; Katz-Nelson, *The patron's payoff*, 37–66.
[6] Wickham, *Framing the early Middle Ages*, 732–6.

were often also active in trade.[7] In the territory of Lucca, of the dozen or so aristocratic families, in the eighth century only two or three lived permanently in the countryside. These aristocrats were prosperous, but not extremely wealthy. Likewise, they nearly all possessed some land, but few owned very large estates. Compared to other parts of Western Europe, the Italian elites were fairly modest and clearly urban-oriented.

After a series of social movements from the tenth century, mainly directed against the noble regimes, the bishops, the crown, and the established order more generally, power in the towns became distributed more broadly. This period of social and political agitation and change, which gained momentum in the eleventh century, included mass actions, demonstrations, and uprisings, as in Milan, where the merchants and middling groups successfully rebelled.[8] One of the main aims of the insurgents, who often also included members of the lesser nobility and urban landowners, was the removal of all forms of arbitrary decision making based on feudal privileges. The insurgents acted to replace this by new forms of administration, with the formation of communes, which in their turn could build on earlier forms of urban organization.[9] As early as the late ninth century, some urban communities had had a role in local affairs, and these now slowly developed into full self-organization and formal self-government in the late eleventh century. In 1097, for instance, the most senior Genoese townsmen formed a *compagna communis*, a sworn association, which in its turn built on earlier organizations, including those of neighbourhoods.[10] The consuls of the *compagna*, who were mainly noblemen, were at least in theory expected to dispense equal justice to all citizens, which again points to a desire to remove arbitrariness and to develop justice and security, at least for those who belonged to the citizenry. After some experimentation with different political organizations, around 1200 a system was adopted in Genoa which strengthened the cooperation between factions and formed a balance between leading families, with policy setting separated from policy implementation.[11]

In Genoa the middle classes did not participate in political life. In other towns, political changes in this period went further, and broader layers of society participated. Middling groups increasingly, and especially in the thirteenth century, organized themselves in neighbourhood associations, guilds, and confraternities, which resulted in a high degree of self-organization of non-elite groups. In the decades after the rise of the craft guilds, around 1200, many communes, especially those in which the aristocratic elites were internally divided, as in Florence and Pisa, saw the establishment of regimes with the participation of the *popolo* (roughly the middle classes of merchants, bankers, the self-employed, and craftsmen).[12] This went along with political clashes, sometimes of a violent nature. In Perugia, in the thirteenth century, regimes dominated by the *magnati*, the older landowning

---

[7] Wickham, *Framing the early Middle Ages*, 211–12 and 605–6, also for the following.
[8] Violante, *La società Milanese*, 173 ff.
[9] Jones, *The Italian city-state*, 103–20 and for the following: 130–4.
[10] Epstein, *Genoa*, 33–4.   [11] Greif, 'On the political foundations'.
[12] For the role of elite divisions: Lachman, *Capitalists*, 58–64.

nobles and knights, or by the *popolo*, continuously alternated, until in the late thirteenth century the commune was transformed into a kind of guild republic.[13] The new regime aimed at making the fiscal system more equitable, lowering grain prices, securing peace, and curbing feudal violence. Although the success of the new regimes was not self-evident, and they excluded the lower classes, totally or partially, these social movements had changed the face of social and political power in the Italian towns and decisively broadened the participation of various social groups.

These developments in the towns were mirrored, although perhaps less markedly and a little later, by those in the countryside. Peasants, village notables, and rural communities organized themselves and fought against lordly power and arbitrariness, in legal battles and sometimes in violent clashes, especially in the late twelfth and early thirteenth centuries.[14] In Tassignano, near Lucca, where relatively detailed sources give us an in-depth view, this process was perhaps not dramatic, but the villagers still struggled for self-determination, through a decade-long process of disputed elections, boycotts, and destruction of documents.[15] In the twelfth century, all over Italy, rural communes appeared, and these asserted their right to choose their own leaders, the consuls, and their village councils. Through their representatives, the communes negotiated and made agreements with their lords, as a legal body, and were responsible for the observation of all agreements. This process was formalized in many regions, as around Lucca or Siena, by 1200. Although these communes were certainly not fully homogeneous and democratic, and were often politically and economically dominated by local elites, they still allowed for fairly broad participation.

A similar picture emerges for the distribution of economic wealth, which was fairly wide. Investigations of some Tuscan villages at the beginning of the thirteenth century show that some 10–15 per cent of the rural population were substantially richer than the rest, while 30–50 per cent of the population owned no land and often were not included as members of the village community.[16] Still, this leaves a large middling group of landowning peasants, comprising about a third or even half of the rural population, who based their position on relative secure ownership titles.[17] Access to wealth and political decision making was relatively broad compared to many other Western European societies of the period.

At the same time, and especially in the areas closest to the cities, towns and urban elites started to extend their influence over the surrounding countryside. In part, this was a natural process, since noblemen moved from the countryside to the towns, or because they were rural noblemen and urban burghers at the same time, and increasingly operated from the towns.[18] Another factor was that urban merchants acquired

[13] Blanshei, 'Perugia', 16–19 and 50–3. See also Cohn's recent book, *Lust for Liberty*, 57–8 and 76–7.

[14] Redan, 'Seigneurs et communautés rurales', 149–56 and 620–6.

[15] Wickham, 'Rural communes', 7.   [16] Collavini, 'La condizione giuridica'.

[17] See for these titles, as offered by the *livello*, for instance, this section, 104–5.

[18] Jones, *The Italian city-state*, 18–24, 80–5, and passim.

land in the surrounding countryside, a process which slowly started in the eleventh century, as shown for Milan.[19] To some extent, however, the process was the result of the deliberate actions by the towns, which brought lordships, abbeys, and estates under their control, if necessary by using military power and destroying the castles of their rivals, and tried to dominate the countryside.

This process had mixed effects on the degree of rural freedom and self-organization. On the one hand, some village communities were crushed by urban power, and villages close to the towns were brought under urban rule. As early as the mid-twelfth century onwards, towns had brought their immediate surroundings under their political and judicial control, taking over the administration of justice and the appointment of village officials, and leaving the rural communities only minimal scope for self-government.[20] Urban dominance in jurisdictional matters, and also the numerous land sales to townsmen, eroded the rural communes and led to their disintegration. Sometimes, if their interest was served by this, towns even sided with the rural lords to fight a rural community, as in cases when a lord wanted to force peasants to pay commercial rents, which the town in its turn expected to help supply the urban market. The city of Florence, for instance, in the period 1230–47 supported its bishop in his capacity as a rural lord when he commuted the traditional levies in the commune of San Casciano Val di Pesa into grain payments and the city helped to break the rural commune's resistance.[21] This is a telling example of how the growth of markets—in this case the lease and product markets—was not always the result of the desires and interests of all parties involved, but rather that of specific interests and power relations, in which the rural community in this case was the losing party.

On the other hand, in most cases the influence of the towns in this period had favourable effects for the rural population. The towns frequently aided country people and rural communities to free themselves of noble rule, arbitrariness, and remnants of manorialism, and allow them to achieve a greater degree of freedom, if only out of self-interest, in order to break the power of the remaining rural noblemen, to be able to replace older feudal jurisdictions by new urban ones or to stimulate reclamation activities under the aegis of the towns.[22]

The Early Rise of Land and Lease Markets

In this context of relative freedom, equity, and self-organization, and the removal of older restrictions on the exchange of land, labour, and capital, factor markets expanded. We are best informed about the land market. There are records of sales of land in various parts of Italy, including sales by peasants as early as the eighth and ninth centuries, and accelerating in the third quarter of the ninth century, probably building on a continuity in the existence of land sales from the Roman period on.[23]

---

[19] Violante, *La società Milanese*, 113–32.
[20] Jones, *The Italian city-state*, 365–70.   [21] For this example: Dameron, 'Episcopal lordship'.
[22] Curtis and Campopiano, 'Medieval land reclamation', 100–2. See for growing urban power section 3.2, 113–17.
[23] Herlihy, 'Agrarian revolution', 29–30. See also the examples in Feller, 'Quelques problèmes'.

A further acceleration of the number of land sales in the market, or at least of the recorded number of sales, took place during the eleventh century, in the areas around Milan and Bergamo, in Tuscany, and also in central Italy, in the Abruzzi, as the land market really took off.[24] Besides outright sales, this period also saw a lot of transactions in which land was pledged or given in tenancy for a certain period, on the basis of a written contract, the *livello*, signed and exchanged between the two parties.[25] The precociousness of Italy in this respect, compared with other parts of Europe, can be understood, firstly, from the high degree of literacy and the use of the written word, making its re-entry on a larger scale in the eighth century, allowing for the registration of property rights and transfers, and thus increasing security and stimulating land sales. The road to dynamic land markets in northern and central Italy was further opened up by the disappearance of manorial, communal, and lordly restrictions on the exchange of land during the high Middle Ages.[26] This happened in a context of thriving output markets and commercialized, market-oriented production, with the markets found especially in the towns. Around 1100, most of the countryside had become firmly integrated in market networks and substantial shares of production were oriented towards the market.[27]

Manorial organization, which formed a major obstacle to the rise of an open land market, had always had less impact in Italy, since it had been introduced there only at a relatively late date, and then in most regions only incompletely and weakly. Classical-type manors with large demesnes and extensive labour services were rare in early medieval Italy.[28] Partly connected to this, the *mansus*, as a standard family holding, protected by manorial custom and not to be divided, did not have much importance in Italy. In eleventh-century Tuscany, except for the mountainous, less fertile parts, the concept of a standard unit of tenant exploitation had already been abandoned, or never been introduced, with tenements first becoming fragmented and later consisting increasingly of constantly changing complexes of scattered parcels, with these changes being made through exchanges or gift giving but from the eleventh century overwhelmingly through sale.[29] Since peasant families thus did not regard particular farms as their ancestral holding, this reduced the land-family bond and their personal attachment to the land, even though land sales always remained to some extent influenced by social considerations and relationships,[30] and it increased the inclination towards alienation and the mobility of land. Jointly, these elements enabled open land markets to emerge in Italy already at the start of the high Middle Ages.

This process was strengthened in the following centuries, as alternative systems of exchange and allocation declined. After the first signs of decline as early as the

---

[24] Wickham, 'Land sales and land market'; Wickham, *The mountains and the city*, 242–56.
[25] Conti, *La formazione*, part I, 97, 123, 128–9, and 243–6. For the *livello*, see also this section, 104–5.
[26] Van Bavel, 'The organization and rise', and the references therein.
[27] Jones, *The Italian city-state*, 163–5.   [28] Toubert, 'L'Italie rurale', esp. 104–11.
[29] Wickham, *The mountains and the city*, 27–8 and 231–5; Herlihy, 'Agrarian revolution', 29–30 and 34–5.
[30] Remaining the case until far into the modern era: Levi, *Le pouvoir au village*, 112–18.

ninth century, the relatively weak elements of manorial organization that were present started to disappear in most of the northern and central parts of Italy from the eleventh century onwards, with this process speeding up in the twelfth and thirteenth centuries. It was only in parts of the south and in some mountainous regions in the north, such as Piedmont and Trentino Alto-Adige, that the manorial system persisted longer; in most regions in the north and centre the classical manor was fully dismantled by the beginning of the fourteenth century.[31] Not only manorial rules, but lordly restrictions on land sales more generally were broken down in this period. In Monticello, in the Sienese countryside, the abbot of San Salvatore, in his capacity as lord of the village, in the mid-thirteenth century still claimed that land sales could only take place with his permission, and resisted sales or bequests of land by the villagers to outsiders, and especially to noblemen and religious institutions, in an attempt to shield the socio-economic homogeneity of 'his' villagers.[32] However, in the legal case that followed, the local witnesses declared that this was something from the distant past, which they had only vaguely heard about, and that land sales were virtually unrestricted.

The commons and communal rights to land, too, were gradually dissolving in this period and gave way to private, alienable property rights, although this process showed diversity. In some parts of Italy, as in the valleys and plains of Liguria, Tuscany, and in the Po Valley, agriculture was highly individualistic and communal rights were limited. Especially in the thirteenth century, stubble grazing, gleaning, and other collective rights were further reduced or abolished, often at the instigation of the towns.[33] Wastelands and open fields were enclosed and fenced. Sometimes, towns and urban elites pursued a deliberate policy to this end, at times even enclosing, privatizing, and selling off common lands in order to solve their financial problems and lack of liquidity, as the towns of Perugia and Cortona did in the second half of the thirteenth century, enraging the rural people in the process. In the later Middle Ages, what remained of the commons in these regions was further parcelled out, privatized, or sold. It was only in some parts of central-northern Italy that extensive common lands remained, in the lower Po Valley, where swamps had not been entirely drained yet, in the Alpine regions in the north, where the villagers with full rights held extensive communal properties and grazing rights, and in Umbria and the Apennines, where the communities did so. They fiercely defended these rights and started to formalize and write them down.[34] In most regions, however, common lands in this period were diminished, and in the following centuries they would almost completely disappear.

Since the village communities mostly did not strive for a tight hold on land sales either, the number of the social organizations that could potentially hinder the rise of an open land market, or was willing to do so, had become very small in many parts of Italy as early as the twelfth century. In the second half of that century, the

---

[31] Jones, 'From manor to mezzadria', esp. 206–14; Epstein, 'The peasantries of Italy', 88–9.

[32] Redan, 'Seigneurs et communautés rurales', 632–4.

[33] Montanari, 'Mutamenti economico-sociali', 89; and for the following: Perol, *Cortona*, 92. For the later period, section 3.3, 125.

[34] Curtis, 'Florence and its hinterlands', 13–14; Casari, 'Emergence'.

land market was further stimulated by improvements in the institutional framework, including the legal clarification of property rights, the introduction of standard measures of land, and the establishment of civil courts guaranteeing and
regulating transactions in the land market. In Italy, registration of land transactions was well developed and mainly carried out by public notaries. As early as the
eleventh century, public notaries were active in this field, mainly operating in the
cities, but also extending their activities from their urban base into the countryside. By c. 1200, the development of an elaborate system of public notaries, whose
decisions had full legal validity, was complete, and written charters had been made
compulsory for more substantial transactions of immovable property in various
Italian city-states by the thirteenth century.[35] The notary's signature provided full
legal validity. This system was very advanced, compared with the contemporaneous
situation in northwestern Europe, for instance, and made the opportunity to register land transfers widely available. In combination, these influences brought
about a further growth of the land market, for example, in the areas around Pistoia,
in Tuscany, in the years 1180–1220.[36]

On the other hand, after the thirteenth century, not all non-market elements in
the sphere systems of land exchange and allocation had disappeared.[37] In the high
Middle Ages, the role of kin had not been very important in the field of land transfer, but in the eleventh and twelfth centuries in Lombardy and elsewhere a degree
of kin control grew again, with consortia of kin groups attempting to get a hold
over strategic patrimonial goods and sometimes reclaiming land transferred to
non-kin.[38] Nor did lordly power fully disappear. This power was generally limited,
and even more so with the decline of manorialism and the rise of urban power over
the countryside, forming a counterweight to the power of rural lords. By contrast,
however, some seigniorial rights were strengthened or introduced in the high
Middle Ages. In Tuscany, from the late twelfth century onwards, lords were able to
levy entry fines on the sale of land and the right to demand licence for alienation.[39]
Also, religious institutions acquired the right of first refusal on the sale of land
under their lordship, often at a beneficial price, and also had the right to prohibit
the sale of land to other lords.

Moreover, existing institutional arrangements sometimes became frozen, thus
losing their favourable effects over time, as they were not adapted to economic and
social changes. This can be observed with respect to types of tenure such as the
livello, a contract written down either in a booklet or as two identical copies, which
offered the tenant possession of a parcel of land for a specified period against the
payment of a yearly sum, and which could be renewed and sometimes transferred
to the heirs or a third party.[40] In the eleventh and twelfth centuries, this type of
tenure could be considered favourable, compared with manorial tenure and the

---

[35] Schulte, *Scripturae publicae creditur*, 100–8.   [36] Huertas, 'Between law and economy'.

[37] For the following: van Bavel, 'The organization and rise'; and van Bavel, 'Markets for land'.

[38] Violante, 'Quelques caractéristiques', esp. 118–24; Herlihy, 'Agrarian revolution', 32–3.

[39] Jones, 'From manor to mezzadria', 215.

[40] Conti, *La formazione*, part I, 97, 123, 128–9, and 243–6; Andreolli, *Contadini su terre di signori*, 39–68.

then prevailing types of tenure in northwest Europe. The *livello* can even be seen as one of the foundations of the position of the small peasantry in the early period and of the dynamism this group displayed. But after the dissolution of manorialism, these Italian tenures became relatively unattractive compared with allodial property which offered absolute and exclusive rights to the land and which now emerged in various parts of northwest Europe, particularly from the thirteenth century onwards. The disadvantage increased as this form of tenure, which was dominant in regions such as the Veneto in the thirteenth century, burdened the tenant with restrictions on inheritance, alienation, and possession.[41] Still, despite these nuances, land markets in northern Italy, especially when compared to other parts of Western Europe in this period, can be considered fairly unrestricted and were accessible to a wide group of participants, while property rights to land were clear, often put in writing, and well protected by the legal system.

The clear property rights to land and their legal protection in turn paved the way for the introduction of short-term, contractual leasing. Northern and central Italy was ahead of the rest of Western Europe in the emergence of this type of leasing. In Tuscany, leasing had already started to appear sporadically in the eleventh century, as with some types of the *livello* contracts, which due to the payment of a yearly sum were akin to leasing, and with commercial short-term leasing gaining momentum from the late twelfth century onwards.[42] In Piedmont, in the twelfth century, the earlier, oral contracts between owners and users of the land, which had been based on customary rules, were replaced by written ones, which in the thirteenth century came to be mostly made for a specified number of years, instead of in perpetuity.[43] By 1300, short-term leasing had become highly important, or even dominant, as an instrument of making landed property profitable to the owner. Some of these owners were former manorial lords or owners of large landholdings, who had lost the opportunity to coerce unfree labour, especially after the dissolution of manorialism. Leasing was also stimulated by the growing share of land owned by burghers, who welcomed the lease as an instrument to ensure that their ownership of land would generate steady revenues. At the beginning of the fourteenth century around Siena, about three-quarters of the rural-owned land was still directly used by the owner, but more than four-fifths of the burgher-owned land was leased out, and this category was growing rapidly at the expense of peasant ownership.[44] In Lombardy and the Po Valley, too, short-term leasing acquired considerable importance, in contrast to peasant-dominated regions, such as some of the mountainous areas, where its role remained more limited.

A crucial element in the organization of leasing is the formulation of the payment of the lease: as a fixed rent or as a share of the gross output of the tenancy. In the plains

---

[41] Jones, *The Italian city-state*, 240; Fumagalli, 'L'evoluzione dell'economia agraria e dei patti colonici'.

[42] Hopcroft and Emigh, 'Divergent paths of agrarian change', esp. 14; Jones, 'From manor to mezzadria', esp. 205 and 220–1.

[43] Panero, *Terre in concessione*.

[44] Cherubini, *Signori, contadini, borghesi*, 73–83, 295–8, and 358–64; for the Florentine countryside: Conti, *La formazione*, 97–102, 245, and 395–411, and III, parte 2a, 25–7, and 37–45 ff. (situation in 1427).

of Lombardy, exceptionally for northern and central Italy, fixed rents predominated, but elsewhere sharecropping became increasingly important in the course of the later Middle Ages. Particularly in the central regions such as Tuscany, Umbria, and the Marches, but also further north, in the southern part of Emilia-Romagna, there was a marked increase in sharecropping from the twelfth century onwards. By the first half of the fourteenth century, half of the lease contracts around Pistoia and three-quarters of those around Siena were already sharecropping contracts. The rise of sharecropping did not stop with the Black Death; in fact it proceeded further, sometimes attributed in the literature to labour shortages requiring landlords to shift from fixed rents to sharecropping.[45] It is striking, however, that *mezzadria* continued to increase in importance even in the following periods of population growth and remained the dominant arrangement of land use here until halfway through the twentieth century.[46] To explain its lasting dominance, one must therefore not look at demographic factors, but at the structural characteristics of this property. In this respect, it is significant that sharecropping was present particularly in regions where urban and burgher power was strong, and practised mainly on land owned by burghers, especially those living in towns further away. At the beginning of the fourteenth century, for instance, four-fifths of the land owned by Sienese burghers was already given out in *mezzadria*, in contrast to merely one-fifth of all land owned by rural persons.[47] Apparently, sharecropping became more popular mainly because it suited the interests of the growing group of landowning burghers, as will be further discussed below.

Initially, in the twelfth to fourteenth century, the rise of sharecropping probably had a positive effect on the level of investments made by urban landowners in the countryside, particularly in cases where it was combined with the process of *appoderamento*, in which large landholdings were divided into consolidated, independent farms, *poderi*, that were leased out to sharecroppers. The farmhouses of these *poderi* were often built of stone, and surrounded by stalls, stables, ovens, and other outbuildings, all of which required massive investments by the owner, who often also invested in the cattle and implements of the farm.[48] These investments, which would otherwise not easily have been made, also because of the lack of capital among country dwellers and the restricted scope and volume of the rural capital markets,[49] pushed up land and labour productivity, as is reflected in the high levels which were reached in this period. Around 1300, according to a recent reconstruction, land productivity in Italy had reached a high point, which was not to be reached again until around 1800, and, even more telling for the level of economic development that was achieved, labour productivity simultaneously attained a highpoint, despite the population pressure of the period.[50] Output per worker

---

[45] See Hopcroft and Emigh, 'Divergent paths of agrarian change', esp. 24–6.
[46] Sabelberg, *Der Zerfall*, 116–46 and 217–19; Emigh, 'The spread of sharecropping'. See also van Bavel, 'The organization and rise'.
[47] Cherubini, *Signori, contadini, borghesi*, 295–301.
[48] Jones, 'From manor to mezzadria', 227–34; Emigh, 'The spread of sharecropping', 433–4.
[49] See below, 109.
[50] Federico and Malanima, 'Progress, decline, growth', 438–44 and 451–8; Malanima, 'Wages, productivity', 166–8, also for the following.

around 1300 was as high as after 1348, even despite the windfall gains caused by the population decline of the Black Death and the fact that people started to work many more hours per year, and it was at a level about 50 per cent higher than elsewhere in Western Europe.

The Early Rise of Labour and Financial Markets

Labour markets in this period also developed in central and northern Italy. Their rise is difficult to quantify, for lack of relevant sources, so we have to rely on indications. In the thirteenth century wage contracts for sailors in Venice were common, and also the urban textile sector, as in Florence, employed large numbers of wage labourers, and the construction sector started to do so somewhat later.[51] Sectors such as glassmaking, minting, and shipbuilding even saw the development of proto-factories, which employed larger numbers of wage labourers in one location. As well as wage labourers, some slave labour was used in the towns, with slaves taken from Muslim areas or purchased in Corsica and Sardinia, as happened in Genoa.[52] Most people in the towns, however, probably still worked independently, especially in the large craft sector. The statement that around 1300 there was a growing division of labour, between a class of merchant entrepreneurs and a mass of largely casual wage labourers, as made by Philip Jones,[53] therefore is probably an exaggeration, but it is clear that the thirteenth century in particular saw a strong growth of wage labour in the towns.

It is possible that the rise of labour markets took place even faster in the countryside than in the towns. The rural population, too, became legally free, because of the traditionally weak position of manorialism in these regions and the early dissolution of the manorial and seigneurial elements that had existed, as discussed above. From the late eleventh century, corvées were reduced or converted into money payments.[54] After the thirteenth century, hardly anyone was still legally bound to the land and hardly any labour services remained, except for some symbolic customary services.[55] This process has been analysed, for instance, for the countryside around Siena, as in the Tintinnano, where the commune in 1207 made an agreement with the lord in which all services owed by the villagers were laid down in an annual, fixed sum, to be paid in kind and money, and all existing arbitrary demands by the lord were ruled out. In a few villages in this area, some labour services remained, most of them somewhere between two and twenty-four days per year per man, but their number was fixed and written down, including their monetary value, which allowed the villagers to buy them off.

Towns had played a part in this decline of unfreedom, since in the second half of the thirteenth century they directly sped up the dissolution of serfdom, by

---

[51] Arrighi, *The long twentieth century*, 180–1; Jones, *The Italian city-state*, 186 and 251–3.
[52] Epstein, *Genoa*, 101–2; Origo, 'The domestic enemy', 323, also for the later rise of their numbers.
[53] Jones, *The Italian city-state*, 185–6 and 251.
[54] Collavini, 'La condizione giuridica', section 2.
[55] For the following: Redan, 'Seigneurs et communautés rurales', 152–64 and 637–45.

condemning the principle of serfdom, as in Bologna in 1257/8 and Florence in 1289, for instance, or by offering premiums on manumission to manorial lords.[56] Even though moral considerations probably played little part in this, and the main aim of the towns was instead to eliminate the rival power of manorial lords in the countryside, the effects on the legal position and liberation of the rural population were real. In turn, this widened the opportunities of the rural population to hire themselves out for wages.

It is impossible to quantify the importance of the rural labour market in the thirteenth century, since information is even more scarce than for the towns. As suggested for the Po Valley,[57] possibly more labour was delivered for wages than would appear at first sight, and there must have been many more day labourers, especially in view of the high population pressure and the concomitant low wages. Entrepreneurs took up the exploitation of ecclesiastical properties there and acted as middlemen, using salaried manpower to work the land, and probably the burgher landholders, such as those from Turin, did the same.

Market exchange was aided by the wide availability of gold and silver coins in both town and countryside, as observed for late thirteenth-century Tuscany.[58] The urban mints produced enormous amounts of coins; not only the high-value gold coins and the larger silver ones, but also smaller silver coins, such as the pennies or *piccoli*, and the black money, containing only small quantities of silver. These small coins were useful for small-scale commodity sales and for day-to-day transactions in land and labour markets. The reconstruction of the output of the Venetian mint, using documentary sources and statistics on numbers of coins and dies that have been found, shows a large increase from the late twelfth century, as output had been virtually nil. Around 1280, the mint produced about 1 million penny coins and 4.5 million of the bigger silver *grossi* per year, while in 1319, these figures were 3 million and 5 million, respectively.[59]

Producing these coins at the Venetian mint required more than 10,000 kg of silver per year, while hundreds of kilograms of gold were also used, the gold being imported to Venice by merchants, often of German origin. Venice had become the main node in the European bullion trade around 1200, thanks to its location and also its favourable market framework.[60] The accuracy of the information supply there, the strictly enforced standards of weight and fineness, and the speedy public registration of transactions attracted bullion traders to Venice. The official assayers and weighers were salaried officials, their fees were standardized and prescribed in the 1266 regulations, and they were not subjected to private interests, since they were not involved in the trade themselves. Both buyers and sellers were well protected, by a number of agencies active in the field, and regular auctioning was used to establish prices.

---

[56] Waley, *The Italian city-republics*, 84–5.
[57] Barbero, *Un'oligarchia urbana*, 116–19. See also Panero, 'Il lavoro salariato nelle campagne'.
[58] Day, *The medieval market economy*, 129–40.
[59] Stahl, *Zecca*, 369–406; Spufford, *Money and its use*, 201.
[60] Lane and Mueller, *Money and banking*, 134–55.

At the same time, especially from the late twelfth century, financial markets developed in the centre and north of Italy, a development mainly limited to the towns, however. In the countryside, credit opportunities remained much more restricted, although the rural credit market was more open in this period than it would become later. In the late thirteenth century, as observed for the countryside around Lucca, there were still all kinds of mutual payments, loans, and investments involving villagers, especially the wealthier ones.[61] This was in contrast, however, to other parts of Tuscany, such as around Siena, or in Emilia-Romagna, around Bologna, where according to a possibly exaggerated lamentation as early as the mid-thirteenth century nobody was left but poor people.[62] The countryside there had been sucked dry of money and was drained of lending capital, it was claimed, making countrymen dependent on the few who offered credit.

This contrasted with the situation in the towns, where financial markets quickly developed from the twelfth century and became ever more sophisticated— especially those aimed at the spheres of public debt and long-distance trade. The campaigns of the Church against usury mostly concerned the activities of pawnbrokers and the sale of rents, not merchant bankers and commercial loans.[63] Also, various instruments were developed in order to circumvent the prohibition of interest. A main example is the *commenda*, a partnership formed for trading missions, and especially used from the twelfth century on, which enabled participants to pool merchandise, financial capital, and human capital. Not only did this help to generate more profits, but it also enabled upward social mobility for those who had the ability but lacked the capital to invest.[64] Also, a market for short-term credit based on foreign trade was in place around the middle of the thirteenth century and became further perfected during the subsequent decades. Within the large cities, and most notably in Genoa, money changers also started to take deposits and make money transfers, with an interlocking banking system developing here in the late twelfth century.[65] This was a revolutionary period in the development of Italian financial techniques.[66] In the same period, the 'Lombards', from Asti in Piedmont but also including bankers from Tuscan cities, who disposed of huge amounts of money, started to lend this out to princes, noblemen, and merchants in Italy and all over Western Europe in the thirteenth century, especially in the Low Countries. Merchant bankers from Siena, Florence, and Lucca were major financial players at the fairs of Champagne and in Flanders and Brabant, specializing in business loans. In this field, and in market development more generally, Italy at this point in time clearly stood out from the rest of Europe.

---

[61] Osheim, 'Countrymen and the law'; Epstein, 'The peasantries of Italy', 98–9. For the later decline of rural credit markets: section 3.2, 117–19.

[62] Cherubini, *Signori, contadini, borghesi*, 74 ('nisi pauperes').

[63] Rubin, 'Institutions', 1314.   [64] Greif, 'The fundamental problem', 267–9.

[65] Spufford, *Money and its use*, 256–7.

[66] Day, *The medieval market economy*, 141–4; Luzzati, 'Firenze e le origine'. For the Lombards active in the Low Countries: section 4.2, 165–6.

The wealthy merchants and merchant bankers who came to prominence as a result of these developments gradually acquired more political weight, as can be observed in Venice, Pisa, and elsewhere. Here, the commune was increasingly dominated by the rich, who were mainly involved in international trade and financial operations, and sometimes had intermixed with older feudal families or grown from their ranks. These elites also became tighter than before. In Venice, in 1286, nomination to the Great Council, which up to then had been fairly open to upwardly mobile men, became more tightly controlled by the elite families, and in 1297–8 the council became virtually closed to outsiders, a shift which is aptly labelled *la serrata*, or the closure.[67] Within the guilds and 'popular' regimes, too, those who had amassed economic power now clearly became dominant, as in Siena, where the commercial elite through its control over the merchant guild was able, in 1287, to establish a narrow mercantile regime.[68] In all respects, we can see how economic power was transformed into, or merged with political power.

Florence, too, in this period saw the rise of the super-wealthy and their firms. During the second half of the thirteenth century, it became home to wealthy bankers and to some super-companies, such as those of the Bardi and the Peruzzi, with their extensive trading networks and banking agencies. The Peruzzi family climbed from having little significance in the early thirteenth century to a role as active businessmen and international traders in luxury goods some fifty years later.[69] Alongside their role as traders, they also acted as money changers and bankers, helping members of the family to acquire big fortunes. In 1300, the total capital of the Peruzzi Company amounted to 85,000 gold florins, with 56 per cent of the shares in the hands of the family. At that time they, together with their peers, started to dominate not only economic, but also political life in Florence. Although these individual companies also experienced misfortune again, as seen in the bankruptcy of the Peruzzi Company in 1347, the process intensified in the following centuries. The rise of such elites in the thirteenth century foreshadowed their economic dominance, their heavy involvement in financial markets and their growing political power that is so characteristic of the following period.

All in all, the period 1000–1300 saw rapid economic development and growth in Italy, both before the time of factor markets and during their emergence and further rise. Real wages in the centre and north of Italy were at a high level. Even in the period 1310–48, a period of huge population pressure and ample supply of labour, real wages still were at a level comparable to, or only slightly lower than that of the period 1500–1800, and clearly higher than elsewhere in Europe. Wage data for the earlier period are scarce, but what is available suggests that earlier, in 1290–1310, real wages had been even higher than in 1310–48.[70] Regarding GDP per capita, the centre and north of Italy stood out from the rest of Europe even

---

[67] General: Acemoglu and Robinson, *Why nations fail*, 152–5.

[68] Jones, *The Italian city-state*, 587–90.

[69] Hunt, *The medieval super-companies*, 15–25 and 127–33, also for the following. See also Jones, *The Italian city-state*, 193–4, 200–1; Luzzati, 'Firenze e le origine', 424.

[70] Malanima, 'The long decline', 176–8 and 186–8, complemented with the data for 1290–1310 on <http://www.paolomalanima.it>, accessed 21 June 2012.

more clearly. GDP per capita around 1300 is estimated by Paolo Malanima at about $1,600, by far the highest level in all of Europe.[71]

Earlier figures are unavailable, but on the basis of these figures from around 1300, and the high levels already attained by then, we may surmise that economic growth had already started before the rise of factor markets. A further rise of GDP per capita was sustained by the emergence of factor markets. These markets were formed during the twelfth and thirteenth centuries in a social context characterized by a relatively wide participation in political decision making, especially in the towns. In the well-balanced social context resulting from this, markets acquired an open, non-biased organization, in which market exchange thrived and all social groups benefited to some extent from participation. Around 1300, the centre and north of Italy was the most developed market economy in western Eurasia. At the same time, this process bred new urban elites, who successfully combined commodity, land, lease, labour, and also financial markets, and who increasingly came to the fore. They further stimulated the growth and development of these markets, but also increasingly monopolized the gains from these markets, as will be discussed in the next section.

3.2. ORGANIZATION, CONTEXT, AND EFFECTS OF DYNAMIC FACTOR MARKETS, EARLY FOURTEENTH TO MID-FIFTEENTH CENTURY

The high levels of GDP per capita and real wages observed for Italy around 1300 were pushed up even further around the mid-fourteenth century, as a result of the windfall gains to those who survived the Black Death. This demographic catastrophe made labour much more scarce and radically altered the capital to labour ratio. Around 1400, as a result, real wages per hour and per working day in Italy reached their highest level before the twentieth century. After 1400, however, real wages started to stagnate and from the mid-fifteenth century they declined dramatically, as did the Italian economy more generally, with real wages per hour being more than halved around 1600.[72]

This economic decline was preceded by changes in the organization of factor markets. Instead of leading to ever more open exchange and equal opportunities, markets in the longer run had adverse effects. As will be shown in this section, both the context in which these markets functioned and their organization started to change and became more unbalanced and skewed towards the interests of the elite, especially in the fourteenth century. This was the critical turning point. As we will also see, these changes were much more pronounced in the countryside than in the towns. This was because the main beneficiaries of the market development were

---

[71] Malanima, 'The long decline', 186–8, using 1990 international dollars. See also van Zanden, *The long road*, 239–43 and 258.

[72] Malanima, 'Wages, productivity, 157–60; Malanima, 'The long decline', 176–8 and 186–8, but without much explicit attention to the windfall effect of the Black Death.

found in the towns. These were the rising urban elites, who were the main victors in acquiring property and market dominance, and who subsequently translated their economic position into political leverage. They exercised their power both within the towns and even more clearly from the towns over the surrounding countryside, the latter by using the urban political and military dominance over the countryside as an instrument for exploitation, often linked to factor markets. This situation was found particularly in the most highly developed city-states, as in Tuscany and Umbria, where the now dominant market elites, and the cities they increasingly controlled, extended their non-economic power over the countryside, including through their dominance within factor markets and their influence over the organization of these markets.

One of the domains in which urban elites started to exercise a negative influence was that of property rights to land. Urban courts extended their jurisdiction over the countryside and often sided with the urban elites, a process found in the thirteenth century and intensifying in the fourteenth. Around 1200 in Lucca, for instance, a new court had been instituted for the Lucchese *contado*. Its judges, the *consules foretanorum*, ruled in cases concerning rural matters, and were prone to find in favour of the urban parties involved.[73] This situation was even more pronounced in Florence and Siena in the fourteenth century, where the courts often ruled in favour of the urban landowners, creditors, and speculators, especially from the capital cities, thus undermining the security of property rights for the rural population.[74] Further, the costs of litigation and legal aid sometimes became prohibitive for villagers. As a result, they had become highly vulnerable to coercion, especially since they had no assets to fall back on.

The early lead of Italy in the registration of land transfers also disappeared. In several parts of northwest Europe in the fourteenth century systems of public courts and public registration developed. Italy, on the other hand, remained dependent on the work of notaries, a type of registration which was fragmented and mostly not organized on a territorial basis, or only for smaller areas. It did thus not provide an overview of complete, larger areas and its records could not easily be consulted. Since it was difficult to find out exactly which notarial register held information on a specific parcel of land, this prevented full transparency and created insecurity for potential buyers.[75] Although the role of notaries in the twelfth century had been an innovation, and Italy at that point had the most advanced system of registration, they now became a drag on developments, compared to the more advanced and public systems that had meanwhile developed in northwest Europe.[76] Still, their monopoly was difficult to break, also because of the vested interests developed by the notaries. These belonged to the most influential occupational groups in the Italian towns, through their guilds, which engaged in effective collective action, and their strong position in society more generally.[77] In Turin,

[73] Wickham, 'Rural communes', 3–4, who illustrates this with a concrete case from 1206.
[74] Osheim, 'Countrymen and the law'. See also van Bavel, 'Markets for land'.
[75] Van Bavel, 'Markets for land', 508.
[76] See section 4.2, 156–7, also for the prohibition of notaries to operate in this field.
[77] Barbero, *Un'oligarchia urbana*, 177–85.

around 1400, more than a third of urban councillors were notaries. Moreover, most of them came from the oligarchy of ruling families, and the indispensible role of the notaries helped these families to strengthen their grip on society, thus leaving little scope for this system to change. Only much later the security of peasants' property rights to land may have improved, as a result of the systematic registration in the *estimi* or *catasti*, since these fiscal registers often had evidential value, as in Treviso, and could be consulted.[78] This took place only from the later fifteenth century, however, when peasants in Tuscany, Umbria, and elsewhere had lost almost all landed property to the urban elites.

The process of dispossession of the rural population indeed proceeded ever further. The urban elites, including those active in trade and finance, continuously extended their landed interests, enlarging their holdings through acquisitions in the land market. In a sample area around Siena, in the early fourteenth century roughly 65 per cent of the land was already owned by burghers, on top of the 26 per cent owned by mainly urban-based institutions. At the time, burgher ownership was still increasing: between 1320 and 1330 in this area approximately 34,000 lire worth of property was transferred from burghers to country dwellers, in contrast to the 77,000 lire worth of property transferred in the opposite direction.[79] As a result, in the centre and north of Italy at the start of the fifteenth century, about half of the rural land in the *contadi* and much more of the movable wealth and liquid assets was owned by the urban elites.[80]

Some of these families also invested in plantations overseas. Federico Corner from Venice, for instance, around 1360 acquired huge sugarcane plantations in Cyprus, including sugar mills and a refinery.[81] He combined these activities with financial transactions, especially lending tens of thousands of ducats to the king of Cyprus, who used this money to finance his wars. In return, Corner acquired a number of privileges in Cyprus, including preferential access to the scarce water supplies, enabling him to outflank all other sugar producers there. He also headed a consortium of Venetians, which formed a cartel and monopolized the export of sugar, salt, and cotton from Cyprus. Federico Corner, with an estimated wealth of 150,000 ducats, making him the richest man in Venice in 1379, thus controlled both production and trade in sugar.

For Corner, the bottleneck in the production was the supply of labour for his sugar plantations and mills, since it was not easy to attract people to perform this arduous work. To this end, Corner used hundreds of Greek freedmen, refugees from the Middle East, as well as serfs.[82] Although they received a wage, paid by the week, they worked in a situation of factual or even formal dependency, a situation which limited their bargaining power. Labour shortages later induced the Corners to take even more drastic steps and to employ Muslim captives bought from pirates or warlords, such as the 1,500 Egyptians kidnapped in 1415 and brought to

---

[78] Scherman, 'La distribuzione della ricchezza'.
[79] Cherubini, *Signori, contadini, borghesi*, 73–99, 278–88, and 304.
[80] Epstein, 'The peasantries of Italy', 89–90.
[81] For the following: Lane, *Venice*, 141–6 and 151.
[82] Ouerfelli, *Le sucre*, 116–26 and 128–9.

Cyprus to work on the plantations as semi-slaves. This is an example of how the capitalist entrepreneurs of this period combined their dealings in financial markets and international trade with the monopolization of commodities and the coercion of semi-free or unfree labour. The heavy involvement of Genoese entrepreneurs in plantations and the slave trade, especially in the years around 1400,[83] shows that Venice was not alone in this.

The *Mezzadria* System

Within Italy, these urban elites, comprising no more than a small percentage of the total population, used their financial power to buy up rural land and to acquire coercive means over the countryside, often linked to market exchange. A case in point is *mezzadria*. As a sharecropping system linking lease markets with the exchange of goods, capital, and labour, *mezzadria* had emerged in the twelfth century, as we have seen, and the system became dominant in northern, and particularly in central, Italy in the thirteenth to fifteenth century, especially on burgher landholdings in regions where urban power was strong. Burgher-owned land, that rapidly grew in this period, was almost all leased out for a share of the crop, through *mezzadria* contracts, and often consolidated into family-sized farms to this end. As we will see, the rise and specific organization of the *mezzadria* system allowed the urban patriciate to obtain a stronger bargaining position in the lease, capital, labour, and product markets, all at the same time. Although the initial effect of the rise of the system was beneficial, as it was associated with huge investments in farms which otherwise could hardly have been made, especially in view of the weakness or non-existence of the rural capital market,[84] its later development turned negative, especially for the rural population.

One of the effects of the way the urban elites had arranged the sharecropping system in Tuscany, Umbria, and elsewhere was that it hindered the rural population from selling their labour for wages and, at least indirectly, it curtailed the rural labour markets. Firstly, the urban landowners did so by creating farms of a size aimed at using the full labour of a family, which in itself was a logical strategy. Urban landowners adapted the size of farms in order to achieve and maintain a balance between land and labour,[85] which indirectly decreased both the supply of and the demand for additional wage labour.

Secondly, sharecropping reduced the scope for the emergence of wage labour through the strict regulations in the contracts. Sharecropping contracts not only stipulated the share of output to be delivered, but also contained extensive regulations on the crops to be cultivated, with an increasing emphasis on a combination of labour-intensive cultures, such as viticulture or olive growing, absorbing all labour all year round. Further, these contracts stipulated the exact type of labour to be performed by the tenant, with specifications concerning the number of ploughings, the dates of sowing and harvesting, the extent of fertilizing,

---

[83] Epstein, *Genoa*, 266–70 and 281–3.   [84] See below, 118.
[85] Malanima, 'Industrie cittadine', esp. 277.

the length of ditches to be dug, the tools to be used, and so on. The Italian share-cropping contracts thus offered little freedom to the tenant in the exploitation and use of the tenancy and almost fully determined the way the labour of the tenant and other members of his household should be applied. In view of the strict regulation of labour, sharecropping can also be considered a labour con-tract, with tenants paying in labour and not having the opportunity to become real agrarian entrepreneurs.[86]

Additionally, the lease contracts sometimes directly prohibited sharecroppers from selling their labour outside the farms, even if this had been possible after carrying out all the tasks outlined above. As a side effect, the Italian sharecropping system thus negatively affected the rural labour market, and contributed to its malfunctioning. It operated as an instrument for the urban landlord to profit from his ability to control labour and to force the sharecropper to put the maximum of his family's labour to the land.

The power of urban landlords to enforce all these stipulations was increased by the fact that they were the main supplier of credit for a large proportion. Often sharecroppers themselves had no property at all, as shown by the fiscal sources, and a rural capital market was virtually non-existent, as observed for Tuscany.[87] Thus, the urban elite landowner was often the sole provider of loans and livestock,[88] and although sharecroppers initially may have welcomed this credit, it also made them dependent, and it may have enabled the creditor to use debt bondage to tie sharecropping tenants to the land and prohibit them from selling their labour on the market. Landowners could also use debt bondage to compel the peasants to work on large projects for relatively low remuneration. The situation of initial economic inequality in which this system developed thus made its organization and effects quite negative for large shares of the rural population. This was true for many sharecroppers, even though some of the disadvantages were compen-sated by the size and quality of the consolidated farm they held in lease, but more clearly for the agricultural labourers without direct access to such a farm or to any land; access which was further reduced exactly because of the consolidation of farms.[89]

In the fourteenth century, urban elites also succeeded in shifting the tax burden to the countryside and to the rural population. Taxes were levied by urban govern-ments, dominated by the urban elite, who had a vested interest in shifting the fiscal pressure to the rural population, and also limiting the taxation of urban landown-ership, which was exactly what happened. In the Florentine *contado* such an exploitative fiscal relationship did not yet exist in the thirteenth century, but it emerged in the following period, as the rural population size was declining as a result of the ravages of the Black Death, while the fiscal demands were rising. This resulted in a doubling of the tax pressure on the rural population between 1330

---

[86] General: Bhaduri, 'Cropsharing as a labour process'.
[87] Alfani and Ammannati, 'Economic inequality', 34 and 46. For rural capital markets: below, 118.
[88] Emigh, *The undevelopment of capitalism*, 136–8.
[89] Emigh, *The undevelopment of capitalism*, 194; Alfani and Ammannati, 'Economic inequality', 46.

and 1400.[90] Particularly in the mountainous areas, where peasant landownership was relatively strong, tax rates were very high: in 1393 they amounted to 3 per cent of the property value in the mountainous districts of the Prato area, compared with 1.6–2.0 per cent in the hills and plains of the *contado*, and 1.4 per cent in the city of Prato. Moreover, urban-owned property in the countryside was exempted from rural taxes, based on the argument that burghers had already contributed by being taxed in the towns. This made owning land more attractive for burghers than for peasants, and this further stimulated the growth of burgher landownership, as peasants sold their tax-burdened landholdings to tax-exempted burghers.

The Florentine tax re-arrangement of 1427 was perhaps partly an attempt to alleviate the tax burden for the countryside, by finding a more equitable distribution and by taxing real estate less,[91] but its effect was modest and its measures were later partly revoked. Although Florence had an extraordinarily strong grip on its *contado*, and Siena adopted a somewhat less exploitative fiscal policy towards its countryside,[92] this situation was not restricted to Tuscany but was also found in the north of Italy. In the provinces of Cremona, Milan, and Pavia, all in Lombardy, plots of land owned by country dwellers in the fifteenth century were taxed at a rate four to eight times heavier than a similar plot of land owned by a burgher.[93]

Moreover, farming happened in a context that increasingly was distorted, as witnessed for instance by the increasing hold the urban elites had over the market for goods. Moreover, many urban landlords decided to market the produce of their landholdings themselves, mostly in urban markets, leaving the sharecroppers hardly any scope to try to benefit from market opportunities.[94] The penetration of urban market influence, landholding, and power in the countryside—especially in the nearby *contado*—thus harmed the rural markets. As analysed for Tuscany in the fifteenth century, rural market institutions were dominated and adapted to suit the interests of urban actors, rural markets were crushed by the concentration of transactions in Florence, and rural participation in output and factor markets contracted again.[95] In this process, rural agency, as strengthened by peasant landownership and the existence of well-functioning village communities, could play a role as a counterweight and help to avoid this, as indicated by the much more favourable developments in the outlying parts of the Tuscan territory, further away from the town. Here, as shown for the Casentino Valley, and further discussed below,[96] the commercialization process did not become subjected to urban interests, but rather allowed rural people to trade through their own village markets,

---

[90] Molho, *Florentine public finance*, 23–36 and 81–7. A more nuanced picture is found with Cohn, *Creating the Florentine state*, 71–81, who shows the diversity in fiscal relations with Florence within the *contado*.

[91] Molho, 'The state and public finance', 116–19.

[92] Caferro, 'City and countryside'. A much more negative view of Sienese fiscal policies: Pinto, 'I mercanti e la terra', 268–9.

[93] Chittolini, 'Notes sur la politique fiscale', 147–8.

[94] Emigh, *The undevelopment of capitalism*, 166–7.

[95] Emigh, *The undevelopment of capitalism*, 43 and 201.

[96] Curtis, 'Florence and its hinterlands', 18–19. See more about the exceptional developments is this area, section 3.4, 138–9.

as witnessed by the growth of local market centres and the number of rural traders in the fourteenth and fifteenth centuries. These outlying areas, however, formed the exception.

The dominance of the urban elites was already established by the time of the Black Death, but this demographic catastrophe,[97] and the simultaneous economic downturn, exacerbated the desire or even necessity for urban elites to use their political and legal powers to distort the operation of factor markets in their own interests. This was because these elites had built their position largely through the operation of these factor markets, in which they now had a large stake. The decline of agriculture and industry, as most specifically the urban industries that were focused on the labour-intensive production of luxury textiles, which were hit hard by the higher wages after the Black Death, induced the Italian elites even more to apply coercion within the market, or to shift their investments from industry and take refuge in financial speculation. The emerging financial markets offered ample opportunities for the latter.

A clear example of the way urban elites influenced the market, and used it to suit their interests, is the erection of the *Monte delle doti* in Florence. This dowry fund, created in 1425, allowed Florentine fathers to deposit a sum of cash, earn interest, and receive a more substantial sum back after a stipulated period, to be used for the dowry of their daughters.[98] Thousands of deposits from the leading Florentine families poured in. The dowry fund prevented the dispersion of their estates, since its existence meant that cash and liquid assets now made up the lion's share of dowries, while real property remained with male kin, and it also gave these elites a handsome gain, since the nominal interest rates were set at an amazingly high level of 15 to 21 per cent. The interest was paid out of fiscal revenues, which in turn pressed disproportionately on others than the urban elites. This instrument, therefore, worked at the expense of those who were unable to participate in the dowry fund, that is, the inhabitants of the Florentine countryside and the urban lower classes. As a result of the steeply rising sums involved in dowry settlements in this period, stimulated by the attractiveness of this fund,[99] the lower and middling groups increasingly remained outside this segment of the marriage market altogether, thus in practice leading to an increase in endogenous marriages among the elites.

Although capital markets had emerged early in the Italian towns, and a wide range of commercial debt contracts and other instruments of commercial credit were adopted here centuries earlier than in other parts of Europe, there are indications that credit was not easily available for ordinary people, in either the towns or the countryside. The *Monti de Pietà*, created in the fifteenth century, as in Perugia in 1462, offered small loans free of interest or with a small interest charge to the very poor, out of charitable considerations, but did not offer credit to craftsmen or small traders.[100] Nor were other forms of credit easily available for such people.

---

[97] For this demographic impact, see section 3.4.
[98] Kirshner and Molho, 'The dowry fund'; Molho, 'The state and public finance', 115.
[99] Herlihy and Klapisch-Zuber, *Les Toscans*, 414–17; Kirshner and Molho, 'The dowry fund', 434.
[100] Pullan, *Rich and poor*, 432 and 443–75.

This was even more clearly true for the rural population, and it was difficult for farmers to procure working capital. Before the Black Death, credit was expensive, as it was elsewhere in Europe, with perpetual annuities (loans secured on real property, mainly land) amounting to at least 9–12.5 per cent per year.[101] Other forms of credit could entail harsh conditions, often leading to default, or usurious interest rates in the range of 20–50 per cent. But not until the centuries following the Black Death did the real contrast with northwest Europe emerge. After 1348 interest rates in capital markets declined all over Europe, as a result of the demographic collapse and the concomitant increase in the supply of capital per capita, and in northwest Europe interest rates remained low thereafter, but credit in the Italian countryside did not witness this decline and remained expensive, pointing to flaws in the institutional framework of this market and associated insecurity and high transaction costs.[102]

Indeed, in the Italian countryside credit markets remained imperfect or even non-existent, as has been established for early fifteenth-century Tuscany. Peasants and other country dwellers had to resort to pawnshops in Florence, to Jews, to notaries, to Florentine patricians, or to professional moneylenders who offered credit at high interest rates.[103] Although usury was formally prohibited, in practice usurers were tolerated in the countryside, since they often formed the only source of liquidity. The government tried to set maximum interest rates, but these were still between 20 and 30 per cent per year, and were not always complied with in practice.[104] At the same time, the countryside was sucked dry of liquidity, through payments to urban merchants and landowners and especially through the high levels of taxation, to be paid mainly in coins. Peasant indebtedness and the inability of peasants to pay off debts were widespread. This is testified, for instance, by sources concerning the Sienese countryside in the second half of the fourteenth century. Urban officials described how village communities and peasants were unable to meet their debts, and how country dwellers were fleeing their land because of debts contracted with urban creditors.[105] In 1394, the situation had become so serious that the city council of Siena intervened and tried to arrange for more equitable settlements between the indebted rural population and their creditors. The authorities in Lucca did the same in their equally impoverished *contado*, also offering the rural population a temporary tax relief, all from fear that the countryside would be fully depopulated and would cease to bring in rents and taxes, as explicitly discussed by the city council.

Particularly in Tuscany and Umbria, the negative effect of the situation in the rural capital market was pronounced, since it was coupled with the creation of medium-sized *mezzadria* farms by urban landlords, entailing an unequal relationship

---

[101] Epstein, 'The peasantries of Italy', 98–101; and a more pessimistic view in Hopcroft and Emigh, 'Divergent paths of agrarian change', 16. See also Herlihy, 'Population, plague', 240–1.

[102] Zuijderduijn, *Medieval capital markets*, 242–6 and 261–7; Epstein, *Freedom and growth*, 16–29.

[103] Botticini, 'A tale of "benevolent" governments', 169–77.

[104] Molho, *Florentine public finance*, 37–41.

[105] Caferro, 'City and countryside', 96–9; for Lucca: Meek, *Lucca*, 77–92. See also Pinto, 'I mercanti e la terra', 268–70.

with their tenants. In this sharecropping system, the landlord would provide a substantial part of the implements, livestock, and seed, or the tenant would acquire the working capital by borrowing it from the lessor in cash advances or advances of tools, livestock, seed, or crops in the field.[106] Either way, this formed an interlinkage of the capital market and the lease market, with the landowner being the source of capital for the farmer who leased the land. This allowed the mainly urban landlords, who also were in a position to use their non-economic power and privileges, to link operations in different output and factor markets within the sharecropping system, creating ample opportunities for rent seeking.

Similarly, the effects of the *mezzadria* contracts and the regulations on labour issued by the town governments complemented and reinforced each other. *Mezzadria* lease contracts prohibited sharecroppers from selling their labour outside the farms, as we have seen, while the sharecroppers were also bound to the urban elites through credit obligations and debt bondage, which was used likewise by these elites to tie people to the land and prohibit them from selling their labour on the market. Agricultural wage labourers in Tuscany were equally subjected to very tight restrictions, especially enacted after the Black Death, as the Florentine city council passed what probably were the most oppressive labour laws in Europe.[107] These laws—directed against rural labourers—froze wages, forced labourers to buy their food at high prices from urban vendors, and restricted their mobility, forcing them to stay on the burgher-owned farms. Those rural labourers and sharecroppers who did leave and violated these laws were designated as rebels, to be buried alive; a law not to be repealed and replaced by less stringent legislation aimed at attracting rural labourers until later in the fourteenth century.

The combination of elements made life for country dwellers, especially those not acquiring a *mezzadria* farm, very hard. It is hardly surprising to find that the reservoir of labourers in the countryside was dwindling. This also applied to the regions more to the north, albeit somewhat later in time. In the Po Valley, too, from the second half of the fourteenth century, wage labour became scarce and labourers were seldom mentioned anymore.[108] In their place appeared the *massari*, tenants who leased separate parcels of land from one owner, and were fully dependent on him for their land and capital.[109] The fact that lease terms were very short and mostly made only orally, in contrast to the written contracts for terms of ten years that in this period came to predominate in the Low Countries,[110] further increased their state of insecurity and dependency vis-à-vis the owner.

Increasingly Distorted Labour Markets and Coercion of Labour

Labour markets were not free, and became increasingly less so, either in an absolute sense, as a result of new restrictive measures by the urban market elites, or at

---

[106] Ackerberg and Botticini, 'The choice of agrarian contracts'; Toch, 'Lords and peasants', esp. 168–77.
[107] Cohn, 'After the Black Death', esp. 468–73.   [108] Barbero, *Un'oligarchia urbana*, 116–29.
[109] Barbero, *Un'oligarchia urbana*, 119–29.   [110] Section 4.2, 157–9.

least in a relative sense, compared to developments elsewhere in Western Europe. After a window of opportunity, offered by the removal of manorial or feudal restrictions, the restrictions on freely selling one's labour in the market grew again, now mainly developed by the town councils and the urban elites and particularly applied to the rural population.[111] The opportunities for country dwellers to migrate or commute to the cities and enter the urban labour market were limited. Often, citizenship or guild membership, or both, were required to work in the towns. From the mid-thirteenth century onwards, urban authorities in northern and central Italy increasingly started to monitor in-migration from the country-side, even preventing it outright on occasion, a policy only relaxed after the popu-lation losses in the mid-fourteenth century. Conversely, some cities prohibited their burghers from going at harvest time to work for wages in the countryside, as for instance Pisa did in 1286.[112] Later, too, the cities regularly closed themselves to rural immigrants, depending on the demographic situation, as shown for fifteenth-century Bologna.[113] With the population growth of the sixteenth century, measures against rural immigrants increasingly became more restrictive again, sometimes stating explicitly that the rural population should remain in the countryside in order to produce the necessary food.[114] As a result, urban and rural labour markets were not well integrated and wage differentials between town and countryside were huge; much bigger than around the North Sea, for instance.[115]

Another type of intervention in the labour market by urban authorities was formed by the forced labour services country dwellers had to perform for cities.[116] Italian towns had ample opportunities to conscript rural labour for all kinds of services, including the building of fortifications for urban military purposes in the countryside, the maintenance of roads and bridges vital to urban trade, work on the city walls, water management works, and transport of materials. Also, hun-dreds or even thousands of the strongest men were conscripted for military service or as oarsmen in the fleet, as happened in the Venetian mainland,[117] with this obligation falling disproportionately—or even fully—on the rural population. Around 1400, they served in the Venetian galleys together with convicts, beggars, slaves, debt slaves, and other types of coerced labourers.

Despite this growing use of coerced labourers, the military was one of the sectors where wage labour did increase during the fourteenth century, and perhaps even most conspicuously. The urban governments replaced the town militias of citizens that were used in the twelfth and thirteenth centuries with professional soldiers hired in the market. This not only increased military efficiency but also ended the necessity for the urban elites to cooperate with their less wealthy fellow townsmen in military matters.[118] From the thirteenth century, thousands or even tens of

---

[111] Van Bavel, 'Markets for land'.   [112] Herlihy, *Pisa in the early Renaissance*, 51 and 158–9.
[113] Guenzi, 'L'immigration urbain'.   [114] Fasano-Guarini, 'Politique et population'.
[115] See for the figures below, 123.
[116] Jones, *The Italian city-state*, 383 and 566–7; a case study: Neri, 'Perugia e il suo contado'.
[117] Rossini, *Le campagne Bresciane*, 242–9 and 260–4. For slaves in the galleys: Origo, 'The domes-tic enemy', 332; and for beggars in the later period: Pullan, *Rich and poor*, 303 and 306–8.
[118] See also section 3.3, 131.

thousands of cavalry, foot soldiers, and archers were hired by the towns. The organization of the military through civic association was thus replaced by using the market for military wage labour combined with coercion of conscripted labour.

In the towns, where the labour market was much more open than in the countryside, wage labour was very important in all sectors of the economy. In Pisa around 1400, for instance, labourers comprised more than half of the population.[119] Their role was particularly prominent in unskilled work such as transporting goods, tying bales, and carrying sand, which was mainly done by casual labourers. In the large infrastructural works, such as the work on the harbour of Talamone on the Tyrrhenian Sea in 1357, most of the labourers were paid by the day. In this case, they were recruited from a wide area, organized into groups by the master craftsmen who were commissioned to do the work, and they stayed for a few weeks or up to six months on this project.[120] Apparently, there was a mobile reservoir available to be hired for wages. Another reservoir was that of the elderly and vulnerable, who tried to make ends meet by earning something. They had no possessions or only very few, and thus were dependent on their labour for a meagre income. The full-time salary of a labourer in Pisa was not enough to cover half of the subsistence needs of an average family, thus requiring other family members to obtain additional income if they were not to go hungry.[121]

In the craft sectors, more independent producers were found. It is difficult to say exactly how large the proportion of wage labour in these sectors was. Often, similar occupational names are used in the sources to indicate both the independent craftsmen and the wage labourers.[122] In the urban textile sector, however, it seems that the producers in this period were increasingly relegated to dependency as wage labourers for big entrepreneurs, or contracted through putting-out systems, even if they retained some ownership of their tools.[123] The production of textiles in Florence was divided into a large number of stages, with an associated hierarchy of workers. The weavers originally held a fairly independent position, but in the decades around 1400 some of them joined the ranks of the labourers, with the exception of a small number of masters who retained their economic independence. Below them were the *ciompi*, who were involved in the primary stages, such as the carding, which were valued much less. Lowest on the economic ladder were the female spinners, who worked both in the towns and in the surrounding countryside. Their numbers were huge: at the end of the fourteenth century, Francesco Datini, the wealthy merchant of Prato, in three years sold 217 pieces of cloth on which 700 female spinners had worked.[124]

Most of the labourers were dependent on large firms, which held a working capital of 10,000 florins or more, but only a few of these workers were directly

---

[119] Cherubini, *Signori, contadini, borghesi*, 435–46.
[120] Cherubini, *Signori, contadini, borghesi*, 538–46.
[121] Jones, *The Italian city-state*, 253–5; Cherubini, *Signori, contadini, borghesi*, 450–3.
[122] Cherubini, *Signori, contadini, borghesi*, 442–3.
[123] Francescoli, *Oltre il 'tumulto'*, 75, stresses more the independence of a substantial share of the weavers.
[124] Stella, *La révolte*, 116.

employed and worked at the site. The wool manufactory owned by Simone di Filippo Strozzi in Florence in 1425, for instance, employed only a manager and a few workers engaged in finishing the cloth.[125] Most labour was done outside the manufactory, mainly for piece wages. This became the norm more generally. In Florence, around 1400, the lower classes, the *sottoposti*, comprising a third of heads of households, and consisting of labourers, construction workers, and wool carders, were sometimes paid by the day, month, or year, but increasingly by the task (*a cottino*).[126] In these decades of economic difficulty in Florence, payment by the task became general, increasing the economic insecurity for these groups. This system also precluded the necessity for the merchant entrepreneurs to invest in equipment; almost all of their invested money was in raw materials and wares, and remained in the sphere of commerce, while investments in instruments or other capital goods remained very limited, even by pre-industrial standards. At the same time, they acquired more means to coerce labour. Regulation of the labour market became stricter and enforcement harsher. The statutes of the Florentine silk industry were reformed in 1458, and these stated that because many offenders were too poor to pay fines, the consuls from now on were empowered to impose corporal punishment, put delinquents in the pillory, and subject suspects to torture.[127]

The willingness of urban elites to coerce labour, if necessary through violence, is also reflected in the growing acceptance, and re-appearance, of slavery in the towns. Especially in Genoa, slave labour was used, with slaves taken from Corsica, Sardinia, and Muslim areas.[128] In Pisa, the number of slaves around 1400 was more limited, with three male and fifty-five female slaves, mainly working in domestic service for the wealthiest families, but in Florence in the same period much more substantial numbers of slaves of Tatar, Russian, Greek, or African origin were used.[129] After their virtual absence in the twelfth and thirteenth centuries, from the mid-fourteenth century slaves had started to reappear there and increase in number again, and in Tuscany more generally. In 1363, by Florentine decree, the unlimited importation of slaves was sanctioned once more in Tuscany. In theory, enslavement was restricted to non-Christians, but in practice many of these slaves were Christians. From Florence, the practice of buying slaves spread to the smaller towns and even to the countryside.[130] Many of the slaves were traded through the slave market of Caffa on the Black Sea coast, and imported into Italy by Genoese merchants. In towns such as Genoa, Pisa, Venice, and Ancona, slave markets were held, with some 10,000 slaves sold in the Venetian market alone between 1414 and 1423. They were sold by auction to brokers, who in turn sold the slaves on to their clients. These could use the slaves themselves, but could also hire them out to others.[131]

Coercive means were also applied to labour in the rural industrial sector. Extensive and free wage labour did not develop there, in part as a result of the intervention of towns and urban guilds. In Tuscany most clearly, the cloth and

[125] Goldthwaite, *Private wealth*, 38–47.   [126] Jones, *The Italian city-state*, 250–5.
[127] Cohn, 'The character of protest', 203.   [128] Epstein, *Genoa*, 101–2.
[129] Cherubini, *Signori, contadini, borghesi*, 434–5; Origo, 'The domestic enemy'.
[130] Origo, 'The domestic enemy', 324–9 and 334.   [131] Origo, 'The domestic enemy'.

linen production was forcibly concentrated in the towns, particularly in the late thirteenth century, with the Pisan and Florentine cloth guilds bringing rural producers under corporate control and restricting textile production in the countryside. By 1305, the Pisan guild had even succeeded in closing down all textile workshops in its *contado*.[132]

From the late fourteenth century, this situation changed, because of increasing labour shortages after the Black Death. In the countryside of Tuscany some spinning and the weaving of coarse, cheap linen and woollen cloth expanded, although always subordinated to the market networks, and sometimes the capital, of the urban merchant elites. A more advanced, high-quality production, or the production of finished goods, did not develop in the Tuscan countryside, since the strict labour laws and urban monopolies in industrial production continued to prohibit this. The situation was somewhat different in the north, because of the weaker power of towns and urban guilds, particularly in the more remote areas, such as the mountain valleys of Brescia and Bergamo in Lombardy, and in Piedmont, where towns generally were smaller and somewhat weaker.[133] Here, from the late fourteenth century, a thriving rural textile sector emerged, as well as the fabrication of iron products, employing increasing numbers of wage labourers. These regions, however, remained exceptions in northern and central Italy.

The effects of the interventions by city governments and urban elites in the rural labour markets and their organization were pronounced. Firstly, there is the effect on wage formation. The openness and integration of labour markets, or lack thereof, is reflected in the differences in nominal wages between town and countryside. In Italy, these were large, because of restrictions on immigration and mobility, and also bigger price differentials in costs of living. In the fourteenth and fifteenth centuries, the difference, for similar occupations/tasks, could amount to 100 per cent, rising to about 200 per cent in the course of the sixteenth century, as established for Florence/Tuscany, but also for the areas further north, compared to 40–90 per cent in the North Sea area.[134]

The effects of the growing institutional blockages can also be seen in the stagnation, or even decline, of the volume of the rural labour market. The only part of northern and central Italy where a large number of full-time, proletarianized wage labourers were found was in the area around Milan in the Lombardy plain. Here, very large farms developed, leased out for fixed rents, with the tenant farmers hiring large numbers of wage labourers, while the rural industrial sectors also started to employ wage labour, as we have seen.[135] Elsewhere, and particularly in Tuscany and the other central regions, however, wage labour in the countryside remained restricted, and perhaps more so than it had been earlier, in the thirteenth century.

[132] Epstein, 'Town and country', esp. 466–9; Epstein, *Freedom and growth*, 115–42.

[133] Epstein, 'Town and country', esp. 466–9; Belfanti, 'Rural manufactures'. See also section 3.4, 139–40.

[134] Malanima, 'Wages, productivity', esp. 136, 156–8, and 165–6. For figures for the North Sea area: van Bavel et al., 'The organisation of markets', 365; and section 4.2, 163–4.

[135] Dowd, 'The economic expansion', esp. 148–9 and 154. See for the large tenants' farms in the fifteenth and sixteenth centuries there also, section 3.4, 139–40.

With all the alternative instruments they had acquired in the fourteenth and fifteenth centuries for binding, using, or coercing labour, there was hardly any need for urban landlords to employ fully free, proletarianized labour, hired on an open labour market. Moreover, most of the labour was absorbed by the *poderi* or other family farms that had been formed by the landlords in the same period, while opportunities for country dwellers to hire themselves out at a favourable rate on an open market were limited by urban restrictions.

3.3. THE CHANGING SOCIAL CONTEXT OF MARKETS: POWER AND PROPERTY IN THE FIFTEENTH AND SIXTEENTH CENTURIES

We observed above how the institutional organization of the markets changed so that they became distorted and skewed towards the interests of the urban wealthy, sometimes causing them to shrink again. These changes can to a large extent be understood from the simultaneous shifts in the distribution of power and property—or more concretely: the concentration of power and property in the hands of these urban wealthy—while conversely the changes in the organization of markets led to a further polarization in this distribution, as we will see in this section. In turn, the growing power of the urban wealthy, who held an ever stronger position in factor markets, went along with a declining role of the social groups who could potentially have offered a counterweight. In the towns, counterbalancing forces were eroded through the curtailment of the political and military role of the guilds, and the restriction of their activities to the economic sphere, and the reduction of the role of the *popolo* in the communes. In the countryside there was the weakening of the roles of the rural nobility and the rural communities. Even if these groups had aimed at acquiring rent-seeking opportunities themselves, if necessary by using non-economic coercion, they had formed a counterweight to the urban market elites, who now became completely dominant and thus were able to distort the operation of markets more than if they had been constrained by these countervailing groups.

In the countryside we can observe this process most clearly. The rural nobility and communities had never held a very firm position in most of the centre and north of Italy, except for the mountainous and more northerly parts, and they were fairly easily pushed aside by the urban elites, who also became more dominant economically, by acquiring ever larger shares of the land and capital. It is this shift in property structures that we will document first, before turning to the effects.

The Growth of Burgher Landownership

The most striking aspect of this growing inequality in property structures is the rapid increase of burgher landownership, resulting in a marked dominance of burghers in the social distribution of land. Burghers accumulated small plots of land, and consolidated them into larger landholdings, by using the land market, but also by lending money to smallholders, especially holders of adjacent parcels of land, or by speculating on their future harvests, in order to annex the land if they were unable to pay the money back.[136] This consolidation of landownership in the hands of urban burghers started in Tuscany in the thirteenth and fourteenth centuries, as noted above, and in the fifteenth century it continued and became more general. To be sure, this growth of burgher landownership did not necessarily have negative consequences, as it could be associated with urban investments in agriculture, as was the case in the first phase.[137] In the later phases, however, the character of the burgher landownership and its effects changed and turned more negative, associated with the organization of the *mezzadria* system—the tenancy system predominantly used by burghers, the decline of productive investments and the loss of agency of the rural population.[138]

Developments were most pronounced in the Florentine *contado*. In 1427, only 18 per cent of the rural property there was owned by country dwellers, and this declined to about 14 per cent by the end of the fifteenth century. In extreme cases, such as in the parish of Montecalvi, 18 km southwest of Florence, all rural householders were either complete paupers or were so poor that they owned no land themselves at all.[139] They worked as tenants of smallholdings or as labourers.

Further north, the growth of burgher landownership started somewhat later, but the situation was not very different. In the early sixteenth century, burghers owned 57 per cent of the land in the *contado* of Cremona in Lombardy, and this even excludes the many properties belonging to urban religious institutions.[140] Similar figures can be observed elsewhere in the north, as in the Po Valley and the Venetian mainland where half to two-thirds of the land was owned by burghers. It was only in the infertile, mountainous areas that rural landownership—organized in small, private plots and large commons—remained important.[141] Elsewhere, the last remaining commons were bought, divided, or even expropriated by burghers, as had happened around Siena in the fifteenth century, or they had been sold by indebted rural communes, as happened later in Lombardy.[142] This opened up ever more land for the market and, subsequently, for accumulation in the hands of wealthy townsmen.

Not only landownership but wealth more generally in central and north Italy was distributed in a highly skewed way, which was biased towards the urban elites. In the province of Brescia, in Lombardy, in the late sixteenth century 26 per cent of wealth was in the hands of country dwellers and 74 per cent in those of burghers—making up no more than 12 per cent of the total population.[143] In Tuscany, in 1427, around 67 per cent of all the taxable wealth was in the hands of Florentines,

---

[136] Alfani and Ammannati, 'Economic inequality', 45.   [137] Section 3.1, 106.

[138] For the negative social consequences also: section 3.4, 137–8.

[139] Conti, *La formazione*, 97–102, 245, and 395–411.

[140] Epstein, 'The peasantries of Italy', esp. 89. Other examples: Cherubini, *Signori, contadini, borghesi*, 73–8.

[141] Casari, 'Emergence'. See section 3.1, 103.   [142] For Siena: Isaacs, 'Le campagne senesi'.

[143] Rossini, *Le campagne Bresciane*, 33, 124, and 195.

making up 14 per cent of the Tuscan population.[144] The distribution of capital and movables was especially highly skewed. Of movable wealth in Tuscany, in 1427, no less than 78 per cent was concentrated in Florence, 13 per cent in the six other large towns, 4 per cent in the Florentine *contado*, and 5 per cent in the more out-lying districts. The wealth of the richest Florentines consisted for a relatively large part of shares in the public debt (about 40 per cent) and of cash, capital goods, and commodities (another 40 per cent).

The three-quarters of the Tuscan population who lived in the countryside in 1427 held only 9 per cent of movable wealth.[145] Liquid assets were almost non-existent in the countryside, with rents and taxes continuously draining the area of cash. An average Florentine household owned 349 florins worth of movable assets, compared with no more than 6 florins worth per household in the countryside. This situation applied not only to liquid assets but also to livestock, which was rarely owned by the sharecroppers, and certainly not by rural labourers.[146] The rural population had hardly any savings or other ways of cushioning themselves against hard times. As a result, peasants became increasingly indebted, with share-cropping peasants in particular becoming the most debt-ridden of the rural popu-lation, tied by these debts to their landlords. Many country dwellers suffered from hunger and were kept alive by small charitable donations. In combination with the effects of the Black Death, villages became depopulated and agricultural land was abandoned.[147]

Growing Financial Markets and Inequality of Wealth Distribution

In the towns, the situation remained more favourable for longer, especially for the upper strata, thanks to their properties, their coercive power, and the gains they made from the development of the financial sector. The late medieval period saw the further growth of large mercantile and banking houses. They formed semi-permanent companies (*compagnie*) with various international branches and the capital divided into shares, as the Bardi and Peruzzi in Florence had done in the first half of the fourteenth century, being among the first in this process, as they became the chief bankers in Europe.[148] The properties of Simone di Filippo Strozzi in 1425 give some idea of the portfolio of the more 'modest' segments of the urban elite. Simone Strozzi held assets with a value of some 7,000 florins, of which 4,500 florins were invested in real estate, including four *poderi* in the Florentine countryside, 500 florins in state bonds, and 1,600 in his merchant enterprises and wool manufactory.[149] Most of the latter sum was in wares, not in equipment, and money investment in the sphere of

---

[144] Herlihy and Klapisch-Zuber, *Les Toscans*, 241–60. See also Zuijderduijn, 'Assessing the rural economy'; Goldsmith, *Premodern financial systems*, 147–70, esp. 148–54.

[145] This is very little compared to elsewhere. For the situation in fifteenth-century Holland: section 4.3.

[146] Herlihy and Klapisch-Zuber, *Les Toscans*, 272–9; and a slightly less pessimistic view—by including the livestock advanced by the landlords to the tenants: Emigh, 'Loans and livestock'.

[147] Curtis, *Coping with crisis*, 70–1. See also, section 3.4, 136–7.

[148] See section 3.1, 109–10; Hunt, *Medieval super-companies*, 127–51.

[149] Goldthwaite, *Private wealth*, 38–50.

production was very limited. Later in the fifteenth century, the members of the Strozzi family shifted their investments even more to banking and financial markets, instead of commerce and production, and they became rentiers rather than merchant entrepreneurs.

Much of the money of the urban elites was invested in public debts, created by the large cities in particular, especially in order to finance their expensive wars.[150] The public debt of Florence, Venice, and Genoa combined rose from less than 1 million florins around 1270 to some 2–3 million florins around the middle of the fourteenth century to 10 million in the late fourteenth century and 18 million in the mid-fifteenth century.[151] These enormous sums can be put in perspective by noting that the properties of all 125,000 people living in the Florentine country-side in 1428 combined had a total value of only 1.7 million florins.[152] The interest payments on these urban debts, amounting to a quarter or more of city-state expenditures, were made mainly from tax revenues. These taxes predominantly applied to consumption in the form of excises, which brought in between a quarter and a third of total revenues and were constantly being raised in the course of the fourteenth century, and on visible wealth, most notably houses and land, and much less on movable wealth, the shares in trade companies and the shares in public debts owned by the urban wealthy. In practice it often happened that these forms of movable wealth, held almost solely by the rich, were not even taxed at all.[153] Taxation, therefore, pressed most on ordinary people and least on the wealthiest.

The wealthier entrepreneurs and capital owners even benefited from the budget deficits of the cities. An inclusive system of the sale of annuities by public authorities in an open market, in which all individuals could participate, such as developed in the contemporary Low Countries, did not develop here.[154] It was not until the sixteenth century that the first life annuities were issued, with Venice in 1536 being the first example, and even there the mint was the issuer, not the city government.[155] Why this instrument was not used is a puzzle, but the answer is probably to be found in the political economy. As a result, in order to attract the necessary capital, urban governments had to offer favourable con-ditions to creditors. One way was to allow creditors to quote the loan in a foreign currency at a given exchange rate, lower than the real rate. This offered the cred-itor a substantial rate of interest, but also allowed him to speculate in various currencies in the international money market.[156] Although this practice had pre-viously been condemned, because it was regarded as usurious and because it diverted money away from commerce and industry, the Florentine government

---

[150] Molho, *Florentine public finance*, 9–21.
[151] Ginatempo, *Prima del debito*, 145–7 and 148–9, for urban revenues. Day, *The medieval market economy*, 155.
[152] Molho, *Florentine public finance*, 25–7.
[153] Alfani and Ammannati, 'Economic inequality', 6.
[154] Munro, 'The medieval origins'; Tracy, 'On the dual origins', 13–24. See for the Low Countries section 4.2, 167–9.
[155] Munro, 'The medieval origins', 533.   [156] Molho, *Florentine public finance*, 171–6.

in 1429 saw itself forced to accept this system and abolish any prohibitions against it. Profits for the financial speculators were huge: on average some 30 per cent per year, or more. Excises, taxes on small-scale property, and forced loans, all levied on the majority of Florentines and on the Florentine countryside, were now used to pay these huge interest rates to those few Florentines who were rich enough and had the liquid cash available to lend large sums to the government. Taxation and debts were now combined in one redistributive system with regressive effects.

At the same time, wealthy creditors used their position to increase their political hold over the heavily indebted city-states. In Genoa, for instance, the position and prerogatives of the government's creditors were strengthened with every financial crisis,[157] including their control over most of the public expenditures and the administration of the Genoese colonies. Gradually, the creditors took over the state.

When looking at social differentiation within the towns, we can see that wealth inequality reached new heights. The Black Death in most localities produced a temporary decline of inequality, but from the late fourteenth century its rise resumed and then continued almost uniformly for the following centuries.[158] This indicates the structural causes of this process. It was found in the countryside, but to a greater extent in the towns and especially in the larger ones. Also, levels of inequality remained lower for longer in the north, as in Ivrea, in Piedmont, where the Gini index for wealth distribution c. 1450–1600 was at a stable level of 0.65–0.7,[159] while they rose faster in Tuscany and other parts of the centre. In the large rural community of Poggibonsi, in Tuscany, the abundant sources show that, after the temporary decline produced by the Black Death, the Gini coefficient rose from about 0.5 in the fourteenth century to almost 0.8 in the eighteenth, in a continuous process.[160]

Polarization was most pronounced in the largest centres. In 1427, in the metropolis of Florence the Gini coefficient was as high as 0.79, compared with 0.75 in the secondary cities of Tuscany and about 0.6 in the countryside, based on the figures in the fiscal sources. When corrected for the paupers not included in the fiscal registration, the figure for Florence was as high as 0.85, which was more unequal than the figures we have for anywhere else in Europe at the time. The wealthiest 1 per cent of Florentine households held 27 per cent of total wealth in the city, and 18 per cent of total wealth in the whole of the Florentine Republic.[161] The situation was not completely black and white, however. Some middling groups of small tradesmen, artisans, and shopkeepers were present in the towns, and they held some wealth. Still, the differences between the wealthiest and the poorest

---

[157] See this section, 132.

[158] Alfani and Ammannati, 'Economic inequality', 11 and 19. For the effect of the Black Death: 19–22.

[159] Alfani, 'Wealth, inequalities and population dynamics'. See for the somewhat different development in Piedmont also section 3.4, 139–40.

[160] Alfani and Ammannati, 'Economic inequality',11–18.

[161] Goldsmith, *Premodern financial systems*, 153–4.

households in the tax registers—that is, even excluding the poor who fell below the fiscal threshold—were huge, at 15,000 to 1 around 1400.

On the lowest rungs of the social ladder was a large segment of poor. One-third of Florentine households around 1400 were considered too poor to pay taxes. Among them were many households headed by wage-earning widows but also wage labourers, including cobblers, blacksmiths, and leather workers, so not necessarily only the unemployed or disabled. In 1371, two-thirds of the workers were listed as 'nihil habentes', and similar figures are found for Prato and Pisa.[162] The position of the urban poor further declined, and their ranks were swollen, because of the influx of pauperized country dwellers, which town governments were unable to stop despite their intermittent attempts. Some of the strains result-ing from the poverty of the urban masses and the sharp discrepancies in wealth were eased by personal bonds between rich and poor and by help offered by their bosses and by the charitable organizations. Total redistribution and formal relief, however, was not impressive at 1–2 per cent of GDP.[163]

Moreover, charity became an instrument of power for the elites, especially from the first half of the fifteenth century, as many Italian towns saw the smaller hospi-tals and charitable foundations being reorganized and consolidated into large organizations, as took place in Brescia (1429), Milan (1456), and elsewhere. In part, this increased the efficiency of poor relief, but it also undermined the role of fraternities, corporations, and associations, with their more varied membership and their independent role in administration, and it brought charity almost wholly under the sway of the urban patriciate. In Cortona, after the reorganization in 1441, it was mainly rich merchants and other economically powerful individuals who acted as administrators, which enhanced their political leverage and social prestige, and enabled them to decide on the disbursement of charity,[164] even apart from the fact that charity was unable to solve the structural mechanisms underly-ing the growth of poverty.

Impotent Revolts, Professional Soldiers, and Growing Power of Market Elites

Begging, pauperism, crime, strains on charity, and antagonism between rich and poor were conspicuous features of this period. City governments responded and tried to minimize popular disorder through a combination of minimal relief offered during crises and extreme dearth, and brutal oppression, including the cutting off of hands, feet, and tongues, as the Florentine authorities did in the fourteenth century.[165] In Venice, as early as 1300 the Grand Council decided that

---

[162] Stella, *La révolte*, 195; Balestracci, 'Lavoro e povertà'. The term does not signify that they were desperately needy but is a proxy of poverty: Alfani and Ammannati, 'Economic inequality', 33–4.

[163] Van Bavel and Rijpma, 'Formalized charity', 167–70.

[164] Perol, *Cortona*, 174–8. For a similar process in late fifteenth-century Bologna: Terpstra, *Lay confraternities*, 179–89.

[165] Cohn, *Creating the Florentine state*, 138–71.

paupers and beggars should be confined in hospitals.[166] Sometimes, urban labourers and smaller craftsmen tried to resist the growing inequalities, as with a series of rebellions, as in Lucca (1369), Perugia (1370–5), Siena (1371), and the *Ciompi* revolt in Florence in 1378.

Some of these rebellions were hardly more than riots, and expressions of the hatred of the poorer people against the wealthy, but others had more clearly voiced programmes. These asked for the opportunity for ordinary people to form guilds, to gain access to offices and to co-determine economic policies. Also, these urban revolts were often aimed against the public debts and the Monte, the system of public debts, of which people knew all too well that the system favoured the rich economically, because of the steady revenues they received from the high interest payments, in their turn financed out of consumption taxes pressing on the ordinary population, and also enabled them to consolidate their control over city states, as public authorities became dependent on the large lenders.[167] In 1339 in Genoa and in 1378 in Florence the rebellions explicitly targeted the Monte. The Florentine rebels demanded a ten-year suspension of all interest payments on the public debts or even the abolition of the Monte, and the introduction of direct, personal taxes, instead of the regressive indirect taxes on consumption goods. This was mostly in vain, however. These revolts, including the scattered rebellions against the tax pressure in the countryside, were futile, in contrast to the successful revolts of the thirteenth century, as the rebel groups could still draw upon strong positions in wealth distribution and social organization. It is illustrative that one of the few examples of successful revolts in the later period is found in the mountainous areas in the Florentine district, where the peasants, by exception, still mostly owned their land and had retained their communal organizations.[168] Here, around 1400, the Florentine government was unable to supress the unrest and saw itself forced to change its policies, by lowering tax rates and offering relief to distressed countrymen.[169]

By far most of the rebellions of the late fourteenth and early fifteenth centuries, on the other hand, were short-lived and, after some initial successes, lost out to the patriciates, through political machinations or bloody repression, by using their mercenaries, as in Siena in 1384.[170] The rebelling labourers, if not killed, were punished and contained through a lock-out, followed by the loss of the right to self-organization. The broader, more inclusive composition of the urban governments of the thirteenth century in most towns now gave way to the installation of oligarchies of wealthy merchant families. Special criminal courts, such as the Otto di Guardia in Florence in 1378, were empowered to put on trial and punish any conspiracy, rebellion, or other threat to the ruling order.[171] Courts like these were

---

[166] Henderson, *Piety and charity*, 241–5 and 276–8. For the later period: Pullan, *Rich and poor*, 220–2 and 296–300.

[167] Molho, 'The state and public finance', 106–9 and 115.

[168] Cohn, *Creating the Florentine state*, passim. For the mountainous area: Curtis, 'Florence and its hinterlands'.

[169] Cohn, *Creating the Florentine state*, 197–202 and 246–65.

[170] Martines, *Power and imagination*, 180–6.

[171] Cohn, 'The character of protest', 199–200, and for the following: 205–9.

often directly placed under the town government and their membership controlled by the leading families—and did not act independently. Fundamental juridical rules, such as a written inquisition of the alleged crime and testimonies of the defence and of the prosecution, were abolished, and the convicted persons were exiled or put to death. In the fifteenth century, suppression through these harsh measures was effective, and ordinary people were no longer able to organize themselves in mass revolts.

The urban patriciates also reacted to the revolts and popular pressure by disbanding the remaining popular militias and employing professional soldiers, hired in the labour market, as we have seen, to maintain order and hold their position. These hired soldiers, sometimes foreigners, were often paid by way of the Monte, and financed by taxing the countryside, by levying indirect taxes on consumption goods and by contracting new debts.[172] The costs were huge. In 1427, Florence hired 6,000 horsemen and 6,000 foot soldiers, and in 1431 these numbers rose to 11,000 and 8,000, plus thousands of crossbowmen, in order to fight its wars with its rival neighbours to the north.[173] Although some of the wages were spent in the towns and the revenue was thus partly returned to the urban economies, the high costs of the hired soldiers put a great strain on urban finances.

The combined use of the labour market and the financial market for hiring mercenaries and developing military power, as happened in an international perspective most conspicuously in the Italian towns from the fourteenth century, allowed the urban elites to strengthen their position. To a large extent they did so by using the state. The high level of public debts even made it easier for them to control the state. In return, the state used its coercive means to protect the property rights of the elite, as the need for protection became increasingly urgent as a result of growing inequality. This process had two negative side effects. Firstly, the organization of the military through financial and labour markets in the fifteenth century resulted in an oligopolistic and later monopolistic market for the provision of the military sector with personnel, capital, and goods. This military market became dominated by a few great captains and elite city administrators who negotiated and made the contracts and reaped the benefits,[174] thus further strengthening inequality.

Second, the use of coercive and military means achieved its own dynamic, which resulted in growing, violent competition between city-states. War making in the fourteenth and fifteenth centuries became more profitable for elites than trade or industry, by way of the gains it offered through pillage, confiscation of wealth, indemnity payments, and fiscal and financial dealings, and as a result surplus capital and investments increasingly found their way to the military sector.[175] At the same time, although elites benefited, the ongoing warfare damaged total output and contributed to economic decline. Mercenary troops supplemented their wages by

---

[172] Martines, *Power and imagination*, 184–5; Caferro, 'Warfare and economy', 179–86.

[173] Molho, *Florentine public finance*, 9–18; McNeill, *The pursuit of power*, 69 ff., also for the following.

[174] McNeill, *The pursuit of power*, 77–8.

[175] Caferro, 'Warfare and economy', 173–6; Arrighi, *The long twentieth century*, 90–3.

robbing, kidnapping, and by pillaging the countryside, which was unprotected, in contrast to the cities which were walled. The cattle seized and the money paid as ransom further robbed the already impoverished countryside of working capital. A mercenary company of Bretons, for instance, in 1377 robbed the Maremma area of 800 head of large cattle and some 20,000 sheep.[176] These soldiers thus destroyed capital, labour, and goods, exerting a negative effect on the supply side of the economy. The economic decline resulting from military depredations drove city-states even more into conflict with each other, in order to get a bigger share of the ever smaller pie, which in its turn led to further decline. As a result, the north and centre of Italy was beset by continuous warfare, lasting up to the mid-fifteenth century, as the Peace of Lodi in 1454 brought some end to it.

All this warfare in turn provided a motivation, and an opportunity, for elites to further increase their hold on local governments and states. The constant need for liquidity, and the growing dependence of states on banks and financial markets, made it even easier for elites to take power into their own hands. In the first half of the fifteenth century, in Genoa, public administration was in practice taken over by the capitalist elites, as administration was put into the hands of the Casa di San Giorgio, the bank of Saint George, ruled by the most prominent Genoese families. San Giorgio assumed a dominant role in capital provision, taxation, and minting, and also started to control government expenses and policies more generally.[177] These policies included the abolition of forms of direct taxation. In 1456, the head tax on all Genoese men above a modest level of wealth was abolished, and in 1490 the same happened to the main property tax, which resulted in making taxation more regressive. In 1453, the Genoese state even gave Corsica and the Black Sea colonies to San Giorgio, as only the latter had the resources to defend and govern them. The state had become a prisoner of San Giorgio. At the same time, San Giorgio itself became controlled by the bigger shareholders, as during the second half of the fifteenth century the number of shareholders was halved and shares were accumulated by the noble and wealthy citizens. Comparable developments took place in Florence, after the financial crisis following the war with Lucca, in 1429–33.[178] As an almost inevitable outcome, the Medici family in a way bought the Florentine republic, and it did so at a bargain price.

In these parts of Italy, political power came more exclusively into the hands of the urban elite. Genoa became controlled by finance capitalists, who were interested mainly in financial networks and power, not in investing in the real economy. In Tuscany, the Florentine elite was interested not only in financial power, but also in territorial power, as it acquired dominance not only within the town, but also by way of the town over the surrounding countryside. Its position was buttressed by the dominance of the same urban elite in financial matters and property ownership. The urban elite combined these two positions and used the town, and its political power, as an instrument of surplus extraction

---

[176] Caferro, *Mercenary companies*, 65–9; Caferro, 'Warfare and economy', 173 and 186–90.
[177] Epstein, *Genoa*, 277–81 and for the shareholders of San Giorgio: 279–80.
[178] Arrighi, *The long twentieth century*, 103–4.

vis-à-vis the surrounding countryside, brought about through the fiscal system and through the markets for landlease, labour, capital, and goods. The position of the tenants through the arrangement of leasing deteriorated in the fifteenth century. Written lease contracts in Tuscany had previously typically lasted for five years, but now most leases were contracted orally and could be renegotiated each year.[179] This led to loss of security, which destroyed the advantages of market exchange. It made the tenants more dependent on their (urban) landlord, who could end the lease each year if he wished, also because of the availability of a reservoir of near-landless rural dwellers who would be willing to take over the lease.

The organization of the rural capital, lease, labour, and product markets, and the social distribution of wealth affected both investment opportunities in the countryside and the degree of independence of the rural population. Initially, in the twelfth to fourteenth century, the rise of sharecropping may have had a positive effect on the level of investments made by urban landowners in the countryside, as full, consolidated farms were built up, to be leased out to sharecroppers, as we have seen. In the process, much more capital was invested in these farms than otherwise would have been available, in view of the scarcity of liquidity in the countryside and the rudimentary nature of the rural capital market. Increasingly, however, from the fourteenth century onwards, the negative effects started to outweigh the positive ones. The investments in the countryside declined or took a different character. Since landlords now had obtained a strong grip on rural labour, through their economic dominance and the organization of the *mezzadria* system, they started favouring more labour-intensive crops over investments in labour-saving capital goods.[180]

As this stifled agricultural improvement, the urban elite in a self-reinforcing process shifted its rural investments increasingly to the extension of landownership or to investments in the countryside that were aimed at increasing status, for instance by building elaborate country villas, a development found in Tuscany from the second half of the fifteenth century onwards and later also in the Veneto.[181] These were used only in part for practical purposes, in agriculture, administration, and storage, but mainly and increasingly for pleasure, escaping from the business of urban life, displaying wealth and signalling the dominance of the urban lord over the countryside, and the sums expended on them can be considered as at least partly unproductive. Their construction came at the expense of real, in-depth investments in rural capital goods and of investments in commerce and industries.[182] Moreover, the drain of surpluses from the countryside to the towns also limited rural investment since it took place at the expense of the investment opportunities for peasants.

---

[179] Emigh, *The undevelopment of capitalism*, 162–3. For the divergent developments in Lombardy, forming an exception in the north and centre of Italy, see section 3.4, 139–40.

[180] See for labour intensification also section 3.4, 135.

[181] Bentmann and Müller, *Die Villa als Herrschaftsarchitektur*, 18–28 and 34–7; Lillie, *Florentine villas*, esp. 23–38 and 147–54.

[182] Pinto, "'Honour' and 'profit'", 85.

At the same time, the rise of sharecropping and the scarcity of money and credit in the countryside affected the independence of the rural population. Since there was almost no semblance of a well-functioning and open capital market in the Italian countryside, and especially not for short-term leaseholders who were unable to offer land as a possible security, sharecropping was the main option open to a tenant for obtaining working capital. This created a situation of personal dependency, as discussed above.[183] In periods when capable candidates to take up a lease were scarce, the effects for the tenants could be mild, and they could even benefit from the personal, long-run relationship with their landlord, through the extension of leases, thus leaving sharecropping farms in the hands of the same family for decades.[184] On the other hand, and especially in the many periods when there were more capable people than there were farms, this situation created ample opportunities for the landowner to exploit his strong bargaining position, often taking the opportunity to link operations on both capital and lease markets in order to increase his security, reduce monitoring costs, and profit from this position. This made the tenant rather unappealingly dependent, and could also be a factor in binding the tenant to the land. The forced interlinkage of markets was found predominantly where capital markets in the countryside were lacking or malfunctioning, as in these parts of Italy, thus leaving tenants without an alternative avenue to acquire some form of economic independence or to become real agrarian entrepreneurs.

Moreover, for the many who had no access whatever to a share tenancy, the situation was much worse, and their opportunities dwindled with the decline of land markets, the long-run leases held by sharecropping families, and the absence of a capital market. This left them without any entrepreneurial opportunity. All they possessed was their own labour, and sometimes they even lost control over that. Growing over the centuries, and systematized by the seventeenth century, was the practice of coercing labour through debt bondage. At Altopascio, for example,[185] Florentine landlords would order their managers to employ indebted labourers fully to this end and even imprisoned debtors for refusing to work. This practice was the outgrowth of a process that had started and grown from the fourteenth century.

3.4. EFFECTS ON ECONOMY, AGRICULTURE, AND DEMOGRAPHY

In most parts of the centre and north of Italy, the fourteenth and fifteenth centuries thus had seen a growing inequality in the distribution of property ownership and political power, in which the urban elites became dominant, and a growing distortion in the organization of markets, which became skewed towards the interests of the same wealthy urban elite, two developments which strengthened

---

[183] Section 3.2, 114–19.   [184] Emigh, *The undevelopment of capitalism*, 145–56.
[185] McArdle, *Altopascio*, 72–8.

each other. The negative effects became evident in all economic domains, for instance in the stagnation of technological development, the decline of GDP per capita, and the fall of urbanization rates. Economic innovation slowed down from the fifteenth century on, especially in the countryside. Exceptions were the spread of the mulberry tree, which provided the raw material for the silk industry, and the very slow spread of maize and rice cultivation from the second half of the sixteenth century. These few innovations, however, did not push up economic growth, but instead increased physical output at the expense of even higher labour inputs, thus decreasing labour productivity. Even authors who see this period in a more positive light, or at least a less negative one, including Guido Alfani, mention only innovations that are labour-intensive and hardly conducive to a rise of labour productivity.[186] For instance, silkworm breeding and the processing of silk was very labour-intensive, and maize production also required much time—about twice the labour per unit land needed in grain production.[187] As far as techniques which could push up labour productivity are concerned, there was hardly any progress, if at all, especially in the countryside.[188] The primitiveness of the ploughs and the scarcity of draught animals, combined with the simultaneous intensification of labour input, forced people to work more hours per year to produce a similar quantity of output. People simply had to work longer hours to avoid poverty, or even to safeguard subsistence.

From the mid-fourteenth century onwards, and in tandem with the decline of agricultural surpluses, the degree of urbanization in central and northern Italy slowly declined, to approximately 18 per cent around 1600. Also, a substantial and long-lasting fall in real wages set in, starting at the beginning of the fifteenth century and most pronounced in the countryside. Although a too gloomy picture would be unjustified, and at least in the towns and a few regions there were periods of recovery or even vitality, as in the second half of the sixteenth century,[189] the long-run trend was downward. At the start of the First World War, real wages per working day and per hour in Italy were still lower than they had been around 1400.[190] After the windfall gain as a result of the population losses during the Black Death, a long decline in GDP per capita started in 1420/40, lasting up to the mid-sixteenth century and followed with some fluctuations by stagnation up to 1860/70. While GDP per capita around 1300 had been $1,600, it declined to some $1,400 two centuries later, while in the North Sea area it grew quickly.[191] Italy had lost its economic primacy by 1500, and it would even drop to the bottom of the economic hierarchy in Europe in the following centuries. Because of the high levels of inequality, the effect of this decline on real wages and average standards of living was probably even more pronounced.

---

[186] Alfani, 'Population dynamics', 36.
[187] Malanima, 'Wages, productivity, 143–7; Federico and Malanima, 'Progress, decline, growth', 453.
[188] Malanima, 'Wages, productivity', 146–7.   [189] See Alfani, 'Population dynamics'.
[190] Federico and Malanima, 'Progress, decline, growth', esp. 456–8; Malanima, 'Wages, productivity', 158–9; Malanima, 'The long decline', 176–8.
[191] Malanima, 'The long decline', 186–9. For the divergence in real wages: Allen, 'The great divergence, esp. 427–31.

In searching for the causes of this decline of the Italian economy, some scholars, perhaps most prominently Paolo Malanima, have pointed to the Black Death and the start of the Little Ice Age, which occurred at about the same time. Indeed, both were destructive. In the late thirteenth century, there was the end of the so-called Medieval Climatic Optimum, a combination of climatic conditions that were conducive to high agricultural yields and had characterized the period from 800 onwards. The ensuing Little Ice Age reduced the cultivable surface of Italy probably by some 6 per cent, especially in the upland areas, and reduced the wheat production by the equivalent of the food needed to feed 1–2 million people.[192] Likewise, the Black Death struck northern Italy very hard. But however negative the effects of these two occurrences may have been, they cannot be held responsible for Italy's economic decline, as is shown by the experiences of the Low Countries in exactly the same period.[193] This part of Europe also underwent a Little Ice Age and was hit by the Black Death, but developed economically over this period and even saw economic growth increase. The sharp population decline caused by the Black Death both in the Low Countries and in Italy should have improved the ratio between capital and people, driven up real wages, stimulated trade, and pushed up GDP per capita, at least as a windfall gain, but perhaps even as an opportunity for structural growth—an opportunity which was captured in this period in the Low Countries, as we will see in Chapter 4. In Italy none of this happened, which indicates that the crucial factor was not the Black Death itself, but rather the social and institutional framework on which this external shock acted. This framework decided whether the resulting responses of society to shocks like these would allow for recovery or would contribute to long decline, as happened in Italy. One example of these divergent responses to the population decline is formed by the strict labour laws that were enacted in several parts of Italy after the Black Death, while in the Low Countries labour mobility and freedom instead increased in the wake of the same population decline.[194] This observation links up with the recent notion in disaster studies that disasters are social occurrences, with hazards of a similar nature and force having very different consequences, depending on the relative abilities of societies to cope with them.[195]

Other disasters of the fourteenth and fifteenth centuries, too, can be linked at least in part to the social and institutional setting that had developed in late medieval Italy. More specifically, some of them were tied to the ecological consequences of the market-induced economic growth of the preceding period and growing pressure on natural resources, combined with a dominant coordination system, namely the market, that was dominated by economic-cum-political elites. One example is the exceptionally large number of floods which hit the Tuscan towns and villages in the fourteenth century, including the terrible flood which hit

---

[192] Capasso and Malanima, 'Economy and population in Italy', 24–5.
[193] See section 4.2.
[194] Cohn, 'After the Black Death'. See also section 3.2, 119–22, and for the Low Countries section 4.2, 160–4.
[195] Tierney, 'From the margins'. See also section 6.3, 277–8.

Florence in 1333.[196] Prominent among the causes are the deforestation of hills upstream, which was associated with the privatization of commons and the sale of wood for the market, and the construction of hundreds of mills and weirs near the city, in part through investments made by urban entrepreneurs.[197] Combined with the impotence or unwillingness of the urban government to act against the harmful effects of these economic activities, this turned the heavy rains into a disaster, which killed hundreds of mostly poor people and caused havoc in the town and its surrounding countryside.

Developments in the countryside were much worse than in the towns, and they led to impoverishment and depopulation. Sped up by the effects of the Black Death, agricultural production declined, villages became empty of people and cultivated fields were abandoned.[198] The rural economy and population numbers in the countryside declined substantially between the thirteenth and fifteenth centuries, as in the district of Pistoia, where the number of inhabitants fell from about 31,000 in 1244 to fewer than 9,000 in 1404.[199] The fact that the decline had already started before the mid-fourteenth century, and that population numbers after the Black Death recovered only slightly and very slowly, suggests that not only epidemics underlay this decline but that there were also more fundamental causes, such as those discussed here. Clear indications of demographic decline are already found in the first half of the fourteenth century, as in the rural territory of San Gimignano and also around Prato and Lucca, where as early as 1333 the commune of Capella San Stefano di Tassignano reported that it had been reduced from the earlier 120 men or more to about twenty-five, and that these were living in abject poverty.[200] These claims were made to get tax reductions, and they may be exaggerated, but they are confirmed by hard population numbers, by subsequent urban inquiries, and by the fact that most petitions were indeed granted. As further evidence against the epidemiological explanation, David Herlihy has noted that the decline in the countryside was often much stronger than in the cities,[201] whereas the latter are mostly assumed to have been hit much harder by the plague.

A more structural, underlying problem for the countryside was its impoverishment, a process starting in the fourteenth century and, after the windfall gains of the Black Death, proceeding in the following centuries. This is also witnessed by the famines which hit the Italian countryside, culminating in the terrible famine of 1590–3, the worst famine to hit Italy in the late medieval and early modern period.[202] The economic and demographic situation in the countryside improved only very slightly, even though there were periods of temporary recovery, and the seventeenth century saw an even further impoverishment of the Tuscan countryside.[203]

---

[196] Schenk, '"…prima ci fu la cagione de la mala provedenza de' Fiorentini…"'; Cohn, *Creating the Florentine state*, 233–8.

[197] Cohn, *Creating the Florentine state*, 235–6. [198] Rao, 'I villaggi abbandonati'.

[199] Herlihy, 'Population, plague'; Herlihy, *Medieval and Renaissance Pistoia*, 62–77.

[200] Meek, *Lucca*, 77–88. For the area around Vercelli in Piedmont: Rao, 'I villagi abbandonati', 44–8.

[201] Herlihy, 'Population, plague'. [202] Alfani, 'The famine of the 1590s'.

[203] McArdle, *Altopascio*, 72, 98–101, and 109–16.

One of the problems for the countrymen was the lack of capital. Much of the wealth was invested in public debts by urban elites, who monopolized access to these secure sources of revenue. Moreover, their land and capital were locked in by fiduciary entails, which immobilized inheritances by allowing the heirs only the usufruct of the property and stipulating that it should be passed undivided to the next generation. This legal instrument was rarely used before 1300 but became prominent especially in the fourteenth and fifteenth centuries.[204] Aristocrats and patrician burghers made their grip on the land more permanent by way of these entails, first informally and ad hoc, but from the fifteenth century onwards in a more structured way. As a side effect, this practice severely limited the possibilities of alienating or re-allocating landownership or of allocating capital to new and better uses, and it thus curtailed the functioning of markets.[205] The wealth accumulated in the hands of a few, in this period of great inequality, was kept in the family and thus shielded from dispersal. In the seventeenth century, in many parts of northern and central Italy more than half the land, sometimes even up to three-quarters, was bound by entails or brought into the dead hand of ecclesiastical ownership, obstructing land mobility and paralysing the land market.

The emergence of these non-market obstructions to the market, in combination with the increasingly biased organization of these markets, contributed to rent-seeking behaviour and further social polarization, and probably lessened the inclination of the non-elite to enter the market freely. This effect can be observed most clearly in the countryside, the area in which three-quarters of the population lived and in which markets were subjected to a growing urban influence and became dominated by powerful urban actors. Here, people retreated from the market and markets contracted, most conspicuously in fifteenth-century Tuscany.[206]

The Regional Variations

These negative developments in the countryside did not happen everywhere to the same extent, however. Regional variations across the centre and north of Italy offer the opportunity to understand this process better and to identify some of the underlying, deeper causes. There are two types of areas in particular in which the developments described above occurred to a lesser extent and markets remained more open and less biased, as we will see, and offered more scope to a broad segment of rural entrepreneurs instead of being dominated by only a few of the urban elite. These are, first, the more outlying and mountainous areas further away from the cities, such as those in the outlying *distretto* of Tuscany, and the Apennine area more generally, and, second, regions in the north, such as Piedmont and most notably the Lombardy Valley. As a result, economic developments in the fourteenth and fifteenth centuries were much more favourable here, with the develop-

---

[204] Zuijderduijn, 'Assets frozen in time'.
[205] Aymard, 'From feudalism to capitalism', esp. 193; Cooper, 'Patterns of inheritance', esp. 277–88. This in combination with the near absence of rural capital markets: section 3.2, 118.
[206] Emigh, *The undevelopment of capitalism*, 6, 43, and chapters 4–7.

ment of a diversified and commercialized economy, which benefited from urban demand instead of being stifled by the distortion of markets by urban interests.

Indeed, developments in the mountainous areas, further away from the towns, were more nuanced, or can even be evaluated as positive. People there had kept a lot of their economic and legal independence, and could therefore avoid becoming subjected to distorted factor markets, while they at the same time benefited from the existence of product markets and the economic opportunities these offered.[207] They entered markets on their own initiative, instead of being forced into them when conditions were unfavourable. The effects become clear when comparing the divergent developments in the fourteenth century between the Florentine *contado*, which was close to the city and dominated by Florentine elites, and the more outlying mountainous areas in the Florentine *distretto*, such as the Casentino Valley.[208] In the latter area, one-half of the households cultivated their own land. This peasant-owner structure remained stable well into the early modern period, as in other parts of the *distretto* and in complete opposition to the situation in the *contado*. Moreover, communal rights and organizations shielded these peasants from risks and enabled them to enter the product markets from a position of strength, using these markets to widen their economic portfolio through the commercialization of silvo-pastoral production.

The other favourable exception, but of a different type, was Lombardy. Here, and particularly in the more remote areas, such as the mountain valleys of Brescia and Bergamo,[209] a thriving rural textile sector emerged, as well as an iron goods industry, employing increasing numbers of wage labourers. This process started in the late fourteenth century and expanded particularly in the second half of the sixteenth century, helped by the fact that towns and urban elites were not able, or not willing, to forcibly obstruct this development. Even more striking are the developments in the plains of Lombardy, where, in the fifteenth and sixteenth centuries, very large farms developed. These farms, 50 to 130 hectares in size, were leased out for fixed rents, paid mainly in cash, not for a share of the crop, as elsewhere.[210] Also, in contrast to the Tuscan farms, the parcels of land of which these farms were composed could be leased separately, if necessary from different landlords, creating a much more fluid and competitive lease market.[211] Moreover, lease terms, from 1430 mostly at nine or eighteen years, were neither too long—thus stifling competition—nor too short—thus increasing insecurity. In general, the tenants in the Lombardy plains had a much more independent position than those within the *mezzadria* system.[212] This is witnessed, for instance, by the fact that more investments were made by themselves, instead of solely by the owners.

Also, labour markets in Lombardy remained more open and competitive, and they were intensively used by the tenants to get access to labour. This was needed,

---

[207] Curtis, 'Florence and its hinterlands'.

[208] A comparison made by Curtis, 'Florence and its hinterlands'. For this difference, see also Cohn, *Creating the Florentine state*, 15–28.

[209] Epstein, 'Town and country', esp. 466–9; Belfanti, 'Rural manufactures'.

[210] See section 3.2, 114–15.   [211] Barbero, *Un'oligarchia urbana*, 108–16 and 122–3.

[212] Sella, 'Household, land tenure and occupation', esp. 491; Dowd, 'The economic expansion', esp. 148–9 and 154.

because of the large size of their farms, and it was possible, thanks to the fact that, exceptionally in the context of the centre and north of Italy, no sharecropping restrictions were imposed by the landlords which bound all labour to the family farms.[213] As a result, the additional labour that was needed on the large farms could be supplied by proletarianized or semi-proletarianized labourers, or seasonal labourers. No less than 45–50 per cent of Lombardy households consisted of labourers in the late sixteenth century.[214] These labourers were hired by the tenants in a fairly open labour market. By combining land, labour, and capital, and by using factor and output markets, the tenants here thus developed into true agrarian entrepreneurs, rather than just providers of labour.

In Lombardy, an open market system was maintained for longer than in the rest of the centre and north of Italy. A main underlying cause of the exceptionality of Lombardy was the socio-political balance there. Lombardy, which was being transformed into a more territorial state from the late fourteenth century onwards, saw the emergence of princely rule, which in turn built on feudal lords, and strengthened their position, thus creating a political counterweight to the towns and their elites.[215] This situation, with its more divided power, also allowed rural communities to gain more leeway vis-à-vis the towns, and the rural farmers vis-à-vis the urban elites, and thus contributed to a more balanced relation in which factor markets remained more open and also rural entrepreneurs could benefit from the opportunities these offered.

Elsewhere in the centre and north of Italy, village communities traditionally had a much weaker position, since as early as the mid-twelfth century the towns had brought their hinterlands under their political and judicial control. The remote hinterlands of the cities (the *distretti*) and the mountainous areas, on the other hand, offered rather more elbow room for the rural communities, even in the hinterlands of Florence in Tuscany as we have just seen.[216] Here, and even more so where the counterbalance of princely rule developed, as in Lombardy and to a lesser extent on the Venetian mainland, in the sixteenth century rural groups were able to formally organize themselves in corporate bodies in order to defend their interests, particularly in the 1560s and 1570s.[217] In these parts of northern Italy, the patriciates, princes or territorial lords, feudal noblemen, and rural communities kept each other in check to a greater extent, and did not allow urban elites to control markets and dominate the economy. These areas, however, were the exceptions.

Wealth and Elite Dominance

When we leave these exceptions and return to the main pattern in the centre and north of Italy, it is clear that the combination of market-related developments, and

---

[213] See for sharecropping and these restrictions more extensively section 3.2, 114–19.
[214] Sella, 'Household, land tenure and occupation', 493–4: examples San Giuliano and Inzago.
[215] Belfanti, 'Town and country'; Epstein, 'The peasantries', 78–80.
[216] Curtis, 'Florence and its hinterlands'.   [217] Zamperetti, '"Sinedri dolosi"'.

the social inequality they brought, reduced productive investments, both in urban and rural industries and in agriculture. In particular, the countryside was sucked dry of liquid assets, and the urban elites did not have the incentive to maintain levels of investment.[218] If investments were made, they were generally not in-depth investments which enhanced labour productivity, as they had been in the first phase of the formation and outlay of sharecropping farms, but mainly concerned the acquisition of more land or public debts. The growing use of fiduciary entails also made it difficult for members of the elite to shift investments to new sectors or opportunities, with socio-dynastic considerations thus prevailing over economic ones. More generally, spending their income on luxuries, status symbols such as rural villas, and means of coercion were much more feasible and attractive for them than making risk-bearing investments, especially in view of the economic stagnation of the period. Spending on the arts and patronage enhanced one's social prestige and formed an attractive outlet for social competition.[219] It also enabled elites to show wealth and munificence.

Earlier, in the thirteenth century, in a situation of relative social equality, this conspicuous display of wealth was not accepted, as a result of both the religious aversion to wealth and the social norms within the communes, which wanted to avoid the jealousy and rivalry it produced. This changed, however, around 1400, after a period of rapid market development, huge profits gained by some through the market and rising social inequality. Urban elites now felt less inhibited by the religious and social norms, or even became cynical about them.[220] This went along with the growing popularity of pseudo-Aristotelian economics, with its opposition to the ideal of poverty and its emphasis on the importance of private wealth for the self-fulfilment of the individual—wealth being a necessary tool for developing virtue—and more generally for the well-being of society. These ideological changes thus legitimized the wealth and social dominance the market elites had now acquired.

This changing atmosphere induced the wealthy to openly display their wealth. In the late Middle Ages, urban patriciates spent increasing amounts on the arts, architecture, and learning. The blossoming of the Renaissance is thus only in part a sign of economic growth. In another respect it is rather the sign of the decadence of a preceding period of growth: the fruit of autumn. Only the urban luxury industries, with their limited scope for scale-enlargement or increases in labour-productivity, benefited from the resulting elite demand, while the economy as a whole declined. The effects of this mechanism were even greater because of the rising inequality of the period. A growing share of total wealth was concentrated into the hands of the same urban elite, with its predilection for luxuries, leaving less for other groups who would be willing to invest in more productive goals. This all contributed to the economic stagnation, or even decline, observed above.

---

[218] Zuijderduijn, 'Assets frozen in time'.

[219] For the big expenses on art: Goldthwaite, *Wealth and the demand for art*, 54–62 and 190–203. See also section 6.3, 278–9.

[220] Baron, 'Civic wealth and the new values of the Renaissance'; Goldthwaite, *Wealth and the demand for art*, 204–6.

At this point in time, at the beginning of the sixteenth century, Machiavelli was contemplating the decline of Florence and the other Italian city-republics. He attributed this decline mainly to the belief of his fellow countrymen that the wealth of individuals would promote virtue. Although he was not an advocate of excessively taxing the rich, he did observe that successful societies instead kept the community rich and the citizens poor, which required the latter to preserve a communal spirit and defend the community.[221] In his view, laws should prohibit political inequality and allow all citizens to put themselves forward for public office, regardless of their wealth or social status. This was not happening, however, in the Italy of his time, where numerous gentlemen were enjoying the fruits of their military-political power or their landed estates, living in luxury. The resulting social inequalities opened the way for the wealthy to use their private economic power to dominate political and legal processes, he argued, and they thus threatened freedom.[222] This would lead, according to Machiavelli, to corruption, an erosion of civic liberty, the neglect of the public good, the end of virtue, and to violent outbursts of poorer people who had lost their interest in preserving civil order, as they felt their grievances were no longer represented. Machiavelli, although he did not highlight the role of markets in this, thus described the last stage of a process analysed in this chapter, a process starting three centuries earlier in a much more balanced context that had allowed for a favourable, open organization of the same markets, that would eventually become distorted and have negative consequences for society as a whole, as a result of the influence exerted by the elites who had strengthened their position through these markets.

---

[221] Pocock, *The Machiavellian moment*, 208–18.
[222] Benner, *Machiavelli's ethics*, 269–79.

Map 4.1. Towns and regions in the late medieval and early modern Low Countries (indicated are the boundaries of present-day countries).

4

Markets in Late Medieval and Early Modern Principalities
The Low Countries, 1100–1800

4.1. THE SOCIAL CONTEXT BEFORE AND DURING THE EMERGENCE OF FACTOR MARKETS, FROM THE TWELFTH TO THE FOURTEENTH CENTURY

The Low Countries in the high and late Middle Ages consisted of a collection of principalities and lordships bordering on, or located near the southeastern shores of the North Sea. Major principalities included the counties of Flanders and Holland, the duchies of Guelders and Brabant, and the prince-bishoprics of Utrecht and Liège. From the eleventh century onwards, this low-lying area of some 80,000 km^2 in size, roughly covering the present-day Netherlands, Belgium, and the northernmost part of France, saw almost continuous economic development and growth. The Low Countries became the most densely populated part of Europe. New, largely uninhabited regions were reclaimed in this period, while old territories were cultivated and used ever more intensively, and both became scattered with towns that sprang up. The population rose no less than sixfold between the tenth and fourteenth centuries, from some 400,000 to 2.5 million people.[1] After the demographic catastrophes in the fourteenth century, which had less impact here than elsewhere in Western Europe, the population rose by a further 50 per cent to the end of the sixteenth century.[2] As a result, the Low Countries caught up with Italy with respect to population density, counting c. forty people per km^2.

Even more striking is the rapid growth of towns, a growth gaining momentum especially in the thirteenth and fourteenth centuries. At the beginning of the fourteenth century, roughly 20 per cent of the population in the Low Countries was living in settlements with more than 5,000 inhabitants, and in the late fifteenth century this share was already as high as 34 per cent.[3] In the sixteenth century this rate rose even further, especially in Holland, with towns such as Haarlem, Delft, Leiden, and rapidly growing Amsterdam. By now, the Low Countries—although

---

[1] Van Bavel, *Manors and markets*, 35–7 and 278–9.

[2] Van Bavel, *Manors and markets*, 278–80; Blockmans, Pieters, and Prevenier, 'Het sociaal-economische leven', 44–5.

[3] Blockmans, Pieters, and Prevenier, 'Het sociaal-economische leven', esp. 44–5; de Vries, *European urbanization*, 28–43 and 271–6.

they had only a few really large cities—had become by far the most urbanized part of Europe and had surpassed Italy, which by then was stagnating.

Notwithstanding the dramatic population rise of this period, and the associated pressure on resources, GDP per capita in the Low Countries remained high, in part achieved by a Smithian process of specialization and division of labour, but also by investments in fixed capital goods, and resulting rises in labour productivity, not only in industries but also in agriculture.[4] In the fourteenth to seventeenth century, these processes can be observed most clearly in one of the core regions, Holland. Around 1600, as Holland was entering its 'Golden Age', GDP per capita here was at a level almost double that of the surrounding parts of Europe, and nominal wages were much higher than anywhere else in Europe, including Italy.[5] Holland became a major global player, and possibly the dominant force in European or even global shipping, trade, and finance.[6] The Low Countries also reached a high point in the arts, first in Flanders and Brabant, and later in Holland, during its Golden Age, pointing to the abundance of surpluses, which were spent on paintings and architecture.

This all happened in the context of market exchange: not only of goods, but also of land, labour, and capital. Factor markets thrived in the Low Countries in this period. It is, therefore, tempting to link this economic florescence to the rise and dynamism of markets, as is often done in the subject literature.[7] But the picture can be sharpened, and perhaps partly corrected, by using recent investigations which enable us to better chart the rise of these markets in the Low Countries, their arrangement, and their effects.

This chapter will do so by making a number of observations. The first is that factor markets emerged earlier here than traditionally assumed; too early to be automatically linked to the so-called Golden Age of Holland in the seventeenth century. In many parts of the Low Countries the market for goods developed in the high Middle Ages, and the factor markets in the thirteenth and fourteenth centuries, so that they had become dominant by the sixteenth century.

A second observation is that the organization and functioning of these markets was favourable especially in the fourteenth to sixteenth century, that is, during the late Middle Ages. In the late medieval period, the institutional organization of these markets, as most conspicuously in Holland, offered flexibility, accessibility, and low transaction costs, which were especially notable in its capital and labour markets, as we will see. This enabled broad groups in late medieval society to participate in market exchange and to benefit from this.

A related, third observation is that the open and inclusive organization of factor markets, and its beneficial effects, were captured especially in the late medieval period. By the mid-seventeenth century, the high point in the organization and

---

[4] Van Bavel, 'The medieval origins'; van Bavel, 'Land, lease and agriculture'.
[5] Van Zanden, 'Wages and the standard of living'; de Vries and van der Woude, *The first modern economy*, 619–32.
[6] Prak, *The Dutch Republic*, 96–101 and 111–21; Israel, *Dutch primacy*, 38–79.
[7] De Vries and van der Woude, *The first modern economy*, 687–99.

effects of these markets had already passed, as again most pronounced in Holland, despite the label of 'Golden Age' placed on its seventeenth century.

This will all be dealt with in this chapter, but we will start by looking at the social context within which the factor markets in the Low Countries emerged, from the thirteenth century onwards. This context was characterized by a relatively wide and fairly equal distribution of power and property among individuals and social groups. Rural nobles, urban patriciates, and territorial lords held each other in check, while peasants, village communities, and urban craftsmen and guilds also all held secure positions in society and participated in legal and political decision making. This situation had emerged in the high Middle Ages, as various parts of the Low Countries developed a relatively high degree of freedom and wide access to decision making, compared with other parts of Europe. The situation was found most conspicuously in the sandy regions such as Drenthe and the Campine, the Frisian areas on the North Sea, and the newly reclaimed coastal areas, such as Holland and coastal Flanders.[8]

On the infertile sandy soils, such as those in Drenthe and the Campine, peasant landholding was predominant. Manorial organization was weak, where it was present at all. Extensions to the cultivated area were small, and took place gradually, mainly from existing peasant farms scattered over the area. This resulted in small landholdings, mainly cultivated by the peasants themselves. Peasant landownership was even more dominant in the coastal area of Holland. The massive reclamations in this extensive peat wilderness, starting in the eleventh century, were carried out in a kind of no man's land, where hardly any settlements or manors existed. People had to be attracted to occupy this inhospitable area. The territorial lords, most notably the count of Holland, had to lure people from outside by granting them favourable conditions for settlement. Thus, the numerous colonists who carried out the hard work of land clearance were granted freedom and in practice became owners of the land, each receiving a family-sized farm of uniform size. They paid only a small nominal rent in recognition of the princely position of the count.[9] Members of the landholding nobility in Holland were very few in number; the land came almost completely into the hands of the peasant colonizers, who also acquired full personal freedom.

Regions such as these are clear, albeit perhaps extreme, examples of a pattern found more generally in many parts of the Low Countries, where peasants had personal freedom and owned their land.[10] This freedom went hand in hand with a large scope for self-organization by ordinary people, not only in the towns but also in the countryside, where large numbers of associations were formed or became formalized in the high Middle Ages and self-organization of the rural population was well developed. In regions such as northern Holland and Drenthe, the village community formed a strong counterbalance to lordly power, even more since feudal

[8] Van Bavel, *Manors and markets*, 83–101.

[9] Van der Linden, *De cope*, 93–5 and 160–82; van der Linden, 'Het platteland', 69–78. See also Curtis and Campopiano, 'Medieval land reclamation', 98–9.

[10] Although a few regions were dominated by manorial, large landownership: van Bavel, *Manors and markets*, 75–86.

lordly power was relatively weak here, thus limiting the opportunities of lords to exert non-economic coercion on the population. In Drenthe, with its infertile sandy soils and large wastelands, the strength of the peasant communities was particularly expressed in their hold over the commons. Here, the commons developed in close relationship to the village communities and were managed by the village boards.[11] In their turn these village boards were made up of free, landholding peasants.

In many of the coastal areas, including Frisia and coastal Flanders, the self-organization of the rural population was also expressed in the context of water management. In these coastal areas, the village community, uniting in jurisdictional, fiscal, military, and ecclesiastical responsibilities, often overlapped with the organization for water management.[12] The latter organizations were formed as *coniurationes* of colonist associations bound by an oath, as can be observed most clearly in Holland. Here, as early as the twelfth century, and possibly even before, free confederations were responsible for water management, under the constant threat of flooding, necessitating co-operation and communal organization. They did so in concert with the princely overlord, the count of Holland, who coordinated and regulated supra-local activities, but without fundamentally damaging the communal character.

In Frisia, the self-organization of the rural population was most highly developed. From the weakness of feudal organization and the near absence of authority of territorial lords, a tradition had developed of free men, viewing themselves as directly subordinate to the king, with no intermediary role for princes or feudal lords. These free countrymen had started to organize their autonomous communities as early as the eleventh century, allowing for broad participation in public matters. In the thirteenth century, the organization of communities here proceeded further, with the appearance of the *redjeven*, judges and representatives, appointed by the community.[13] Also, some twenty-five districts were formed, with their own boards, consisting of the joint representatives of the communities. Even though this independent nature and the autonomous associations of the Frisians, with little control from secular or higher ecclesiastical authorities, often irked neighbouring territorial lords and church leaders,[14] the self-government of the Frisian communities largely remained unbroken up to the fifteenth or sixteenth century.

Similar social and political movements were also found in the towns, which have traditionally been better investigated and more generally discussed in the literature. Here, too, the eleventh to thirteenth century had seen the emergence of horizontal associations, such as fraternities and occupational associations. The merchants were the first to form these, followed by other groups of burghers. In this process, the south of the Low Countries—where urban development was most marked—took the lead. An example is the *Caritet* in Valenciennes, a burgher

---

[11] Van Zanden, 'The paradox of the marks'.

[12] Van der Linden, *Recht en territoir*, 10–26; Soens, 'Floods and money', 336–7.

[13] Ehbrecht, 'Gemeinschaft, Land und Bund', esp. 154–60; van Bavel, *Manors and markets*, 96–7.

[14] Oexle, 'Gilden als soziale Gruppen', esp. 322–3.

association rooted in an older merchant guild, aimed at offering mutual support.[15] Communes with their own representatives sprang up in Tournai, Saint-Omer, and Cambrai, aiming to ensure internal peace and to offer security to the people living in the growing centres and conducting trade here. Another major goal was freedom from arbitrary seigniorial judgements and some self-government,[16] which was obtained by way of struggles against lordly influence and the power of the old, closed patriciates and by gaining a clear demarcation and registration of mutual rights and duties. The next group of people in the towns to form associations were the craftsmen, increasingly organizing themselves by way of guilds. In the first half of the twelfth century, proto-guilds appeared in cities in the Meuse valley and Flanders as religious and charitable fraternities organized according to occupation. Arras had such fraternities among the tailors, minters, and shearers.[17] In the course of the thirteenth century these organizations increasingly developed into professional guilds, operating as social and economic pressure groups, as can be observed around the middle of the century in Huy and Dinant, and later also in the Flemish cities.

From the middle of the thirteenth century onwards tensions arose between the increasingly better organized craftsmen and the old patriciate, particularly in the cities of the Meuse Valley, but also in Ghent and later in a number of other Flemish cities.[18] The craftsmen demanded better working conditions, social improvement, but also reform of the city governments and the breaking down of the oligarchy of the narrow, ruling elites. They also demanded increased control over urban finances. Often the rebellious craftsmen were supported by the newly rich who were denied access to the old patriciate. The urban uprisings were sometimes bloodily repressed, as in Saint-Omer in 1280, where a number of weavers who revolted were banished by the town magistrate, and others buried alive, and in Ypres,[19] but in many cases they were successful. In several towns, as a result of the strength of the craftsmen and the new rich, the guilds succeeded in their struggle for reform. Sometimes they even acquired control over the urban government, as in Utrecht in 1274, although here the patriciate succeeded in regaining most of its previous control in 1276 after a bloody battle. In many other towns, however, the success of the guild revolts was more enduring, particularly in Flanders.[20]

As a result of the success of these processes of association and self-organization, the ordinary population in the Low Countries acquired ample scope for participation in political, economic, and social decision making, both in town and countryside. This was through the urban communes and guilds, but also through village communities and commons, and through religious and charitable organizations, such as parishes, poor tables, and hospitals, and also the water management boards.

---

[15] Godding and Pycke, 'La paix de Valenciennes'.
[16] Dhondt, 'Les "solidarités" médiévales'; Boone and Prak, 'Rulers, patricians and burghers', 101–3.
[17] Bijsterveld and Trio, 'Van gebedsverbroedering naar broederschap', esp. 26–34.
[18] Dumolyn and Haemers, 'Patterns of urban rebellion', esp. 374–8.
[19] Boogaart, 'Reflections on the Moerlemaye'; Cohn, *Lust for liberty*, 54.
[20] Blockmans, *Metropolen aan de Noordzee*, 316–23.

They were all voluntary organizations, formed mainly by medium-scale, independent producers who formed associations, often confirmed by an oath, and based on consensus.[21]

The rise of these organizations, in the eleventh to thirteenth century, and the goals they set themselves, can only be understood in combination with the growth of output markets, which occurred at exactly this time and was very pronounced in the Low Countries. The interaction worked in both directions. The increased security the horizontal organizations brought, the reduction of the lordly rights to impose arbitrary decisions they entailed, the advances in administration they brought and the growing safety of property rights, all helped reduce transaction costs and increased opportunities for trade and specialization. They thus increased the quality and efficiency of product markets. Conversely, the growing self-organization enabled the people to absorb the shocks and disruptive effects caused by growing trade, market competition, and market dependency, including sharp inequality or insecurity caused by the vagaries of the market.[22] This buffering was achieved especially by securing the economic independence and welfare of the producers—the medium-sized ones in particular—by limiting the accumulation of capital and production facilities, and by restricting the market exchange of land, labour, and capital. This was carried out, up to and into the early modern period, by the urban guilds, through setting maxima on sizes of workshops, numbers of labourers, and working hours, for instance, and likewise this was done in the countryside by the village communities and the commons, through allocating and restricting usage rights and limiting numbers of cattle.

As a result, during the eleventh to thirteenth century, on the one hand the output markets grew and increasingly thrived, whereas on the other hand the exchange and allocation of land, labour, and capital remained firmly embedded in non-market organizations. Among these organizations, family and kin had traditionally played a primordial role, and in some regions lordly seigneuries and manors also did so, but now, associations such as the commons and the guilds also assumed a prominent role in the allocation and exchange of land, labour, and capital. This role is exemplified by the influence of the guilds on the allocation of labour and capital, observed above, and that of the commons in the allocation of land and the regulation of the use of the rights to land, by limiting the number of cattle to be grazed, for instance.[23]

The associations produced only limited amounts of written sources, especially for this early period, and their role in exchange thus left much fewer traces than market transactions did, but in many regions and localities their role was important, as reconstructed for the commons in the Campine area, where they played a primordial role in the organization of economic and social life.[24] In these cases, guilds, commons, and other associations regulated and facilitated the exchange

---

[21] See Oexle, 'Gilde und Kommune'; Blickle, *Kommunalismus* II, esp. 132–53.
[22] De Moor, 'The silent revolution', esp. 197–201 and 207. For the role of the guilds in a later period: DuPlessis and Howell, 'Reconsidering'.
[23] For the role of the commons: van Zanden, 'The paradox of the marks'.
[24] Van Onacker, *Leaders of the pack?*, 112–41.

and allocation of land, labour, and capital outside the market. In doing so, they valued other considerations more than the price mechanism, as most notably the protection of the independence and welfare of the medium-sized producers.[25]

As we have seen, the associations played yet another role in relation to the market, that is, by combating the negative effects of market exchange. These could be social excesses, such as sharp polarization or poverty—as fought against by the guilds, the commons, and the charitable organizations—but also ecological excesses, as in cases in which intense commercial exploitation or profiteering threatened to result in the exhaustion or pollution of natural resources. Lastly, and equally important, these associations and other forms of self-organization offered a counterweight to elites in the formation of the institutional rules of market exchange. Even though guilds and commons represented only part of the population, and could be a vehicle for the peasant or craft elites to dominate their sectors and defend their own interests,[26] associations in this period were fairly inclusive, especially when compared to the earlier situation of more arbitrary decision making by feudal lords.

The effects of this constellation, in which expanding output markets were combined with a highly diversified and largely non-market allocation of land, labour, and capital, were positive. This was a period full of technological innovations, and it saw the successful introduction and wide application of many labour-saving tools, with the Low Countries being at the forefront of these developments in Europe, as evidenced by the relatively high levels of welfare reached, or maintained, even despite the highest population growth in Europe.[27] These technological innovations often required huge sums of capital, as most clearly with the construction of mills. The investments were made without recourse to the capital market, by associations or communities, or by manorial or seigneurial lords, with the lordly exactions used as an instrument to charge the population, but also as a way to bear the costs of expensive investments in cranes, sluices, ovens, breweries, and mills.[28] The more efficient overshot waterwheels were introduced all over the Low Countries from the thirteenth century on. These mills required canalization of the watercourse and construction of a mill pond, water race, and sluice gates to guarantee a regular water supply entering the mill from above, requiring large expense,[29] and again the Low Countries were in the lead.

Economic progress was also made within the systems for communal agriculture, developed by the rural associations and village communities. In the high Middle Ages, these succeeded in reorganizing the layout of the arable, to create open fields, to implement more efficient rotation systems, and to introduce new implements,

---

[25] For the guilds: DuPlessis and Howell, 'Reconsidering'.

[26] Ogilvie and Carus, 'Institutions and economic growth', 421, 431–2, and passim; van Onacker, *Leaders of the pack?*, 267–79 (a broad elite in the Campine).

[27] Thoen, 'Le demarrage économique'; van Bavel, *Manors and markets*, 133–6 and 158–61. For population growth: this section, 145–6 and 152.

[28] Van Bavel, *Manors and markets*, 148–9, 159–60; Genicot, *L'économie rurale Namuroise*, iii, 99–103.

[29] Examples from the Brussels area: Deligne, *Bruxelles et sa rivière*, 19–23 and 36–43. See for windmills Bautier, 'Les plus anciennes mentions', esp. 606–20.

including long-handled scythes and reaping hooks, thus making much more efficient use of land and labour.[30] This period, that is, before the rise of factor markets, also saw the massive introduction of heavy ploughs and horse traction.[31] To be sure, these labour-saving techniques were introduced more generally in Western Europe, but nowhere as massively as in the Low Countries, as is witnessed by the fact that here productivity was hugely increased, while living standards were sustained, or even pushed up, and this despite the very rapid rise of population numbers. Between c. 1000 and c. 1300 the number of people in the Low Countries rose five or sixfold—forming the biggest rise in all of Europe and making this into the most densely populated part of Europe, aside from Italy.[32] Despite this huge rise, living standards remained relatively high, and this can be considered a momentous achievement of the Low Countries' society of the period, without factor markets having yet developed.

The fairly equal distribution of property and power, and the high degree of self-organization, combined with the opportunities offered by the dynamic output markets, gave ordinary people a relatively favourable position. These farmers, peasants, craftsmen, and petty merchants generally were able to defend their freedom against possible infringements by noblemen and ecclesiastical and secular lords. In the Low Countries, and especially in the Frisian parts, the coastal area stretching from Holland in the west far into present-day Germany in the east, revolts and armed resistance had been a recurrent phenomenon during the eleventh and twelfth centuries.[33] Their incidence actually intensified in the thirteenth and early fourteenth centuries, and reached a peak in number and intensity as the people in these regions defended their freedom, or now won it. These successful revolts thus resemble those in northern Italy in the eleventh to thirteenth century, rather than the powerless unrest of a weakened populace observed there in the fourteenth and fifteenth centuries.

One example of this success, in 1274–5, is the revolt by the people of the Kennemerland, in the north of Holland.[34] The rebels demanded recognition of their self-governing powers and of their own, customary organization of taxation. They resisted the growing power of noblemen and comital representatives, who were trying to undermine the power of the village communities, and the erosion of their rights and customs in general. The rebels succeeded in destroying most of the fortified houses of the noblemen in the region and then pushed further south. They marched on Utrecht, the largest city of the northern Low Countries, some 50 kilometres away, in an attempt to bring the entire prince-bishopric of Utrecht, which covered large parts of the present-day Netherlands, into one community.[35] The Utrecht craftsmen joined their revolt, took control of the town government and banished the noblemen and patricians from the town. Frightened by the successes of the rebellion, the count of Holland after some time decided to meet most

[30] For Hainaut: Sivéry, *Structures agraires*, 83–6, 98–105, and 138–42.
[31] Thoen, 'Le démarrage'.   [32] Van Bavel, *Manors and markets*, 278–81 and 372–3.
[33] Schmidt, 'Hochmittelalterliche "Bauernaufstände"', esp. 416–28.
[34] Blok, 'Drie boerenopstanden'.
[35] Blok, 'Beke's bron'; van Bavel, 'Rural revolts'.

of the demands made by the rebels, thus bringing the revolt to an end in 1275. The concessions in the sphere of self-government in local justice, fiscal policy, water management, and the administration of collective goods were laid down in a charter.[36]

Even though some revolts were quickly put down, the considerable degree of success they achieved is still striking. In a number of cases the rebellious people resisted for several years or decades, and in other cases they were even victorious. The Low Countries' revolts are thus among the very few successful rural insurrections of the period found in Western Europe. Even more successful were the urban populations, in their struggle against the nobility and the urban patricians. The position of the guilds became especially strong in the years around 1302, as the Flemish troops, consisting mainly of urban militias with an important guild component, defeated an army of French knights in the Battle of the Golden Spurs.[37] The effect of this spread to other parts of the Low Countries, where the guilds increasingly extended their influence over the urban economy, society, and politics, often with the use of force against the old patriciates. Their success can be explained by the rapid growth of industries in the Low Countries' towns and the large number of people involved in these sectors, the relatively weak position of the old patriciates and the fact that new elites (merchants, elite craftsmen, or the princes) were sometimes inclined to support the claims of the guilds. Elites in the Low Countries, due to their diversity, were thus less united than elsewhere in Europe, opening up possibilities for these revolts.

The success of these revolts was not complete, however. The old elites, sometimes supplemented with the new rich, still retained a large part of their economic and political power.[38] Also, the largest of all revolts, the Flemish revolt of 1323–8, eventually failed.[39] This revolt, in which peasants, farmers, and urban craftsmen fought side by side, had turned against taxation and the monopolization of power by the small patriciate, favouritism, and abuses in town government, and in the second, more radical phase of the revolt, it became directly aimed against the nobility and patriciate, against large landownership and against the levying of tithes, thus acquiring a revolutionary character. This revolution, however, failed, as the insurgents were defeated by a coalition of large numbers of noblemen from all over Western Europe. This defeat destroyed some of the aspirations of the rural population, but it had much less of an adverse effect in the towns. There, the guilds would retain their influence for several centuries and often succeeded in defending the interests of the medium-scale, independent craft producers.

In the late thirteenth and early fourteenth centuries, the Low Countries thus witnessed a massive wave of revolts, in both town and countryside. This wave can be understood as a clash between the freedom and right of self-organization of ordinary craftsmen, peasants, and farmers, won in the previous period, and the

---

[36] Hoppenbrouwers, 'Rebels with a cause'.
[37] Blockmans, *Metropolen aan de Noordzee*, 303–17; Nicholas, *Flanders*, 192–203.
[38] Uytven, 'Plutokratie'.
[39] Sabbe, *Vlaanderen in opstand*, 22–35, 55–62, and 77–85; TeBrake, *A plague of insurrection*, 57–60, 71–86, 112–22, and 139–56. See also section 4.3, 178–9.

intensifying infringements on this self-organization. A main infringement came from the rise of princely power and the growth of central bureaucracies, with their associated fiscal systems and new elites.[40] As a result of this rise, the roles of the associations of ordinary peasants, farmers, and craftsmen in jurisdiction, legislation, administration, religion, water management, and exploitation and exchange of land, labour, and capital, came under pressure. Despite their successes, the associations did not thus acquire a dominant position, but had to share it with other groups and organizations, including the rising princes and their bureaucracies, while the old elites in town and countryside also retained some of their position. Still, the old, feudal nobility had lost its monopoly of power, and now had to share it with associations, merchants, princes, and state elites.[41]

Associated with these developments, the older systems of exchange of land, labour, and capital that were dominated by this old, feudal elite declined and its arbitrary power was reduced. Not only the manors owned by the feudal elite disintegrated in the twelfth to fourteenth century, but also their power as local lords became restricted.[42] This opened up the possibility that new systems of exchange of land, labour, and capital, most notably the market, would rise. This happened in a context of social balance, with a number of countervailing powers, which had developed in many parts of the Low Countries, more conspicuously than in any part of contemporary Europe. In turn, this balance did not allow any social group to dominate the exchange and allocation of land, labour, and capital, a situation which was the best guarantee for a favourable institutional framework of the factor markets that now started to rise, as we will see in the next section.

4.2. THE EMERGENCE OF FACTOR MARKETS IN THE THIRTEENTH TO FIFTEENTH CENTURY

Land and Lease Markets

Before the rise of land markets, much, or possibly even most, of the exchange of land was within the family, with informal or formal arrangements among family members, and hereditary practice, shaping exchange to a large extent, even though the monetary value of the land could be included in the considerations. Non-familial exchanges generally did not take place through the market either. As in other parts of Europe, in the Low Countries such transfers were generally regulated within the multitude of social organizations which had developed in the early Middle Ages, such as the manor, or in the high Middle Ages, such as the lordship, the village community, and the commons. Exchange of land among members of the elite was also largely dominated by non-economic motives, as with gift exchange—establishing a lasting bond between the two parties involved, with benefactors making a donation of land to a religious house, or with the establishment

---

[40] Van Bavel, 'Rural revolts'; Cohn, *Lust for liberty*, 32–3 and 54–7.
[41] Boone and Prak, 'Rulers, patricians and burghers', 102–6.
[42] See for this process section 4.2, 155–6 and 160–1.

of a feudal relationship, with the social, political, and ideological implications of the exchange being predominant.[43]

Before the rise of the land market, land transfer was thus primarily a social instrument, firmly embedded in social organization and in the formal and informal rules these organizations had developed. This organization of land rights restricted the quick transfer of land and the working of economic mechanisms, but should not automatically be judged as a negative one, since it potentially had all kinds of social and ecological advantages. It could, for instance, help in preventing one single party from reaping short-term benefits at the expense of all other parties or to the detriment of long-term social, ecological, or economic sustainability. Thus, as argued for types of common property regimes,[44] it could offer more long-term security to all parties involved.

In the twelfth and thirteenth centuries, this situation started to change in some parts of the Low Countries with the emergence of a land market. Rights to land became more absolute and exclusive, with restrictions and the non-market mechanisms for distributing land being gradually replaced by market transactions. This was a long and protracted process, but it started earlier in the Low Countries and evolved more quickly there than in the rest of Europe, except for Italy, as discussed in Chapter 3. An important element in the process was the decline of the manorial system, which occurred in the eleventh to thirteenth century in many parts of the Low Countries, first in the western, coastal parts and later also on the fertile clay and loamy soils, in regions such as the Guelders river area.[45] Another important change was the dissolution and privatization of common lands, making these much easier to buy and sell. There were significant regional differences; in Drenthe, the Campine, and the Ardennes, characterized by poor soils and dominated by landholding peasants and their rural associations, extensive common wastelands and village restrictions survived until well into the modern period.[46] In most regions, however, communal rules had largely disappeared before the fourteenth century. The rural associations there had helped in breaking down traditional structures, but they had not become dominant, as we have seen in the preceding section. No single group could thus control the exchange of land by non-economic means and this situation opened up land to be exchanged in the market.

The erosion of these non-market systems was accelerated by the rise of factor markets. The emerging labour and capital markets made social actors less dependent on the land as a binding element, as a form of security, or as an instrument of power or coercion. More specifically, the growing opportunity for manorial lords to use land and lease markets to exploit their property rights to land, and derive an income from it, made clinging on to the manorial system less attractive to them. Also, they could now avail themselves of the dynamic product markets for their provisioning and they no longer needed the manors to provision them directly. The emerging land and lease markets now offered all actors an option to use land

---

[43] Bijsterveld, *Do ut des*, 18–27 and 32–6; van Bavel, *Manors and markets*, 162–4.
[44] Van Zanden, 'The paradox of the marks'.   [45] Van Bavel, *Manors and markets*, 86–92.
[46] See the overviews by Hoppenbrouwers, 'The use and management', esp. 98–108; de Moor, 'Common land', esp. 113–27.

as a commodity, with both lords and peasants in the thirteenth century entering the land market, as witnessed by a multitude of sales, including small plots or fragments of land.[47] The fact that many parts of the Low Countries, such as the Frisian areas on the North Sea, the sandy, peasant-dominated regions such as Drenthe and the Campine, and the newly reclaimed coastal areas such as Holland and coastal Flanders, had large amounts of land in the hands of ordinary peasants—up to 90 per cent of the land[48]—and these were relatively unencumbered by feudal rights and increased the openness of land markets and the number of potential participants in this market.

The rise of the land market was further promoted by the security of market transactions and property rights to land. In the Low Countries, registration of land transfers had been mainly carried out by lords or lordly courts up to the thirteenth century. This role of the lords was often related to their desire to exercise some control over transactions in land and the opportunity to levy a tax.[49] In the southern parts of the Low Countries, such as Flanders and Brabant, this lordly tax on the sale of land could amount to 8–16 per cent of the selling price. In the later Middle Ages, and especially in the northern parts of the Low Countries, however, registration was taken over by public courts. These courts were mainly instituted by towns and village communities and proceeded from the associative wave of the eleventh and twelfth centuries, but were later recognized by the princely lords and incorporated in their administration. From the fourteenth century, the voluntary registration of private land transfers by public courts in the record books of the aldermen became common practice in the cities, and from the fifteenth century this practice spread to the village courts.[50] This process developed very early compared to other parts of Europe, and as a result, an increasing proportion of land transfers was registered by the public courts, in both town and countryside. It also precluded notaries and their fragmented administration from fulfilling this role, in contrast to areas in the south of Europe, such as Italy.[51] Often, public authorities even explicitly prohibited notaries to engage in registering land transfers, also because the registration by public courts could be more easily used to check the tax returns.

The early development of public registration in these parts of the Low Countries, and the fact that it became more important there than anywhere else in Europe, was connected to the strong influence of the authorities and public courts in legal matters, and the development of a network of public courts in the countryside, to some extent formed under the influence of village communities. Parties engaging in a transaction increasingly preferred to transfer land in a public court, and to have the transfer registered there, rather than performing a private transfer, mainly because of the stronger legal security vis-à-vis third parties.[52] The court books or

---

[47] Van Bavel, 'The land market in the North Sea area'. For Flanders: Thoen, *Landbouwekonomie*, 878–94.
[48] Van Bavel, *Manors and markets*, 83–6 and 242–6.
[49] For the following: van Bavel, 'The land market in the North Sea area', esp. 130–3.
[50] Van Bavel, 'The land market in the North Sea area', 131–2.
[51] See section 3.1, 112–13.
[52] Van Bavel, 'The land market in the North Sea area'.

protocols had both legal validity and evidential value. Registration entailed some costs, and small sums were charged for looking into the protocol or copying it, but the amounts involved were minimal.

Proof and accessibility of registration at a central and public place greatly enhanced transparency and security for potential buyers. Even more so, as the same procedure was increasingly applied to transactions in the financial market, with the growing registration of new mortgages and the selling of rents on real estate by public courts.[53] This practice, which was even made obligatory in the early sixteenth century, prevented a buyer of a plot of land from being confronted with an unexpected rent burden on the land. The position taken by the authorities on these matters thus reduced the insecurity and the information costs on the land market, and gave all participants in this market—both urban and rural—an equal position. Even though land markets have never functioned as perfectly open markets with complete competition, where supply and demand are the only factors determining price movements, non-economic factors gradually lost most of their influence within the land markets in the Low Countries. In the course of this process, the volume of land markets quickly grew.[54]

Compared to the land market, the lease market was even more important for increasing the mobility of land. In most parts of the Low Countries, the ten-year term was predominant, while terms of nine, eight, six, or even three years were also used.[55] In practice, leaseholds could be longer, if the lease contract was extended or renewed, but still mobility of land in the lease market was very high. These were mainly contractual leases, of separate parcels of land, a few hectares in size, resulting in a dynamic, flexible lease market. This differed from the full holdings or farms leased out in most parts of central Italy, where the relationship between landlord and tenant was more personal and at the same time had greater overtones of dependency.

In the Low Countries, from the first half of the thirteenth century onwards the contractual, short-term lease made its appearance. This happened first in the most urbanized regions, such as Flanders, Brabant, and the Rhineland, and next, around 1300, even more forcefully in moderately urbanized regions such as the Guelders river area and Salland, which had been dominated by large landownership but had seen the lords losing their non-economic power with the dissolution of manorialism.[56] In the resulting situation there, in which the lords lost their coercive power over labour but retained their grip on landownership, and in which product markets offered a ready outlet for agricultural output, these former lords started to lease out most of the land. In the fourteenth and early fifteenth centuries, the majority of the land here was already given out on short-term leases, rising to approximately 75–80 per cent around 1500. In regions dominated by peasant landownership, such as Drenthe and inland Flanders, most of the owners continued

[53] Zuijderduijn, *Medieval capital markets*, 66–7 and 200–14.
[54] As is evident from the high turnover rates: see section 4.3, 171.
[55] Van Bavel, 'The land market in the North Sea area', 137–9.
[56] Van Bavel, 'The emergence and growth', esp. 185–9.

to farm the land themselves, and the proportion of land leased out to tenants remained smaller, at 40–45 per cent.

These lease markets were fairly competitive. It was only in some regions, such as Holland, and in the northern regions, that tenants were able to claim more enduring rights to the land they leased. In Groningen, for instance, tenants had strong, lasting rights, especially if they owned the farmhouse, buildings, plantings, and other improvements on the leased land.[57] Lease prices there became almost frozen, and leases were normally renewed or transmitted by inheritance. In practice, this system of leasing led to a kind of hereditary lease or even outright ownership for the tenant.

This contrasts sharply with the situation in other parts of the Low Countries, as in the Guelders river area or Namur, where the time of termination of the lease was strictly enforced, and continuation was only possible if the tenant had a strong economic position on the lease market. This arrangement encouraged a high mobility of land use, open competition, and flexibility of the lease market. It also offered unconstrained use of the land to the tenant for the duration of the lease, with contractual clarity for both owner and tenant. Security for both parties was enhanced by an elaborate system of administration, including lease contracts for the two parties involved, lease agreements recorded by courts in protocols, lease books in which the landholder administered the land leased out, and lease accounts or account books which noted the lease sums and payments.[58] Also, since most lease agreements contained clear rules for the reimbursement of investments made by the tenant, it formed a stimulus for investment.[59]

As a result, in many parts of the Low Countries the mobility of leased land was high. In these areas, in the fifteenth century, a competitive, market-determined situation existed, in which parcels of land were rarely let for a second time to the same tenant or to his son.[60] The landlord granted the lease to the highest bidder, regardless of the wishes or alleged rights of the previous tenant. This applied particularly where land was let by public bidding. Markets for leased land were thus even more mobile and accessible than sales markets. In the Guelders river area, each piece of leased land (forming about three-quarters of all agricultural land) entered the market on average every six to ten years, whereas each piece of land that was sold entered the market on average once in fifty to seventy years.

In almost all cases the rent was fixed as a monetary amount, and for the major part paid in money. Sharecropping in the Low Countries, in contrast to Italy, from the thirteenth and fourteenth centuries onwards diminished in importance. The use of sharecropping became mainly limited to highly infertile soils and to insecure times, such as periods of war; otherwise it had almost completely disappeared. The rise of short-term leasing thus went hand in hand with a monetization of agriculture; most of the rents were not only fixed in money but were in practice also paid

---

[57] Formsma, 'Beklemrecht en landbouw', esp. 13–27.   [58] See also section 1.3, 25–6.
[59] Van Bavel, 'Land, lease and agriculture', 29–30 and 37.
[60] Jansen, *Landbouwpacht*, 77–80. See for Namur: Genicot, *L'économie rurale Namuroise*, 283–5 and 292.

in money.[61] Even small-scale tenants paid their rent in cash, a development facilitated by a strong increase in the number of coins in circulation.[62] Also, agricultural production became more commercialized. Tenant farmers were more inclined than other farmers to focus on the market and to specialize, since they needed to do so in order to increase profits and compete successfully for the lease land. In regions of highly competitive lease markets, such as the Guelders river area and coastal Flanders, highly specialized agriculture can be observed, almost fully oriented at the market.

Labour Markets

From the fourteenth century onwards, the Low Countries saw a marked rise in wage labour, both in the towns and in the countryside. Some wage labour must already have existed in the early and high Middle Ages. In ninth-century property lists, such as that by the abbey of Lobbes, labour services are often shown as equivalent to amounts of money, showing that there was an awareness of the monetary value of labour. Moreover, many hundreds of labourers are mentioned in these lists, as well as in various other sources from the ninth to eleventh century, mainly for Brabant and Hainault. Such labourers lived on the manors and were personally bound to the lord, but had no land of their own, or only a small garden around their cottage, and no usage rights in woods or pasture, and they must have been largely dependent on work performed on the demesne or on larger farms, probably for wages.[63] But, apart from a few mentions, all the evidence on wage labour is only indirect and often in a situation of dependency on the lord.

The picture becomes clearer in the thirteenth and fourteenth centuries. In the growing cities of the Low Countries, labour was still mostly small-scale and independent, but some sectors witnessed a clear increase in wage labour. This particularly applies to work in which relatively large numbers of labourers were needed, such as building, infrastructure, and transport. For instance, dozens of carpenters, masons, and slaters could be employed as wage labourers in the building of churches. Even larger numbers were employed in public works, and especially the construction of walls and gates, which were undertaken in many cities in this period. In 1382 in Bruges, up to 150 master masons, 160 journeymen masons, and 720 diggers were employed per month in the construction of fortifications, although most only for some six days a month on average.[64] This, and the highly seasonal nature of building works, points to the fact that such labourers were not exclusively dependent on this wage, but must have had other sources of income or access to poor relief to survive periods of unemployment. In other urban sectors, as well, paid labour increased from the thirteenth century onwards, since some artisans expanded their production and required labour from outside the household,

---

[61] Thoen, *Landbouwekonomie*, 539–50 and 569–73; van Bavel, *Manors and markets*, 177.

[62] For coin production, see this section, 164.

[63] Devroey, *Le polyptyque*, xcv–xcvi, cvii–cviii, cxvii, and cxxi; Kuchenbuch, *Bäuerliche Gesellschaft*, 249–60.

[64] Sosson, *Les travaux publics*, 232–55.

often in the form of apprentices and journeymen within a guild system. In exceptional cases, this came close to real wage labour, as suggested for the Flemish textile centre of Douai, where in the second half of the thirteenth century the merchant and entrepreneur Jehan Boinebroke had already made numerous artisans dependent on his commissions, monetary loans, instruments, or the raw materials he supplied, while he also dominated the supply of wool and the finishing of the cloth.[65] This, however, was an exception. Small-scale, independent production for the market remained dominant in the cities, and was often successfully defended there by the guilds, certainly in production and services aimed at the local market but even in export-oriented industries.[66]

In the countryside, the rise of wage labour was more rapid and affected larger numbers than in the towns. Part of this growth was found in the proto-industrial sectors, as most conspicuously in Holland, where brick production, peat digging, and also fishing in the fifteenth century were predominantly done by wage labourers.[67] An even more profound effect on the demand for wage labour was caused by the emergence of large tenant farms, which required additional labour, either at peak times during the harvest or all year round, often in the form of farm servants. This process remained limited in regions dominated by peasants, where the small or medium-sized family holding remained dominant, and the need to hire additional labour remained small, but from the middle of the fifteenth century onwards it grew tremendously in regions such as coastal Flanders and later the Guelders river area, Salland, and coastal Frisia, which were dominated by large landholdings and leased out land.[68] Many people were available to hire themselves out for wages, and they could freely do so, since hardly any elements of unfreedom or personal dependency existed any longer. This personal freedom was a major prerequisite for the rise of a labour market.

A large part of the population in the Low Countries had already been free in the high Middle Ages, as in those regions where manorialism traditionally had been weak (the Campine, Drenthe, Frisia), in newly reclaimed regions (Holland), and in the rising towns (Artois, Flanders, and elsewhere). In most regions, the last remnants of unfreedom were removed in the thirteenth and fourteenth centuries. A conspicuous role in this was played by the princes, who grew in power in the process of developing territorial principalities. They were instrumental in attacking elements of unfreedom and manorialism, with the aim of breaking the rival power of manorial lords, for instance by granting franchises to village communities, as happened in Brabant.[69] The towns also played a role, one more generally found in Western Europe, by giving freedom to former serfs residing for a year and a day in the town, thus offering the rural population an alternative to serfdom. Serfs did

---

[65] Espinas, 'Jehan Boine Broke', although the exact nature of his entrepreneurial activities is disputed. See also Blockmans, *Metropolen aan de Noordzee*, 122.

[66] Dambruyne, *Corporatieve middengroepen*, 59–83; DuPlessis and Howell, 'Reconsidering the early modern economy'. For the role of the guilds, see 161–2.

[67] Van Bavel, 'Early proto-industrialization', 1151–61.

[68] Van Bavel, 'Rural wage labour'. For the shares of labour performed for wages in these different regions: section 4.3, 147.

[69] Steurs, 'Les franchises'.

indeed run away to the towns, as is shown, for instance, by the decrees of lords, and the treaties signed between them, in order to stop this practice, but mostly in vain.[70]

Apart from the initial weakness of manorialism in the Low Countries, and the growing infringements and attacks on this system in the thirteenth century, there was also a positive inducement to the manorial lords to dissolve their manors. This was the fact that the rise of towns and urban markets, being stronger than anywhere in Europe, aside from Italy, offered them interesting economic opportunities, for marketing products and buying them, without having to resort to the manorial system. Moreover, the emergence of lease and labour markets enabled these lords to exploit their landownership by using these markets, instead of binding serfs, and often much more profitably, in view of the growing population numbers and the associated low wages and high lease prices of the period.[71] These parts of the Low Countries thus offered a unique combination of growing costs of coercion, also because of the revolts and self-organization of ordinary people, and a growing attractiveness of factor and output markets, a combination which induced these elites in a positive feedback cycle to use these markets and release their non-economic grip on land and labour.

Many obstacles to free labour and the rise of labour markets in the countryside were, therefore, removed in this period. This is not to say that labour markets were fully free, however. In some parts of the Low Countries, most clearly in Flanders, new restrictions were introduced, now by the towns and urban elites. Although not as vigorously as their Italian counterparts, urban authorities in Flanders regularly intervened in the labour markets—both urban and to a lesser extent rural markets. This was associated with the strong position of the guilds, and their direct or indirect influence on town governments, starting from the victories of the guilds in these places around 1300, and with the desire of these guilds to protect the employment and living standards of their members, the urban craftsmen.[72] Under conditions of labour scarcity, the migration of labourers from the town to the countryside was sometimes prohibited, unless the consent of the town aldermen had been obtained. Conversely, when the supply of labour was large, immigration and access to the urban labour market in Flemish and other guild-dominated towns were often restricted.

Guild-dominated town governments, as found most conspicuously in Flanders, also interfered in rural labour markets, particularly in the fourteenth and fifteenth centuries. As the cities in this region were faced with a crisis in the production and export of cloth, in the years around 1300, they tried to avert this crisis not only by switching to the production of higher quality cloth, but also by eliminating rural competition.[73] Thus, they turned against rural cloth production: not against spinning

---

[70] Epperlein, *Bauernbedrückung und Bauernwiderstand*, 67–75, for examples from the Rhineland in the thirteenth century.

[71] See more extensively, van Bavel, 'The emergence and growth'.

[72] Van Houtte and van Uytven, 'Wirtschaftspolitik und Arbeitsmarkt'.

[73] Van der Wee, 'Structural changes and specialization', esp. 217–10; Nicholas, 'Economic reorientation and social change', esp. 8–11.

and other simple, preparatory activities, which were left unimpeded, but against rural weaving and finishing of cloth. On the basis of privileges obtained from the count, the Flemish cities, and Ghent in particular, tried to wipe out this industry in the surrounding countryside,[74] and did not hesitate to apply brutal force in doing so. Other rural activities, too, such as river transport, trade, and brewing, were hampered or even prohibited.[75] Thus, only simple, labour-intensive activities, performed by independent peasant households producing on their own account, remained in the Flemish countryside. Moreover, the towns succeeded in concentrating the markets for the output of these proto-industrial activities within their walls, forcing rural producers to bring their products there. The scope for rural agency was further limited as urban merchant entrepreneurs made the rural producers dependent on them by advancing raw materials or credit. In some of the proto-industrial sectors in Flanders, urban merchant entrepreneurs in the fourteenth century thus combined privileges, monopolies, and sometimes even outright violence with their economic power, and they successfully linked their activities in capital, labour, and product markets in order to create a division of labour that suited them and to make rural producers dependent on them.

Where guilds or urban elites became dominant, they thus restricted the development of open labour markets. This, however, was exceptional in the late medieval Low Countries. Outside Flanders these practices were much less apparent, partly because of the political weakness of the urban guilds, which were often kept in check by the territorial princes. In Holland, the guilds in this period were few and had almost no political role; this was explicitly denied them by the count.[76] Labour markets there were fairly open to country dwellers and other migrants. Moreover, due to their success the economies of the booming Holland towns were able to absorb large quantities of rural labour. In the countryside, too, the labour market in the northwestern parts of the Low Countries was open and flexible. In Flanders, servants in particular were subjected to some restrictions. The breaking of contracts by labourers and servants was a criminal offence, for which the ordinances prescribed corporal punishment. In fifteenth-century Flanders, runaways could count on a whipping.[77] In Holland, by contrast, labour legislation was to be found only in some urban by-laws, applied mainly to wage labourers in urban industries, and was primarily aimed at the prevention of strikes. Labour legislation for agricultural workers and servants was virtually absent and remained so.

Wage earners could move freely from one place to the other. The count of Holland or the parliamentary estates never fixed wages, nor did they issue penal laws against wage payments above customary levels. Labourers and servants were supposed to serve the usual terms, but in all economic sectors they had contractual freedom and therefore a strong bargaining position in setting the terms of the labour contract they entered into. This did not change with the Black Death and

---

[74] Thoen, *Landbouwekonomie*, 1011–14; van Uytven, 'Die ländliche Industrie', esp. 65–6; Nicholas, *Town and countryside*, 99–116 and 188–221.
[75] Van Bavel, 'Early proto-industrialization', 1124–6.
[76] De Munck, Lourens, and Lucassen, 'The establishment and distribution'.
[77] Van Bavel et al., 'The organisation of markets', 355–7, also for the following.

the demographic decline of the mid-fourteenth century. In the by-laws of Holland towns there are signs of labour shortages in the early fifteenth century, but compulsory labour was not the solution adopted by the authorities.[78] Instead, they typically decided to open the market to immigrants. More generally, in the fifteenth and sixteenth centuries, arrangements there between employer and labourer were market-determined and based on a money wage, which was paid regularly, for instance on a daily, weekly, or monthly basis.[79] Labour contracts in these regions were mostly for short terms: verbal agreements for the day or written one-year contracts. Because labourers had full legal freedom and there were hardly any formal restrictions, their mobility was very high. Even though their security may have been low, and perhaps lower than with longer contracts or in a more dependent position, it did offer them freedom and it fuelled a dynamic labour market.

Moreover, there was by then virtually no conscription of country dwellers by urban authorities in the Low Countries. Earlier, towns were often entitled to coerce rural labour for specific tasks, but in the fifteenth century this was no longer the case, not even for large-scale activities such as the building of city walls or hydrological infrastructure which might perhaps even be regarded as a shared responsibility of the urban and rural population. From the late fourteenth century onwards, these large infrastructural projects were mostly carried out by wage labourers, hired by master contractors, with a large share of the labour force coming from the countryside.[80]

The effects of these factors on the development of the labour market were pronounced. Firstly, there was the effect on wage formation. The freedom and integration of labour markets in most parts of the Low Countries is reflected in the small differences in nominal wages between town and countryside.[81] In Italy, as we saw in Chapter 3, because of restrictions on immigration and mobility, and also larger price differentials in costs of living, this difference could amount to no less than 100–200 per cent for similar occupations or tasks, as established for Florence and elsewhere in Tuscany, and for other parts of Italy in the fourteenth to sixteenth century.[82] In some parts of the Low Countries, too, there were some restrictions on mobility, and access to the urban labour market was not always easy for the rural population, as we have seen for Flanders, but it was easier to obtain there than in Italy. This is reflected in much smaller differences between urban and rural wages. In inland Flanders, nominal wages in the countryside were still close to the urban rates in the early fourteenth century, but in the late fourteenth and fifteenth centuries an urban/rural wage differential emerged of some 50–70 per cent, possibly because it was in this period that urban and guild restrictions on immigration and entry into urban occupations became tighter.[83] In Holland, where restrictions were

[78] General on labour legislation: Cohn, 'After the Black Death'.
[79] Van Bavel, 'Rural wage labour', esp. 65–6. Compare the contemporary developments in Italy: section 3.2, 119–22.
[80] Sosson, *Les travaux publics*, 167–78 and 215–16; Soens, 'Floods and money', 341–2; van Dam, 'Digging for a dike'.
[81] Van Bavel et al., 'The organisation of markets', 365–6.   [82] Section 3.2, 123.
[83] Stabel, *De kleine stad in Vlaanderen*, 185–92; Thoen, *Landbouwekonomie*, 955–60. See also van Bavel et al., 'The organization of markets', 365–6.

weakest, the difference at this time was very small, at 10–30 per cent, or even absent altogether, witnessing the openness of the labour market there.

Money, Credit, and Capital Markets

As a result of the growth of wage labour,[84] and also of the growing importance of leasing, commodity trade, and monetary taxation, the demand for coins greatly increased in the course of the late Middle Ages. This growing demand was met by a growing supply in the Low Countries beginning in the late twelfth century, both locally produced and imported. Large numbers of coins were available, as exemplified by the production of the *lion groat* as well as the silver esterling, of which some 90 million pieces were struck in the Low Countries in the period 1290–1300 alone.[85] These coins were struck in princely workshops which employed large numbers of wage labourers: in 1300 there were forty in Hasselt, 100 in Namur, and 200 in Leuven and Brussels.[86] Louis de Male, Count of Flanders (1346–84) struck some 15 million gold and some 135 million silver coins, or no fewer than 150 pieces of gold and 1,350 pieces of silver per Flemish household.[87] Some of these coins ended up in England, particularly in payment for wool purchases, or they were hoarded. As silver from the mines dried up in the late fourteenth century and resulted in a bullion famine, some mints in the Low Countries were temporarily closed for lack of bullion,[88] as were mints throughout northwest Europe. Around 1460, as new silver mines were opened, this problem was solved, but until that happened, the scarcity of coins must at times have been an obstacle to the functioning of markets.

Solutions to this problem were found in the form of barter, payment in kind—which was important especially in the lease market and reduced the need for coined money—and delayed payment and forms of credit, the solutions we will turn to now. Credit and financial markets experienced a quick rise in the Low Countries, from the thirteenth century on, as we will see below. As such, they further pushed up the commercialization of the economy. They were vital, for instance, in the emergence of land markets, since much of the land was paid for by credit. Conversely, credit was often obtained by using land as collateral. Land and financial markets were therefore intimately linked. The same applied to the lease market, since the choice between either fixed rents or sharecropping was determined in part by the accessibility of the capital market, with sharecropping being a solution to the difficulty of getting access to working capital by way of the market.[89] Sales of output also often depended on credit, which thus formed a crucial element in the commercialization process and in the rise of the market for goods in the high

---

[84] For a quantitative reconstruction of this growth: section 4.3, 174–5.
[85] Mayhew, 'The circulation', 61; van Bavel, *Manors and markets*, 197–9.
[86] Baerten, *De munten van de graven*, 38 and 59.
[87] Van Werveke, 'Currency manipulation'.
[88] Spufford, *Money and its use*, 339–62, especially 356–62.
[89] As we have observed for Italy, where rural capital markets were very weak: section 3.2, 118.

Middle Ages and the markets for land and leases in the thirteenth and fourteenth centuries.

The emergence of capital markets in the Low Countries had started in the eleventh century. Initially, this was a slow, protracted process. As was true elsewhere in Europe, their rise was impeded by the insecurity inherent in providing credit, the condemnation by the Church of interest on money loans, the contempt for credit operations, and the weak institutional framework of the capital market.[90] These factors led to high transaction costs and high interest rates. In the eleventh century, as a response to this, the *mortgage* as a formalized type of credit appeared in the Low Countries.[91] In this system, the debtor offered as security for the loan some immovable property to be used by the creditor. Formally, the creditor did not receive interest, and thus did not break the usury laws. At the same time, this type of pledging of real estate offered the creditor ample security, since he had a firm hold on the pledge.

Between the late twelfth and early fourteenth centuries more fundamental changes took place, leading to a more open and extensive capital market in the Low Countries, more so than anywhere else in Western Europe. In the first phase, these changes were led by foreigners, particularly Jews and Lombards, operating in the field of credit on a personal basis, not in an anonymous market. Jews, being exempt from Christian usury laws, started to operate in the Low Countries in the early thirteenth century, although not in such large numbers as elsewhere in Western Europe. As Lombards started to take over from the Jews the larger loans to elite debtors in the decades around 1300, Jewish moneylenders increasingly concentrated on local business, lending small sums of money for short terms on pledge or on security of movables, with very high interest rates of around 65 per cent. In 1349, seven out of the nine Jews living in Hainault were active in the money market, with 390 outstanding debts in total, mainly sums of a few pounds, the equivalent of the yearly lease sum of a parcel of land. A large share of the debtors, up to half, were female, and many of them were living in the countryside.[92] The economic hold of Jewish creditors over these people, who probably often were immiserated, in combination with latent anti-Semitism, provoked hatred towards the Jews, which flared up with the pogroms of 1309 and 1348–9. Expulsions and massacres reduced the number of Jews in the Low Countries after the fifteenth century to virtually nil.[93]

In the thirteenth century, Lombards gradually took over the role of Jews in the Low Countries. The first wave of Lombards came mainly from Asti, Chieri, and other Piedmontese towns. They often operated in consortia of shifting compositions, primarily through strong family bonds, and using the capital they had accumulated, especially in the trade in textiles, grain, and wine, in the north of Italy in

---

[90] Munro, 'The usury doctrine', 976–9, although he nuances the real effects of anti-usury doctrines. See also Rubin, 'Institutions', 1313–14.

[91] Vercauteren, 'Note sur l'origine'.

[92] Cluse, *Studien zur Geschichte der Juden*, 18–38, 50–8, and 132–60.

[93] Speet, 'Joden in het hertogdom Gelre'.

this period. This capital they now also used for financial and banking activities.[94] They opened dozens or possibly even hundreds of small banking houses and loan offices in the Low Countries, particularly in the last quarter of the thirteenth century. Around 1300, there were some forty of them in Brabant alone, even in the smallest cities.[95] The Lombards—a term which by now had become shorthand for all Italians active in the money trade, including those from Genoa, Florence, or Siena—were more active in the Low Countries than anywhere else in Europe north of the Alps. This was how the capital that was accumulated in Italy, where the economy now started to stagnate,[96] found its way into the emerging economy of the Low Countries. Lombards operated at all levels of the money trade, from the lowest to the highest. They lent smaller sums of money for short terms, mainly on security of movable goods or on promissory notes, as well as larger sums to merchants, patricians, nobles, and senior clergymen. By pooling money within their consortia, Lombards were also able to lend large sums to territorial princes, up to tens of thousands of pounds.

This is where the emerging financial market clearly met the process of state formation. It was in this period that princes needed large sums for their state-building projects, while fiscal instruments had not yet fully developed or resistance against fiscal levies was too strong. The Lombards provided the princes with the liquid capital they needed to realize their political and military ambitions. Although the Lombards' position was slightly better than that of the Jews, it still was not secure. At best, their activities were tolerated, but if the debtor was too powerful and the debt too large, he might still default or have the creditor arrested on the charge of usury. Moreover, there always remained a constant threat of violence. In Utrecht, in 1267, three Lombard bankers were murdered by a mob in the cathedral.[97] These risks resulted in very high interest rates. The three Utrecht bankers had charged 87 per cent per annum in the first four-year period of their concession, and 65 per cent in the following years.

Insecurity in the capital market was thus significant, leading to high interest rates, which in turn often caused severe social problems. Public authorities tried to counteract this by reducing insecurity and increasingly restricting the short-term loans provided by Lombards to a maximum interest rate, mostly fixed at 43 per cent. At the same time these princely authorities were the main protectors of the Lombards, by offering them concessions to provide financial services, allowing them to use separate judicial procedures, giving physical protection, and sometimes even granting them the right to collect arrears themselves, if necessary through the seizure of goods.[98] Princes were induced to do this because of the revenues from selling concessions and the opportunity to obtain credit from the Lombards for themselves.

---

[94] Spinelli, *I Lombardi in Europa*, 14–20. See for Italy also section 3.1, 109–10.
[95] Reichert, 'Lombarden zwischen Rhein und Maas'; Murray, *Bruges*, 138–48.
[96] Section 3.4, 134–6.   [97] Melles, *Bisschoppen en bankiers*, 31.
[98] Reichert, 'Lombarden zwischen Rhein und Maas', 210–16. For Bruges: Murray, *Bruges*, 140–1.

Lombards did not have a monopoly on credit operations, however. To an increasing extent, local people became involved and between 1249 and 1291 in the industrial centre of Ypres in Flanders, no fewer than 5,500 debt recognitions are recorded by the aldermen.[99] These were mainly promises of payments at a future time, often at one of the Flemish fairs, for goods delivered or services rendered, almost always between inhabitants of the town. The role of local people extended even to high finance, as testified by the many large bankers from Liège, Artois, and Flanders, of whom the financiers from Arras were the most notable examples. From the early thirteenth century, burghers from Arras, and especially the Crespin family, were advancing huge sums to dozens of cities, lords, and kings in the form of loans and life annuities. In 1275 the city of Ghent had debts amounting to 38,500 pounds, of which 37,700 were held by six Arras burghers. In 1304 Bruges owed 140,000 pounds, mainly to the Crespins.[100] This type of voluntary loan by wealthy people to towns other than one's own was pioneered here; towns in Italy had mainly confined themselves to *Monte* loans or forced loans from their own citizens. Although default remained a problem, and financiers such as the Crespins still ran the risk of being accused of usury—as happened in 1296—these loans in the Low Countries were apparently relatively secure for the creditors. This is reflected in the low interest rate of about 10–12 per cent, and up to 20 per cent at most.[101] These relatively low interest rates were in part the result of the safer position of these local creditors, as compared to that of the foreign Lombards and Jews, and the more credit-worthy debtors they chose, but also partly attributable to the institutional improvements in the financial market, taking place in this period.

Ecclesiastical courts now lost influence in the sphere of financial markets, and secular authorities became increasingly reluctant to follow ecclesiastical prohibitions. Moreover, after a last flare-up of anti-usury campaigns by the Church in the early thirteenth century, the attitude of churchmen towards financial transactions became more nuanced, as a result of the emergence of new instruments allowing for the advancing of credit without violating the usury laws.[102] Most prominent among these new instruments were the perpetual annuities and life annuities secured on real estate, mainly land and houses. These annuities were formally sales, not loans, and were not labelled usurious, while the security they brought led to a decline in interest rates, to levels that were considered morally acceptable, in contrast to the earlier loans provided by Lombards, with their huge, usurious rates.

The sale of these life annuities by towns emerged in the first half of the thirteenth century in the border zone between the north of France and the south of the Low Countries, and was possibly even stimulated by the radical anti-usury campaigns of the period, which required creditors and debtors to employ a non-usurious

[99] Nicholas, 'Commercial credit'.
[100] Bigwood, 'Les financiers d'Arras'; Derville, 'La finance Arragoise'. For loans in Italian towns: section 3.1, 109.
[101] Wyffels, 'L'usure en Flandre', esp. 861–3.
[102] Munro, 'The usury doctrine', 975–89; Munro, 'The medieval origins', 518–24.

instrument.[103] Around the middle of the thirteenth century, towns such as Arras, Douai, Saint-Omer, and Ghent were already heavily involved in life annuity sales. The practice spread to Brabant, Holland and other parts of the Low Countries around 1300.[104] One pre-condition for its rise was the formation of the towns into corporate associations in the twelfth to thirteenth century, acquiring legal person-hood and able to own property, enter into contracts, and thus sell annuities.[105] Apparently, there was then enough trust that the town magistrates would honour the towns' obligations, even to foreign creditors. The trust was enhanced by the impartial legal practices of the urban courts in the Low Countries. Thus, the town associations and their legal bodies, and the trust they produced, helped in the rise of the financial market, perhaps the most complex of all factor markets, in view of the chain of future payments and the high degree of security and trust it requires. The increasing expenses incurred by these growing towns in financing walls, infra-structure, a civil service, and military duties must have stimulated the rise of the life annuities too, on the demand side, while the supply was offered by the wealthy Arras burghers, whose willingness to lend their money out was stimulated by the comparative stability of currency there.

Since cities had hardly any land to offer as collateral, urban excises were used to fund the annuities, in Flanders and Artois from the second half of the thirteenth century, and even more significantly from the fourteenth century onwards in the Holland cities. At times, soft coercion was applied by the towns in selling these annuities. Some cities requested, and sometimes even forced, their own burghers to provide credit at low interest rates. This method can mainly be found in the old cities which disposed of the non-economic instruments of power to coerce their burghers. In Bruges, in 1297, such a semi-voluntary loan was used to pay for the construction of fortifications.[106] Most cities, however, lacked these means of coer-cion or preferred to sell their annuities on the open market.

Life annuities were sold in the Low Countries in massive numbers from the early fourteenth century onwards, making credit at relatively low interest available to towns and other sellers, and to convert short-term debts into medium-term obligations. Religious institutions in particular, with ample capital available, were attracted to buy annuities to secure a steady income flow, and they found numer-ous potential sellers in the cities and among private individuals needing to attract capital. The importance of this instrument, and the security it offered, becomes evident from the huge numbers sold. Dordrecht sold hundreds or even thousands in the fifteenth century, in order to finance works on its harbour, town walls, and bridges, and to fulfil its fiscal duties to the central government.[107] In the same period private individuals, too, started to sell life annuities in large numbers in the market. The Low Countries led the way in this field.

---

[103] Tracy, 'On the dual origins'; Munro, 'The usury doctrine', 983–9, also for the connection with the anti-ususry campaigns.

[104] Bangs, 'Holland's civic lijfrente loans'; Houtzager, *Hollands lijf- en losrenteleningen*, 19–27.

[105] Tracy, 'On the dual origins', 13–24. Apparently, these or other conditions were not met in Italy, where this instrument did not develop until much later: section 3.3, 167.

[106] Blockmans, 'Nieuwe gegevens'.   [107] Dokkum and Dijkhof, 'Oude Dordtse lijfrenten'.

The availability of credit, especially at low interest rates, could promote investments in capital goods, in agriculture, and industry. This is not to say that these investments, especially on a smaller scale, would not have been possible without a formal capital market. Resources could be concentrated by way of coercion, as in the manorial system or banal lordship, or be voluntarily or quasi-voluntarily pooled, using soft coercion, as done by village communities or water management organizations in the Low Countries from the eleventh to thirteenth century, in order to allow for costly investments.[108] Also, credit could be arranged in informal ways—between relatives or friends—using kinship ties, or between lord and peasant. Since creditors in these informal systems were well informed about the creditworthiness of the debtors, risks were limited and credit was relatively cheap. On the other hand, there was the drawback that informal loans remained personalized, and thus limited to a relatively small and localized group of people who knew each other and were linked by familial or communal ties.

These types of pooling resources or informal credit remained important, but became less feasible as the scale of economic operations became larger. This required more formal capital markets, with new credit instruments and the institutions offering protection and security to the participants in the market, as happened in the Low Countries. More anonymous, impersonal forms of credit and larger credit operations now became possible, and in their turn these opened up the fortunes amassed during the first phase of market development.

In the course of the late Middle Ages, the functioning of the capital market improved further, resulting in a larger, more open and anonymous market, with very many participants, and no longer dominated by creditors specializing in the money trade, such as the Jews and Lombards. Intervention by the authorities played a large part in the process. In the fourteenth century, urban authorities became aware of the negative aspects in the massive creation of annuities and the overburdening of land and houses with interest obligations, and they started to make perpetual annuities redeemable, including the older annuities which had no redemption clause.[109] This measure improved the position of the rent payers. Moreover, as capital and possible creditors became more widely available, the debtors acquired more freedom in bargaining and became less dependent on the creditors.

In the Low Countries, well-functioning credit markets also emerged in the countryside. The most important instruments for obtaining credit here, too, were perpetual annuities and life annuities, mainly secured on land and houses. These were created in large numbers from c. 1300 onwards, and this made long-term credit at relatively low interest rates available to much of rural society, including farmers and even peasant smallholders, while at the same time offering security to the annuity buyer: security enhanced by public courts under princely surveillance.[110] This credit system became even more attractive to prospective lenders with the continuous decline of interest rates. This decline reflected the improvements in

---

[108] See section 4.1, 147–50. [109] Godding, *Le droit foncier*, 205, 213–16, and 220–31.
[110] Zuijderduijn, *Medieval capital markets*, 183–90; Thoen, *Landbouwekonomie*, 897–940.

the organization of the capital market in the Low Countries. After the windfall gain caused by the Black Death, and the resulting increase in the capital to capita ratio, interest rates kept on declining even as population numbers started to rise again in the fifteenth century, due to the growing security offered by the framework of the capital market. In Flanders, the interest rate for perpetual annuities sold by private parties and secured on land was 10 per cent in 1275–81, but it had declined to 8 per cent by 1429–31.[111] Also, in the meantime, these annuities had become redeemable, and hence more attractive to the annuity payer. The decline in interest rates was even more pronounced in Holland, where they went down from about 12 per cent around 1300 to 6 per cent by around 1500.[112] All this testifies to the quality of the organization of the capital market, and of factor markets more generally, and the security they offered. In turn, this stimulated the growth of the volume and the functioning of these markets, which had emerged in the Low Countries especially in the thirteenth century and became ever larger, more sophisticated, and more dynamic in the following centuries.

4.3. THE FUNCTIONING AND EFFECTS OF DYNAMIC FACTOR MARKETS FROM THE FIFTEENTH TO THE MID-SIXTEENTH CENTURY

The preceding story is a very positive one. Factor markets in the late medieval Low Countries were organized in a relatively favourable way, by multiple types of actors which counterbalanced each other and to a considerable extent prevented these markets from being used for rent seeking or being hijacked by specific interest groups. Even in regions where a few social groups held or acquired a relatively strong position, as the owners of the former manors who now became large landholders in the Guelders river area, or the independent craftsmen and their urban guilds in Flanders, these were not able to arrange the factor markets to fully suit their own interests. As a result, the open and dynamic factor markets in this period had many favourable effects. They enabled flexibility, the rapid re-allocation of labour, land, and capital when circumstances changed, and they promoted an intense process of specialization and division of labour.[113] These effects are observed in the towns and also in the countryside, and they played an important role in the economic growth observed in the Low Countries in this period, first mainly in the south, in Artois and in Flanders, and later, from the second half of the fourteenth century, in Holland. Especially in this latter region, the factor markets were so open and so favourably organized that transaction costs must have been very low, as evidenced by the small differentials in interest rates between town and countryside, and between various types of lenders, and by the low wage differentials between town and countryside.[114] In its turn, this situation stimulated investments

---

[111] Thoen and Soens, 'Appauvrissement et endettement', esp. 710–11. See also section 4.3, 176.
[112] Van Zanden, *The long road*, 22–3; Zuijderduijn, *Medieval capital markets*, 242–6.
[113] See the classical work by de Vries, *The Dutch rural economy*.
[114] Van Bavel et al., 'The organisation of markets', 363–6; and this section, 176.

in expensive capital goods, which increased labour productivity and added 'modern' growth to the positive effects of Smithian growth there.

Accumulation through Land and Lease Markets

In the fifteenth and early sixteenth centuries factor markets were further improved and became even more dynamic, which had positive economic effects, but also caused profound social changes. In the land market, for instance, security further increased as, in several parts of the northern Low Countries in the decades around 1550, the princely authorities made compulsory the judicial conveyance of transacted land in a public court, often on penalty of nullification of the transfer, and ordered the courts to register all enacted deeds.[115] The governments did so not only for the protection of the participants in the land market, but also because of their own fiscal interests. Through the protocols or registers, they were able to check the property returns of all taxable persons. Still, proof and accessibility of registration at a central and public place greatly enhanced transparency and security for potential buyers. In its turn, this security fuelled the dynamism of the land market. In the Guelders river area, on average, 1.5 per cent of the total cultivated area was transferred in the market each year in the period 1515–57. This average was high by Western European standards.[116]

These open and dynamic land markets enabled rich burghers to buy up land in the countryside, although not to the extent found in late medieval Italy. Burgher ownership first started to grow in Flanders and Brabant, the first core of economic growth and urbanization in the Low Countries, as in the surroundings of Ghent in the thirteenth century.[117] In the fifteenth century this growth came to a standstill, however, and burgher ownership never became dominant here. The same applied to the surroundings of Antwerp, the metropolis of the fifteenth and sixteenth centuries, where burgher landownership also was relatively limited. Only in the immediate environs of the town, and in a small area to its north, was burgher landownership substantial, reaching 20–30 per cent of the total area in the second half of the sixteenth century.[118] Owners were mainly merchants, looking for a secure investment. Some of them accumulated 100 hectares or more, in exceptional cases even up to 300 hectares, and these properties often included a country house or villa. City dwellers, however, never came to dominate rural landownership structures here.

Holland shows a somewhat different picture. At the beginning of the sixteenth century, the province was still dominated by peasant landownership. Holdings were small and mostly worked by the peasant owners themselves, a situation dating back to the eleventh to thirteenth century, as Holland was occupied and reclaimed

---

[115] Ketelaar, 'Van pertinent register', esp. 39–42.
[116] Van Bavel and Hoppenbrouwers, 'Landholding and land transfer', 28–31.
[117] Thoen, *Landbouwekonomie*, 512–27.
[118] Limberger, *Sixteenth-century Antwerp*, 189–213.

by free peasant colonists, who had received the land with full property rights.[119] Circa 1500, the landed property of burghers was as fragmented and small-scale as that of peasants. This began to change only during the mid-sixteenth century, as the acquisition and accumulation of land by wealthy town dwellers took place on a larger scale, certainly in the central, most urbanized part of Holland.[120] Around 1560, more than 40 per cent of the land there was in urban hands. That in all of the Low Countries the level of encroachment of town dwellers in the market for rural land was most profound in Holland, where the social and political landscape most clearly showed a balance between different interest groups, is striking. It suggests that polarization was endogenous to markets and not the sole effect of distorted markets or unequal starting positions in new markets.

At the same time, this balanced context in Holland meant that burghers from one town found it impossible to dominate the surrounding countryside. The urban landownership here was spread between burghers and institutions from a multitude of towns, with overlapping spheres of influence, and with no single city dominating landownership structures, in contrast to the Italian situation. Likewise, in contrast to Italy, the impact of the growth of burgher landownership on the distribution of the fiscal burden over town and countryside was limited. In Holland, these fiscal effects were completely absent, as burgher landownership was not exempt from central taxes and burgher landowners were not favoured over their rural counterparts. From the late fourteenth century onwards, the count of Holland had enforced the levying of taxes on burgher-owned land, despite opposition from the cities.[121] Moreover, at the same time, the counts of Holland had become less and less dependent on taxation of landownership for their revenues, and correspondingly more dependent on taxation of the towns and burghers.[122] These provided an increasingly large part of taxes and loans.

The land market, therefore, in this period did not yet bring about any fundamental socio-economic changes. The lease markets, however, did produce such changes, from an early date. This was particularly the case in regions of extended and competitive lease markets, such as the Guelders river area and coastal Flanders, where land for prospective users was only accessible through competition in that market. To be able to offer the highest lease sum in competing for lease land, tenant farmers there had to specialize in producing for the market and engage in a market-driven, competitive process. In the longer run, this led to social differentiation and went with the concentration of lease land in the hands of the successful farmers, a process which can be clearly observed in both of these regions and even accelerated in the Guelders river area in the sixteenth century, when this

---

[119] Van der Linden, *De cope*, 93–5 and 160–82; van der Linden, 'Het platteland', 69–78. See also Curtis and Campopiano, 'Medieval land reclamation', 98–9.

[120] Van Bavel, 'Rural development', 167–96. See also de Vries, *The Dutch rural economy*, 45–6. For the later growth of burgher ownership: section 4.4, 193–4.

[121] Bos-Rops, *Graven op zoek naar geld*, 76, 96, and 225–6. See also Hoppenbrouwers, 'Town and country', esp. 73.

[122] Bos-Rops, *Graven op zoek naar geld*, 225–6, 240, and 253–4; Blockmans, 'The Low Countries in the Middle Ages'.

was the region most clearly dominated by open, competitive factor markets.[123] Again, this shows that factor markets, exactly in their purest form, acted as drivers of inequality.

In the course of the sixteenth century, this situation of competitive leases for limited terms also began to prevail in Holland, one of the parts of the Low Countries where country dwellers up to then had retained more enduring, or even perpetual rights to the land.[124] This change was associated with the disappearance of the original peasant character of the Holland countryside due to the growing influence of land, lease, labour, capital, and output markets, and the associated commodification of land and labour, and the acquisition of peasant land by urban investors. These processes were sped up by the erosion and subsidence of the peat soils, which made grain farming for subsistence impossible and pushed peasants to the market ever more vigorously.[125] At the same time, the authorities, under the influence of the rising urban investors or sometimes themselves being among these investors, started to prohibit the traditional, informal claims of peasants to re-letting or inheritance of leases and acted more severely against such informal claims, as emerges from the verdicts of courts and councils.

Sub rosa, personal arrangements, such as those between landlords and sitting tenants or their sons who wanted to extend or renew the lease, were increasingly replaced by selling or leasing through public bids. In the coastal areas of the Netherlands, for example in Holland, leasing by public auction of tithes, mills, tolls, and all sorts of excises began to take place as early as the fourteenth century, and for leasing out land this method became more common at the end of the sixteenth century. In a number of provinces, around 1580, it was decreed that all public leasing should be announced in church well in advance, that the bidding should take place in the presence of government officials, and that no pact or arrangement should be made in advance.[126] This increased competition for land assured landowners of the best possible lease price, and it also increased the mobility of land.

The open, competitive organization of lease markets allowed for the easy transfer and accumulation of lease land by successful tenant farmers. Especially under the economic circumstances of the late fifteenth and sixteenth centuries, with their rising food prices and relatively declining wages, large tenant farmers benefited. They were able to market sizeable surpluses, make capital investments, and reduce labour costs, and they used their growing profits to retain the upper hand in the lease market and further expand the amount of land they leased. This process was mainly observed in regions such as coastal Flanders and the Guelders river area and the Frisian sea clay area. These had ample land available for lease, since they were traditionally dominated by large landownership and, in the fourteenth century, saw these large landowners almost completely switch to leasing as a means of exploiting their landownership. Already around 1400, as we have observed above,

---

[123] See below, 174.   [124] Van Bavel, 'The emergence and growth'.

[125] For the process of subsidence: van Bavel, *Manors and Markets*, 44–5; van Zanden, *The rise and decline*, 30–1.

[126] Kuys and Schoenmakers, *Landpachten*, 26 and 34.

most of their land was leased out for short terms. Via a highly flexible lease market, this land could be freely accumulated by the financially powerful farmer entrepreneurs, who gradually pushed aside small and medium-scale tenants.[127] The result, especially combined with the population growth of the fifteenth and sixteenth centuries, was the emergence of a large group of proletarianized and semi-proletarianized country dwellers. Around the middle of the sixteenth century, more than half of the population in these regions had no or little land at its disposal. Some of them left for the cities, in search of work there, but many became employed in the countryside as wage labourers by the large tenant farmers.

The Further Growth of Labour and Capital Markets

Many of the proletarianized country dwellers were thus pushed on to the labour market. This market was able to absorb many labourers, also thanks to its favourable, open organization that we have observed above. In combination, these push and pull factors resulted in a massive growth of the importance of wage labour in the Low Countries. For the middle of the sixteenth century this importance can be quantified fairly accurately. In central Holland, almost half of all rural labour was performed as wage labour, and in the Guelders river area, far more than half, whereas in inland Flanders this share was a quarter.[128] The highest percentages were thus not necessarily found in highly urbanized areas (such as inland Flanders), but instead in those areas where obstacles to freely hiring out labour were weakest and the transition of the rural economy to agrarian capitalism had proceeded furthest, as in the Guelders river area. Of the wage labour performed in the latter region, perhaps a quarter was performed by live-in servants, another quarter by people working for wages in order to supplement other means of subsistence, and more than half by fully proletarianized wage labourers. Not all of them were living there, since migrant labour was fairly substantial. Sometimes the migrant workers came from other villages in the region to work in harvesting and also in diking, but there were also groups of labourers from regions further away, up to 150 km.

In Holland, wage labour was also very important, but mostly it was not offered by fully proletarianized country dwellers but by small-scale peasants, who still dominated the countryside at the start of the sixteenth century. They often combined work on their own mini-holdings with wage labour outside the holding, mostly in a seasonal labour cycle.[129] This created a large reservoir of part-time wage labourers in the countryside, allowing huge infrastructural works in town and countryside to be carried out by wage labour. In some cases the employment of wage labourers assumed enormous proportions. For instance, during the repair of the Spaarndam dike in the years 1510 and 1515, many hundreds of labourers were working at any one time.[130] The workers, paid on an individual basis, were recruited by contractors all over Holland, and particularly in villages dominated by

---

[127] Van Bavel, 'Land, lease and agriculture'.
[128] Van Bavel, 'Rural wage labour', also for the following.
[129] Lucassen, *Naar de kusten*, 160–71.
[130] Van Dam, 'Digging for a dike'; de Vries, 'The labour market', esp. 59–60.

smallholdings, with the peasants combining the exploitation of their own mini-farms with wage labour in peat digging, fishing, or infrastructural works. In 1510 and 1515, over 10 per cent of the male labour force of some villages was working at Spaarndam at the same time.

The share of wage labour in the countryside (about 50 per cent of total labour input) was probably even greater than that found in the towns. Part of the cause seems to be found in the policies of the urban guilds and town governments. Among the main goals of the guilds and guild-influenced governments, as found in many cities in Flanders and Brabant, were full employment, guaranteeing a decent living for small masters or guild members, and securing economic independence for the producers. The guilds tried to shape and restrict the labour market. They aimed to determine the number of workdays, how many journeymen could be employed, and the conditions of hiring journeymen, and these restrictions were often embedded in the urban by-laws. Also, they tried to limit accumulation of the means of production—by setting maxima on the possession of capital goods, for instance—and to slow down increases in the scale of production.[131] Their measures protected small-scale commodity production undertaken by independent masters, who possessed their own workshops and tools and were assisted by a small number of labourers, often partly from the masters' own household.[132] Even though they did not obstruct the increase in market orientation and large shares of the production indeed were aimed at the export market, their influence slowed down the growth of wage labour in many towns.

In the Holland towns, the situation was different. Guilds were formed later there, and they had little direct political power.[133] Urban wage labourers, such as weavers and fullers, thus tried to use other weapons, such as strikes and walk-outs, to put pressure on the town governments to meet their demands. The fullers in particular, the most proletarianized among the urban workers, used this instrument. In the textile centre of Leiden, in the period 1370–1480, they went on strike no fewer than seven times and attempted to do so five more times.[134] Their actions were well organized, mainly through informal contacts and religious brotherhoods, and they had a clear set of economic demands, including higher wages, prohibition of the truck system, and better working conditions. Although the strikes were occasionally successful, they were mostly repressed by the magistrates, often in collaboration with the count of Holland and the central authorities, and the leaders were severely punished, either by execution or by lengthy banishment. Wages here remained subjected to supply and demand, without much opportunity for the labourers to engage in collective bargaining, and labour markets were open, flexible, and highly competitive, and they grew quickly.

[131] De Munck, 'One counter'. Reality could be more fluid: Stabel, 'Guilds in late medieval Flanders'.

[132] DuPlessis and Howell, 'Reconsidering the early modern economy', 50–1 and 83–4. For the use of subcontracting to evade these restrictions: De Munck, 'One counter', 27–8.

[133] For the chronology: De Munck, Lourens, and Lucassen, 'The establishment and distribution'. See also section 4.4, 196.

[134] Boone and Brand, 'Vollersoproeren'.

In the meantime, the organization of the capital market had also been further developed and its volume increased. The option of redemption of annuities by the rent payer, for instance, was now included in all contracts and even made compulsory by central legislation, as in Flanders in 1529. This strengthened the position and the security for the rent payers. Still, capital became cheaper for them and interest rates declined further. In Flanders, interest rates decreased from 8 per cent in the fifteenth century to 6.3 per cent by 1569–71.[135] Their decline was even more pronounced in Holland, to about 6 per cent around 1500, and credit was easier to obtain here, even for peasants with smallholdings. A fiscal register from Waterland, a not particularly progressive area north of Amsterdam, shows that in the late fifteenth century a quarter of all peasants were active in the capital market, rising to about half in the first decades of the sixteenth century, and almost all village communities were also involved in this market, in their capacity as public bodies.[136] Peasants, farmers, craftsmen, and traders there used credit in order to finance all kinds of transactions, including buying houses and land and shares in ships, wharfs, mills, and fishing nets.

The division of property into shares, up to 1/256 share of a ship, was a common practice in this region. Combined with the open and dynamic capital market this instrument created flexibility, pushed up investments, and stimulated markets in land, houses, and capital goods.[137] The capital market worked as a lubricant, and was even used between relatives, to smooth transactions in real estate and capital goods. Virtually all individuals were able to obtain credit at low costs within an institutional framework offering maximum security to both creditor and debtor. Interest rates in the Holland countryside fluctuated between only 5.3 and 5.8 per cent on average, compared with 5.6 and 5.7 per cent in the nearby town of Edam. Differentials between government annuities and private annuities were almost equally small, that is, 5 per cent versus 5.6 per cent, and private households, including peasants, could obtain credit at interest rates almost as low as the state could.[138] The near absence of rent differentials shows how the capital market was better integrated in Holland than elsewhere, and offered security to both private and public parties, reflecting the favourable institutional framework of the capital market here.

In some parts of the Low Countries, it even became possible to sell annuities without land as collateral, funded only by movables. This innovation was particularly important for tenant farmers, who had no land to offer as collateral and would otherwise have been dependent on their landlord for credit in order to obtain working capital, a situation that could create personal dependency.[139] The security of the capital market and the guarantees offered by the public authorities

[135] Thoen and Soens, 'Appauvrissement et endettement', esp. 710–11. For the theological debate about redemption: Munro, 'The usury doctrine', 987–99.

[136] Zuijderduijn, 'Assessing the rural economy'; Zuijderduijn, *Medieval capital markets*, 242–6.

[137] De Moor, van Zanden, and Zuijderduijn, 'Micro-credit'. See for shares also: Gelderblom, 'The Golden Age', 164–5.

[138] De Moor, van Zanden, and Zuijderduijn, 'Micro-credit', 658–9.

[139] Van Bavel, 'The organization and rise', 38–9. For this situation in Italy, see section 3.2, 118–19.

at the local and central levels enabled annuities funded by movables to develop not only in highly urbanized regions, but also in some rural areas in the Low Countries. In turn, a secure and accessible capital market was crucial in balancing power relations between the various parties involved in the lease, most notably the landlords and the tenants, contributing to the rise of open, flexible, and competitive lease markets.

Output markets were also large in the Low Countries, a situation which was made possible by the thriving factor markets—that helped in successful specialization, for instance. Also, factor markets, and most particularly the lease market, to some extent forced producers to orient their production more towards the market, since this was the most direct way to increase profits and keep on winning the competition for land in the market. Factor and output markets thus stimulated each other. In the sixteenth century, by far the greatest part of the agricultural and industrial production was brought to market, and no longer was consumed within the household or exchanged by systems other than the market. Of the services and the end products of agriculture and industry in Holland, as early as the mid-fourteenth century an estimated 60–66 per cent was destined for the market, a figure increasing to 87–94 per cent around 1500.[140] In Flanders, the growth of market orientation had started earlier, with a share of 63–74 per cent reached as early as the mid-fourteenth century, but in guild- and peasant-dominated inland Flanders this growth stopped afterwards, while in coastal Flanders it proceeded to 82–89 per cent around 1500.

The Social Effects of Extensive and Dynamic Factor Markets

Many parts of the Low Countries reaped the benefits generated by these favourable, dynamic markets, as these offered their economies the ability to swiftly adapt to changing patterns in supply and demand, and to take advantage of new trade opportunities, by combining land, labour, and capital in new ways that had been less feasible in cases in which these production factors were accessible only through non-market mechanisms.[141] As a result, these regions witnessed clear economic growth spurts, as most conspicuously Artois and later Flanders in the thirteenth and fourteenth centuries, and even more clearly Holland, where this spurt started in the mid-fourteenth century and lasted with some hiccups, until the seventeenth century, as shown by reconstructions of GDP per capita, urbanization rates, and other indicators of growth.

In Holland, strong interactions among the various factor markets can be observed. In particular the emergence of a well-functioning capital market enabled and reinforced the rise of land and labour markets. The resulting feedback cycle in Holland had a positive character, speeding up the growth of markets and stimulating that of the real economy, especially within the tertiary sector,[142] being an example

---

[140] Dijkman, *Shaping medieval markets*, 313–32.
[141] Van Bavel and van Zanden, 'The jump-start'. See also van Bavel, *Manors and markets*, 378–406, for these and other growth spurts.
[142] Van Bavel et al., 'The organisation of markets', 362–9.

of the positive effects the rise of factor markets had on economic growth. The service sector, which grew to employ no less than 22 per cent of all labour and to produce 30 per cent of GDP in Holland at the beginning of the sixteenth century,[143] benefited most clearly from the favourable capital and labour markets, and in return stimulated their further development.

Still, even in this favourable context and with these beneficial economic effects, the markets in the Low Countries, and the competition they brought, in the long run had profound, and often quite negative, social effects. The most notable was social polarization, with a growing inequality in the social distribution of land and leaseholding, and in the distribution of wealth. These changes can first be observed in thirteenth-century coastal Flanders, where factor markets developed rapidly and relatively early, especially in the countryside. There was the introduction and spread of short-term leasing—mainly of separate parcels of land—which pushed up the mobility of land in the market. Also in the second half of the thirteenth century there was a rise in wage labour, the extension of urban landownership, and the beginning of the expropriation of peasants, who suffered under mounting debts contracted in the emerging rural capital market, also in order to pay for the high water management costs, and sold their land, sometimes compelled by economic necessity, to urban investors.[144] New forms of inequality made their entrance in rural society. In the thirteenth to fifteenth century, the developing factor markets took over the role of the associations in the allocation of land and capital in the countryside, while the social polarization the markets brought at the same time eroded the foundations of these rural associations, much more so than in the Flemish towns, where the guilds were successful in tempering this process.

In the countryside of coastal Flanders, these changes were furthered by the major revolt of 1323–8. This was primarily directed against the noble and patrician elites, but can also be seen as the last trumpet call of the rural associations there.[145] These associations, such as the village communities and their regional assemblies, formed the backbone of the revolt. In contrast to the earlier, thirteenth-century revolts in the Low Countries, and despite its initial success, however, this revolt in the long run was not successful. Nobles and princes from all over Western Europe set aside all their internal conflicts to jointly combat this threat. An army of 3,000 to 4,000 mounted noblemen and 12,000 soldiers and foreign mercenaries, led by the king of France, defeated the rebels in 1328 and killed more than 3,000 of the insurgents.[146] The repression was harsh, with the horrific execution of the leaders of the revolt—burning some of them with hot iron and breaking their arms and legs before killing them—the execution of thousands of insurgents—sometimes without trial—and the confiscation of their goods. Also, there was the imposition of enormous indemnity payments, the withdrawal of the privileges of towns and rural districts, and the reduction of their rights to self-organization.

[143] Van Zanden, 'Taking the measure of the early modern economy'.
[144] Soens and Thoen, 'The origins of leasehold'; Thoen and Soens, 'Appauvrissement et endettement'.
[145] Van Bavel, 'Rural revolts', 254–5, 257, and 264.
[146] TeBrake, *A plague of insurrection*, 119–22.

The direct, negative consequences for the rural insurgents were accompanied by more structural developments, as a result of the further dynamics brought by the factor markets, including the growth of large landownership at the expense of peasant landholding, and the rise of large tenant farms on burgher-owned land, a process that had already started before the revolt. The social changes also had fundamental consequences for the organization of water management, a primordial aspect of this coastal society. Here, too, the high degree of self-organization and grip of the ordinary population on the organization of water management became eroded, as these boards in coastal Flanders increasingly operated independently of the village community and became dominated by landowners, or even purely by wealthy landowners, who to some extent turned them into an instrument to defend their own interests.[147] Since the large landowners were now increasingly from outside the area, and were living in the cities, for instance, and were mostly interested in short-term gains, this resulted in falling investments in water management and a growing vulnerability of fragile coastal lands to storm floods. In a negative feedback cycle, occurring in the fifteenth and sixteenth centuries, this further eroded the viability of peasant landholding and caused peasants to leave their land.[148]

Simultaneously with, and enabled by, the dynamism of the factor markets, profound social changes occurred, most conspicuously in the countryside. In Holland, wealth traditionally had been quite evenly distributed over town and countryside, but this now started to change. In the Holland town of Edam and the surrounding rural district of the Zeevang, for instance, investigated for the period 1460–1560, urban and rural households were still assessed as having a similar level of wealth.[149] Most peasants owned some land, almost all owned their homes, and almost four-fifths of rural households owned cattle. Liquid assets were less equally distributed between the town of Edam and its hinterland, but still about a quarter of peasants did have substantial savings. This situation changed in the late sixteenth century, however, as the peasants' liquid assets diminished, their ownership of cattle decreased, and many lost the ownership of their land, with the dominance in wealth shifting increasingly to the towns.

This was part of a more general trend in Holland. Whereas this region had maintained its traditionally equal social distribution of resources up to the start of the sixteenth century, wealth now became concentrated in the towns, and within the towns especially in the hands of a small group of merchants and merchant entrepreneurs. From the early sixteenth century, the wealth and purchasing power of urban elites grew due to favourable developments of trade and industry, the profitability of trade ventures, and the handsome, safe returns on investments in land and in financial markets.[150] Also, there was the increasing concentration of proto-industries in the hands of urban merchant entrepreneurs. The peasants

---

[147] Soens, 'Polders zonder poldermodel?'.
[148] Soens, 'Floods and money', 342–5; Soens, 'Polders zonder poldermodel?'.
[149] Zuijderduijn, 'Assessing the rural economy'.
[150] Van Bavel, *Manors and markets*, 256–62. This process was further sped up from the late sixteenth century: see section 4.4, 192–5.

involved in rural industries and other non-agricultural activities in the countryside gradually lost their hold over land, raw materials, and equipment. The non-agricultural activities which emerged in the Holland countryside—such as brick making, peat digging, fishing, and shipping—often had a strong capital-intensive element, and this was the case to an increasing extent. This went hand in hand with the growing dominance of urban investors in these sectors.[151] They bought up and accumulated the means of production, including peateries, shipyards, and brick ovens. This process directly affected the position of the labour force. In the four-teenth century, these activities were still mainly performed independently and on their own account by peasant families who also worked their own smallholdings, but in the course of the fifteenth and sixteenth centuries they were increasingly carried out by semi-proletarianized wage labourers, who were employed by large-scale, often urban-based entrepreneurs. The latter made ample use of financial markets, labour markets, and output markets.

In inland Flanders, the peasant sector was more resilient and rural industries there largely kept their peasant character, most notably in the linen sector. In the rural tapestry sector, however, with its more expensive capital goods, developments mirrored those in Holland. This sector became completely divided in the sixteenth century between entrepreneurs who owned the relatively expensive tools and the costly dyed yarn on the one hand and the proletarianized tapestry weavers on the other. Tapestry weavers from the villages generally had to come to their employers in the town of Audenarde each Sunday to deliver the products, to collect their wages, and to pick up fresh supplies of wool and yarn. Many weavers worked for piece wages, and, additionally, the tapestry workers themselves often employed some hands. Although the number of journeymen was limited formally to three per entrepreneur, the number of other employees was unrestricted and various forms of subcontracting were used.[152] The Flemish tapestry sector thus saw the emergence of hierarchical concentrations, dominated by a few urban entrepre-neurs, who also possessed the contacts with the most important market, the metropolis of Antwerp.

A similar process of proletarianization was found in several urban industries and services. Again, this was mainly in those sectors which were capital-intensive and now witnessed an increase in scale, often combined with strong rises in labour productivity. This was most apparent in the brewing industry. Total output of breweries in the three major beer producing towns in Holland rose from 30 million litres in 1400 to 100 million litres around 1570. Three-quarters of this was produced by only 100 breweries in the city of Delft alone. Indicative of the increase in scale and rise in labour productivity in this sector was also the fact that in 1514 Holland had 377 breweries in the towns, employing some ten workers each, whereas at the end of the sixteenth century there were only 183 breweries with an

[151] Van Bavel, 'Early proto-industrialization'; van Zanden, 'A third road to capitalism'.
[152] Van Bavel, 'Early proto-industrialization', 1148–50; Stabel, *De kleine stad in Vlaanderen*, 191–4.

average of sixteen workers each, producing a larger total volume of output.[153] These rises in labour productivity were the result of a continuous stream of numerous small investments in fixed capital. Economic growth here was thus not only Smithian growth, thanks to specialization and division of labour, but also real, or 'modern' economic growth, thanks to investments in labour-saving technology.[154] In the course of this process, small-scale and rural brewing was wiped out, and the importance of wage labour greatly rose.

Developments such as these were also found in Antwerp, where the entrepreneur Gilbert van Schoonbeke was their most notable protagonist.[155] Starting as a land speculator and real estate developer, around 1550 he acquired a dominant position in the building industry and public works there, after he was commissioned by the town government to build a new part of the city and the new city walls. He developed a large, vertically integrated building enterprise, including brick ovens, lime kilns, and peateries, employing many thousands of wage labourers. Through his vertical organization of production he could undercut all competition, particularly that of small independent masters, driving them out of the market. As soon as he achieved an actual monopoly in Antwerp, backed by the town government which had become increasingly dependent on him, he started to push wages down. Admittedly, van Schoonbeke was exceptional, even in the booming metropolis of Antwerp. Also, he was successful in such sectors as the building industry, in which guild power was weak, but not in sectors with strong guild organization.[156] Still, his rise is illustrative of broader developments found not only here but everywhere in the sixteenth-century Low Countries, both in town and countryside.

Simultaneous with these developments there was a growing inequality in wealth distribution. The rise of wealth inequality was found especially where factor markets were most extensive and open. In the industrial centre of Leiden, for instance, in 1498 the poorest 60 per cent of the population owned only 3 per cent of total wealth.[157] In the period 1500–1650 total capital wealth in Holland, where market development at that point was most conspicuous, further increased from 10–12 million guilders to 500–50 million guilders, i.e. more than tripling per capita wealth in real terms.[158] This wealth was mainly concentrated in the cities, in the hands of a small urban elite.

Much of this wealth was invested in the financial market, whose organization became even more advanced in the fifteenth and sixteenth centuries. The authorities increased security in the financial market by having sales of annuities registered by public courts, a practice that was well established in Holland and other

[153] Unger, *A history of brewing*, 104–13 and 163–80; van Bavel, 'Early proto-industrialization', 1136–7.

[154] Unger, *A history of brewing*. More generally: Gelderblom, 'The Golden Age', 159–62; Davids, *The rise and decline*, 116 ff.

[155] Soly, *Urbanisme en kapitalisme*, 275–80, 301, and 419–24; Lis and Soly, *Poverty*, 70–1.

[156] Soly, *Urbanisme en kapitalisme*, 411–47.

[157] Posthumus, *De geschiedenis van de Leidsche lakenindustrie* I, 386–99.

[158] Van Zanden, 'Economic growth in the Golden Age', esp. 13–16 and 21–3. More extensively on wealth distribution: section 4.4, 193–5.

regions as early as the fifteenth century, and was made compulsory in 1529 by emperor Charles V.[159] As noted with transactions in the land market, this legislation was partly inspired by the fiscal needs of governments, as they started to tax annuities, but at the same time it also had advantages for participants in the market. The public registration of land and annuity sales, and the monopoly local authorities held on ratification, offered the strong advantage of enabling possible creditors to see how many annuities were already funded on a plot of land or other collateral, since it was clear what the jurisdiction was for every transaction. This reduced information costs and increased security, further facilitating the development of a more anonymous market in which personal trust was less vital.

A further innovation was made in the fifteenth century, as letters obligatory or IOUs became popular in the Low Countries, and these were increasingly made payable to bearer and thus transferable.[160] Debt assignment was initially not fully secured by legal enforcement, thus limiting the circulation of such IOUs to narrow circles of acquaintances. Decisive steps in offering full security were made in Antwerp in 1507, in Bruges in 1527, and by central decree for the Low Countries as a whole in 1537/41. The bearer now received all the rights of the principal, fully secured by legislation, thus greatly increasing the security for the person who took over the letter. From that point such titles could pass through dozens of hands before payment in cash took place. These IOUs were increasingly used to raise money for commercial or industrial enterprises, for medium terms, with not only land but also ships, merchandise, and even jewellery used as security.

A major centre of financial transactions, remittance of bills obligatory, insurance, and other financial operations was the new Antwerp Bourse, opened in 1531. The Antwerp money market at that point held supremacy in northwest Europe.[161] Many merchants in Antwerp started to devote themselves exclusively to the money trade. As a result of the introduction of new financial instruments, but also of that of maritime insurance, lotteries, and new opportunities in exchange arbitrage, a speculative atmosphere developed, which was punctuated by crises.[162] The Antwerp market also offered opportunities for monopolization. Guicciardini, when visiting Antwerp in 1560, observed how large merchants, by amassing money and loans, were able to manipulate the financial markets and enrich themselves at the expense of others.

The authorities also used the markets to find new ways to finance their debts, which were needed to cover their rapidly rising expenses, especially for warfare and state formation. Forcing citizens to lend money to them was traditionally one of these ways, although used to a much lesser extent in the Low Countries than in Italy, for instance. In the late fifteenth century, there was a wave of involuntary loans to the Flemish cities, often converted into perpetual annuities, as well as in

[159] Zuijderduijn, *Medieval capital markets*, 50–2 and 138–66, also for the following.
[160] Van der Wee, *The growth of the Antwerp market*, 337–49; Munro, 'The medieval origins', 545–56; Gelderblom and Jonker, 'Completing a financial revolution'.
[161] Van der Wee, 'Antwerp and the new financial methods'; van der Wee, *The growth of the Antwerp market*, 199–207.
[162] Van der Wee, *The growth of the Antwerp market*, 126, 202–3, 363–6, and 409–12.

Utrecht, where in 1481, 1492, and 1495 hundreds of burghers were persuaded to make loans to the city.[163] The largest lenders, mainly patricians, could derive political benefit from the situation, because their position as creditors offered them opportunities to exercise influence on the town government and the use of public resources, and possibly also to take preference over others as excises were leased out or public works were put out to contract. This has been detailed for Bruges in the late fifteenth century, where a small group of urban creditors used their leading participation in the urban debt in order to strengthen their political power.[164]

Most cities in the Low Countries did not use this route of forcing, persuading, and profiteering, however, and instead preferred to sell life and perpetual annuities in the open market in order to raise cash. In the long run this strategy potentially offered much better opportunities for obtaining credit. Despite huge debts, and interest payments which often absorbed 30–50 per cent of the urban revenues, as in 's-Hertogenbosch, Antwerp, and Dordrecht c. 1500, towns still succeeded in selling new annuities.[165] Also, they were able to attract credit at relatively low costs, at interest rates of 5 per cent (as in Bruges in the late fifteenth century) or 5–6.7 per cent (in 's-Hertogenbosch), in an open annuity market. Here, too, the urban elites benefited. These rates offered a handsome and secure source of revenue for them, while the payments were mainly financed out of the collection or leasing out of the urban excises, which pressed most on ordinary consumption goods, including beer, wine, flour, bread, and meat. This system of public finance, therefore, although more open than the system in vogue in Italy,[166] had similar regressive effects. Since those who bought the annuities mostly came from the wealthier strata of society, and those who paid the excises from the middling or poorer strata, the whole system can be considered an instrument of income transfer from the ordinary urban population to the rich.[167]

Annuities were also developed for use at a higher political level: that of the province, most notably in Holland. This was exceptional, from a European perspective.[168] A major cause for its emergence in the Low Countries was that central authorities there were not able to force their subjects to advance credit as their power was limited and various interest groups would have opposed this, so they instead entered the open market and tried to offer security to creditors to attract capital. The provincial estates of Holland were especially successful in this respect. As early as the fourteenth century the count of Holland had used the cities as intermediaries to sell annuities in the capital market, and in the course of the fifteenth and sixteenth centuries the estates of Holland developed the instruments to directly fund debts, not on immovable properties, as was usual, but on future tax revenues at the provincial level. This required a high level of trust. From 1515, this innovation was tried in the Habsburg Low Countries as a whole, as Charles V persuaded

---

[163] Berents, 'Gegoede burgerij in Utrecht'.
[164] Derycke, 'The public annuity market', 176–7.
[165] Hanus, *Tussen stad en eigen gewin*, 35–9, also for the following on interest rates.
[166] Section 3.3, 127–8.   [167] Munro, 'The usury doctrine', 994–1000.
[168] Zuijderduijn, *Medieval capital markets*, 100–9, extending the pioneering work by Tracy, *A financial revolution*.

the estates of four provinces to make a first issue of heritable annuities funded by provincial revenues.[169] These annuities were sold at a low interest rate, usually 6.25 per cent, reflecting the trust placed in this organization, although in war time rates could go up to 8.33 per cent.[170] In the following decades, millions of guilders were raised this way by the Habsburg government. At the same time, this made the central authorities more dependent on the financial power and the willingness of urban elites to offer them credit, and it strengthened the political leverage of these elites, although not to the same extent as with the Italian instruments of financing public debt.

A major part, or even the lion's share of the money they raised in the financial market was used by the public authorities to finance the build-up of a state apparatus, developing military means and war making. These costs rapidly increased, especially as the state formation process went into a higher gear under the Burgundians and later the Habsburgs, who strove to build a central state apparatus in the Low Countries, with a growing bureaucracy, integrating parts of the older and new elites, as governors, councillors, jurists, and other civil servants.[171] Besides noblemen, and increasingly so, it was professionals who as *homines novi* moved upward and enriched themselves in the service of the state. In fifteenth-century Flanders, no fewer than half of the higher offices came to be held by burghers, a few originating from the craftsmen elite, but by far the majority from the patriciate,[172] who often combined merchant and entrepreneurial activities with operations in the capital markets and/or landholding, and who greatly benefited from the opportunities the factor markets offered. In this sense, too, the state apparatus and the urban elites came to overlap more.

The growing state apparatus employed its means of coercion, including the professional soldiers who were hired in an international market, against competing sovereigns and foreign enemies, but likewise against internal opposition groups and revolts. This internal opposition was sometimes the result of a distributional struggle for non-economic control of resources, as when privileged groups tried to avert the loss of privileges and rent-seeking opportunities, or new groups tried to acquire them. But this opposition was also often provoked by the radical social and economic changes of the period, and by the social polarization resulting from the working of the dynamic, competitive markets, and it was sometimes directly aimed against these changes. The main platforms for this opposition were the associations of ordinary people formed in the high Middle Ages, most notably the guilds. These guilds, and the guild-dominated urban governments, irked the central authorities also because they formed an obstacle in the state-formation process, as the princes had difficulties in imposing their hold on the semi-autonomous and self-willed cities, as found mainly in the southern Low Countries.[173] This led to a series of clashes between the central authorities—who relied on financial markets for their

---

[169] Tracy, *A financial revolution*, 45–6 and 57.
[170] Tracy, *A financial revolution*, 45–6, 57–60, 89, 92–3, and 132.
[171] Blockmans, *Metropolen aan de Noordzee*, 472–80.
[172] Dumolyn, 'Dominante klassen en elites', esp. 87–93.
[173] Boone and Prak, 'Rulers, patricians and burghers', 104–8.

financial means and on labour markets for hiring soldiers—and the local opposition—which relied on its associations.

These clashes became more violent in the second half of the fifteenth century and the sixteenth, as in many towns the guilds and their participation in urban government were targeted by the central government. Sometimes this was done by using brute force. In Dinant (1465) and Liège (1466–8), two towns with strong guild power, the uprisings against the increasing Burgundian influence and its centralizing tendencies were brutally crushed by Duke Charles the Bold. He killed about a quarter of the (mostly unarmed) population of Liège, drowned hundreds in the Meuse river, and set fire to the city, which burned for seven weeks.[174] Here and elsewhere, the Burgundians and later the Habsburg emperor Charles V put an end to the participation of guilds in urban governments, which had been established in many cities around 1300. In Utrecht, too, where the guilds held powerful military and political roles for a long time, their hold was broken by Charles V in 1528, partly in reaction to their insurrection in 1525, when they had revived all their traditional guild claims, chosen a new town magistrate, and demanded a more equal distribution of taxes and excises.[175] In all these instances, Habsburg rule clearly chose the side of the urban elites, who were heavily involved in factor markets, and acted against the associations of independent craftsmen. The political role of the latter, therefore, was crushed between central state formation, rising urban elites, and the opportunities the factor markets offered to states and elites to raise capital and hire soldiers.

Another example was Antwerp, where Charles V stepped in to repress a rising against the economic dominance and monopolies of the entrepreneur Gilbert van Schoonbeke. This entrepreneur and real estate developer, as we have seen, intensively used land, labour, and financial markets, but at the same time obtained de facto monopolies in the building and brewing sectors, made profits of around 50 per cent on the tendered sums by way of subcontracting and speculation, and acquired all kinds of prerogatives from the city authorities.[176] Under pressure from thousands of people—craftsmen, proletarians, and outcasts—the city government was compelled to curb Schoonbeke's position and withdraw his privileges. Charles V, however, had a few thousand of his German mercenaries in 1555 put down this Antwerp revolt.[177] Elsewhere, too, disturbances were quelled by the central Habsburg authorities, who often used hired soldiers, followed by the execution of the leaders of revolts and the withdrawal of urban privileges.[178] Also, restrictive measures were forced upon the towns, such as the tightening of the night watch and the introduction of the obligation to register residence.

In the same period, new instruments of repression and coercion were devised by the authorities, increasingly on a central level. An example was the reorganization

---

[174] Boone and Prak, 'Rulers, patricians and burghers', 106–11. For Flanders in this period: Dumolyn and Haemers, 'Patterns of urban rebellion', 380–2.

[175] Van Kalveen, 'Bijdrage tot de geschiedenis'.

[176] Soly, *Urbanisme en kapitalisme*, 263–8, 279–82, and 302–5. See also above, 181.

[177] Soly, *Urbanisme en kapitalisme*, 298–302 and 440–7.

[178] Dumolyn, 'The legal repression'; Blockmans, *Metropolen aan de Noordzee*, 605–11.

of poor relief in the second quarter of the sixteenth century, which was combined with harsh legislation and the prohibition of the activities of mendicants and beggars, and that restricted poor relief to the 'deserving poor'. As a side effect, these measures increased the availability of labour in the market and kept wages down, both directly by forcing beggars and 'lazy people' to work and indirectly by preventing poor people from dying.[179]

Another conspicuous element of the period is the growing employment of professional soldiers by the authorities. This was part of a general development in which urban militias, feudal noblemen, and conscripted peasants were replaced by soldiers hired in the labour market. These economically dependent military personnel were hired by the princes and elites, and successfully so, to crush any rebellion or revolt. In Friesland, the rise of hired soldiers corrupted the century-long system of feuding in the late fifteenth century, when feuding parties started to hire mercenaries in ever larger numbers. Feuding, and taking revenge on a perpetrator and his relatives, aided by one's own kin, is often judged negatively, but it was bound by the rules of fair play and often resulted in reconciliation and indemnification of the family of the victim, at least, if these rules were kept. Now, however, foreign mercenaries came into play, instead of kin, and these did not obey the rules of feuding.[180] The hired soldiers did not capture people, but killed them, leading to escalation and anarchy. The established system of feuding now degenerated into private wars without rules, as in late fifteenth-century Friesland, leading to destruction and ever heavier burdens on the population. In the end, the situation was ended by Duke Albrecht van Saksen and his mercenary captains, who used the anarchy in Friesland to step in and establish his princely authority there.

The sixteenth century saw the processes of accumulation and social polarization proceed almost everywhere in the Low Countries. Many producers lost access to the means of production, for example through the accumulation of lease land by large tenant farmers, leading to the loss of access to lease land for many country dwellers, as we have seen. Also, there was a process of proletarianization in urban industries and services, and also in some rural industries, mainly in those sectors which were capital-intensive and had scope for increase in scale, as in brewing, ship building, or brick production. In the sixteenth century, these processes of proletarianization and polarization were joined by population growth and the resulting rise of food prices and decline of real wages.[181] In combination, this led to immiseration of large groups of people who had increasingly become dependent on markets: for food (with rising prices), for land and lease land (with ever sharper competition and polarization), and for labour (with declining real wages). At the same time these people lost their opportunities for self-organization and the exercise of political power, and they were confronted with ever more wealthy and powerful merchants and entrepreneurs, who dominated these markets.

---

[179] Lis and Soly, *Poverty*, 82–96; van Bavel, *Manors and markets*, 311–13.

[180] Mol, 'Hoofdelingen en huurlingen'.

[181] Even in economically successful Amsterdam real wages stagnated, or even declined, from the first half of the sixteenth century: Allen, 'The great divergence', 428.

This situation led to protests, unrest, and criticism, voiced by writers such as Cornelis Everaert, a fuller and member of the chamber of rhetoricians in early sixteenth-century Bruges.[182] In his plays, whose performance was repeatedly prohibited by the authorities, Everaert condemned the abuses by entrepreneurs and merchants, the vicissitudes of the market, the manipulation by employers, and the risks brought by market dependence. He did not advocate any type of revolution, however. Rather, he came up with more corporatist medieval solutions, and in the end submitted to governmental rule. This attitude was found more generally. Apart from some intellectuals arguing for the abolition of private property, no new socio-economic programmes emerged. The focus in the sixteenth century was on practical problems and abuses, and while there was widespread hatred of the rich by the poor, there was no coherent ideology.

The only major exceptions were the Anabaptists, the most radical offshoot, or the left wing, of the Reformation. They entered the picture around 1526, and gained a strong presence in the northern areas of the Low Countries. In addition to their religious beliefs, the Anabaptists also developed ideas on reforming economy and society. Many of them believed that property should not be used solely for the benefit of the private owner but also for others, and they strove for a voluntary community of goods.[183] Their supporters consisted mainly of small, often pauperized craftsmen and proletarians, and some small-scale merchants, and they were led by craftsmen such as the tailor Jan van Leiden. In 1535 the Anabaptists revolted in many places, such as in Amsterdam, where they had many supporters, but the repression by local and central authorities was severe, with hundreds of the rebels being killed.

Although this insurrection was unsuccessful, the Anabaptists did manage to take power in the town of Munster in Westphalia. Many Anabaptists from Holland and Friesland decided to go to Munster, where an Anabaptist state came into existence, presided over by Twelve Elders and their leader, Jan van Leiden. This state implemented a social and economic revolution, more extreme than the original Anabaptist ideas, with the abolition of private property. Communal property was introduced, not voluntarily, but compelled by the new authority.[184] Accounts and titles were burned and personal valuables and moneys were collected. The town council was supposed to provide food, clothing, and housing; community houses were erected where free meals were distributed. When the voluntary collection of individual property did not yield very much, the authority resorted to confiscation. The full rejection of private property and markets as allocation system, and the threat this posed to elites and their profitable market involvement, explains why its subsequent suppression was so harsh, as was the suppression of any Anabaptist activity in the Low Countries. Among Protestants executed by the authorities, the Anabaptists were by far the majority, and this remained the case in

---

[182] De Vries, 'Rederijkersspelen'.
[183] Klassen, *The economics of Anabaptism*, 28–34 and 42–5.
[184] Klassen, *The economics of Anabaptism*, 47–8.

the following decades.[185] The harsh repression was whole-heartedly supported by the urban elites, including those who had converted to Calvinism, who had become frightened by the revolutionary aspects of the movement.

With the Anabaptists, the only substantial group able to formulate and pursue a new economic and social programme was defeated. At the same time, the old types of associations, dating from the high Middle Ages, such as the guilds, commons, and village communities, in most regions were forced onto the defensive and sometimes even became marginalized, at least as autonomous economic and political actors. This happened, for instance, to the guilds in the Flemish, Brabantine, and Liègois towns, which were targeted by the Habsburg regime, as we have seen, and to the village communities and organizations for communal agriculture in the coastal regions. In the fifteenth and sixteenth centuries, growing factor markets and the process of state formation increasingly had strengthened each other, and both processes eroded the role of the associations. This happened indirectly, because factor markets took over the role of associations in the exchange and allocation of land, labour, and capital, and also directly, since states and public authorities targeted the associations as rivals in exercising authority and power, and aimed to limit their position. In doing so, the public authorities indirectly promoted factor markets, while they also used these markets, especially the capital and labour markets, in order to perform their attacks on the rivalling power of the associations. At the same time, the authorities and market elites increasingly came to rely on each other. The latter process would persist in the next century, and was even intensified in Holland, where the positive and negative effects of market development were most evident. It is, therefore, on this province that the next section will mainly concentrate.

4.4. EFFECTS OF DYNAMIC FACTOR MARKETS FROM THE MID-SIXTEENTH TO THE SEVENTEENTH CENTURY

Holland, and several other parts of the Low Countries, had become thoroughly market-dominated societies by the mid-sixteenth century, with a high mobility of land, labour, and capital in competitive and flexible markets, and ample opportunities for accumulation and increases in scale of production, more than anywhere else in Europe. Not all regions were involved in this process, however, since even within the Low Countries differences in market development were very big.[186] Some regions remained largely unaffected by the rising markets and the commodification of land and labour. One of these was Drenthe. In the seventeenth century, and although it was located only a short distance from the highly commercialized agrarian regions of Groningen to the north and Salland to the southwest, still only

---

[185] Marnef, *Antwerpen*, 119–22: 89 per cent of all Protestants executed in Antwerp were Anabaptists.
[186] This is the central theme of van Bavel, *Manors and markets*.

a quarter of people in Drenthe lived mainly on wages and only a quarter to a third of the land was transacted through lease markets.[187]

The case of Drenthe shows that the expansion of markets was not an automatic process, but rather one directly linked to local and regional structures of power and to the strength of alternative systems of allocation and exchange. In Drenthe, and likewise in the Campine, the dominant social group consisted mainly of the fairly large number of substantial peasant farmers, possessing family-sized holdings complemented with extensive common lands. They felt that their interests in the long run were served best by their more communal forms of agriculture and restrictions on the commodification of land and usage rights, enabling them to steer clear of factor markets. Communal rules were vigilantly kept and commercialization of the common lands was resisted.[188] The fact that in market-dominated Holland, despite relatively high nominal wages, the living standards of producers (in that case mainly wage labourers) were quite low,[189] suggests that they may have been right. Also, it shows that resistance against factor markets and the commodification of land, labour, and capital is not a sign of backwardness, but a question of social relations and power, both in resisting them and in promoting them, even against the interests of large shares of the population.

Not by coincidence, the main sector in Drenthe in which wage labour, large-scale capital investment, and fully market-oriented production emerged, was the peat extraction sector, which was created and organized by wealthy and powerful outsiders. This sector was developed from the early seventeenth century on by merchant entrepreneurs from Holland, who pooled their capital in consortia in order to finance the heavy investments in canals, sluices, and other infrastructure.[190] In the year 1636, thousands of boats loaded with peat departed from the Drenthe market town of Meppel, destined for Holland markets. This development was not exceptional. In the mid-sixteenth century, a similar development had taken place in the barren borderlands between Utrecht and Guelders, where a consortium of Antwerp merchant entrepreneurs and real estate investors, including the notorious Gilbert van Schoonbeke, had organized a massive peat-digging operation.[191] The consortium invested tens of thousands of guilders up front, mainly in canal building, and leased many hundreds of hectares of land from various large landowners. More than 10 million kg of peat was dug there annually, with the hard work performed by hundreds of labourers and much of the peat shipped to Antwerp, some 130 kilometres away. Those who had bought the thirty-two transferable shares of the consortium received a handsome profit, paid out by way of yearly dividends.

[187] Bieleman, *Boeren op het Drentse zand*, 131–51 and 252–61.
[188] Van Zanden, 'The paradox of the marks'. See for the commons in the Campine: van Onacker, *Leaders of the pack?*, 128–40.
[189] See this section, 204–7.
[190] De Vries and van der Woude, *The first modern economy*, 39–40 and 182–3.
[191] Stol, *De veenkolonie*, 61–78; Soly, *Urbanisme en kapitalisme*, 251–62. See for Gilbert van Schoonbeke also section 4.3, 181 and 185.

These examples show how a number of parts of the Low Countries were partly integrated into factor markets by actors from the market cores, but often not as economic equals and with few positive effects for the local inhabitants. In other cases, even within these cores of market development, the positive effects material- ized only for a limited segment of the population. An example is the Guelders river area, which we encountered as the region where agrarian capitalism in the mid- sixteenth century had developed most fully, with large tenant farms, a highly com- petitive lease market, a predominance of wage labour, and a market-oriented agricultural sector.[192] The two branches of agriculture growing most conspicuously were oxen fattening and horse breeding, sectors which were fully geared towards the market, which was often found in the Holland towns, and which were highly capital-intensive, with cattle traders, farmers, and landowners deeply immersed in credit relations and financial markets. As a result of reductions in labour inputs and simultaneous investments in capital goods there, labour productivity in the agricultural sector was pushed up. This process was brought about through factor and output markets and it was driven by the large landowners and big tenant farm- ers, who were also the main beneficiaries of the developments. At the same time, the majority of the rural population had to cope with decreasing employment and declining real wages, and saw its position deteriorate, witnessed by the growing numbers of paupers and declining population numbers in the region.[193] The dis- crepancy between rising labour productivity and decreasing real wages shows that the big tenant farmers, through their market power, increasingly dominated access to the lease land and reaped the benefits of this development, leaving the majority of the rural population with either low pay, poverty, or migration as options.

Holland probably formed the pinnacle of market development in the Low Countries in this period and as such it will be the main focus of the remainder of this section. At first sight, market developments there did not work against the interests of large shares of the population, but rather seem to have had very favour- able effects. With respect to economic growth this indeed was the case, at least up to the beginning of the seventeenth century. The flexibility in the exchange and allocation of land, labour, and capital through the markets, and the opportunities for specialization and increases in scale which these markets offered, pushed up investments and allowed for increases in labour productivity once again, as reflected in a further rise in GDP per capita, at least up to c. 1620, as growth in Holland levelled off, also because of a growing incidence of crises and instability of the economy.[194] To be sure, a rise of GDP per capita does not automatically translate into rising real wages for ordinary people, as we will see later on.

The markets themselves in Holland and other parts of the Dutch Republic also saw further development, in volume and complexity, with the emergence of new market institutions and the further growth of markets, mainly in long-distance

---

[192] Van Bavel, 'Land, lease and agriculture'. See also section 4.3, 172–4.
[193] Van Bavel, 'People and land'; Curtis, *Coping with crisis*, 158–9 and 163–7.
[194] Van Zanden and van Leeuwen, 'Persistent but not consistent', 123–4. For the older, more positive view (with growth assumed to have lasted to the 1660s): de Vries and van der Woude, *The first modern economy*, 672–6.

trade and in the financial sector. These segments of the economy expanded, as we will see, but due to the risks and fluctuations involved in them, they were also responsible for the growing instability of the economy.

In the sixteenth century, financial markets had already grown to a huge size and scope, with active engagement of public bodies such as towns and provinces, and private individuals, for larger and smaller amounts, through all kinds of financial instruments. This growth proceeded, after a setback during the first phase of the Dutch Revolt, in the early seventeenth century. In 1609, the Holland public debt had reached 14.4 million guilders, and between 1621 and 1648 it had further risen to 125 million guilders.[195] In the latter year, the interest payments absorbed 60 per cent of public revenue.

In the field of public debts and other financial transactions, Amsterdam became the main international centre.[196] In 1609, the Exchange Bank of Amsterdam, the *Wisselbank*, was founded. It took deposits, made transfers between accounts, and paid out bills of exchange, with high efficiency and low bank charges. The estates of Holland and the estates general developed the bank into a well-structured public body, while private cashiers linked the bank to the Amsterdam market. Also, the first stock exchange in permanent session, the Amsterdam Bourse, was developed in this city and was housed in a new, grand building, erected in 1611. Amsterdam attracted money from all over Europe, thanks to the relative security, the flexibility, and the profits the stock market, the bank, and other financial instruments offered, if only by way of their scale and scope.[197] Some of this money came from the southern Low Countries, and especially from Amsterdam's precursor as a financial centre, Antwerp, brought to Amsterdam by Antwerp immigrants,[198] but also flowing in from elsewhere in Europe. The Amsterdam bank and stock exchange became the main European mechanisms through which accumulated capital was made profitable, and the Amsterdam elite controlled these money and financial markets.

Amsterdam also offered the most advanced and secure business instruments, including all kinds of insurances, instruments for commodity trading, and price quotations, and all this on a permanent basis. Moreover, further steps were taken in the organization and funding of large companies, although these built on institutions that had developed here in the late Middle Ages, including trade partnerships with numerous members and transferable shares. One of the most conspicuous steps was the foundation of the United East India Company, the VOC, in 1602. The VOC possessed various characteristics of the modern corporation, including permanent, shielded capital, a clear-cut separation between ownership and management, transferability of shares, and limited liability of the shareholders.[199] The company was funded with a capital of 6.4 million guilders, of which 57 per cent

---

[195] Gelderblom and Jonker, 'Public finance and economic growth', 6, 10, and 15.
[196] Arrighi, *The long twentieth century*, 140–4; Braudel, *Les jeux de l'échange*, 80–6; de Vries and van der Woude, *The first modern economy*, 113–58.
[197] Israel, *Dutch primacy*, 73–9.
[198] Although less than once thought: Gelderblom, *Zuid-Nederlandse kooplieden*, 60–71.
[199] Gelderblom, de Jong, and Jonker, 'An admiralty for Asia'; Prak, *The Dutch Republic*, 99–100 and 116–21. For the political-military characteristics of the VOC, see below, 199–200.

was supplied by 1,100 participants from Amsterdam, with a substantial share of this coming from immigrants from the southern Low Countries.

Big companies such as the VOC, but also smaller businesses in both town and countryside, attracted wage labourers from a large area. Labour migration had a long tradition in Holland and was encouraged by the seasonal character of the most rural activities there, causing a peak demand for labour. This was the case for herring fishing, peat digging, bleaching, and brick production, which had short, overlapping production seasons, mainly in summer.[200] Since these seasons largely coincided with the busiest period in agriculture, as the mowing, hay making, and crop harvesting had to be done mainly in June and July, this resulted in a seasonal labour scarcity. Hence, alongside local wage labour, migrant workers from neighbouring regions were also employed in Holland, attracted by the relatively high nominal wages. Especially in the peat sector, in which demand for labour was very strong in the short digging season, numerous people from elsewhere found a job, notwithstanding a few scattered attempts of local authorities to restrict this by way of stipulations embodied in the local by-laws.[201] The rise of migrant labour in Holland thus had late medieval roots. What did change, however, from the fourteenth century on, was the number of people involved in migrant labour and the distances to the areas of origin of the labourers, associated with the enlargement of scale in Holland agriculture, industries, and services. Particularly from c. 1570 onwards, migrant labourers from inside Holland were replaced as seasonal workers by foreign migrant labourers, mainly from the peasant regions in the eastern, sandy parts of the Netherlands and Westphalia in present-day Germany.[202]

Growing Economic Inequality

Although factor markets around 1600 generally were open and accessible, as discussed in the previous section, not everyone benefited from these markets to the same extent. There were clear economic winners and losers. Increases in scale, for instance, as in shipping and trade, and in some industrial sectors, caused some of the most profitable capital ventures to become exclusive to economic elites. Whereas it was possible to subscribe to public debt by investing small amounts of money in the late Middle Ages, under the Dutch Republic entry sums increased. Similarly, while at the beginning entry sums for shares in the East India Company were quite low, and hundreds of small savers invested sums of up to 150 guilders in shares, there were also wealthy persons who individually invested tens of thousands of guilders in VOC shares, and gradually large numbers of shares were accumulated in the hands of a few, with these large shareholders coming from the ranks of the already wealthy.[203] Economic growth coincided with demands for new types of funding, which may have been efficient from a strictly economic perspective, but in practice cut out large parts of the population.

---

[200] Lucassen, *Naar de kusten van de Noordzee*, 93, 95, 102, and 107; van Bavel, 'Rural wage labour'.
[201] Van Bavel, 'Proto-industrialization', 1157.
[202] Lucassen, *Naar de kusten*, 159–71; van Zanden, *The rise and decline*, 157–67.
[203] Gelderblom and Jonker, 'Completing a financial revolution', 654; Adams, *The familial state*, 51.

The accumulation of capital in Holland was further driven by the high profits made by merchants, especially in long-distance trade. The average annual increase in the wealth of Amsterdam merchants in the years between 1590 and 1609 may have been as high as 12.5 per cent.[204] Hans Thijs, who traded in jewels and other commodities, possessed a few thousand guilders at the time of his marriage in 1584, but had amassed 63,000 guilders by the time of his death in 1611. This was not exceptional. The merchant Louis Trip, to give a later example, invested 46,000 guilders in two family businesses in 1632, but by the early 1660s his assets ran to 600,000 guilders and around 1685 they totalled more than 900,000 guilders.[205] Of the latter sum, about a quarter was invested in real estate, more than a quarter in government bonds, and about one-eighth in VOC shares. The VOC itself had enlarged its assets from 6.4 million guilders in 1602 to more than 40 million in 1660, by retaining profits, while at the same time it paid 62 million in dividends to its shareholders.

This period also offered ample opportunities for financial dealing. As early as the 1550s, futures trading was practised by Amsterdam merchants. With the growth of trade and the development of more advanced commercial and financial instruments in the following decades, these activities grew enormously, especially from the start of the seventeenth century, either through futures trading, options, short selling, or stock index purchases.[206] This also enlarged the opportunities for speculative behaviour, associated with booms and busts of ever growing intensity.

A large portion of wealth was invested in landed property. In the period 1580–1620, burgher landownership in Holland increased, to much higher levels than had been reached in the highly urbanized parts of the southern Low Countries, near Ghent or Antwerp. There, the share of urban landownership had remained fairly modest, not exceeding a quarter of the total area in most cases, that is, less than half of the Italian amounts we observed above.[207] This started to change in Holland around 1600, however, as the share of burgher landownership there now reached the high percentages found in northern and central Italy. The share of land in the hands of burghers in the central parts of Holland in 1620 had risen to 50 per cent or more of the 'old' land, by way of acquisitions through the dynamic land market, and it reached 80–90 per cent in the newly created polders.[208] These investors were merchants, merchant entrepreneurs, high officials in the developing state bureaucracies, and noblemen residing in the towns, all heavily involved in factor markets. Amsterdam merchants such as the Trip family, for instance, invested heavily in some of the new polders, sometimes adorning their newly acquired property with a rural mansion. Apart from these mansions, almost all of this urban-owned property in the countryside was leased out for short terms, in larger

---

[204] Gelderblom, *Zuid-Nederlandse kooplieden*, 122–44 (Hans Thijs) and 162–3. In general: de Vries and van der Woude, *The first modern economy*, 669–70.

[205] Klein, *De Trippen*, 42–6.

[206] De Vries and van der Woude, *The first modern economy*, 150–3.

[207] For burgher landownership in the southern Low Countries: section 4.3, 171, and for Italy: section 3.3, 124–5.

[208] Van Bavel, 'Rural development'. For the property of the Trip family: Klein, *De Trippen*, 50–5. See also section 4.3, 179–80.

farms, and used for market-oriented production. To be sure, landholdings formed only one component in the portfolios of these new elites, and the importance of government bonds and shares was rising even quicker.

Another conspicuous phenomenon in this period was the sharp increase in social inequality. As far as we know, income inequality in the Low Countries—including Holland—had been relatively low before 1500, when compared to later periods, even though in some large towns inequality was already on the rise. Inequality in thriving, dynamic Holland towns such as Haarlem and the industrial city of Leiden was markedly higher than in small towns such as Edam and Alkmaar.[209] Around the mid-sixteenth century, however, the smaller towns, too, saw growing inequality, as shown by figures for Alkmaar. For Holland as a whole, income inequality in 1561 had already reached a high level, with a Gini coefficient of 0.56.[210] The inequality in wealth distribution also increased substantially, especially in Amsterdam. The Gini coefficient there moved up to about 0.74 in 1585.[211] Of the 391 people who paid the highest taxes in 1585, and whose occupation was mentioned, no fewer than 278 were merchants, and forty-five were industrial entrepreneurs. The predominance of merchants was even greater among the highest taxpayers.

Even though becoming more concentrated in the course of the sixteenth century, in an absolute sense the wealth of the richest people was still fairly limited around 1600. In the opening decades of the seventeenth century, however, really huge fortunes were amassed through the enormous profits of wealthy merchant entrepreneurs, which was accompanied by a further increase in inequality.[212] At the other end of the social scale, inequality was driven up by the stagnation, or even decline, of the average real wages of craftsmen and labourers.[213] The effects are evident in further rising Gini coefficients and growing shares of the richest households in total income and wealth, especially in Amsterdam, where the distribution became most skewed.

The Amsterdam wealth distribution moved up from a Gini of about 0.74 in 1585 to 0.85 in 1630, that is, as skewed as it had been in highly unequal Florence in 1427.[214] In 1630/1, of the total taxed wealth in Amsterdam of 63 million guilders, one-third was owned by the top 1 per cent, all of them individuals active in long-distance trade and often combining this with commercial landholding and activities in financial markets.[215] In other towns, the concentration of wealth was only slightly less marked, as can be seen in the cities of Leiden (1622: 0.79) and The Hague (1627: 0.76) in Holland. The smaller towns and the countryside showed less inequality, but the general picture of increasing inequality of wealth distribution is clear. With regard to income developments were no less marked. In

---

[209] Van Zanden, 'Tracing the beginning', 645–6 and 649.
[210] Milanovic, Lindert, and Williamson, 'Measuring ancient inequality', 54 and 77.
[211] Goldsmith, *Premodern financial systems*, 204–6; van Zanden, 'Tracing the beginning'.
[212] Gelderblom, 'The Golden Age', 163–4. For figures on inequality see directly below.
[213] Allen, 'The great divergence', 428.
[214] Goldsmith, *Premodern financial systems*, 204–6; van Zanden, 'Tracing the beginning'.
[215] Goldsmith, *Premodern financial systems*, 204–6. See also Gelderblom, *Zuid-Nederlandse kooplieden*, 225–8.

1732 the Gini coefficient for income inequality in Holland had reached the figure of 0.61, which for income distribution in a comparative perspective is astonishingly high.[216]

These calculations of inequality are mostly based on tax records and are hampered by the non-recording of the exempt households, which were too poor to pay taxes at all, a share often comprising a third of the total population or even more. Including them would make the inequality even more marked than the tax figures show. On the other hand, some nuances can also be discerned, at least for income inequality. Recent research looking at other sources of income, including revenues from property, arrives at somewhat lower estimates of income inequality.[217] Another nuance would be that a fairly big share of GDP in Holland, or in the Dutch Republic as a whole, was transferred through public assistance. In seventeenth-century Holland, the share distributed by way of formalized relief has been roughly estimated at some 2–4 per cent of GDP, and this was much higher than anywhere else in Europe, with the exception perhaps of England.[218] Still, much of this relief was aimed not at the poorest strata of society, but at those just above—as a kind of insurance—and much of it was not paid for by the wealthy segments, but by the middling and lower groups themselves, especially where relief was organized within the guilds.[219] Also, relief was much scantier for wage labourers who fell outside the guild system, and had lost most of the traditional safety networks, including kinship and community ties. They became ever more dependent on highly competitive markets, declining real wages, and a volatile and unstable economy, and relief just blunted the sharpest edges of poverty and economic insecurity somewhat for them. Moreover, the high level of *wealth* inequality, of course, was not at all reduced by relief systems.

Growing Political Inequality

The economic inequality of the period went along with a growing political inequality. The merchant entrepreneurs encountered ever less counterweight in the sphere of political decision making. The stormy development of open and flexible markets undermined the role of associations of independent producers. The associations, and especially those in the countryside, were marginalized, lost political influence, or became dominated by elite groups. This marginalization had happened, as we have seen, through the limitation of the political and military role of the guilds by the town magistrates and princes, through the dismantling of the autonomy of village communities, through the dissolution of the commons, and through the growing dominance of large landowners within the associations for water management, as in coastal Flanders.[220] All this eroded the contribution of

---

[216] Milanovic, Lindert, and Williamson, 'Measuring ancient inequality', 54 and 77; Soltow, 'Annual inequality through four centuries'.
[217] Blondé and Hanus, 'Beyond building craftsmen'.
[218] Van Bavel and Rijpma, 'Formalized charity'.
[219] Van Leeuwen, 'Guilds and middle class-welfare'.
[220] For the latter: Soens, 'Polders zonder poldermodel?'. See also section 4.3, 179.

associations to social balance. Even where new associations were formed, as with the guilds set up in Holland in the seventeenth century,[221] this balance was not restored. The guilds in Holland traditionally had almost no political role; this had been explicitly denied them by the count of Holland. The guilds that were formed there anew in the seventeenth century hardly formed a political counterweight to the elites either, since they had no formal constitutional position, as opposed to the eastern parts of the Dutch Republic, where they participated more directly in the political process and the election of urban officials.[222]

At the same time, the merchant elites strengthened their grip on urban governments, as evidenced most clearly by the fact that urban administrative boards became more closed to non-elite members. The citizens in the Holland towns did not play a direct role in recruiting the council, since this was done through co-optation. The new members who were co-opted were recruited from an ever smaller number of families, a development reaching its apex in the late seventeenth century. At that point, about four-fifths of the newly appointed members of the city council of Rotterdam were relatives of the sitting board.[223] Nepotism became ever more widespread, with elite members appointing their sons, or having them appointed, in offices, for instance as mayors, members of city councils, or directors of companies.[224] This dominant group came to form a regent oligarchy, with economic and political leverage increasingly overlapping each other.

The enormous capital accumulation by merchant entrepreneurs and rentiers, who used the factor markets and the opportunities they brought, also strengthened their political power more directly. Public bodies, both for taxation and for financing their debts, became increasingly dependent on the financial resources of these wealthy market elites, and especially those of the trade metropolis of Amsterdam, who used this position to strengthen their hold on government and society. This process accelerated with the Dutch Revolt and, after its success, the formation of the Dutch Republic. The dominance of the Amsterdam market elites now became further consolidated, as they were able to create their 'own' state and use it to defend their interests.[225] During the revolt the power of rival groups, including the king and his court, large parts of the nobility, and the ecclesiastical hierarchy were done away with, to be replaced with a relatively small stadtholder court. The overwhelming influence of Amsterdam merchants on state policies was further based on the fact that, as a result of their dominant economic position, they came to pay half of the provincial, Holland taxes and a quarter of the taxes of the Dutch Republic as a whole.[226] Holland paid almost all costs of the government administration, the embassies, and the expenditure on ammunition and the military, in order to get a hold on these strategic sectors. The policy of the Dutch Republic,

---

[221] De Munck, Lourens, and Lucassen, *The establishment and distribution*.

[222] Boone and Prak, 'Rulers, patricians and burghers', 116–19.

[223] Prak, *Gezeten burgers*, 64 and passim.   [224] Adams, *The familial state*, 81–92 and 148–9.

[225] Adams, *The familial state*, 39–42. See also Ogilvie and Carus, 'Institutions and economic growth', 422–3.

[226] Swart, 'Holland's bourgeoisie', 45. See also 't Hart, *The making of a bourgeois state*, 79–81; Prak, *The Dutch Republic*, 77–9.

particularly its foreign policy, was strongly influenced, or even dictated by the Holland market elites, directly and in part indirectly, through the dominant position of the provincial government on national decision making.

The effects of this can be seen, for instance, in the low taxation of foreign trade and commercial capital. In the late Middle Ages, the towns had prevented much of this taxation, and this resulted in a relatively lower tax burden in the towns compared to the countryside. This difference had been reduced, however, in the period c. 1470–1540, and the fiscal reforms by the Habsburg regime in 1542 and again in 1568 even aimed at introducing taxes on exports and on commercial and industrial capital, and by making the tax on real estate strictly proportional.[227] Emperor Charles V also was the first to tax long-term loans and mortgages, in 1542. All this could have led to an equitable distribution of the tax burden, but the moves in this direction were halted by the Dutch Revolt and the opportunity this offered to the merchant entrepreneurs and rentiers to take control over state power and the making of fiscal arrangements.

As a result, wealth taxes in the seventeenth century came to be levied only very intermittently and their size was very modest, mostly at 0.5 per cent of wealth. The property inventories used were often old, and they shifted the burden from merchants with liquid wealth to the owners of less mobile forms of property, most notably land. Although the creation and transaction of long-term loans came to be taxed, there were also opposite developments: the public debt created by the states of Holland increased rapidly, and to promote Holland bonds, the buyers received tax exemption.[228] The thresholds for tax reductions, moreover, favoured the large-scale wealth owners over the small-scale owners. Also, some of the wealth levies took the form of forced loans, thus not being a real tax but an interest-bearing loan.[229] Taxes on transactions of goods, land, or capital existed, but they mostly had a flat rate, thus burdening the small owners most.[230] At the same time, most real taxation consisted of indirect excises, which had most impact on the middling and lower segments of society.[231] In 1600, two-thirds of taxes in Holland were levied on basic necessities, used mainly to pay interest on the public debts and cover military costs, rising to three-quarters in 1650. In this period, compared to the mid-sixteenth century, inequalities in taxation thus increased. Consumption goods (through excises) and land were heavily taxed, but export trade and capital and capital goods much less so. The result was a further sharpening of economic inequality. In its turn, the result of this inequality was that, despite the regressive taxation system, most of the taxes were paid by wealthy market elites, which formed a component in this political leverage.

Conspicuous also is the growing coercion exercised by Holland merchant entrepreneurs. Initially, their dominance was based on capital and property accumulation,

---

[227] Grapperhaus, *Alva en de tiende penning*, 42–54 and 286–93.
[228] 't Hart, 'The merits', 13.
[229] Gelderblom and Jonker, 'Public finance and economic growth', 10–11 and 19.
[230] 't Hart, *The making of a bourgeois state*, 123.
[231] Brandon, 'Marxism and the "Dutch miracle"', 112; Prak, *The Dutch Republic*, 78. See also for the following numbers: 't Hart, *The making of a bourgeois state*, 123–31 and 137–9.

by making use of the opportunities offered by the free and dynamic factor and out-put markets. At a later stage, however, and especially from the late sixteenth century on, these elites started to employ more non-economic coercion, using their eco-nomic and political leverage to develop these coercive instruments. This happened, for instance, in the organization of trade in Holland, where a host of trading venues had traditionally offered open access to markets, but around 1600 gave way to a more closed system that privileged a few urban markets, thus limiting marketing opportunities for country dwellers in particular.[232] In the towns, the guild system formed an instrument to control the urban wage labourers, to regulate the labour markets and to impose increasing segmentation and restrictions for country dwellers. Also, semi-forced labour relationships now appeared. In Holland, the system of houses of correction with forced labour became the most fully developed in all of Europe.[233] Even if these workhouses in themselves were not economically viable, they helped in getting some economic use out of otherwise idle labour and they contrib-uted to forcing people onto the labour market, in combination with the simultane-ous repression of begging and the stricter organization of charity, which now limited relief to the 'deserving' poor only.[234] Some large manufactories emerged using semi-forced labourers who were paid rates below the market wage, as in the bridewells and rasp and spinning houses, or by employing orphans.[235]

Outside Holland, too, the same Holland elites started to employ coercive means, especially from the late sixteenth century, mainly by way of the Dutch state. The newly emerging Dutch Republic became increasingly dependent on the financial resources of the market elites from the Holland towns, who strengthened their grip on government and political decision making.[236] Holland merchants and urban elites next used the framework of the newly emerged Dutch Republic, for instance, to extend their power over the eastern and southern parts of the Netherlands. Military force was used to dominate the north of Brabant and Twente, regions which were situated on the fringes of the Dutch Republic and formed a military buffer for Holland and used as a war zone.[237] These regions also offered cheap labour, to be tapped by Holland textile entrepreneurs and taxed in order to finance the Dutch policy, which was particularly aimed at defending the interests of Holland merchant entrepreneurs.

The same Holland elites from the opening decades of the seventeenth century also subjugated parts of the East Indies, using violence and military force in order to coerce labour and monopolize production of, and trade in, spices and other goods. The interests of this relatively small group of merchant entrepreneurs were served by expensive wars at sea, against the English, for instance, in order to main-tain naval dominance and protect shipping routes, and also by the establishment of monopolies, forts, and trading posts overseas, using coercion and force if needed.

---

[232] Dijkman, *Shaping medieval markets*, 148–50.
[233] Van Bavel, *Manors and markets*, 313 and references therein.
[234] Van Bavel and Rijpma, 'Formalized charity'.
[235] See the nuanced account by Spierenburg, 'Early modern prisons'.
[236] Adams, *The familial state*, 39–42 and 69–72.   [237] Adriaenssen, *Staatsvormend geweld*.

The Dutch East Asia Company, the VOC, is a fine example of this process. While its predecessors, the various overseas companies, or *voorcompagnieën*, were true trade organizations, aimed at making a profit through trade, the VOC departed from this practice. From the outset, the VOC was involved in the political-military ambitions of the Dutch oligarchy and the republic and it received a monopoly in Asian trade in order to achieve these ambitions.[238] The VOC became an instrument of power, for instance in subordinating the spice-producing areas in the East Indies by brute force, including the killing of the population of the Banda Islands, of whom only a few hundred were spared.

The same VOC became fully dominated by the merchant-rentier elites, who had furnished most of its capital, and the estates general, who used it as a political-military instrument.[239] It was not the shareholders who held authority over the VOC, as they had done over the earlier overseas companies, but the directors, the *Heeren XVII*. These were not elected democratically by the group of shareholders as a whole, but rather selected via procedures favouring the large shareholders, and as a result these posts were increasingly held by members of the ruling oligarchic families.[240] Also, the administration was largely at their discretion, as accounts were not made public. In 1623, shareholders targeted this situation, but the republic's government—largely dominated by the same oligarchy—came to the aid of the directors. To be sure, the situation with the VOC was not an exception, as the members of the Dutch admiralty councils in the seventeenth century also belonged to the richest families, often the very rich ones. All this increased the possibility that these positions of power would be used to serve private interests instead of public ones.

Indeed, these developments further enlarged the profits and the wealth amassed by the large shareholders of the VOC and its counterpart for the West Indies (the WIC) and by the merchants involved in overseas trade. They also made it possible to shift much of the costs of the military power exercised by the VOC and WIC, which were huge, to others in Dutch society. The Dutch Republic was almost continuously at war throughout the seventeenth century and spent vast sums of money on this, as in the wars against England, and in armed conflicts in Denmark, Brazil, and East Asia, mainly fought to protect trading interests.[241] Although part of these costs were internalized by the VOC, which itself produced part of the protection it needed,[242] more generally a substantial share of the Dutch military expenses costs was borne by the taxes on consumption goods paid by the middling and lower groups.

The results of these wars were, in an economic sense, not necessarily negative, but the benefits accrued to relatively small segments of Dutch society: to the merchants, entrepreneurs, shareholders, rentiers, military officers, and middlemen.

---

[238] Steensgaard, *The Asian trade revolution*, 126–8 and 132–5; van Zanden, *The rise and decline*, 67–85. See also Israel, *Dutch primacy*, 69–73.

[239] Steensgaard, *The Asian trade revolution*, 128–31; Gelderblom, De Jong, and Jonker, 'An admiralty for Asia'.

[240] Adams, *The familial state*, 48–51.

[241] Israel, *Dutch primacy*, 146–9, 160–4, 184–5, and 247–53.

[242] Steensgaard, *The Asian trade revolution*, 151–2.

The other side of the coin consisted of stagnation or declining living standards for the rest of the population.[243] Most conspicuously, this applies to the labour overseas, especially those coerced through the slave trade or, from 1596 onwards, through the use of slave labour on plantations in Surinam and Brazil, and the forced cultivation and coerced labour in the East Indies by the VOC and WIC. Also, there was the establishment of monopolies and the use of slave labour in the Cape Colony, where slaves outnumbered the free population by the late seventeenth century.[244] At the same time, these companies were also intimately linked to factor markets, as witnessed for instance by the use they made of the labour of thousands of wage labourers, in the form of sailors and soldiers, mainly hired through the labour market.[245] Labourers, escaping from even worse conditions elsewhere, where nominal wages were often lower or opportunities for wage labour scarcer, were attracted from all over Europe, or sometimes pressed or lured in. In 1600, most of the military in the Dutch army consisted of foreign soldiers, while on Dutch fleets the proportion of foreign sailors also rose, especially on the longer voyages with higher risks.[246] The VOC developed the combination of factor markets with coercion most perfectly, by intensively using the labour markets for sailors, soldiers, officers, and administrators, by using the financial market for funding its debts and transacting its shares, and by using the market for both the purchase and sale of goods, but it combined these market transactions with the use of military power, coercion, and monopolies. Factor markets and coercion were thus not hostile to each other, but became integrated. Both the organization of factor markets and the socio-political context in which they functioned, in a process of interaction, thus lost their favourable characteristics.

Stagnation of the Economy and Decline of Welfare

The investments in the financial market and those in exercising force and coercion gradually seem to have become more attractive to the possessors of capital than the more risky and often also less remunerative real investments in capital goods and new technologies. The rise of the financial market and its financial instruments initially had a positive effect on investments and the opportunities it opened for entrepreneurs. This effect in part still applied to the opening decades of the seventeenth century, at least in a few sectors, as in the Holland brewing industry or sugar refining, for instance. Capital intensity there grew even further and money invested in breweries often came to exceed 100,000 guilders per brewery, with about half of this invested in fixed capital goods. Trade profits were not sufficient to finance these large investments, so brewers often used a mixture of financial instruments, including short-term loans from relatives, mortgages, long-term debts, and partnerships.[247]

---

[243] See below, 205–7. [244] Van Zanden, *The rise and decline*, 88–90.
[245] Van Zanden, *The rise and decline*, 38.
[246] Van Lottum and Lucassen, 'Six cross-sections'.
[247] Gelderblom, 'The Golden Age', 164–8.

In the course of the seventeenth century, however, the financial market largely lost this positive effect and instead contributed to economic stagnation by diverting capital from productive uses to speculation and financing non-productive activities, including war making. Speculation was part of the functioning of the market itself, while the leaking away of money to unproductive uses was at least facilitated by the financial market. Conversely, the decrease in profitable investment opportunities in the real economy, as a result of the levelling off of growth in the Dutch industrial and agricultural sectors from c. 1620, and the rise of international import restrictions, in combination with the huge capital stocks accumulated by the wealthy elites, drove up the size of the public debt, which formed the main outlet for this idle capital.[248] In this sense, and especially from c. 1650 on, the growth of public debt was to a large extent supply-driven, with otherwise idle capital entering the market, even though interest rates were very low. The relative attraction of investing in the public debt is shown, for instance, in 1653, as the government's proposal to redeem annuities met with clear disapproval by the creditors.[249]

It is striking that the great wealth that was amassed to a declining extent found its way into the real economy in the form of productive investments. The investments in the extension of the canal system, city extensions, and the drainage of lakes and reclamation, and the associated investments in drainage mills, water management works, and new farms, remained large in Holland up to the 1660s.[250] They can, however, be largely considered as elements of extensive growth, that is, in cultivated area or numbers of people. Moreover, after the 1660s these investments seriously declined. The growth of large-scale, in-depth investments in capital goods in Holland seems to have halted even earlier, from the early seventeenth century on, apart from a few exceptions such as the brewing industry and the fleet. The growth of labour productivity and total factor productivity, that in Holland had reached the highest level in Europe, in this period levelled off.[251]

The relative decline of labour-saving and productivity-enhancing investments in the economy in the seventeenth century can be understood from the fact that investments in industries and technology remained risky compared to those in real estate, while the profits were limited compared to those made in trade, coercive activities, financial speculation, and state debts. Holland merchants remained strong in international trade because protective costs were partly borne by the state. In the field of public debts, Amsterdam remained the financial centre of the world until well into the eighteenth century.[252] This is the field in which Holland's dominance lasted longest, also through the development of new financial techniques. Around 1650, for instance, the directors of the Amsterdam Exchange Bank

---

[248] Gelderblom and Jonker, 'Public finance and economic growth', 2–3, 13–16, and 26–7. See also Adams, *The familial state*, 69–72; and for the levelling off of the growth of GDP per capita below, 203.

[249] Gelderblom and Jonker, 'Public finance and economic growth', 16–17.

[250] De Vries and van der Woude, *The first modern economy*, 672–3.

[251] My interpretation of van Zanden and van Leeuwen, 'Persistent but not consistent', 126.

[252] Arrighi, *The long twentieth century*, 142–4 and 202–10.

introduced the tradable receipt for bullion deposited at the bank. This attracted even more bullion to Amsterdam, and lowered the price for obtaining liquid funds to levels much lower than elsewhere. In its turn, this created a rush of people searching for credit at low interest rates. It was only in the late eighteenth century that Amsterdam lost to London its position as the financial centre of the world.[253] In agriculture and industry, on the other hand, Holland had lost its pre-eminence much earlier. Developments in these sectors were less favourable, because the fully proletarianized labour in Holland remained more expensive than forced or peasant labour elsewhere, which was able—or forced—to accept a remuneration below the full costs of subsistence,[254] while investments in labour-saving technology in Holland remained relatively limited, because wealth found other, more attractive outlets.

The latter is linked to the more structural causes for the decline of real investments in vital sectors of the economy. This decline can also be observed elsewhere in the Low Countries, in other regions where factor markets had become dominant. After an initial positive effect of these markets on labour productivity, stagnation set in. In coastal Flanders, where the rise of factor markets and the transition to becoming a market economy had taken place as early as the late thirteenth and fourteenth centuries,[255] there had been a clear decline in investments in agriculture and water management infrastructure in the following period. The Guelders river area saw the same happening after its agrarian transition c. 1450–1600. While this transition to a market-dominated economy went hand in hand with the reduction of labour inputs and growing investments in capital goods, and it resulted in a rise in labour productivity, after the completion of the process in the late sixteenth century, stagnation set in. Although agriculture continued to be market oriented, there were no further gains in investments, labour productivity, or innovation. Moreover, competition in factor markets was instead reduced in the seventeenth and eighteenth centuries, as many tenant farms came to be leased by subsequent generations, or family groups.[256] Also, wealthy tenants started to buy up their farms, allowing them to increase their status and political influence, with their capital now invested in land instead of capital goods.

These were agricultural regions, but in more industrialized Holland development and growth came to a standstill too. The dominance of merchant interests in Holland and their advocacy of relatively free trade, while neighbouring countries resorted to trade restrictions, may have been a factor.[257] Another was the state of technology, disallowing further large advantages of scale and competition with regions where labour was cheaper, which reduced the attraction of investments in industries.[258] More importantly, however, Holland elites shifted their capital in the

---

[253] See section 5.1, 222.

[254] Van Zanden, *The rise and decline*, 84–5 (forced labour in the East Indies) and 103–9 (proto-industrial peasants).

[255] See section 4.3, 178–9.

[256] Brusse, *Overleven*, 177–87; Curtis, *Coping with crisis*, 167–70.

[257] De Vries and van der Woude, *The first modern economy*, 409–12, although many trade economists would downplay this argument, as discussed below, 204.

[258] See the careful discussion by Lis and Soly, 'Different paths of development', esp. 230–6.

seventeenth century increasingly to the more secure and relatively profitable public debts, investments abroad, and the acquisition of privileges and public offices. In 1652, a complaint was made that the directors of the VOC, the *Heeren XVII*, were not merchants anymore, but had shifted their attention to investments in landed property, conspicuous consumption, and war making.[259] The same change of focus (with the exception of war making) happened in the rural areas where factor markets had become dominant, including coastal Flanders and the Guelders river area. Here, too, as highlighted above, economic growth came to a standstill in the seventeenth century, as opportunities for further specialization, increases in scale, and capital investments had been exhausted, and investments shifted to acquiring landed property, status, and political power.

Even though the seventeenth century is traditionally labelled the Golden Age of the Dutch Republic, and Amsterdam in this century reached the peak of its cultural splendour, as a result of all the preceding elements the economic growth in Holland had already levelled off around 1620, as the newest calculations show.[260] To be sure, GDP kept growing longer, mainly as a result of massive immigration and concomitant population growth, but the growth of GDP per capita declined and, some decades later, started to stagnate. The Dutch Republic in the second half of the seventeenth century lost its position of economic leadership to England, first in agriculture and industry, later in trade, and yet later also in finance.

The economic rise of the Low Countries in the late Middle Ages and its relative decline in the seventeenth century cannot be solely attributed to the endogenous processes within factor markets and their social and political context analysed here. We also have to look at exogenous factors. On closer inspection, however, these only played a minor role.[261] This applies, for instance, to climatic changes, which are sometimes attributed the role of historical protagonist. The Little Ice Age that had commenced at the end of the high Middle Ages reached new depths in the sixteenth century, as the northern parts of the Low Countries experienced weather extremes in the 1560s and 1570s, followed by frequent severe winters in the seventeenth century, and otherwise recurring episodes of big climatic variations.[262] These did have an effect on the economy and society, and short-term crises based on harvest failures did ensue, but within this highly diversified economy, with its direct access to international markets, the relatively low transaction costs in these markets and the high nominal wages allowing a high purchasing power in foreign goods, including Baltic grain, the effects of an unfavourable climate were mitigated to the point that its economic consequences were limited.[263] Moreover, the adverse climate had not prevented economic growth in the fourteenth to sixteenth century,

[259] Adams, *The familial state*, 69–72 and 80.

[260] My interpretation of van Zanden and van Leeuwen, 'Persistent but not consistent', 123.

[261] See also Adams, *The familial state*, 137.

[262] De Vries and van der Woude, *The first modern economy*, 21–3.

[263] De Vries and van der Woude, *The first modern economy*, 21. For easy access of Holland to international grain markets and the strong links Holland had established already in the fifteenth century, see also Dijkman, *Shaping medieval markets*, 305–11.

and neither can it be held accountable for the stagnation in the later seventeenth century, as climatic conditions were already improving again.

Another exogenous development that in the literature is often held responsible for the Dutch stagnation is the rise of mercantilist policies in the neighbouring countries around the middle of the seventeenth century and the large demographic and military weight of these larger, far more populous countries.[264] This factor may have had a negative effect on the opportunities for further economic growth, although some trade economists would argue that unilateral free trade is often still beneficial, even in an international context of protectionism, and thus would disagree with the argument. Moreover, this element cannot explain the whole of the endogenous process analysed here, particularly not the growing wealth inequality, the ensuing shifts in investments, and the translation of economic wealth into political power. Also, a large part of this endogenous process, and the ensuing levelling off of economic growth, had already started before the emergence of these mercantilist policies, which also disqualifies a causal link.

Nor can these exogenous factors explain the declining living standards of ordinary Dutch people, since these had already started to deteriorate in the period when the economy was still prospering. Although GDP per capita in the sixteenth and seventeenth centuries had risen to by far the highest level in Europe, this rise did not translate into better conditions for the majority of the population. Firstly, the economic fruits of market developments mostly accrued to the market core, Holland—that is, only one part of the Netherlands. Especially in the later phases, as Holland market elites used their economic, political, and military dominance in order to apply coercion, often within markets, developments did not benefit all parties involved, as could have been the case in a situation of more open markets, but may well have been at the expense of living standards in other areas, such as the southern and eastern fringes of the Dutch Republic and even more clearly those in the East Indies. Moreover, where growth did take place in the late sixteenth and seventeenth centuries, it was mainly found in the financial sector, long-distance trade, and other international services, which formed an ever larger part of the Dutch economy, and especially that of Holland. These expanding sectors were much more volatile and unstable than agriculture and industry, and they can be held responsible for the high instability and sharp fluctuations which characterized the Holland economy as a whole from the mid-sixteenth century on.[265] These fluctuations hit the poorer segments of society hard and created insecurity.

An even more weighty nuance on the high GDP per capita figures is that the polarizing tendencies of the period also prevented economic growth from having a favourable effect on the living standards of large shares of the population. The urban elites in the Low Countries—and especially in Holland—amassed unprecedented wealth, but living conditions for most people did not improve, and sometimes declined. Many parts of the Low Countries in the sixteenth and seventeenth

---

[264] De Vries and van der Woude, *The first modern economy*, 409–12. See also Israel, *Dutch primacy*, 339–46.
[265] Van Zanden and van Leeuwen, 'Persistent but not consistent', 123–4.

centuries, and especially those with vibrant factor markets, witnessed a sharp social polarization, as we saw above. Ever sharper differences between rich and poor could be encountered in the booming market centres. Very many people in seventeenth-century Amsterdam were totally pauperized.

More generally, the economic growth of the sixteenth and early seventeenth centuries, and the resulting Dutch Golden Age, to a large extent came at the expense of large parts of the population. Especially the formerly independent craftsmen, peasants, and retailers, and the wage labourers, lost position and became submerged in an ever poorer substratum. Criticism was voiced, for instance, by Jan van Houtte, the town secretary of Leiden, the textile centre in the vanguard of market development.[266] In a detailed report he wrote in 1577, he criticized the organization of the textile industries and the dominance of a few wealthy drapers, who had made numerous miserable workers dependent on them. Since the employers and the town authorities were interrelated, resistance by the workers was futile. In his words, the workers were forced to work like slaves, and on their day off, on Sundays, they had to go begging in order to supplement their meagre income.

The economic growth of the fourteenth to seventeenth century did not even have uniform positive results for the able-bodied, adult workers who were employed full-time. The social polarization prevented an increase of the purchasing power of such people. Industrial workers and construction workers in the seventeenth century had lower real wages than their counterparts around 1300, the first period for which wage and price data are available.[267] Even around 1345—at the peak of pre-Plague population pressure—real wages of labourers in Holland had been higher than they were in the sixteenth century. In the Golden Age, real wages in Holland remained fairly constant and did not undergo the erosion found in other parts of Western Europe at the time,[268] but neither did they rise above the late medieval levels, even despite the technological leadership and big capital accumulation of the period.

In the period of dominant factor markets, the fifteenth to seventeenth century, the consumption patterns of ordinary people remained bleak, despite economic growth. Their diet in this period consisted of very basic foodstuffs, such as bread, peas, and beer, which took by far the largest share of their budget. This can be inferred from a report by Vicente Alvares, a Spanish visitor. While travelling through the Low Countries in the mid-sixteenth century, he observed that people's daily food was very scanty, consisting mainly of salted soup with cheese and black bread, and stew, washed down with huge quantities of cheap beer.[269] Thus, for the majority of the population, after having shifted from wheat bread—if any was eaten at all—to rye bread, from meat to cheese or peas, and from woollen clothes to linen,[270] there was not much scope for further cutting back.

---

[266] Lis and Soly, *Poverty*, 69.   [267] Van Bavel and van Zanden, 'The jump-start', 510–16.
[268] Van Zanden, *The rise*, 134–6; de Vries and van der Woude, *The first modern economy*, 627–32. See also Allen, 'The great divergence', 428–30.
[269] Van der Wee, 'Nutrition and diet'.   [270] Unger, 'Prices'.

If the already precarious situation of the poorer part of the population was further threatened by disastrous events, such as crop failures and resulting price rises, this led to crises. In the second half of the sixteenth century, there were several years of crises, which brought serious want, a sharp decline in the standard of living, epidemics, and high mortality, as in 1556–7 and 1565–6, the so-called hunger year.[271] At price peaks, this caused severe problems for large sectors of the population, exacerbated by speculation and hoarding by the rich. The latter happened despite the attempts by town governments to reduce price fluctuations in grain and bread by regulating or even freezing the price of bread, prohibiting speculation, buying and storing grain, and distributing it, combined with the distributions by charitable organizations.[272] Market integration also helped in the mitigation of the shocks. Grain imported from the Baltic, for instance, reduced price fluctuations and made rye relatively cheaper. Still, this was a positive element in a general picture of worsening living conditions for many. It was especially the wage labourers who, having become fully dependent on the market, were hit most severely. Their fate was not very different from that of their peers in other parts of Western Europe, as also evidenced by the fact that thousands of immiserated foreigners flocked into Holland,[273] where labour markets were open, opportunities for wage labour were abundant, and nominal wages were high, but the relative numbers of the poor in Holland were larger, their dependence on the market bigger, and their plight was more striking because they were living in a society in which GDP per capita and accumulated wealth had reached levels never seen in world history before.

We can get a keener insight into the development of general welfare thanks to the recent results of archaeological investigations into bones and dental remains. Probably the best indicator of the welfare position of common people, as observed in Chapter 1, is the development of average human stature, since this is determined by the quality of the diet, diseases, housing, and environmental conditions, that is, by the main elements of welfare.[274] The archaeological data show a clear decrease in stature over the period 1000–1800. In the Netherlands the average height of men in the early Middle Ages was 1.73/1.74 metres, declining to 1.71 in the thirteenth/fourteenth centuries, and to 1.69 in the fifteenth/sixteenth centuries. This low level remained all through the seventeenth and eighteenth centuries, to reach its lowest point in the first half of the nineteenth century, at 1.67 metres.[275] In the Golden Age, the shortest men (1.67) were found in Leiden, Holland's main industrial centre. This is not surprising, in view of the low wages, the hard work, the use of child labour, and the poor living conditions in this town, where the masses of textile workers lived in very small dwellings that mostly consisted of only

---

[271] Kuttner, *Het hongerjaar 1566*, 193–210.
[272] De Vries and van der Woude, *The first modern economy*, 621 ff. For the importance of charity: van Bavel and Rijpma, 'Formalized charity'.
[273] Lucassen, *Naar de kusten van de Noordzee*, passim.
[274] Steckel, 'Strategic ideas'. See also section 1.3, 26–7.
[275] Maat, 'Two millennia of male stature development'; van Bavel, *Manors and markets*, 143 and 378.

one or two rooms. More generally, living conditions and the quality of the diet decreased for most people in the northern Low Countries from the fifteenth century onwards.

At the end of the Golden Age, both real wages and average stature were lower than they had been around 1300, that is, before the rise of the factor markets. These observations, again, cast doubt upon the assumed favourable effects of factor markets. The Low Countries in the period from the eleventh to the thirteenth century, by using non-market systems for the exchange and allocation of land, labour, and capital, and combining these with output markets, had been very successful in coupling unprecedented growth in population numbers and area cultivated to real growth and maintaining relatively high standards of living. Also, this period had seen the development of the social balance of power and property, which stood at the basis of the favourable organization of factor markets; a balance which became eroded in the fifteenth to seventeenth century by the working of the same markets, as these gave rise to the market elites who increasingly succeeded in coupling political leverage to their economic dominance.

5

Epilogue
Markets in Modern States: England, the United States, and Western Europe, 1500–2000

Taking over the role of world economic leaders from the Netherlands after the seventeenth century were first England and next the United States. Both societies are pre-eminent examples of market economies, and will be discussed in this chapter, albeit tentatively. Since the book is not primarily focused on these modern cases, but on the pre-industrial ones, this chapter will be relatively brief and tentative. It will perhaps provoke criticism on account of its lack of extensiveness and depth. Also, scholars familiar with the English and American cases might feel unease in seeing these cases being treated in the same long-run perspective as the pre-industrial ones, whereas we are used to studying these cases more in detail and for shorter time frames only. The latter, however, may lead to a kind of myopia, resulting in an overestimation of the complexity of modern patterns and, in the opposite process, an underestimation of that of a more distant, pre-modern past. In this chapter, therefore, I will do the same as in the rest of the book: using a long-term perspective and focusing on the broad lines of one particular set of mechanisms in these societies, that is, those connected with market development.

Discussing these modern cases, albeit in a sketchy way, will to some extent enable us to see whether the process analysed in the preceding chapters did or did not change fundamentally after the Industrial Revolution. Leaving fully open the possibility of such a fundamental rupture would compromise the relevance of the insights gained in the preceding chapters, and probably unnecessarily so. The Industrial Revolution and the further technological advances of the nineteenth and twentieth centuries brought increase in scale and a growth of productive power, but the following discussion of the modern cases will enable us to assess to what extent the social and institutional processes, and their effects on economic development, have remained essentially similar.[1] In order to illustrate this point, and to invite further research along these lines, the following therefore concentrates on the essential aspects of the process, found in the realm of the organization of market exchange and its social context. These aspects perhaps have not received the attention in the subject literature they deserve, starting with, for instance, the fact that in both England and the United States these markets developed in a relatively

---

[1] See also section 6.3, 284–6.

egalitarian situation, just like the pre-industrial cases analysed before, as will be shown in the following discussion.

5.1. ENGLAND AND ITS NORTH AMERICAN COLONIES, 1500–1800

England experienced a first rise of factor markets in the twelfth and thirteenth centuries. The development of more secure property rights to land, in the late twelfth century, was instrumental in promoting the rise of land markets. Also, at the end of the thirteenth century, about a fifth or even a quarter of all labour in England was performed for wages.[2] Some have argued that this first, cautious development of factor markets promoted a much more effective allocation of resources and a strong growth of GDP per capita.[3] The latter assumption has become discredited in recent years, however, and seen as overly optimistic. Recent calculations instead show a very bleak picture for the twelfth and thirteenth centuries. It is assumed now that GDP per capita in England in the eleventh century was higher than earlier estimates and that subsequently, during the period of market development, it did not rise, but rather declined to a low level of $700–800 around 1300.[4] Moreover, the same period was characterized by growing inequality, to a large extent due to the working of land markets in a context of population growth, which led to accumulation of landholding, polarization, and widespread poverty.[5] Around the mid-fourteenth century, and following the Black Death, the factor markets in England stagnated and declined again.[6] Moreover, even though these markets had been important in the high Middle Ages, they had not become the dominant system of allocation of land, labour, and capital.

The Rise of Factor Markets to Dominance

The definite breakthrough of factor markets and the development of England towards being a market-dominated economy took place in the following centuries. The process is quantitatively not well documented, even though qualitative statements in the literature about this rise of markets are sometimes bold. We will try to assemble the quantitative material available. It shows that this rise was a slow process. With respect to land transfers, for instance, the lords and manorial courts retained their influence for a long time, even in Norfolk and other areas of eastern England—where manorialism was relatively weak in comparison with other parts

---

[2] Campbell, 'Factor markets'.

[3] Snooks, 'The dynamic role of the market', 49–54 even assumed a doubling of GDP per capita. The assumptions by Graeme Snooks were already criticized by Nicholas Mayhew and Christopher Dyer in the same volume as they were published, see Dyer, 'A note'.

[4] Figures for England kindly supplied by Bas van Leeuwen, 4 February 2013 (using, again, 1990 international dollars).

[5] Bekar and Reed, 'Land markets and inequality', where they demonstrate this effect through a simulation. See also Dyer, *Standards of living*, 287–96.

[6] Campbell, 'Factor markets', 98–9.

of England and freehold land was substantial.[7] This influence was slowly eroded, and by the sixteenth century the land market had become highly active, as is shown by various quantitative indicators. On the manor of Slaidburn, in Yorkshire, in the period 1520–70 on average 1.3 per cent of the area of copyhold land was transferred per year by way of extra-familial transactions, in the period 1570–1620 this was 1.4 per cent of the area, rising to more than 2 per cent in the period 1620–1720.[8] On a manor in the Lea Valley, north of London, in the period 1528–62, nearly 5 per cent of the copyhold land was transferred in the market each year.[9] Although this extraordinarily high figure is only a partial indicator, for a mobile type of land, figures for earlier periods were not nearly this high, and it does point to a strong rise in the sixteenth century.

Leasing out of demesnes had increased in the fourteenth and fifteenth centuries, and the majority of them continued to be leased, and subletting of customary and freehold land was also ubiquitous. Some of the customary and freehold land was turned into leasehold, not in a rapid switch produced by aggressive landlords, but in a gradual process.[10] As a result, by 1600, more than half or even up to three-quarters of all agricultural land in England was leased out to tenants.[11] Even if rents were not always fully market-determined, and social considerations and traditions continued to play a role in lease relationships, these figures signal that land—still by far the most important factor of production—by that time through large and active land and lease markets had become a commodity and it was mainly allocated through the market.

Credit and financial markets in the later Middle Ages also grew, though at a slow pace, slower than the land and lease markets. Available instruments of credit included bonds and bills of exchange, but most credit was informal and depended on personal relations.[12] This makes its importance more difficult to quantify, although samples of probate inventories indicate a clear expansion in the sixteenth century. More formal forms of funding debts developed more slowly. The legal rules that helped secure the investments of creditors seem to have been so rigorous that they discouraged debtors from contracting mortgages, at least initially. Also, the divided rights to land and the fragmented registration of these rights among several jurisdictions hindered the emergence of a mortgage system.[13] Several seventeenth-century pamphleteers noticed this situation and pressed for a reorganization of legal systems and registration, which was realized only up to the end of the century and resulted in a decline of litigation, also because households grew accustomed

---

[7] Whittle, *The development of agrarian capitalism*, 93 and 99.

[8] French and Hoyle, 'The land market'.

[9] Glennie, 'In search of agrarian capitalism', esp. 20. These figures are placed into a comparative perspective by van Bavel and Hoppenbrouwers, 'Landholding and land transfer'.

[10] Whittle, *The development of agrarian capitalism*, 305–10; Whittle, 'Leasehold tenure', nuancing the earlier stress of Brenner, 'The agrarian roots', 51–5 and 83–8, on the role of aggressive landlords.

[11] Whittle, 'Leasehold tenure', 150–1.

[12] Muldrew, *The economy of obligation*, 96 and 115 (mortgages).

[13] Schofield, 'Access to credit'; Allen, *Enclosure and the yeoman*, 102–4. See also van Bavel et al., 'The organisation of markets', 354–5.

to dealing with substantial amounts of credit secured along these now more efficient lines.[14]

As early as the late fourteenth century, a very substantial share of labour in England was allocated through the market. About a third of the population obtained most of their living from wage labour,[15] while many more peasants and townsmen performed some part-time wage labour, without being fully proletarianized. For the sixteenth century, most calculations of the importance of wage labour in the English countryside show that the share of wage workers in the total rural population at that point amounted to between a quarter and a third.[16] In Norfolk in around 1525, for instance, 20–35 per cent of the rural population consisted of wage labourers, and similar figures are found for Leicestershire and Lincolnshire. This hired labour was not fully free, especially not in the case of full-time wage labourers, since labour legislation was very strict. It led to the foundation of specialized courts and in many parts of the country to intensive prosecution of breaches of contract or violation of maximum wage rates.[17] Justices enforced the established wage levels while contracting was regulated in the quarter session courts. This structure was still in operation in the sixteenth century, as new statutes renewed both the obligation to work and the obligation to serve long terms.[18] Still, even though many customary and non-market determined elements continued to play a role, factor markets in England after their growth in the fifteenth and sixteenth centuries had become quite substantial and dynamic, with large shares, or even most, of land, lease land, and labour allocated through the market.

The Social and Political Context

Factor markets in England emerged, were organized, and grew within a relatively egalitarian context, at least where political influence is concerned, and during a period characterized by social and political revolts and reforms. Several authors have noticed this before, but they have put the emphasis too exclusively on the Glorious Revolution of 1688, as can be seen with North and Weingast, and with Acemoglu and Robinson, who all saw this event as the decisive step towards secure property rights and a market economy.[19] This emphasis on 1688 is misplaced. Factor markets had been developing from a much earlier period, and in a much more gradual process, as we have seen, and the social and political context in which they did so was shaped not only by the Glorious Revolution but also by a host of earlier revolts and movements from the late fourteenth century to the seventeenth. The context in which factor markets in England developed was greatly influenced by the collective protests in 1377 and the Peasants' Revolt of 1381, which—even

---

[14] Muldrew, *The economy of obligation*, 239.   [15] Dyer, *Standards of Living*, 211–14.
[16] Whittle, *The development of agrarian capitalism*, 227–31. An overview for England: van Bavel, 'The transition in the Low Countries', 288–9.
[17] Clark, 'Medieval labor law'; Steinfeld, *The invention of free labor*, 22–4 and 28–32.
[18] Whittle, *The development of agrarian capitalism*, 287–96.
[19] North and Weingast, 'Constitutions and commitment'; Acemoglu and Robinson, *Why nations fail*, 102–3.

though some legislation was even tightened after its suppression—hastened the decline of manorialism and unfreedom, while also strengthening the confidence and assertiveness of the peasant elites. This revolt was followed by a multitude of local and regional revolts.[20] Some of these later revolts spilled over to larger areas, and had a bigger effect, such as the Kent rebellion of 1450, with village notables, peasants, and craftsmen taking London, the revolts of the Sussex rebels with their radical and egalitarian ideas in 1450/1, targeting the gentlemen, the customary dues and the lordly exactions, or the Cornish rebellion of 1497.[21] Even despite suppression and defeat, the arbitrary and lordly dues and services in the areas where these revolts had taken place were often abolished or converted into fixed monetary payments, thus extending the opportunities for the market exchange of land and labour.

Equally important in the erosion of non-economic power of lords and the development of a social balance were the numerous cases of individual or local resistance. There were the refusals to pay rent, by way of active local resistance, individual or collective rent strikes or the refusal to perform customary services, with an increasing determination shown by peasants in the fifteenth century, as reconstructed for the West Midlands.[22] Even though this area saw hardly any large-scale revolts in the fourteenth to sixteenth century, small-scale resistance abounded. Dues associated with servility and the legal power of the lords were especially resented and targeted. This was not solely the work of peasants, or marginalized people, since large farmers, graziers, rich butchers, lawyers, and merchants in this period likewise participated and eroded the lordly power. Moreover, the growing security of more absolute and exclusive property rights, and the opportunities offered by emerging markets, made it more attractive for lords to let go of their now heavily contested non-economic, coercive instruments and to concentrate on using their wealth and property rights to land, as these brought ample revenues through the lease market.[23] The pressure exerted by other social actors and economic attractiveness thus reinforced each other in this process.

In the sixteenth century, social revolts often intermingled with religious movements or religiously inspired radicalism. There was the Pilgrimage of Grace in 1536, the Prayer Book Rebellion of 1548/9 in Cornwall and Devon, with the slogan 'Kill all the gentlemen', and the risings in Somerset, Wiltshire, East Anglia, and elsewhere in the same year.[24] In East Anglia, one of the motivations of the rebels was to counteract the attempts of lords to reimpose serfdom or to monopolize the local economy, which the rebels vehemently resisted. Actors from all groups in society, including the lower ones—who actively engaged in politics and eagerly criticized authority and the established order—therefore contributed to the emergence of a social balance. Even if their rebellions were suppressed, they helped to break the

---

[20] See, however, Cohn, 'Revolts of the late Middle Ages', who downplays the number of revolts, especially in the countryside.

[21] Mate, 'The economic and social roots'; Vallance, *A radical history of Britain*, 87–99.

[22] Dyer, 'A redistribution of incomes'.   [23] Brenner, 'The agrarian roots', 83–9.

[24] Wood, *The 1549 rebellions*, 21–6 and 40–69; Vallance, *A radical history of Britain*, 100–22.

power of the old rural magnates.[25] Jointly, these groups—each with their own interests and motivations—eroded the coercive and arbitrary power of lords and broke much of the remaining non-economic power they had over the exchange of land, labour, and capital.

The next steps in this process, which further freed up the factor markets, were taken in the seventeenth century. The latter part of the sixteenth century was characterized by growing social cleavages in the countryside, with a developing division between yeomen, who benefited from market opportunities and were socially mobile, and the poor. This cleavage perhaps temporarily precluded joint rural action,[26] but only as the calm before the storm. Around the mid-seventeenth century, England became the home of a wave of social revolts, in both towns and countryside, with a general mood of social agitation and the desire to change everything.[27] The revolutionary movement of the Levellers, which had strong egalitarian and democratic overtones, for instance, made a heavy impact in the 1640s, during the Civil War.[28] They put forward a programme of reforms including elections for parliaments, a wide franchise, reform of the legal system, equal rights before the law, an equitable tax system, and the abolition of monopolies, excises, and tithes. More radical, and less focused on constitutional reforms, was the movement of the Diggers, or True Levellers, which called for protection of the interests of the poor, communal ownership, and the abolition of land and labour markets.[29] Their numbers remained small, however, in contrast to the Levellers, who had massive support. The ideas of the Levellers perhaps represented most closely those of smaller tradesmen, yeomen, and craftsmen, that is, small-scale, independent producers in possession of the means of production, who seem to have longed for a lost, ideal world, but at the same time lived in a context in which markets became ever more important.

The Levellers were defeated in 1647 and again in 1649 by Oliver Cromwell, who was more conservative, and aborted the far-reaching ideas on communal property and full democracy. Still, Cromwell after the Civil War effectuated some reforms, perhaps more effectively than the Levellers could have done, as in the abolition of feudal rights and arbitrary taxation. These reforms did, at least indirectly, further broaden the opportunities for market exchange. Acts of 1656 and 1660, for instance, removed feudal levies and insecurities, and made land subject even more to the forces of supply and demand. As studies at the local level have shown,[30] this did not always translate into drastically higher turnover rates of land, but instead fitted into a longer developing pattern of fairly mobile landownership, substantial extra-familial, economic transactions, and land and lease markets becoming an integral aspect of rural society.

---

[25] Lachman, *Capitalists*, 180–5.   [26] Wood, *The 1549 rebellions*, 187–95 and 202–7.
[27] Hill, *The world turned upside down*, 13–15 and passim.
[28] Aylmer, *The Levellers*, 25 and 76–81 (petition of 1647); Macpherson, *The political theory*, 107–36 (franchise).
[29] Hill, *The world turned upside down*, 88–111, esp. 107–8.
[30] French and Hoyle, 'English individualism'. See for seventeenth-century market dynamism also below, 215–17.

This episode was followed by the Glorious Revolution of 1688, whose possible economic effects have been much more thoroughly investigated. This episode saw the intervention of Dutch troops, who invaded England—in part financed by Amsterdam bankers—were victorious and helped to bring about a regime change, in concert with allies and popular uprisings in England, Scotland, and Ireland. The Glorious Revolution helped to consolidate the earlier gains against lordly arbitrariness and it stimulated further institutional innovation, with various elements of fiscal policy, banking, and finance, and the political system with its greater degree of accountability of the executive, possibly borrowed from, or inspired by, examples from the Dutch Republic, but also building on social movement and thoughts developed within England.[31] Also, the Glorious Revolution sped up the inflow of Dutch capital into England that had started in the middle of the seventeenth century. Especially in the 1710s, millions of pounds of Dutch capital were invested in the English national debt and in shares in English companies.[32] The two market economies in different phases of their cycle now clearly interacted with each other. The Dutch cycle was in its final phase, with an abundance of capital, low interest rates and ample coercive, military instruments, which were now employed in England, and sped up developments there.

Some researchers have highlighted the supposed, direct effect of the Glorious Revolution on the organization and functioning of markets. More particularly, North and Weingast called attention to its effects on government funding.[33] The improved position of the English parliament guaranteed that the sovereign would commit to financial institutions—and would no longer renege on debts as was the practice before. This should have had a favourable effect on the amounts the kings could borrow in the capital market and the interest rates they paid. North and Weingast therefore used the decline in interest rates as an indicator for improved property rights. Again, they have underestimated earlier developments, however. Epstein, for instance, demonstrated that the interest rates in England did not drop sharply after 1688 but rather showed the continuation of a declining trend that had started in the fourteenth century, while Clark showed that there was hardly a discernible effect on rates of return on farmland, on rent charges, or on farm land prices.[34] Rather, the Glorious Revolution, the growing security of property rights, and the growth of the capital market all were part of a much broader and more gradual process, starting at least in the sixteenth century.

This process took place within a relatively equal distribution of property and, especially, power. Compared with other parts of Europe, broad sections of the population had access to the vote; in 1688 a robust 15 per cent of men were

[31] Scott, *England's troubles*, 484–90. Pincus, *1688: The first modern revolution*, 221–53 and 366–99, stresses the endogenous developments within England, as also done by Murphy, *The origins of English financial markets*, 4, 13, and 43–9.

[32] Arrighi, *The long twentieth century*, 206–7. See also Adams, *The familial state*, 151; and section 4.4, 201–3.

[33] North and Weingast, 'Constitutions and commitment'.

[34] Epstein, *Freedom and growth*, 16–29; Clark, 'The political foundations'. See for criticism on the focus on 1688 also Murphy, *The origins of English financial markets*, 4, 13, and 43–9; Ogilvie and Carus, 'Institutions and economic growth', 426–8.

enfranchised.[35] Also, calculations suggest that in 1688 the English elite extracted about 60 per cent of the surpluses available within society. This rate is relatively low, compared to other pre-industrial societies.[36] Income inequality around 1688 was fairly average, at a Gini of about 0.45, but the 9 per cent of total income earned by the top 1 per cent is, again, very low by the standards of the time.[37] The fact that wages were in theory regulated by statute, but in practice often set through bargaining, while servants were highly mobile, can likewise be considered a sign of an equal balance between servants and employers.[38] The position of poorer wage labourers or seasonal workers was relatively favourable, also thanks to the Poor Law. Out of the complex web of late medieval arrangements, in the late sixteenth century a national poor law system had been set out and codified. Rates were set by parliament and the system was funded by a compulsory tax on property. The amount of money redistributed in this way to the poor, alongside some 1 per cent of GDP redistributed through other forms of formalized relief, was fairly substantial: it amounted to 1 to 1.5 per cent of GDP during the seventeenth and eighteenth centuries.[39] This was not on the basis of arbitrary charity, but was a uniform entitlement. It offered security to poor people and made it more attractive to enter the labour market, as it made them less vulnerable to irregular employment and wage fluctuations.[40] As a result, the system helped to maintain a large and growing pool of wage labourers.

Dominant Factor Markets

Within this context, early modern England became a full market economy, with the market becoming the main allocation system of land and labour. The extent and importance of market exchange in England is sometimes sketched in brilliant colours, as by Macpherson, who claimed that England had become an individualistic market society by the seventeenth century, with market relations permeating all social relations, a claim others later extended—probably too far—to periods even further back in time.[41] The dominant role of markets in seventeenth-century England is also evident from the changes in thinking about economy and society, that clearly sought to capture the influence of the market.[42] These new ideas, in part taking inspiration from the Dutch and their market economy—which was watched with a mixture of jealousy and admiration by English observers—were

---

[35] Acemoglu and Robinson, *Why nations fail*, 102 (the optimistic view); Lindert, *Growing public*, 72 (figures). See also Williamson, *American suffrage*, 20–2 and 62–5.

[36] Milanovic, Lindert, and Williamson, 'Measuring ancient inequality', 17 and 50–1.

[37] Milanovic, Lindert, and Williamson, 'Measuring ancient inequality', 71 and 76–8.

[38] Muldrew, *The economy of obligation*, 41; Kussmaul, *Servants*, 35–9 and 49 ff.

[39] Lindert, 'Poor relief before the welfare state'; van Bavel and Rijpma, 'Formalized charity'.

[40] Solar, 'Poor relief'.

[41] Macpherson, *The political theory*, 53–68. For the later, more extreme—and contested—claim: Macfarlane, *The origins of English individualism*. For a nuanced criticism of Macfarlane: French and Hoyle, 'English individualism'.

[42] Appleby, *Economic thought and ideology*, 19, 73–98 (the Dutch example), and 245–8.

geared towards redefining social priorities, with an emphasis on economic, market-determined relationships.

Indeed, in this period, many of the non-economic considerations that had remained were now being removed.[43] The remaining manorial and customary restrictions on land transfer were targeted, while the growing availability of mortgage finance also pushed up the activity of the land market, which was buoyant in the seventeenth century.[44] Especially after c. 1650, market competition for land led to small peasant landowners losing their landed property to yeoman farmers or large landholders, who subsequently leased out the land.[45] Also, customary tenancies and life leases were gradually replaced by short leases for a specified number of years. The lease market became highly dynamic, as shown for Romney Marsh in the second half of the seventeenth century.[46] Here, some two-thirds of the land was leased out for short terms and tenancies frequently changed hands. Tenants used the lease market to create large-scale capitalist farms, often formed by leasing land from various owners at the same time, and in the process ousting the small-scale farmers.

In the labour market, contracts or agreements were voluntarily entered into. Contracts were often for long terms, of a year or even more, and they offered the employer ample scope for rigorous control over the labourer during the term.[47] At the end of the contract, however, mobility of farm servants was high, with hiring fairs forming a main occasion for masters and prospective servants to meet. Casual labourers, hiring themselves out for the day or the task, had even more autonomy, and were fully free after completion of their task. Wages for labourers were often on credit, giving rise to numerous law suits about credit, also by poor people who had performed work and were owed their wage. To a surprisingly large extent poor people were prepared to sue their wealthier employers or neighbours for wages or other payments owed, and were successful at this, as is shown for the Norfolk town of King's Lynn in the seventeenth century.[48]

During the eighteenth century, a large amount of additional labour was released on to the market, as a result of the rises in agricultural productivity, the enclosures, and the related shift to less labour-intensive pastoral farming.[49] This does not mean that labourers did always find themselves in a favourable position, in view of the low level of wages in the period. As noted, however, their insecurity was somewhat lessened through the Poor Law. The effects of the Poor Law on labour mobility are harder to assess. The workers now were no longer solely dependent on kin networks, and this may have increased mobility, but legislation also tied them to their own parish in order to be eligible for relief.[50]

[43] Macpherson, *The political theory*, 61–2. For the rural economy: Overton, *Agricultural revolution*, 147–88.

[44] French and Hoyle, 'The land market', 353–9.

[45] French and Hoyle, 'The land market', 360–3.   [46] Hipkin, 'Tenant farming'.

[47] Steinfeld, *The invention of free labor*, 25–41; Kussmaul, *Servants*, 31–4 and 49–69 (mobility and hiring fairs).

[48] Muldrew, 'Credit and the courts'.

[49] See the careful discussion by Allen, *Enclosure and the yeoman*, 150–70.

[50] For the eighteenth century: Kussmaul, *Servants*, 66–9.

Although the cash nexus became more important, these early modern factor markets were not fully anonymous, but often embedded in social relations. In particular, the fact that credit, and credit-based exchange of labour or land, needed trust, suggests the importance of social and moral elements, to some extent embedded in non-market communities, while issues of power—both at the household and the societal level—also played a major part.[51] At the same time, the development of clear and secure market institutions, often upheld and enforced by the public authorities as a third party, paved the way for a more anonymous exchange of land and labour, and of capital in particular, also outside communities.

The financial market grew, especially in the late seventeenth century. At that point, investment capital had become abundant and financial services more advanced, while newly established joint-stock companies offered new opportunities for investment and speculation. These developments, centred in London, gave rise in the 1690s to the first small boom in the stock market and an active trade in derivatives.[52] Initially, the amount of wealth invested in joint-stock companies remained limited, however, at 1–2 per cent of total wealth in 1695. Even though in the past some have argued that an efficiently organized banking and stock market in Britain was among the main causes of the Industrial Revolution, it is clear that the eighteenth-century financial landscape was very heterogeneous and private alternatives for financing investments, based on trust and networks, were predominant, even up to the nineteenth century.[53] Banks were important not so much for providing long-term credit for founding factories, which was relatively inexpensive anyway, as for smoothing financial transfers and allowing for short-term credit.[54] More important in the rise of English financial markets were the needs of the state, with public expenditures from the late seventeenth century quickly rising and the increase in taxation not being able to keep pace. The state thus resorted, first, to short-term borrowing and later to the sale of annuities and long-term loans in the open market. The associated financial innovations, and the checks placed on the arbitrary powers of the ruler, necessary in order to attract capital, laid the foundation for the further growth of financial markets and of public debts.[55]

In agriculture, developments were equally fundamental and they were intimately linked to the dynamism brought by factor markets. Enclosure broke and removed the customary and communal rights to land and opened up more land to be privatized and freely exchanged through the market. Large landholdings were leased out and accumulated by large tenant farmers, who specialized their agricultural production for the market, as equally done by the medium-sized farmers, the

---

[51] The first stressed by Muldrew, 'Interpreting the market'; the second by Daunton, *Progress and poverty*, 16.

[52] Murphy, *The origins of English financial markets*, 11–25 and 37.

[53] Mokyr, 'Entrepreneurship and the Industrial Revolution', 191–2; Cull et al., 'Historical financing'.

[54] Pollard, 'Fixed capital', 301 and 308–9.

[55] Murphy, *The origins of English financial markets*, 37–43; North and Weingast, 'Constitutions and commitment' stress more the role of the Glorious Revolution.

yeomen.[56] Together, they drove the agricultural revolution of the seventeenth century, with its advances in technology and agrarian techniques, including the introduction of advanced crop rotations, mechanization, selective breeding, and agrarian specialization. This resulted in a marked rise of per capita output after 1600. By 1750 output per agricultural worker exceeded that of all other European countries.[57] How this increased the ability of agriculture to sustain a growing population, freed an increasing portion of the population for non-agricultural activities, and fed the industrial workforce, and also sped up the accumulation of capital later invested in other sectors, is by now a quite familiar story. It also formed a main component in the growth of GDP per capita in England, which in the eighteenth century approached the levels reached in the Dutch Republic, in order to overtake them around 1800.[58]

These developments led to a steady rise in urbanization rates, especially from the beginning of the seventeenth century.[59] The late medieval period in England had been one of stagnating or even declining urban population numbers, but the sixteenth and seventeenth centuries saw renewed urban growth, and London was in front during this process, with a huge population spurt from c. 75,000 in the 1550s to c. 400,000 in the 1650s. At that point, London became the largest city in Western Europe; only Paris was of a comparable size. London sustained this process of rapid growth into the late seventeenth and eighteenth centuries, with its population rising to almost a million around 1800. The total urbanization rate in England rose simultaneously, to c. 33 per cent or more around 1700, and to no less than 42 per cent around 1800, the highest level in the world.

The American Colonies

At the same time, in the British colonies in North America, large towns were almost non-existent. In 1700 the largest city was Boston with only 7,000 inhabitants, rising to 15,000 around 1750. In the eighteenth century, cities started to grow, but the level of urbanization remained very low and the colonies remained overwhelmingly rural.[60] In 1800, New York and Philadelphia were the largest cities with a little more than 60,000 inhabitants, still only one-fifteenth the size of London. On the other hand, and despite their small size, the North American cities were favourably located near the sea and formed important transport links between their hinterland and the world market. These were not consumer or extractive cities, but producer and trade cities, operating in a society in which a lot of the ideals of seventeenth-century England were realized and markets could develop unhampered by coercion and arbitrariness.

[56] Allen, *Enclosure and the yeoman*, passim, while the role of large landlords and tenant farmers is stressed by Brenner, 'The agrarian roots'. See also Overton, *Agricultural revolution*, 135–67.

[57] Allen, 'Economic structure', 22.

[58] Broadberry et al., *British economic growth*, 380–1. For the role of the agricultural sector: Brenner, 'The agrarian roots', 105–13.

[59] De Vries, *European urbanization*, passim.

[60] Wells, 'The population of England's colonies', 100–1.

Society in the British colonies in northern America, especially in the northeastern colonies, or Free States, on which we will focus here, was shaped in a way that created a wide distribution of social, political, and economic power. Especially when focusing on the population of white settlers, and leaving aside the native population, this broad distribution was much wider even than had emerged in England. After the first English settlers arrived in Virginia in 1607, there was some experimentation with feudal types of colonial organization, in which a key role was assigned to aristocrats, but these attempts were quickly aborted. In 1618, the Virginia Company turned to attracting settlers by offering them land and a form of self-rule.[61] In Virginia, all adult, white, propertied men had the right to vote for a representative assembly, and in the following decades, other American colonies would follow the same practice. This linked up with the mindset of many of the immigrants coming to the American colonies. Among them were substantial numbers of unorthodox thinkers and dissenters who valued equity and placed great value on equality in speech, manner, and work relationships.[62] These settlers, including thousands of Puritans, also brought their relatively advanced and recently developed legal institutions, representative forms of governance, and communal ideals from England, including their desire to be free of lordly arbitrariness, resembling the ideas of the English reformers and Levellers.[63]

A strong, land-owning nobility, as was found in England, remained absent here. Attempts to introduce a more hierarchical society with a strong elite at a later stage failed, also because of the ample availability of land, offering too many opportunities for settlers to be coerced.[64] The absence of large numbers of natives to be exploited as workers and the comparative disadvantage in the production of plantation crops using slave labour made the northern parts of the British colonies more dependent on European labourers. Some of these were indentured servants and unfree labourers, but more crucial were the free people and their human capital. This, in combination with the abundancy of land, contributed to the growth of a relatively equal society. Moreover, many free settlers wanted a society in which the highest and lowest ranking were eliminated, and noble privileges and claims would be erased. This ideal, shared with many of the mid-seventeenth century English rebels, was realized here more fully than in the motherland.

One element in this was the economic independency of the common people. The English settlers were obsessed with acquiring their own land, preferably by way of ownership of a family-sized farm. It was the ideal of many to become an independent yeoman, an ideal likewise imported from Britain, where this status had become much harder to realize.[65] Even though wealth in the American colonies was not equally distributed, at a Gini of 0.64–0.67 in New England and other

[61] McFarlane, *The British in the Americas*, 38–49 and 191–5.

[62] Belich, *Replenishing the earth*, 157–63; McFarlane, *The British in the Americas*, 47–9, 63–8, and 159–60. For indenture: Steinfeld, *The invention of free labor*, 129, 173, and passim.

[63] Konig, *Law and society*, 17–22.

[64] Acemoglu and Robinson, *Why nations fail*, 19–28; and—with more emphasis on the role of factor endowments—Sokoloff and Engerman, 'History lessons'. See also Acemoglu and Robinson, *Why nations fail*, 351–7, for the different trajectory of the south of the United States.

[65] Kulikoff, *The agrarian origins*, 37–41.

parts of the north,[66] freeholding indeed became widespread. In eighteenth-century New Hampshire, the proportion of freeholding men varied from 50 to 90 per cent per village, and figures were similarly high in Virginia, Connecticut, and elsewhere. Also, income inequality in the colonies was much lower than in England. At a Gini of a little over 0.4, and the richest 1 per cent of households only having 7 per cent of total income, colonial America in 1774 was the most equal society in the documented parts of the eighteenth-century world.[67] The fact that 40 per cent of households in the middle of the distribution received 42 per cent of total income shows the presence of a large and strong segment of middling groups in American society, and again confirms the egalitarian picture.

Another element was political equality. Even before 1776, there was a relatively wide franchise, as this was based on freehold landed property, which was widely distributed, while for local elections the qualifications were often set even lower, for instance opened up to all householders.[68] During the American Revolution, many called for abandoning the qualifications for suffrage altogether.

It was within this context of relative equity in the eighteenth century that output markets quickly grew, while the social and institutional foundations of factor markets, with open access to broad groups, were also laid. Notwithstanding the high value they placed on economic independence and owning one's own farm, at the same time many colonists used credit and they became involved in lease markets and, in particular, output markets from an early date. This was in interaction with a process in which these output markets were becoming large and easily accessible, through a dense network of local markets, merchants, and retailers, well-established in town and countryside by the eighteenth century, and helped by the dissemination of information about prices, supply, and demand through regularly published lists.[69] Based on the structure of the family farm, most farmers produced not for subsistence but for the market and were geared towards increasing surpluses.

Common and civil law, in part imported from England, helped to protect property rights, stimulated trade in land and facilitated borrowing, even though it did not result in the rise of big, anonymous factor markets right away. Loans in the early period, for instance, remained mostly embedded in social relations, between people who knew each other, and usually did not entail the payment of interest or at most charged the 'lawful interest' fixed at 6 per cent.[70] Impersonal transactions in a formalized credit market remained limited, at least in the countryside, up to c. 1780.

Likewise, there were some limitations on the rise of a labour market. One of these was the importance of systems of indenture and the widespread use of indentured

---

[66] For the second half of the eighteenth century: Rothenberg, 'The emergence of a capital market', 785.

[67] Lindert and Williamson, 'American incomes', 755–8.

[68] Williamson, *American suffrage*, 12–19, 22–39 (freeholding), and 92–116 (effect of the Revolution). For the high share of freeholders also: Kulikoff, *The agrarian origins*, 39–40.

[69] Atack, 'America', 537–41.

[70] Rothenberg, 'The emergence of a capital market', 787–90. For the seventeenth century: Konig, *Law and society*, 83–8.

servants, and, in Virginia and further south, of slavery.[71] Also, free English settlers often resented the idea of selling their labour in the market and felt this to be degrading.[72] If wage labour was performed, in the seventeenth century this was often controlled by religious and social norms about the 'just wage', while wage rates were sometimes fixed by statutes, even though pockets of wage labour existed.[73] By the mid-eighteenth century, however, many of these norms were eroded and wage labour grew, and closer to the end of the century labour markets became competitive and integrated, as indicated by the wage convergence observed in New England.

For land, these developments had begun at an earlier stage. Land was increasingly granted out or sold and organized as private property, and could be freely transacted through the market, sometimes giving rise to speculation, as shown for mid-seventeenth century Maryland.[74] In other areas, as in Massachusetts, the abundance of cheap land caused land sales to be recorded in a careless way, with land titles only vaguely defined. It was only as land became more scarce, and sales to non-residents became more important, that litigation over landed property grew and recording became more exact, a process that did not develop fully until c. 1700.

Building on these emerging markets and their sound institutional foundations, and on the wide distribution of property, the American economy started to grow. This is reflected by the important position the American colonies acquired, for instance, in maritime commerce and iron production, in the latter respect surpassing Britain by 1776.[75] There is some debate about the rate of economic growth in the eighteenth century, and whether and how to include the indigenous population in the calculations. Angus Maddison's estimates of GDP per capita show a substantial rise of 0.7 per cent per annum from 1700 to 1820, to reach $1,250 in the later year, that is, quickly catching up with the level of Western Europe, while other scholars have put growth in the eighteenth century on a much lower level.[76] The most recent figures endorse the optimistic view, indicating substantial growth up to 1774 and average incomes already reaching a higher level than in England, followed by a setback as a result of war damages in the period 1774–1800.[77] Even despite this temporary setback, income levels around 1800 were fairly high, and they would quickly rise in concert with the development of factor markets in the decades around 1800, to be discussed in the next section.

---

[71] Steinfeld, *The invention of free labor*, 11–12, 129, and 173. See also Atack, 'America', 543–5.

[72] Kulikoff, *The agrarian origins*, 37–8.

[73] Rothenberg, 'The emergence of farm labor markets', 548 and 550, and passim for the following. More emphasis on the freedom of wage labour: Innes, *Labor in a new land*, 73–7, 180, and passim.

[74] Smith, 'The indentured servant and land speculation'. For the following on Massachusetts: Konig, *Law and society*, 40–4 and 186–7.

[75] Larson, *The market revolution*, 61–2.

[76] Maddison, *The world economy*, 249–50 and 262–4. For more pessimistic estimates: Mancall and Weiss, 'Was economic growth likely'.

[77] Lindert and Williamson, 'American incomes'.

England as the Leading Economy

In the meantime, in England a growth of factor markets proceeded and, now, financial markets also grew. Private investments in agriculture and industry remained predominant, and most capital until the nineteenth century came from private funds or local networks, but the well-functioning financial markets in England, and the trust placed by foreigners in them, also made capital available for investments. English financial markets increasingly formed an outlet for the accumulated capital of the Dutch elites. At the beginning of the eighteenth century, about a quarter to a third of the British national debt, the stock in the Bank of England, and the stock in the East India Company was held by Dutch investors and Dutch capital kept on flowing into England, also to finance private enterprises.[78] This was how the last phase of the Dutch cycle interacted with, and accelerated, developments in England.

In the process, London slowly gained ground on Amsterdam as the world centre of finance, and in the late eighteenth century it fully took over this role. At the same time, the English national debt was growing quickly, to more than the national income in the 1760s, and it reached a peak in the 1820s at twice the national income.[79] The spread of these debts over the population was fairly wide. Around the mid-eighteenth century there were 50–60,000 public creditors in Britain, rising to 300,000 three-quarters of a century later. Among them were tens of thousands of single, middle-class women who lived on annuities and typically possessed government securities of several hundreds or thousands of pounds.[80] In total, they held about a quarter of these securities. Most of the debt, however, was held by a much smaller group of rentiers, who formed a monied interest that grew in power, to the minds of some thinkers even threatening free government.[81]

In the period when Adam Smith was living and working, in the second half of the eighteenth century, this accumulation of resources through factor markets had only just started and it was hardly apparent as yet. Output markets in England were thriving, factor markets had become relatively free, and the effects of these dynamic markets on economic growth were positive. For Adam Smith, apart from the slavery used on English-owned plantations, some guild regulation, and the mercantile inclinations of its trade policy, England was the model society of his time. It would be the first society able to enter his stage of 'natural liberty'.[82] Adam Smith formulated his ideas during the most favourable phase of the English cycle, as factor markets exerted a positive influence, which probably in part explains his positive judgement on the functioning of markets. His ideas therefore need to be placed in their historical context, instead of being generalized.[83]

---

[78] Arrighi, *The long twentieth century*, 205–7; Brezis, 'Foreign capital flows', 52–5, although her estimates of the exact amounts involved have later been criticized.

[79] Daunton, *Trusting Leviathan*, 47–9; Clark, 'Debts, deficits and crowding out'.

[80] Green and Owens, 'Gentlewomanly capitalism?'.

[81] This view can be found with David Hume: Daunton, *Trusting Leviathan*, 38–9.

[82] Smith (Campbell and Skinner, eds), *Wealth of nations*, 606–7 and 687–8.

[83] See section 1.3, 21–2, for the more negative expectations Adam Smith himself had of the market economy in a more mature stage.

Still, together with Adam Smith, one cannot but be impressed by the rapid changes and growth in eighteenth-century England, and these changes would proceed in the first half of the next century. Monopolies, tariffs, and privileges were further removed. There was a growing and almost general belief that these obstructions to free markets were wrong. In other Western European countries, these views were also expressed at the time, but in England they won and were actually put into practice.[84] In their turn, the highly dynamic and well-organized factor markets sustained entrepreneurship and technological innovation, in a process helping England to become the workshop of the world.[85] First, agriculture had been revolutionized, with the commodification of land and labour, and the growth of commercialized production, using increasing amounts of capital and helping to substitute capital for labour.[86] Next, factor and output markets offered the infrastructure to combine the labour of workers released from agricultural work, the surpluses of food, and the accumulated capital in order to boost industrial production and the services sector. Especially striking is the ample use of wage labour in the domestic industries, factories, mining, and services, with labourers often hired by way of internal subcontracting. Wage labour grew rapidly, while short-term contracts, payment per output, and the hiring of overseers became instruments for entrepreneurs to push up the productivity of hired labour.[87] In an often painful process, for instance, tens of thousands of semi-independent hand-loom weavers were turned into factory workers, or replaced by them, and subjected to the factory discipline and its fixed working hours.[88] The associated use of machines and fossil fuels made it possible to greatly push up labour productivity. In the eighteenth and nineteenth centuries, and especially from c. 1780 on, English GDP per capita leaped forward, and the English economy clearly became the leading economy in the world.[89]

5.2. THE DECLINE OF ENGLAND AND THE RISE OF THE UNITED STATES, 1800–1950

At the same time, in the first half of the nineteenth century, factor markets in England were further opened up. In the 1820s, there was a crusade to further stimulate market exchange, to free up land, labour, capital, and goods for the market, and to remove anything which was perceived to be a hindrance to free markets. In part this crusade was propagated by the rising industrialists, traders, and bankers, and motivated by self-interest, but there was a more general notion within English society that free markets were a good thing, resulting from the

---

[84] See section 5.2, 223–4.
[85] Mokyr, 'Entrepreneurship and the Industrial Revolution', who stresses the role of informal institutions.
[86] Overton, *Agricultural revolution*.   [87] Daunton, *Progress and poverty*, 182–4 and 229–31.
[88] Thompson, *The making of the English working class*, 297–321; Daunton, *Progress and poverty*, 178–86.
[89] Broadberry et al., *British economic growth*, 197–9, 376 and appendix 5.3; Maddison, *The world economy*, 97.

growing belief that market exchange was not a zero-sum game but something that would benefit all involved.[90] This crusade was successful especially in the 1830s and 1840s, and it resulted in the adoption of policies and legislative measures to this end. One example is the Poor Law Amendment Act of 1834, promoted by the large manufacturers, which reduced poor relief and subjected labourers more to the price-setting mechanisms of the labour market. Also, labourers were increasingly paid only with money wages, while non-monetary entitlements and rights to perquisites were banned.[91] From 1821, the Mint began to produce large numbers of small, copper coins, making it possible for employers to actually pay their workers in cash. The same period also saw restrictions on the use of coercion over groups of vulnerable workers, including the Factory Act of 1833, which tried to stop the worst excesses in the employment of child labour, and the Slavery Abolition Act. In the output market there was the Anti Corn Law Bill of 1846, which removed import restrictions on grain.

Financial markets were promoted by the adoption of the gold standard and the convertibility of the pound, measures that also enhanced the position of the City of London in global capital markets, at the instigation of new commercial and banking elites in the City.[92] Land markets were also further stimulated, for instance through parliamentary enclosure, which reached a peak between c. 1760 and 1830. This process, in which common rights and collective agricultural practices were removed through acts of parliament, opened up more land for market exchange, but in a coercive way, in which only the interests of the owners of farms and landed property were served and those of the owners of use rights on the land were largely neglected, as the outgrowth of a process in which their rights had already become more marginalized.[93] Also, the lobby begun in the 1820s to adapt the land laws to the working of the market, and the actions of the agitators for 'Free Trade in Land', resulted in more reforms of the land market around 1870 and increased its accessibility and the liquidity of landed property.[94]

These nineteenth-century policies are sometimes regarded as the start of modern free markets—this is how Polanyi saw them.[95] Rather, however, they should be seen as a final phase in this process, and not as the first stage. As we have noted above, recent research pushes back the first phase in the rise to dominance of English factor markets instead to the fifteenth and sixteenth centuries, and locates a further acceleration in the seventeenth century, with England having already become a market economy by then. These measures in the first half of the nineteenth century did indeed stimulate the further growth of factor markets, but now to a substantial extent through the pressure and political leverage of those who had gained wealth and power through the functioning of the same markets, as

---

[90] Mokyr, 'Entrepreneurship and the Industrial Revolution'; Daunton, *Progress and poverty*, 533–45. See also Polanyi, *The great transformation*, 143.

[91] Daunton, *Progress and poverty*, 421–5 and, for the production of small coins, 425–6.

[92] Ingham, *Capitalism divided?*, 97, 101–12, and 126–7.

[93] Overton, *Agricultural revolution*, 158–61.   [94] Offer, *Property and Politics*, 23–40.

[95] Polanyi, *The great transformation*, 82–9 and 141–5, who particularly emphasizes the Poor Law Amendment Act of 1834.

industrial entrepreneurs and merchants. Through the process, these market elites were enabled to further accumulate wealth, and they reached the position where they could use the state machinery to change the rules of market organization, to enforce these pro-market measures or even to coerce others to subject themselves more to factor markets.[96]

Inequality, Counter-Reaction, and Stagnation in England

GDP per capita in England in this period grew quickly. Real wages also increased, but much more slowly. In combination with the deteriorating living conditions of many workers, this even makes it difficult to say whether the lot of most people in this period improved. The optimistic view holds that real wages reached a low around 1800, but in the 1820s surpassed the levels of the mid-eighteenth century and then grew substantially to reach in the 1860s a level even higher than the fifteenth-century high, while others hold a more pessimistic view and posit that real earnings of manual workers only slightly grew over this period.[97] At the same time, despite the improvement of the position of children brought by the Factory Act of 1833 and possible gains in wages, it is clear that the non-monetary aspects of the lives of the great majority of people in this period remained gloomy or even deteriorated. The period saw lengthy working days, monotonous work in unhealthy factories, bad living conditions in urban slums, pauperization, and a worsening of the diet on average. The decline in average welfare is reflected in the decrease of average height in England, starting around 1730, with the low reached around the mid-nineteenth century.[98] The Poor Law Amendment Act of 1834 greatly reduced poverty relief, which had already started to decline from c. 1820 onwards and around 1850 had been reduced as a share of GDP by more than 60 per cent.[99]

This happened in a context of rising inequality. Income shares at the top rose and those at the bottom fell. The share in the national income of the wealthiest part increased, slowly, from 1688 to 1801, and sharply rose in the next half century, and the share of capital owners in national income rose to an unprecedented high of more than 40 per cent, reached in the mid-nineteenth century.[100] Wealth inequality, even though already at a high level in Britain, continued to rise until the outbreak of the First World War, as the top 1 per cent owned almost 70 per cent of total wealth.

This process was halted, and even reversed, from the mid-nineteenth century onwards, and even more clearly from the First World War, starting with the rise of real wages. Between the 1860s and the 1920s real wages in England more than

---

[96] As highlighted by Polanyi himself: *The Great Transformation*, 145–7. See also Elbaum and Lazonick, 'The decline of the British economy'.

[97] Clark, 'The condition of the working class', 1311 and 1317–19. A much more pessimistic view is found with Feinstein, 'Pessimism perpetuated'.

[98] Komlos, 'Shrinking in a growing economy?'. For a nuanced discussion of well-being and heights: Daunton, *Progress and poverty*, 439–41.

[99] Lindert, *Growing public*, 46–8, 54, and 71–3.

[100] Williamson, *Did British capitalism breed inequality?*, 200–1 and passim; Piketty, *Capital*, 200 and 343–4.

doubled.[101] In part, this was the effect of innovation, technological progress, and gains made in labour productivity. This progress, however, had already been there for some three-quarters of a century but it had not improved living standards of workers and ordinary people earlier, due to the simultaneous growth of inequality. More crucial than technology, or an almost automatic drive towards equality as a result of rising GDP per capita or sectoral changes, were the growing self-organization of workers and the threat of revolution.[102]

Labour movements in England could draw on older radical ideas that were kept alive among domestic workers and artisans, and which were further provoked by the growth of manufacturing towns, forming a fertile ground for the rise of labour associations.[103] Among the now emerging movements were those of the Luddites, with the discontent of the workers turning against the labour-saving machines of entrepreneurs who paid low wages, and later that of the Chartists, pressing for political reforms in the period 1838–48. These, and other social movements, arose out of anger or aversion to the abuses and excesses produced by the now dominant market economy and the desire to develop some social protection.[104] Local unions were established, as in Birmingham in 1830, even despite restrictive legislation, and also the attempts to form national, general unions became more concrete and successful, while trade unions became legalized in 1871. Fuelled by the depression of the 1870s and 1880s, there was a series of bitter disputes and strikes in the urban centres, with the successful strike of the London dock workers in 1889 being the most famous. Now, unskilled and casual labourers also became involved in labour conflicts and trade union activities. Moreover, trade unions could draw upon the workplace organizations and their substantial autonomy vis-à-vis the employers.[105] In the last quarter of the nineteenth century, the position of trade unions had become well entrenched.

The rise of these movements, and their success, can to some part be attributed to the exogenous influences, which at this stage of history had become stronger than ever before and affected England more than the earlier cases discussed in this book, where the cycles had been almost fully endogenous. Revolutionary ideas and the threat of revolution emanated especially from the United States and France, as with the revolutions of 1776 and 1789. These evoked sympathy from some in England, and helped stimulate the heightened radicalism and the formation of workers' organizations in the 1790s, and they provoked anger and fear among others.[106] The revolutions of 1848 in France, Germany, and elsewhere in Europe and the Paris Commune of 1871 had a similar effect.

In the decades around 1900, interaction with socio-political developments elsewhere even further increased in force, especially that with developments in continental Western Europe, an area that in the latter part of the nineteenth century

---

101 Clark, 'The condition of the working class', 1325.
102 See for similar arguments made against the 'Kuznets curve' section 6.2, 260–1.
103 Thompson, *The making of the English working class*, 207–13. Chase, *Early trade unionism*, 40–4.
104 Polanyi, *The Great Transformation*, 175–82.
105 Elbaum and Lazonick, 'The decline of the British economy', 70.
106 Vallance, *A radical history of Britain*, 255–82. See also Chase, *Early trade unionism*, 78–83; Thompson, *The making of the English working class*, 111–203.

started its first stage of a new cycle, characterized by growing self-organization, political struggles, and the rudimentary development of state welfare provisions.[107] Both in continental Western Europe and in Britain in this period the franchise was widened and more people were granted access to decision making. The extension of the vote in 1884–5, to about two-thirds of English men, quickened the decline of the parliamentary influence of the large landholders and, through the ensuing legal changes, had direct effects on social spending and redistribution. After a low in social transfers as a share of English GDP had been reached in the period 1840–90, at less than 1 per cent of GDP, first pensions were raised and next, from 1920, poor relief was raised, resulting in a rise of social transfers to 2 per cent of GDP. Despite these rises, however, England now lagged behind the countries on the European continent in the development of a welfare system.[108]

Instead of directly entering the latter phases of the cycle, accompanied by further growing inequality of property and power, England thus in some respects saw a countervailing process, at least for almost a century, in part under the influence of the new cycle starting for its continental European neighbours.[109] In other respects, however, the developments in England took a course similar to that of the earlier cases. For one, enormous sums were invested in the extension and preservation of a colonial empire that spanned the globe and mainly benefited merchants, bankers, shippers, and entrepreneurs, and those involved in securing and administering the colonies. The profits accrued only slightly to society as a whole, while costs and deficits were paid for mainly by ordinary people.[110]

Also, the second half of the nineteenth century saw English money move out of trade and production into finance; a shift also found with the three earlier cases discussed. Perhaps as a result of the sharp competition in output markets, and the declining profit margins, investing in financial markets became more attractive for the owners of wealth, and ever more money flowed there. British provincial banking networks expanded and became better integrated with the City of London. As a result, they became geared more towards investing in big joint stock companies, financial activities, and overseas ventures than in funding local, small-scale start-ups and domestic industries.[111] After the crashes of 1866 and 1873, and the ensuing depression, English banks cut back their investments in England and shifted them elsewhere, in large-scale projects overseas such as railways and industries in the United States, where higher profits could be made. While England in the eighteenth century had attracted capital, especially from the Dutch Republic, now it saw capital being exported, with the volume of these exports rising from an average of 8–10 million pounds per year in the period 1815–55 to over 200 million pounds per year in 1914.[112] Even though the ample availability of local savings and the relatively small capital requirements of English industries still prevented a scarcity of capital in England, the English-financed industrial boom elsewhere did hurt

[107] See section 5.3, 239.   [108] Lindert, *Growing public*, 46, 72, 81–2, 172, and 175.
[109] For the later, full resumption of the English cycle, see section 5.3, 240–50.
[110] O'Brien, 'The costs and benefits', 176–81 and 186–95.
[111] Ingham, *Capitalism divided?*, 143–50; Arrighi, *The long twentieth century*, 161–2 and 165–6.
[112] Ingham, *Capitalism divided?*, 62–5; Piketty, *Capital*, 116, 120–1, and 369–70.

English industries and industrial workers. At the same time, the revenues and interests from overseas investments, amounting to some 10 per cent of national income, lined the pockets of the English wealthy.[113]

That English industries were hurt by international competition, and gradually lost out to foreign competitors, still needs to be explained. Viewpoints on the relative decline of English industry differ, but two possible causes stand out, namely: institutional rigidity and vested interests. Some scholars have suggested that the obsessive focus on self-regulating factor markets and market competition, partly due to lobbying groups, and the resulting institutional rigidity, was at the cost of England's loss of industrial leadership.[114] More specifically, it is argued that the small, fragmented English firms, and the extreme competition among them, precluded the rise of large corporations which were able to make large-scale investments in technological innovation and mass production.[115] Also, English industrialists and the City's financial elites were deeply suspicious of state interference and staunchly defended the openness of the economy and free movement of capital.[116] Perhaps also induced by their reliance on market forces, British governments refrained from interfering in labour markets and supplying better technical education or research facilities. Britain's poorly-adapted education system did not produce the human capital needed for English firms in the second Industrial Revolution. Compared to continental West European countries and the United States, it was less able to provide appropriately trained managerial and technical personnel,[117] while the well-entrenched trade unions further reduced the opportunities for technological innovation by defending labour-intensive production methods. As a result, the profit rates in English industries declined and investments stagnated, while industries in countries such as the United States and elsewhere boomed.

Strikingly, as in the other cases discussed, retailing and commodity trade were not hit, and the financial sector even grew. Still, overall, this period saw the start of the relative decline of the English economy. It experienced a slowing down of growth and saw itself being overtaken by others, first and foremost the United States. During the Victorian era, England still enjoyed a level of GDP per capita that was higher than that of all other European countries as well as that of the United States, but its relatively low growth rates already foreshadowed the end of English economic hegemony. Between 1870 and 1913, these rates were lower than the Western European average, while GDP per capita in the United States even grew at a rate almost twice as fast as that of the United Kingdom.[118] At the latter date it had decisively overtaken the British level.

---

[113] Phillips, *Boiling point*, 207–8.

[114] Elbaum and Lazonick, 'The decline of the British economy'. See also the nuances made by Kirby, 'Institutional rigidities and economic decline'.

[115] Elbaum and Lazonick, 'The decline of the British economy', 569–74.

[116] Kirby, 'Institutional rigidities and economic decline', 653 and the literature cited there, and 654–5 for the following.

[117] For England's lag in education: Lindert, *Growing public*, 113–15.

[118] Maddison, *The world economy*, 262–3; Elbaum and Lazonick, 'The decline of the British economy', 576–7.

Freedom, Equity, and Rising Factor Markets in the United States

In the narratives on the American rise to economic prominence strong emphasis is often placed on political and legal freedom, the security of property rights, and the open organization of markets—and understandably so. However, that the white settler population in the United States in the eighteenth and nineteenth centuries also formed one of the most egalitarian societies in the world, both in power and property distribution, or perhaps even the most egalitarian one, is equally relevant in the light of the argument this book seeks to make. To start with, the United States—that is, the northern and central parts on which this argument focuses— had a relatively equal distribution of land.[119] Rights to land for 'people of modest means' were institutionalized, in part at the expense of the indigenous population. Land grants, as with the Land Ordinance of 1785 and later the Homestead Act of 1862, benefited especially the smallholders and gave rise to the predominance of family-sized farms.[120] This predominance remained in being for a long time. The American farmers already at an early stage became geared towards production for the market, with markets found even overseas, and towards the increase of sur- pluses, but the basic model remained that of the family farm, mostly worked by the family's own labour. Engrossment of landed property remained limited, at least up to the mid-nineteenth century.[121]

After 1776, the elements of equality that had already developed in the colonial period were consolidated and embedded in the proclamations, founding princi- ples, and legislation of the independent republic. Thomas Jefferson, for instance, in his draft constitution for Virginia, written in 1776, brought into practice some of the main ideas of the seventeenth-century English radicals, who imagined social and public virtues such as generosity, justice, and liberty to be linked up with an equitable distribution of landed property. In this vein, Jefferson proclaimed that lands be distributed so that each adult would own 20 hectares of land in full prop- erty.[122] For leading revolutionary activists such as Thomas Paine, the link between liberty and economic equality likewise was primordial, and breaking aristocratic large landownership and promoting widespread freeholding was one of the ways of achieving this.

After the Revolution, voting was open to all men holding landed property over a certain minimum, which in the United States was met by many. Equity was fur- ther strengthened by the westward colonization movement, which started in the 1780s and really took off in the first half of the nineteenth century. The egalitarian values brought to the United States and further developed there, encompassing equality in dress, manners, speech, and social interaction, including the relation- ships between employer and employee, became most outspoken on the western

---

[119] See also more extensively section 5.1.

[120] Belich, *Replenishing the earth*, 334; Kulikoff, *The agrarian origins*, 39–44. See also Weaver, *The great land rush*, 6, 12, and 58.

[121] Appleby, 'Commercial farming'.

[122] Allen, *Enclosure and the yeoman*, 303–7. For the following: Williamson, *American suffrage*, 136–7 and 162–6.

frontiers.[123] Egalitarian tendencies were also strengthened by the influence of the French Revolution and by the influx of populist immigrants and those with non-conformist religious beliefs.

Within this atmosphere, labourers started to resent the hierarchy between masters and servants and the ways hired labour was coerced. This coercion was eroded, labourers acquired more freedom, and also, outside the South, chattel slavery was abolished.[124] In the first half of the nineteenth century, the practice of indenturing labour came further under pressure and the legal independence of labourers, their personal freedom, and their rights to mobility became acknowledged. Another step in the emancipation of labourers was that wealth or property requirements for the suffrage were abandoned and wage labourers were allowed the vote. The franchise in the United States was thus extended relatively early, compared to Western Europe.[125] Four states had universal suffrage—for white men—already by 1815, and the number further increased in the following years. Wage labour, personal freedom, and suffrage now became compatible with each other.

Within this context, factor markets from the beginning of the nineteenth century rapidly grew.[126] This development could draw upon a favourable institutional framework, including secure property rights to land, labour, and capital, in part already implanted by the colonizers.[127] Path dependency played a large role in this, as shown by the continuities from the colonial era, while the new institutions were developed within a balanced, equitable social context that also built on the society formed in the colonial period. Relevant formal institutions included laws on limited liability, legal protection of debtors, limitation of indenture, rules for the formation of private corporations, a banking system, and land laws. Informal rules, too, smoothed the rise of markets or at least adapted to markets early, as through the rise of Methodism from the 1790s to the 1840s, a religious strand far from hostile to markets, and increasingly even favourable to them and to seizing market opportunities.[128]

The development of a market economy or—as some would even have it—a market revolution, took place first on the east coast, especially in the decades around 1800. New England is one of the areas where this is observed, even though the focus in the literature is more on the growing market orientation of production and the rise of markets for output, than on the rise of markets for land, labour, and credit, which are central to my analysis of market economies.[129] Still, there is sufficient evidence that these factor markets became more formalized, impersonal, open, and voluminous in the decades around 1800. In rural Massachusetts, for

---

[123] Belich, *Replenishing the earth*, 157–63.
[124] Steinfeld, *The invention of free labor*, 122–38, also for the following.
[125] Sokoloff and Engerman, 'History lessons', 225–6; Steinfeld, *The invention of free labor*, 185–7; Williamson, *American suffrage*, 182–222.
[126] Sellers, *The market revolution*, passim.
[127] Acemoglu, Johnson, and Robinson, 'The colonial origins'. Sokoloff and Engerman, 'History lessons', rather stress the role of natural endowments and the resulting comparative advantages.
[128] Carwadine, 'Methodists and the market revolution'. For the formal rules: Cain, 'Entrepreneurship in the Antebellum United States', 332–8.
[129] Sellers, *The market revolution*.

instance, credit and capital markets swiftly rose from c. 1780 onwards, as shown by an investigation of probate inventories.[130] Suddenly, securities, shares in bridges, banks and insurance companies, and state notes, start to appear among the goods of rural households, especially the wealthier among them. Also, interest rates now became market-determined and flexible, the number of creditors and debtors per household increased, and their networks covered larger areas, showing the thickening and widening of credit markets. This was helped by changes in the institutional framework, as courts tempered the legal remedies against debtors and brought debtors and creditors onto an equal footing, while debt also became transferable to third parties.[131] Also, limited liability became established, a process finalized in 1830, not coincidentally the moment that shares in manufacturing companies start to show up in inventories in rural Massachusetts.

The rise of factor markets was also evident further west, as in the wave of land speculation in the years 1800–20, propelled by the credit programme launched by Congress in order to enable pioneers to buy a farm on credit. This led to a westward flood of farmers and speculators, who bought and sold land, used credit markets, hired wage labourers, and stimulated transport and banking services.[132] More generally, land markets in the first half of the nineteenth century boomed, and both rural and urban land were frenetically bought and sold, sometimes in speculative markets.[133] Land sales in the midwest, for instance, increased dramatically in the first half of the nineteenth century. In Illinois, land sales rose from 40,000 hectares annually in the years before 1829 to 140,000 hectares in 1835 and even 800,000 hectares in 1836, suggesting very high annual turnover rates, sometimes of a speculative nature, underpinned by credit.[134]

Wage labour, too, grew, especially in industries, first through apprenticeship and putting-out systems and later also within sectors in which mass production emerged, as in woollen cloth and cotton industries, as early as from c. 1810 onwards.[135] By the mid-nineteenth century, some 100,000 wage labourers were employed in cotton textile production alone. Around 1850, factor markets had become dominant in the northeastern, central, and western United States. The Civil War sealed this development. Labour was made fully free, and made available to be hired for wages, now slavery, indentured labour, imprisonment for debt, and apprenticeship were limited, or even abolished, while collective and community rights were also done away with in the north.[136] During and after the Civil War markets and the concept of freedom became even more clearly conflated.

The state and public authorities were not absent in this development, especially not in the west of the United States. The building of roads and bridges, canals, and

---

[130] Rothenberg, 'The emergence of a capital market', also for the following.
[131] Rothenberg, 'The emergence of a capital market', 786–7.
[132] Larson, *The market revolution*, 29 (land speculation), 63, and 71–2 (wage labour); Kulikoff, *The agrarian origins*, 44.
[133] Weaver, *The great land rush*, 76–81.
[134] Belich, *Replenishing the earth*, 226; Clark, 'The agrarian context', 18–20.
[135] Sellers, The market revolution, 24–8.
[136] Larson, *The market revolution*, 162 and 164–7.

railroads was often organized or even funded by the federal government, the states, and local, municipal governments.[137] Public authorities also bore the expense of military protection, subsidizing railway construction, surveying areas, and offering settlers a homestead. The role of public authorities was especially pronounced in the big westward movement, which really took off at the beginning of the nineteenth century. The states in the midwest made a huge effort in the period 1825–45. The investments they made were in part financed by taxes, but mainly by land sales and contracting public debts. In the 1840s, local governments took over the leading role in developing infrastructure.[138] In other respects, too, the rise to dominance of factor markets in the newly occupied areas was partly the result of the investments made by public bodies. Labour markets, for instance, were hugely promoted by the state. Large numbers of wage labourers were employed in public works, as in the 1850s annually some 100,000–200,000 workers in railroad construction alone. At first, using wage labourers may have been seen as a temporary solution for large works like these, but increasingly wage labour came to stay, especially as a wage-based factory system developed.

Above we have focused on the northern, central, and western parts of the United States. The south, with its conspicuous dominance of an elite of plantation and slave owners, followed a different trajectory. Here, labour was to a substantial degree supplied by slaves, up to the abolition of slavery in 1865. This did not stand in the way of ample involvement of southern elites in land, capital, and product markets, thus creating a kind of capitalist farming with slave labour.[139] Markets were not free, however, and their social context was not balanced. Even after the defeat in the Civil War and the abolition of slavery, the organization of markets, and of society at large, remained characterized by unfreedom, coercion, and power imbalances. Plantations were not redistributed, the elite remained in place, and black labourers, who were poorly educated and were paid low wages, remained dependent on this elite.[140] Their mobility remained restricted, also by the patriarchal authority of the employers, and no open, competitive labour market emerged there.

The geographical differences in credit and financial markets were much less pronounced. Financial markets developed everywhere in the United States, they quickly became integrated and grew explosively, albeit with booms and busts. There was a rapid growth of bank loans, based on the institutional framework devised in the 1790s, with a new currency (the dollar), chartered banks, financial corporations, and a central bank. Large numbers of banks were set up in the United States, helping the development of an impersonal monetary economy and credit system, and eroding personal bonds in credit relations.[141] In the American west alone, loans increased four or even fivefold between 1830 and 1837, to over half a

---

[137] Belich, *Replenishing the earth*, 185–6, 226–8, and 333–4; Atack, 'America', 546–8.

[138] Wallis, 'American government finance'.

[139] Dunaway, *The first American frontier*, 16, 88–91, and 120–1, although she perhaps overstates the capitalist character.

[140] Acemoglu and Robinson, *Why nations fail*, 351–7; Clark, 'The agrarian context', 26–7.

[141] A positive account: Wright, 'The first phase'.

billion dollars.[142] Money poured in from Britain and the American east coast. More generally, between 1815 and 1914 enormous amounts of British capital were invested in the United States.[143] Credit was almost limitless and participants in financial markets were at times possessed by a kind of mania for speculation and the drive to take risks, sometimes even when devoid of vital information.[144] As a result, almost half of the business ventures in the 1840s and 1850s ended in bankruptcy and there were regular crashes, with banks failing or being wiped out, as happened during the busts of 1818–19, 1837, 1857, and 1873.[145] During the Panic of 1837, for instance, brokers failed, banks called in their loans, and investors did not pay the bills. Wage labourers temporarily had no money or credit to buy necessities. Criticism and anger, however, mostly targeted government policies, privileges, and officials, corrupt or not, but not the market economy.[146] The ensuing attacks on government instead gave leeway for the further growth of the market.

People became used to the occurrence of crises and bankruptcies and came to see them as a natural, or even indispensable, element of a market economy that otherwise offered them growing welfare. Also, the sharpest edges of financial failure were softened, through the legislation on bankruptcy enacted in the 1840s. At the same time, however, bankruptcy laws helped to line the pockets of all kinds of professionals active in the sector, including sheriffs, lawyers, and speculators. Bankruptcy became a business.[147] Still, positive steps taken were that information on the creditworthiness of debtors was made more widely available and credit reporting became more systematic.

Also, in the settler areas where these booms and busts were most pronounced, after each bust the economy recovered, based on cheap credit and built on the strong economic position of family-sized farmers and medium-sized producers. Financial markets were instrumental in this. For instance, when settler families built their farms acquired through the Homestead Act of 1862, they were allotted 60 hectares each, but were obliged to develop their farm within five years, which required large investments in buildings, fences, seed, and livestock, only to be made through credit or mortgages. Credit was in part provided by insurance companies and, increasingly, specialized mortgage companies issuing bonds on the east coast and in Europe.[148]

Even though landownership remained widespread, family farmers thus became ever more dependent on credit. Also, the distribution of landownership became more skewed. Engrossment increased and, from 1860, the independent family farmers were on the wane.[149] Although around 1900 almost three-quarters of all

---

[142] Sylla, 'Financial systems and economic modernization', 283–5.
[143] Belich, *Replenishing the earth*, 114–20.   [144] Belich, *Replenishing the earth*, 200–6.
[145] Balleisen, 'Vulture capitalism'; Clark, 'The agrarian context', 18–20.
[146] Larson, *The market revolution*, 92–7 and 147.   [147] Balleisen, 'Vulture capitalism'.
[148] Brewer, 'Eastern money', shows that this was not a smooth process, but one hindered by lacking information and other obstacles.
[149] Kulikoff, *The agrarian origins*, 52–3. Continuity is stressed more by Appleby, 'Commercial farming'.

American rural households still owned at least some land, the family farmers were increasingly replaced by larger, capitalist farmers and landowners, and by the labour offered by wage labourers. Also, land became more scarce and expensive. This, and their lack of working capital, made country dwellers more dependent on sharecropping as a way of accessing land.

The increasingly more precarious position of small-scale producers and ordinary participants in output, land, and credit markets in the later nineteenth century was sometimes sustained by trade unions and cooperatives. Small labour unions or societies had been formed by factory workers, journeymen, and artisans around the middle of the century, although these were attacked, sometimes even vehemently, or prosecuted in court, and labelled as criminal conspiracies in order to raise wages and as obstacles to entrepreneurship. Larger unions were developed after the Civil War, and they achieved some success in bringing direct material improvement to the workers in the 1890s and 1900s, to some extent through collective bargaining, but at the same time these unions abandoned the hope of structurally changing the organization of the economy or building an alternative to the dominance of markets and private entrepreneurship.[150] Still, exceptions to fully market-determined development existed. Cooperatives, big companies, and public authorities sometimes jointly developed new markets and sustained commercialization. A successful example was the California fruit sector around 1900. Here, state agencies, large railway companies, and cooperatives of producers with smaller and medium-sized farms allied in production, marketing, and transport, and made a great success out of this sector, especially by accessing markets on the east coast.[151] The use these producers made of their cooperatives increased their success in output and credit markets.[152] In many other cases, however, independent farmers lost out to the economic leverage of big railroad owners, commodity merchants, and monopoly capitalists.

In this period, and in tandem with these developments, the American economy boomed. GDP per capita had already been fairly high around 1800, at a level similar to that of Western Europe, but the real take-off took place in the nineteenth century. Between 1800 and 1860 America's growth rates were substantial, at 1.5 per cent per year, surpassing those in Western Europe, and with growth concentrated in New England.[153] Around 1900, after yet another round of growth, American GDP per capita surpassed that of Britain, and the United States became the wealthiest economy in the world.[154] Real wages were also rising, even if this did not translate into direct welfare gains for many ordinary people, as evidenced by the declining average heights of Americans from the 1830s up to the 1850s, caused

---

[150] Tomlins, *The state and the unions*, 36–36 (for the 1840s) and 60–82 (for the 1890s). For movements in the first half of the century also: Larson, *The market revolution*, 108–16.

[151] Belich, *Replenishing the earth*, 488–9.

[152] Saker, 'Creating an agricultural trust'. The following, much more negative view in Kulikoff, *The agrarian origins*, 57.

[153] Lindert and Williamson, 'American incomes', 751.

[154] Maddison, *The world economy*, 264. See also the latest GDP per capita figures: the Maddison Project, <http://www.ggdc.net/maddison/maddison-project/home.htm>, 2013 version.

by the rising income inequality, the growing variability of income, and food budgets and the negative side effects of urbanization.[155]

Dynamic factor markets and economic growth thus went hand in hand. At the same time, during the process, markets changed in character. The period between the mid-nineteenth and early twentieth centuries saw a number of processes which were generated by dynamic, free, and highly competitive markets and at the same time limited their functioning. First, inequality increased dramatically. The first phase of rising inequality, a steep one, took place as early as the period 1800–60, that is, simultaneous with the rise of big, dynamic factor markets. Income inequality in the east of the United States rose from a Gini of 0.4 to 0.53 and the top 1 per cent increased its share from 7 to 10 per cent of total income.[156] Also, there was the accumulation of wealth, growing in the following decades. Wealth inequality in the United States had been low at the beginning of the nineteenth century, with the richest 1 per cent owning about a quarter of total wealth, being much less than in Western European countries for instance, but this share rapidly rose in the course of the nineteenth century, and around 1900 the richest 1 per cent already owned almost one-half of all real estate and private property.[157] This wealth increasingly consisted of financial assets and was accumulated through the markets. The ownership of government bonds, likewise, became heavily concentrated in the hands of a few, and even despite attempts to market bonds to the masses and thus widening the circles of bond ownership, in 1880 the top 1.4 per cent of bond holders held about half of the public debt.[158] The interest payments on these bonds were financed through the taxes paid mainly by ordinary Americans.

Another development interacting with markets, and at the same time limiting them, was the rise of big business, often in the form of corporations. After a slow start in the eighteenth century, the rise of corporations gained speed in the 1860s and especially during the Great Depression of 1873–9, as large-scale corporations emerged which strove for the vertical integration of production and distribution, and offered limited liability to stockholders. This was a response to declining profit margins, the rising costs of making investments in ever costlier technology, and the experienced disruptions of price-making markets, and also from the will to dominate or even supersede these markets.[159] Also, in the 1890s, there was a wave of mergers, in which competitors in a sector merged into huge enterprises. While these large corporations were virtually non-existent in the United States before the Great Depression of the 1870s, they dominated many sectors around 1900, with Standard Oil forming a notable example. These corporations largely organized the flows of capital, labour, raw materials, and commodities within the firm or

---

[155] Komlos, 'Shrinking in a growing economy?'. See the remarks on this indicator: Bodenhorn, Guinnane, and Mroz, 'Problems of sample-selection bias', 7.

[156] Lindert and Williamson, 'American incomes', 755–8, with the figures found in the 2011 version of the paper, p. 27 and tables 6 and 7.

[157] Piketty, *Capital*, 150–5 and 347–50.

[158] Hager, 'What happened to the bondholding class?'.

[159] Atack, 'America', 556–61; Arrighi, *The long twentieth century*, 285–95. For the pioneering role of the railway sector: Chandler, *The visible hand*, 79–187.

corporation, and thus internalized the costs otherwise involved in market exchange and reduced the insecurities and price fluctuations associated with the market.[160] They, or at least the survivors of the process, were also large enough to bear the costs of the big investments in technology needed in capital-intensive sectors. At the same time, these large corporations gained market control and monopoly power, and they achieved a position in which they could limit the entry of competitors.

Often, these corporations were joint-stock enterprises, which were rare before, and also had been rare in Britain. The consolidations and mergers of the late nineteenth century were often financed through the issue of securities, thus promoting the link between industries, financial markets, and wealth holders, and favouring the large companies that had better access to capital. In the process, a number of sectors through the large corporations became dominated by big shareholders or owners. This was the era of the rise of great tycoons, including John D. Rockefeller, Andrew Carnegie, and Cornelius VanderBilt, also pejoratively named the Robber Barons, for their alleged, or real, dishonourable practices. They did not hesitate to use their wealth to acquire political influence or even outright power.[161] Respect for their success increasingly yielded to public fears about their political influence and monopoly power, and to calls for regulatory legislation.

A related fear was that financial markets and investment funds would come under the control of a few actors, as in the case of the powerful investment bank led by J. P. Morgan.[162] The Panic of 1907, and the way J. P. Morgan was able to organize a bail-out by channelling and controlling large capital streams, disclosed the financial power of one single man. Alerted by this, the US congress ordered an investigation into the concentration of finance in the United States. The Pujo Committee, established to this end, concluded—although not undisputed—that a few leaders of finance formed a community that controlled money and credit. Initially, not much changed, however. Accumulated capital in the 1920s kept on finding a welcoming outlet in financial markets, thanks to innovations including the development of investment trusts, and a host of new stock issues, with stock market prices being fuelled by easy credit and speculation.[163] This, combined with great trust in the market, continued up to the bursting of the bubble, as the boom came to a painful end with the Wall Street crash of 1929.

The Great Depression of the 1930s, and the resulting fear for job losses, and perhaps even concern that the American economic system was failing, caused a policy change.[164] For one, it enabled the Democrats to break the long-standing Republican dominance in politics. The shock caused by the crash and the ensuing high unemployment gave legitimacy to state interventions in markets, as happened especially under President Theodore Roosevelt and his New Deal. Now, stricter

---

[160] The classical account: Chandler, *The visible hand*, 285–339; Lamoreaux, 'Entrepreneurship', 381–6.

[161] For anti-monopoly legislation: Lamoreaux, 'Entrepreneurship', 388–90.

[162] DeLong, 'Did J. P. Morgan's men add value?'.

[163] Eichengreen and Mitchener, 'The Great Depression as a credit boom'. For market optimism: Shiller, *Irrational exuberance*, 103–7.

[164] Shiller, *Irrational exuberance*, 115–16.

anti-trust and anti-monopoly legislation was enacted. Also, legislation including the National Labor Relations Act of 1935 endorsed the right of workers to form unions, to make collective bargains, and to strike, and made them into a corner-stone of the economic recovery policies, placed under the aegis and control of the state.[165] This temporary period of state intervention and redistribution was length-ened by the Second World War and the ensuing Cold War, and the necessity of mobilizing the masses to fight for the United States. This required governments to soften the effects of competitive markets and to distribute more evenly the fruits of the profits made in the markets, even if state coordination, central planning, and social consultation and cooperation remained less in the United States than in Western Europe, especially in the absence of the powerful associations and cooper-atives found there and the continuing presence of large businesses and big wealth, that was weakened but not gone. The period of the Great Depression and the Second World War thus formed a temporary interlude, as is also reflected in the temporary low in wealth and income inequality,[166] but no more than an interlude, especially when seen in the long time frame used in this book. This interlude did not bring a fundamental rupture, and after this period of three or four decades developments resumed again in the 1960s.

5.3. THE WESTERN WORLD BROUGHT IN SYNC AND DOMINATED BY FACTOR MARKETS, SINCE 1950

Developments in the United States in the second half of the twentieth century returned to, and in part built on, the structure of economy and society that had emerged in the late nineteenth century, a period dominated by large corporations and wealthy capital owners. This structure, after a counter-current of a few decades, now became reinforced, also by the growth of the geographical scale and volume of market transactions. This, and the increasing anonymity of market participants, also influenced thinking about economics. It stimulated abstract modelling of eco-nomic behaviour and developments, fitting in with more emphasis on neo-classical economics, so-called rational decision making, and the opportunities offered by mathematical and statistical techniques.[167] From the late 1940s on, there was a revival of neo-liberal economic thinking, with F. A. Hayek and Milton Friedman at the forefront. Although still on the defensive because of the dominance of Keynesian politics and reasoning that had emerged in the 1930s, the neo-liberal thinktanks were well funded by capitalists, as in the case of the Volker fund, which was financed by super-rich businessman William Volker, and grew in strength.[168]

---

[165] Tomlins, *The state and the unions*, 100–2. For the restraints imposed in this process by the judi-ciary: Acemoglu and Robinson, *Why nations fail*, 325–9.

[166] Piketty, *Capital*, 291–4 and 298–300; Milanovic, 'The return of "patrimonial capitalism"', 7–8.

[167] For the growing role of these techniques in the 1930s and 1940s: Hodgson, 'The great crash', 1211–12.

[168] See for these thinktanks also Cohen, '"Economic freedom"', 8.

Labour markets were now opened up again. After the Second World War, legislative measures, such as the Taft-Hartley Act in 1947, also labelled 'the slave-labour bill' by union leaders, increased the obstacles for collective bargaining and curtailed collective action by workers, limiting its scope to direct material matters.[169] The act was promoted by effective lobbying by large corporations. This happened in an atmosphere in which trade unions were increasingly regarded as obstacles to economic growth.

Still, the late 1950s saw growth declining and profit rates falling, and the economy even went into a recession in 1957. US banks and enterprises responded by shifting their attention more to short-run financial gains, to be made by investments overseas and through financial markets, less by investments in technology, and even less so by long-run investments in human capital. Also, companies succeeded in regaining their position in export markets and pushing profitability back up again by reducing labour costs, in part achieved by breaking the position of the labour unions.[170]

Economic growth rates as measured by average GDP per capita recovered, however, also through the impetus of massive, regressive tax cuts in 1964, by the Johnson administration, the growth of public and private borrowing, and the huge expenses of the Vietnam War.[171] Thousands of billions of dollars were spent on military exploits, in part for ideological reasons and the defence of democracy and free-market capitalism—in line with the ideology linking freedom, democracy, and free markets[172]—but arguably also in order to get a grip on the world's resources and markets. Even if the latter is harder to prove, it is clear that the revenues flowed mostly to large companies (arms companies, constructors, oil companies) and their shareholders, as happened when companies close to President Lyndon B. Johnson received lucrative contracts in Vietnam, while the costs were mainly paid through regular taxes on labour incomes and consumption, pressing especially on the middle and lower groups in society. A close link developed between government, the military sector, financial markets, and large private companies. The resulting military-industrial complex, and the risk of public policy becoming the captive of this complex through lobbying, political donations, and shared interests, became a grave concern to some, a concern expressed by President Dwight Eisenhower in his last presidential address in 1961.

The influence of American developments on other Western countries, and especially on northwest Europe, in these decades after the Second World War was profound. Up to this point, the continental northwest European and Scandinavian countries were in a completely different phase of development. They had seen a massive wave of self-organization, starting around 1870, with the foundation and rise of cooperatives, cooperative insurance companies, cooperative banks, farmers'

---

[169] Tomlins, *The state and the unions*, 282–316.
[170] Brenner, *The economics of global turbulence*, 61–6 and 114–17.
[171] For borrowing: Streeck, 'The crises'.
[172] See for the often assumed link between the three elements: section 1.1, 4–5, and 1.2, 17–18.

unions, trade unions, et cetera.[173] Also, these countries saw the rise of all kinds of boards, councils, and independent bodies, representing the interests of various social groups, often including ordinary people. These organizations aimed at acquiring decision-making power and enhancing political equity, also by cooperating and bargaining with other organized interest groups, thus complementing the rise of parliamentary democracy and the extension of the franchise, with an associated rise of socialist and other left-wing political parties.[174] At the same time, these councils, cooperatives, and unions formed a reaction against the liberal economy of the nineteenth century and aimed to enhance economic equity. The struggle of these social movements had started already before the First World War, and it reached new heights during this war and shortly thereafter, fuelled by the need of national elites to win the loyalty of people needed to fight for their countries. The concrete, material results were reaped by ordinary people especially in the decades after the Second World War, with the build-up of the social welfare states.[175]

This process also affected the United Kingdom, where social polarization had been rising in the nineteenth century and living standards were under pressure, especially those for the middle classes. The period between 1900 and 1914 saw a fall of real wages and consumption patterns there becoming scantier.[176] In the military and ideological struggle between European states, this development was reversed, however, by the aforementioned need of the elites to retain the loyalty of the people needed to fight. For the lower groups in the United Kingdom, as a result, many of the social problems were remedied in the period between the First World War and c. 1960, by unemployment benefits, income redistribution, and the build-up of a state-sponsored educational system and a social welfare state.[177] Enabled by economic growth, and stimulated by the experiences of the crisis of the 1930s and the Second World War, and also by the threat of revolutionary movements and communism, the post-war years in particular saw an expansion of social arrangements. The extent of this expansion in the United Kingdom was not nearly as large as in continental Western Europe, however. Changes were less fundamental, thus forming more of an interlude than a rupture.

In continental Western Europe, not only did large shares of the economy come into the hands of the collective sector, up to 50 or 60 per cent of GDP, but additional, large segments of the economy came to be organized by cooperatives, mutual associations, and other non-market systems. Since the 1950s, these countries, sometimes labelled social democratic or corporatist welfare states or Rhineland states, are characterized by cooperation between stakeholders, substantial income redistribution, employment protection, encompassing systems of social security,

---

[173] For the Netherlands: van Zanden and van Riel, *The strictures of inheritance*, 291–5 and 329–30.

[174] For Germany: Müller-Jentsch, 'Gewerkschaften und Korporatismus'; for the Netherlands: van Zanden and van Riel, *The strictures of inheritance*, 249–54 and 340.

[175] For this process: Lindert, *Growing public*, passim, where he also discusses other causes of the growth of welfare states.

[176] Phillips, *Boiling point*, 201–4.

[177] Lindert, *Growing public*, 11–14, 171–5, and, for the following, 176–89.

and modest income inequality.[178] Their alternative labels, 'coordinated market economies' or 'social market economies',[179] may even be wrong for this period, as the market played a relatively small role in the transaction and allocation of land, labour, and capital.

This situation constituted a balanced social and economic context, just like the one found earlier in the United States in the decades around 1800. Just as in the American case, factor markets thus could have gradually started growing within this balanced context. Since the 1980s, or somewhat before, factor markets did indeed grow in Western Europe, but not gradually, however, and not predicated on this balanced context. Rather, Western Europe became rapidly involved in, or absorbed by, the United States' cycle.[180] European companies in the 1970s hugely increased their foreign investments and developed into multinationals, as happened in the United States too, and they oriented more towards American models of organizing their operations.[181] Also, the concept of deregulation became more widely accepted, especially with respect to financial markets. This happened first and foremost in Britain, where as early as the 1950s the Conservative governments sought to restore London as a financial centre, by making the pound sterling convertible, and by reopening and liberalizing markets.[182] London immediately attracted speculative funds, and it was here that a foundation was laid for the later financial boom.

It is in this boom, and in international financial markets, that the growth to dominance of factor markets can be seen most spectacularly and affecting all countries around the northern Atlantic. The next steps of opening up financial markets around 1970, and especially the wave of deregulation from the 1980s, led to an explosion in new financial instruments, new markets, and highly sophisticated financial systems, increasingly operating at a global scale, not hindered by national boundaries. The opportunities for wealth holders to hold capital in foreign money markets and for speculation in currencies grew tremendously. By the mid-1970s, the volume of purely financial transactions already exceeded the volume of world trade several times, in 1979 this had grown to eleven times and in 1984 already twenty times, with London and New York as the main centres.[183]

This growth of financial markets affected other domains, including the political one. Finance capital boosted its position vis-à-vis the nation-states, for instance, gradually forcing these heed more closely the rule of the financial market.[184] Also, economies became more affected by financial activities and considerations. In the United States, the share of the financial sector in corporate profits doubled in the 1950s and 1960s, from 10 per cent to 20 per cent.[185] Moreover, non-financial firms derived an ever greater part of their cash flow and profits from financial activities,

---

[178] Pontusson, *Inequality and prosperity*, passim.
[179] Hall and Soskice, 'An introduction to varieties', 18–21; Pontusson, *Inequality and prosperity*, 3–6.
[180] See more extensively below, 245–50.   [181] Arrighi, *The long twentieth century*, 306.
[182] Ingham, *Capitalism divided?*, 206–8.
[183] Arrighi, *The long twentieth century*, 299–300; Ingham, *Capitalism divided?*, 50–8 (London).
[184] Streeck, 'The crises'.
[185] Krippner, 'The financialization', 178–81 and, for the following, 184–6.

a process starting in the late 1960s. A related effect was that financial experts and bankers gained a strong presence in the boards and directorships of non-financial institutions, and their interests converged with those of the non-financial market elites.[186] Jointly, they decided on investments, the organization of production, and the distribution of profits, possibly in part explaining the success of the 'share-holder value' model.

In other respects, too, the market economy became more pervasive in the real economy, especially from the 1980s on, as market-oriented governments, most conspicuously those led by Margaret Thatcher in the United Kingdom and Ronald Reagan in the United States, came to power. They were dedicated to removing the obstacles to the free operation of markets for land, labour, and capital, an example followed later in many northwest European countries. Labour unions and welfare schemes became increasingly considered as obstacles for a proper functioning of the labour markets.[187] Factor markets became more important, or even dominant, in Western countries, including Western Europe. While people earlier could choose to use the market, they now increasingly became forced to do so. Not only did most people lose direct possession of the means of production or access to non-market systems of exchange or allocation, but also financial needs and stag-nating real wages pushed people into labour and credit markets, as shown by the rising numbers of households depending on two wage incomes or on loans or mortgages.[188]

Also, alternative systems of exchange and allocation, such as cooperatives, mutual funds, or public arrangements, were replaced or dissolved, in order to make way for the market. This happened in the Western world and also outside, in other parts of the world. An extreme, violent example of the latter was the coup against President Allende in Chile in 1973 and the pro-market reforms that were effectu-ated in the following years. This coup was ideologically inspired and underpinned by the blueprints for a Chilean free market economy drawn up by Milton Friedman and his 'Chicago boys', a select group of Chilean students who between 1955 and 1963 had been invited to study economics in Chicago with Friedman and became leading figures in the pro-market shock doctrine applied in Chile.[189] A programme of the retreat of the state, deregulation of markets, banning of trade unions, and privatization of the economy was put into practice with force. In a more peaceful, but at times still coercive manner, using economic compulsion, the same goals were pursued by organizations such as the International Monetary Fund and the World Bank. They inspired, or even forced countries to liberalize and deregulate markets and privatize banks and services. More specifically, the loans advanced in the 1980s to countries in Latin America, Africa, and Eastern Europe, including to Poland in 1989, were provided with strong policy recommendations to this end.[190]

---

[186] Krippner, 'The financialization', 201–2.
[187] Brenner, *The economics of global turbulence*, 147.
[188] For private indebtedness: Crouch, 'Privatised Keynesianism'.
[189] Silva, 'Technocrats and politics', 390–5.
[190] A critical account: Klein, *The shock doctrine*, 202–6 and 221–9.

These international organizations created after the Second World War to bolster global stability thus became instruments for forcing neo-liberal reforms.

These developments were sped up by a large economic literature arguing that the liberalization of capital and labour markets, and free markets more generally, would promote growth and actually had saved the United States and Western Europe from the economic stagnation of the 1970s and 1980s. The policies of President Reagan in the United States and Prime Minister Thatcher in the United Kingdom, after some initial scepticism, came to be widely seen as an economic success.[191] The idea that free markets generate growth became the dominant view and was promoted by international organizations and economists all over the world. Keynesianism lost much of its attraction, and seemed outdated, while neo-liberal and pro-market ideas won ground, also in academia.[192] Conversely, top economists promoted the implementation of neo-liberal policies, as Nobel prize laureate Milton Friedman did in 1973 in Chile, as we saw, or later, when visiting Prime Minister Thatcher in London in 1981, as he convinced the members of her cabinet of the necessity of deregulation and privatization.

There was more, however, than only literature and ideology in the spread of these ideas and their effectuation, in the Western World but also in developing countries. Select cases did indeed suggest a positive effect of economic liberalism on economic growth, as did the rapid growth in Chile in the period 1978–81, after the pro-market shock doctrine applied by the Pinochet regime in 1974/5, and portrayed as an economic miracle, even if this period was preceded and followed by severe economic crisis.[193] The decade-long boom in stock markets in the Western World and the acceleration of growth in the 1990s were also taken as proof of the soundness of deregulation and opening up factor markets. More generally, several studies found a positive relationship between the degree of economic liberalism (as measured by the Economic Freedom of the World index, for instance) and economic growth in the period from 1980.[194] Even though, when viewed in a longer perspective, actual growth levels were not impressive,[195] and these studies have been criticized for errors in methodology and measurement, and for leaving out the effect on growth of simultaneous changes that had no relation to market liberalization, they seemed to endorse the general assumption that free markets generate growth.

Also, special interests played their part in the propagation and realization of these ideas, that is, interests of large corporations, shareholders, and professionals in the West, and also elites and businesses in the developing countries. Another element in the growing prominence of factor markets was the fall and dissolution of the Soviet Bloc in 1989, in itself often considered proof of the failure of non-market systems, and the ensuing implementation of free market policies

---

[191] Cohen, '"Economic freedom"'.
[192] Stiglitz, *Freefall*, 238 and 251. See also section 1.2, 16–18.
[193] Silva, 'Technocrats and politics', 395–7. See for these Chilean reforms also above, 241.
[194] Cohen, '"Economic freedom"', also for the following criticisms.
[195] See below, 247.

there under the impetus of the World Bank and the International Monetary Fund. A similar rapid growth of free factor markets was also found in the free trade zones or special economic zones, starting with the one set up in Ireland in 1959, and speeding up from the 1980s, with large numbers of such zones set up in China, the Philippines, and many other developing countries. In 1975 there were still less than 100 special economic zones around the world, a number rising to some 500 in 1995 and 3–5,000 in 2005.[196] In many of these zones, restrictions on the free trade of commodities, land, labour, and capital were lifted, regulations were removed, trade unions were banned, and private property rights became strictly, or even violently, enforced. This led to the formation of market-dominated econo- mies, but without the political democracy or freedom linked by some neo-liberal thinkers to the market.

In other market-dominated economies, too, unfreedom and coercion were instead strengthened. This especially applies to the United States, where relatively large shares of the population, much larger than elsewhere, are held in prison. Also, the United States came to stand out internationally in the share of labour devoted to maintaining order, through policing, guarding activities, supervision, and sur- veillance.[197] At the same time, state violence became increasingly privatized and put into the hands of companies such as Blackwater, who use mercenaries hired in the labour market. Drafted civilians were increasingly replaced by professional sol- diers and hired security personnel.[198] The fruits of military exploits and coercion exercised overseas were mainly reaped by large companies, often with close ties to the American government, as had happened earlier in Vietnam and later in defeated and occupied Iraq in the 1990s and 2000s, where large contracts were offered to the construction and engineering company Halliburton, closely linked to the US vice-president, its former CEO, Dick Cheney.[199] Also, the inequality in wealth and build-up of large fortunes are likely to have led to the increasing hold of the wealthy over the state and society at large. This may be through bond-holding, with the top 1 per cent of wealthiest households in the United States owning 42 per cent of public debts in 2010, or through the lobbying or financing of political candidates, or through the ownership of media, and voicing a clear pro-market view, as in the case of the Fox Network and the News Corporation, owned by billionaire Rupert Murdoch.[200]

One of the changes in thinking, in part stimulated by these media, is the rise of the principle of shareholder value. The idea was that maximizing shareholder value, and thus disciplining managers towards the goal of cost cutting, downsizing, and profit maximizing, would make everyone better off, including workers and consumers, and it would benefit the economy as a whole. It would also free up otherwise unused capital and superfluous workers and thus stimulate labour and capital markets. The prominence of this principle is a fairly recent phenomenon, emerging in the 1980s, first in the United States and later, in the late 1990s, in

---

[196] Moberg, 'The political economy', 167–9.   [197] Bowles, 'Liberal society', 77.
[198] Avant, 'Private security companies'.   [199] Chatterjee, *Halliburton's Army*.
[200] Arsenault and Castells, 'Switching power'; Hager, 'What happened to the bondholding class?'.

Europe.[201] Associated with this, the corporate principle of retaining and reinvesting profits gave way to a focus of managers to distribute corporate revenues over the stock owners, resulting in a sharp rise of the share of profits paid out as dividends. More generally, top managers, by adopting the principle of shareholder value, now aligned themselves with the owners and their financial interests rather than with the organizations and their stakeholders. More specifically, this resulted in a downward pressure of wages of American workers, job losses, and the dwindling of the corporations' interest in investing in the education and skills of workers.[202] This may be one of the main elements in the decline of investments in human capital and that of the relative performance of students in the United States between c. 1970 and 2000.

Another conspicuous element in the recent developments is the further growth of flows of capital around the world. From c. 1970, enabled by the liberalization of financial markets, the volume of purely financial transactions increased tremendously, and in 1979 already exceeded the volume of world trade eleven times, as we have seen, rising to twenty times in 1984 and no less than seventy times in 2010.[203] Associated with this development, transacting in financial markets has become a better way for wealth owners to obtain maximum profits in the short run than investing in industries or other capital goods. From c. 1990, the financial sector has been the dominant economic sector in the United States, as it generates more profits than manufacturing or services, while even for non-financial firms financial activities account for almost half of profits on average.[204] The profitability of financial dealing was greatly enhanced by all kinds of innovations in financial markets. In the 1980s, for instance, there was the quick rise of junk bonds, more euphemistically also labelled high-yield bonds.[205] In the early 1980s, banking laws in the United States were liberalized, and the separation between banking and commercial finance was gradually lifted, allowing savings banks to buy these bonds and further pushing their popularity up. Facilitated by the availability of junk bonds and big private wealth, the leveraged buy-out appeared on the scene, in the United States and Western Europe. Companies were taken over, stripped, made profitable by budget and employment cuts, and then sold to other investors for a profit. This process may have helped these companies in finding new growth strategies, but it is unclear to what extent it helped in generating long-run value,[206] let alone what the net effects were for society as a whole.

Also, in the years around 2000, first in the United States and next in Europe, there was a rapid rise of derivative trading, in which bets are placed on the upward or downward movement of currencies, asset prices, interest rates, or stocks. Investment banks get most of their profits out of derivative trading, but commercial

---

[201] Lazonick and O'Sullivan, 'Maximizing shareholder value', 27–30; de Jong, Roëll, and Westerhuis, 'Changing national business systems', 776–8.

[202] Lazonick and O'Sullivan, 'Maximizing shareholder value', 13–15; for the following: Lindert, *Growing public*, 136.

[203] Arrighi, *The long twentieth century*, 299–300; Ingham, *Capitalism divided?*, 50–8.

[204] Krippner, 'The financialization', 179–81 and 188–9.

[205] Taggart, 'The growth of the "junk" bond market'.

[206] Cumming, Siegel, and Wright, 'Private equity, leveraged buyouts and governance'.

banks also entered the territory. More generally, the financialization of business and the whole of the economy that had started in the 1960s and further took off in the early 1980s had now reached new heights around 2000.[207] (The effects on the real economy were mixed at best, most particularly by its negative effects on the real investments made by firms, as financial investments become more profitable and offer more rapid returns or better help to drive up stock prices than real investments do.[208])

Northwest Europe Brought in Sync with the American Cycle

In continental northwest Europe, the changes from the 1980s were even more profound, because these countries originally were in a different phase of the cycle. In a relatively short time span, these countries shifted from being mixed economies, with state and social security sectors of more than 50 or even 60 per cent of GDP in the 1970s and a well-developed corporatist organization, to a social variety of market capitalism, in the 1990s.[209] In the years thereafter, this process of marketization proceeded, or even accelerated, and many of these countries turned even more towards market-oriented or Anglo-Saxon-type arrangements. One conspicuous element in this process was the breaking up of cooperatives, semi-public corporations, foundations, and associations, as their activities were either brought under government control or left to the market, with a clear emphasis on the latter option from the 1980s onwards. In northwest Europe, the independent bodies and consultation boards that had been founded from the beginning of the twentieth century on, in order to form a counterbalance to economic liberalism and inequality, were now marginalized or abolished, exactly on the charge of distorting or obstructing the market. The consultation system, collective bargaining, and labour regulation have come under pressure, also aided by the growing influence of the European Union, which has made an explicit choice for the free movement and market allocation of goods, labour, and capital.

These shifts were in part stimulated, or even brought about, by influences and pressures emanating from the United States, where market development had already proceeded much further and market elites had obtained a dominant position. These influences were sometimes very apparent, as with the organization of the operations of European companies along American lines in the 1970s, noted above, but at other times they were hardly visible to the wider public, as with several seemingly practical, impartial changes that contributed to bringing the northwest European economies in sync with the American or Anglo-Saxon cycle. One example is the process leading to the international uniformization of accounting rules, in the 1980s and 1990s, under the impetus of the growing role of international companies, the globalization of capital markets, and foreign investments.

---

[207] Krippner, 'The financialization', 179–81 and 188–9.

[208] Orhangazi, *Financialization and capital accumulation*. More generally on the role of financial markets: section 6.2, 271–4.

[209] De Jong, Roëll, and Westerhuis, 'Changing national business systems', 778–94. For these varieties: Hall and Soskice, 'An introduction to varieties'.

The result of deliberations in the sector was that European countries practically adopted the Anglo-Saxon rules for accounting, rules that place more emphasis on the protection of investors, offer more influence to financial actors, and sever the links between financial reporting and tax accounting, as existed before in Germany, for instance.[210] This technical change thus directly affected the strategies and behaviour of economic actors, in line with American practices.

More visibly, organizations such as the International Monetary Fund, the World Bank, and the World Trade Organization, often under the aegis of the United States, have inspired, or even forced countries to liberalize and deregulate markets and privatize services. Also, chief executive officers of large corporations embraced the beliefs, opportunities, and the financial rewards offered by the American market system. Ideologically, the idea of shareholders' value became dominant over that of stakeholders' interests. This idea was propagated by the Organisation for Economic Co-operation and Development, as it declared in 1999 that corporations should principally be run in the interests of the shareholders.[211] American investors, investment bankers, and consultants also promoted the virtues of this concept and exported it to Europe and elsewhere around the globe. Moreover, as companies increasingly relied on financing by way of the capital market, and not by retained profits, they had to give in to the pressure of shareholders who wanted to have more influence on the way the company was run. The internationalization of share ownership, and the growing need to attract foreign investors, especially English and American ones, made it ever harder for companies to resist the urge for shareholder value, as happened in the Netherlands from the late 1990s.[212] More generally, in society as a whole, the acceptance of this pro-market ideology also was helped by the seemingly effective way in which economic growth was sustained, even despite the budget cuts of governments. This was done by deregulating financial markets, abolishing restrictions on credit, and allowing households to create more debts, for instance by taking a large mortgage on their house, and have them spend part of this credit on consumption.[213] Part of this debt was even unsecured, enabled by instruments now massively used in global financial markets, including derivatives and futures. Large and deregulated financial markets thus became essential in consumption and economic growth.

Another element in the growing dominance of markets, and that of market elites, was the loss of autonomy and power of the nation states, losing ground to the influence exercised by global capital and output markets, or to global players on these markets. Democratic, national governments run the risk of being 'punished' by global capital markets and financial investors, and in a way they have become subjected to them, losing legitimacy in the process.[214] Moreover, and at the same time, they are also losing authority and competence to international bodies, as in Europe, most notably the European Union. National states, and their governments

[210] Botzem and Quack, 'Contested rules'.
[211] Lazonick and O'Sullivan, 'Maximizing shareholder value', 14.
[212] De Jong, Roëll, and Westerhuis, 'Changing national business systems', 792–3.
[213] Crouch, 'Privatised Keynesianism', 390–4.   [214] Streeck, 'The crises'.

and parliaments, thus increasingly become unable to offer a counterweight to the market and the internationally operating market elites.

Even if several negative effects of privatization and unregulated markets did become apparent over time, as with the financial crisis starting in 2007, and this provoked nuances or even criticisms on too firmly held neo-liberal beliefs, this is still the dominant view, in northwest Europe, just as in the United States and the United Kingdom. As a result, these areas are now immersed in the same cycle, which can be labelled a northern Atlantic cycle.

These developments hardly had a positive effect on economic growth, perhaps even on the contrary. Despite all assumptions about the beneficial effect of neo-liberal policies and free markets on economic growth,[215] growth rates actually declined. The exact figures differ, but the tendencies are the same. The figures assembled by Angus Maddison, for instance, show how global growth fell from 2.9 per cent per year in the period 1950–73 to 1.3 per cent per year in what he labels 'the neo-liberal era' after 1973.[216] Even more telling, perhaps, is the decoupling of growth rates between the northern Atlantic countries and the rest of the world during recent decades. Growth rates in the flagship of these policies, the United States, were low, and especially the growth of labour productivity slowed down more markedly than elsewhere. The slowdown of growth happened despite the artificial boost for the demand side created by the growth of first public, and then private indebtedness, with debts as a share of GDP in many northern Atlantic countries reaching a high around 2010, at one and a half times GDP, or more, and with household debts forming an ever larger proportion of this.[217]

Much more apparent than economic growth in the northern Atlantic countries is the mounting inequality. The beginning of the twenty-first century displays growing inequality in income, and also in housing, health, and educational opportunities, but especially in wealth. These inequalities are most evident for Anglo-Saxon countries such as the United Kingdom and the United States. In the northwest European welfare states the picture is more nuanced, but the contrast is decreasing, with income inequality in northwest Europe slowly moving upward, up to the Organisation of Economic Co-operation and Development average, and with wealth inequality approaching the high level of the Anglo-Saxon countries. The distribution of wealth has become highly skewed, with Gini coefficients in many northwest European countries at the beginning of the twenty-first century of 0.8, or even higher.[218] Part of the skewedness is related to the massive rise of the fortunes of the super rich, the owners of hundreds of millions or even billions of Euros. These investments yield revenues several times the

---

[215] See above, 242, and section 1.2, 14–18.
[216] Maddison, *The world economy*, 128–9, 132, and 136 (figures for 1973–98). See for declining growth rates also Piketty, *Capital*, 93–5.
[217] For private debts (or 'private Keynesianism'), see above, 246, and below, 248.
[218] Van Bavel and Frankema, 'Low income inequality, high wealth inequality', revising the figures by Davies et al., 'The level and distribution'. See also Skopek, Buchholz, and Blossfeld, 'Wealth inequality'.

economic growth levels, thus resulting in an ongoing increase of their weight and the levels of inequality.[219]

As for another factor the high inequality figures are related to the growing indebtedness of households at the bottom of the distribution. The latter, paradoxically, was partly caused by the development of the welfare states after the Second World War. The publicly funded lifetime income security and collective pensions rights lowered the propensity to save and enhanced private debt creation, which skewed the wealth distribution. At the same time, the redistributive taxes required to finance this social welfare system were, and are, targeting labour income and consumption rather than wealth.[220] That governments deregulated financial markets and lifted limitations on credit, perhaps being induced by the will of both governments and households to sustain high consumption levels, has further stimulated debt creation by ordinary households.[221]

The organization of taxation further pushes up wealth inequality. The lion's share of state revenue in the northern Atlantic countries is derived from taxes on income and consumption, and the share of consumption taxes in many countries has been growing over the decades around 2000. Taxes on wealth at the same time are relatively low and have been reduced or even abolished, as happened in many countries with dividend and inheritance taxes.[222] Apart from the question whether there is sufficient political leverage to tax wealth, practical obstacles also play a role. The costs of monitoring and levying wealth taxes are higher than in the case of income or consumption taxes. Asset mobility has increased enormously in the last decades of the twentieth century, as a result of the deregulation and globalization of financial markets, and the wealthy have the means to hire legal-fiscal advisers in order to find optimal fiscal arrangements, or loopholes—all elements that make it easier to escape wealth taxes.[223] Increasing asset mobility by way of the global financial markets since the 1970s thus has contributed tremendously to the relaxation and declining revenues of wealth taxation.

As a result, wealth inequality and the importance of inherited wealth have increased since the 1970s or 1980s in the northern Atlantic countries, including northwest Europe, as demonstrated by Germany and Sweden.[224] The effects of this growing inequality on welfare are partly compensated by the access ordinary people have to publicly funded education, health services, and social security systems, but to a decreasing extent, now that budget cuts are causing the social welfare state to retreat. The growing difficulties of states to finance welfare systems through taxes is a process directly related to the growth and opening up of factor markets,

---

[219] Piketty, *Capital*, 25–7, 52–5, and 447–552. More extensively on this mechanism: section 6.2, 260–5.

[220] Van Bavel and Frankema, 'High wealth inequality'.

[221] Crouch, 'Privatised Keynesianism'; Streeck, 'The crises'.

[222] Bertocchi, 'The vanishing bequest tax'; van Bavel and Frankema, 'Low income inequality, high wealth inequality', 12–3.

[223] Zucman, 'Taxing across borders'.

[224] Frick and Grabka, 'Wealth inequality'; Roine and Waldenström, 'Common trends'. See also Piketty, *Capital*, 344–5 and 425–6, although he perhaps underestimates trends in these continental European countries.

more specifically the opportunities and mobility offered by capital markets—which make it difficult for states to tax wealth, as we have seen. Also, it is related to the opening up and liberalization of labour markets, as within the European Union—which exercises a downward pressure on wages and taxes to be levied on labour income—and the mobility of businesses and trusts, which similarly exercises a downward pressure on fiscal rates. As a result, especially in social welfare states, the effective rates of corporate income tax are substantially lowered; in some cases over the period 1982 to 2001 more than 20 percentage points.[225] In turn, this reduces possibilities for states to finance welfare systems, a development legitimized by the idea that markets are more efficient and effective than states in generating welfare.

Compared with the earlier market developments, or cycles, observed in this book, in continental northwest European countries it runs its course faster, beginning in the late nineteenth century with a wave of revolts, emerging self-organization of ordinary people, and growing freedom and equality. This opened up opportunities for a gradual development of factor markets within a balanced setting. However, this development was sped up, especially after c. 1980, as these countries rapidly shifted towards a more Anglo-Saxon organization of economy and society, and they converged with the American cycle.

This was part of a more general development, as the cycles in the modern period go faster and interact more with each other. This increase in speed in the modern cases is particularly the result of advances made in technology, infrastructure, and transport, which cause the interaction of new leading cases with the older ones becoming ever stronger and the force of this interaction ever larger.[226] As a result, the old leader in the last phase of its cycle ever more clearly speeds up the cycle in the new ones. Developments in eighteenth- and nineteenth-century United States, for instance, were clearly sped up by English influence, most notably through the flows of English capital to the United States in the nineteenth century.[227] Conversely, the continental northwest European countries in the first phase of their new cycle, starting in the second half of the nineteenth century, have influenced Britain and have contributed to partly reversing her cycle.

In the second half of the twentieth century, interaction was even more pronounced between the northwest European countries and the United States—which had entered the final phases of its cycle of market development since c. 1960, characterized by growing economic inequality and a growing political leverage of the market elites. During these phases, and especially since c. 1980, America heavily influenced northwest European societies, resulting in an acceleration of the cycle which had started there in the late nineteenth century. This growing interconnectedness of societies is found not only in the economic sphere, but also extends to the political, institutional, and ideological spheres, with the economically leading countries and their market elites in the course of history exerting an ever stronger influence over other areas. Alternative arrangements and

---

[225] Devereux, Griffith, and Klemm, 'Corporate income tax reforms'.
[226] More about this process: section 6.3, 284–6.   [227] Section 5.2, 233.

counter-developments are eroded, and ever more areas are drawn into the cycle of the leader instead. As a result, northwest Europe is brought in sync with the American cycle, instead of pursuing its own, and will now enter the last phase of the cycle of market development, together with the United States, and thus partake in its inevitable decline.

6

Conclusion

The Fundamental Incompatibility of Market Economies with Long-Run Prosperity, Equity, and Broad Participation in Decision Making

6.1. THE CYCLE

The three main cases analysed in the book, and also the three modern cases that are more tentatively discussed, show a similar pattern in the interaction of society, market institutions, and economy. In this pattern, an originally positive feedback cycle—between increasing freedom, growing factor markets, and economic growth—turns into a negative one, with increasing social polarization, institutional sclerosis, markets that become increasingly skewed towards the interests of market elites, and economic growth stagnating and turning into relative or absolute decline. Before placing these developments in the context of the current academic debates, this chapter starts with a more elaborate description of the cycle, using the reconstructions made in the previous chapters for the separate cases.

The Positive Phases of the Cycle

In the first phase of this cycle, these societies already possessed relatively high levels of living standards and GDP per capita, situated well above the bare subsistence level and being higher than in the neighbouring societies in their respective time. They had achieved this position by using a combination of various non-market mechanisms of exchange of land, labour, and capital—including those organized by (semi-)public authorities, local lords, kin, village and town communities, and horizontal associations such as guilds—and combining these with thriving output markets. This first phase, which is not extensively discussed in this book because of its focus on market economies, was found in Iraq in the fifth to seventh century, in Italy in the tenth to twelfth century, and in the Low Countries in the eleventh to thirteenth century. The high levels of GDP per capita in these societies were maintained even despite the high population growth characteristic of these cases in this phase. All of them, including the modern ones, but perhaps excluding Iraq, saw a massive extension of cultivated area and huge population growth, and all of them saw substantial technological progress during this period, that is, before the emergence of factor markets.

This subsequent emergence of factor markets in all of these cases took place within a situation of social balance, that is, a wide distribution of power and property over social groups and people at all levels of society. In all three cases analysed, and also in the modern cases discussed, this balance originated from a series of large-scale social revolts, social upheaval, and growing freedom and self-organization of ordinary people, in which the power of old, feudal elites was broken and gave way to a relatively wide dispersal of property and power. At the same time, the systems of exchange and allocation connected to these old elites were undermined or even done away with, whether they were systems of serfdom and manorialism, arbitrary levies by lords, or heavy taxation by state elites.

The destruction of these allocation systems also meant that exchange and allocation of land, labour, and capital by way of the market became more feasible. The restrictions on the transfer of land, labour, and capital that were connected to these older systems and imposed by these older elites, as within the systems of manorialism, state taxation, and lordship, were now weakened or removed by the new social groups and associations of ordinary people rising in this period. When serfs succeeded in shaking off their compulsory labour services and their ties to the land and their lord, for instance, they also gained a better position to become involved in flexible, competitive labour markets. At the same time, the resentment of peasants against serfdom, and their growing resistance and flight, made it more attractive to former lords to switch either to leasing out the land in competitive lease markets or to hiring wage labourers in the labour market. Growing self-organization and resistance of ordinary people, and the growing social balance resulting from this, therefore stimulated the development of markets for land, labour, and capital in various ways, and in their turn these markets made the removal of the remnants of unfreedom more feasible. This is the phase in which increasing freedom and growing factor markets were linked up and stimulated each other.

In this reconstruction, social revolts and upheavals were a major starting motor of the cycle, in all the cases investigated, but they are not sufficient to explain the start of the cycle (see Figure 6.1). Social revolts, and even a series of intense, successful ones, did not invariably lead to such a cycle, of course. More elements were needed, and tentatively we can point to an already well-developed economy, relatively well-functioning systems of exchange and allocation outside the market, relatively high levels of wealth and welfare, and the presence of well-developed output markets and trade networks as important conditional factors. At least, all three cases—and also the modern ones described—possessed these elements at the start of the cycle.

In the next phase of the cycle, and within the favourable social context which had emerged in the first stage, and which was characterized by a relatively broad distribution of property and political influence, factor markets rose and grew further. As a result of this context, these markets acquired a favourable institutional organization which offered security, transparency, and broad accessibility. This was because the social balance resulting from the preceding period, and the strength of self-organized ordinary people, made sure that all social groups could influence this organization and denied each other the opportunity to skew these markets towards their interests. Also, the use of these markets was open to participants who were in a fairly equitable bargaining position, because property was distributed relatively broadly between them and also because they had access to alternative mechanisms of exchange outside the market and therefore were free to choose whether to use factor markets or not. Functioning in this way, and under these conditions, factor markets grew and helped to sustain economic growth and increases in living standards.

The crucial element in this was the presence of a social balance, based on a wide distribution of property ownership, relatively wide access to political power, and possession of the means of self-organization, which originated in a preceding period of great social upheaval. In all three cases, this balance was consolidated by further revolts or social movements, but now often of a more defensive nature. These movements, like the guild movement in the Low Countries around 1300, or that of the Levellers in seventeenth-century England, despite their differences, were similar in that they both aimed at defending the gains that were made by non-elite people against the eroding effects of competitive factor markets on the position of the independent self-employed peasants and craftsmen in particular and against the new market elites of merchants and merchant entrepreneurs who tried to make use of the opportunities offered them by rising factor markets, both politically and economically. At the same time, at least indirectly, this second wave of social movements and revolts contributed to the removal of the remnants of feudal power and further opened up land, labour, and capital to the market, as happened in Iraq with the Abbasid revolution and in England with the Glorious Revolution.

Up to this point, the balance between the social actors did not yet enable one group to incline the market institutions to their own interests at the expense of

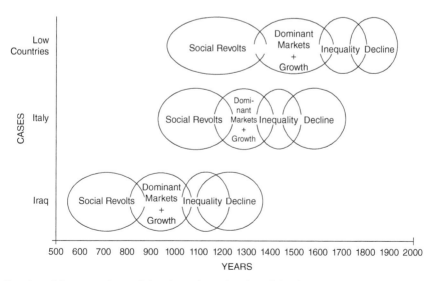

Fig. 6.1. Schematic chart of the chronological order of developments in the three cases discussed.

others. Rather, this social balance enabled a continuous adaptation of the institutions to changing economic conditions and opportunities, and increased the likelihood that individual, private interests and collective, public interests would be aligned. This balance also explains the positive role played by public authorities and the state, at least at this stage of development, since no interest group was powerful enough to use the state as an instrument to promote its own, specific interests. This started to change, however, with the last wave of revolts, which enabled new, non-feudal, and pro-market elites, who had built their strength partly on their use of markets, to get a stronger hold over the state. This was the case with the Abbasid revolution (in Iraq), the takeover of power by small, closed patriciates (in Italy), the Dutch Revolt, the Glorious Revolution (in England), and the American Revolution.

In this period, the economic and political role of non-market associations was slowly eroded. These organizations, including the commons and the guilds, which had been mostly formed by independent producers, were built on informal institutions such as mutual trust, cooperative behaviour, desire for equity among their members, and sociability, and they attempted to avoid or alleviate the corrosive effects of the market on the position of the independent producers. Within the nuclei of market development these organizations and the values that had become formalized within them were slowly eroded, in a process sometimes lasting several centuries, as the roles of guilds and commons were usurped or superseded by the market, and many of these organizations became marginalized or even dissolved. This marginalization often happened through the actions or even outright attacks by the new market elites and public authorities, using land, labour, and capital markets to this end. It could thus be argued that the market operated in a destructive way, eroding the values formed outside and before the market.

On the other hand, in a positive vein, the rise of factor markets initially improved the well-being of most people, both in material respects by way of economic growth, and also in immaterial respects, by replacing slavery and serfdom with wage labour, by banning arbitrariness, perhaps even by freeing lower groups from the constraints imposed by middle-class-dominated guilds and commons, and generally by offering more freedom and agency to people. These are the positive effects witnessed by Adam Smith and which were evident in the eighteenth-century Britain he was living in, inducing him to link markets and freedom to each other in his thoughts. A similar link may have been made by commentators in the Netherlands around 1600 and was surely made in the United States around 1800, and understandably so.

In the next stage, however, these positive effects were phased out and became outweighed by new, negative ones. Old dependencies and traditional hierarchies had been removed, but now came to be replaced by new ones, installed by new market elites who had come to the fore through the functioning of factor markets. The new dependencies they created were now often linked to the market, including the dependency of pauperized wage labourers or debtors on powerful entrepreneurs or creditors, a type of economic dependency growing with the rise of inequality that was also connected to the functioning of factor markets. In each of the cases, wealth inequality rose to high, or even unprecedented levels. Unfreedom grew even further as the new market elites started to use their growing economic wealth to turn this into political leverage and, next, used this to introduce 'new' forms of unfreedom, including market monopolies, slavery, and fiscal exploitation. The leverage they had acquired through the functioning of factor markets now thus came to be used by these markets elites as a hold over the wider political and institutional organization of society, even outside the realm of markets, as will be discussed in the next subsection.

A Closer Inspection of the Negative Phases of the Cycle

Now we have reconstructed the chronology of developments more carefully than has been done before, we can thus see that the causal link between markets and freedom rather was the other way around. More than being the result of markets, freedom was at the basis of market development, and it was used up and eroded by economic unfreedom once markets had become dominant. Factor markets, therefore, are a parasite using freedom rather than the harbinger or promotor of that freedom.

By analysing the main cases of market economies, the book shows that the balance between social groups of the first phases is bound to become disrupted when, in the next phase, the market becomes dominant as the mechanism of allocation of land, labour, and capital. This phase occurred in Iraq in the eighth and ninth centuries, in Italy in the thirteenth and fourteenth centuries, in the Low Countries in the sixteenth and seventeenth centuries, and in England from the mid-seventeenth century to the nineteenth. Even if alternative exchange and allocation systems did not fully disappear, the market at that point assumed a dominant position. This enabled the group, or groups, who benefited most from this organization of exchange and the ensuing economic developments to gradually acquire a dominant position, by the accumulation of property and, subsequently, of political leverage. This process occurred particularly as a result of exchange and allocation being organized by way of *factor* markets, because of the keen competition and the high mobility in the exchange of production factors they bring, and the opportunities they offer for accumulation of land and capital, that is, of wealth.

In this sense, the markets for land, labour, and capital are suitable instruments for nascent elites to break up the old, feudal restrictions on the accumulation of land and capital, to better gain access to surpluses, to acquire and accumulate more capital and land, to make it easier to invest surplus capital, to make it more profitable to possess more land and capital than needed for subsistence, and to get access to wage labour in order to make land and capital goods profitable. This formed an incentive for these groups to further stimulate the rise of markets, and especially factor markets, either directly by attacking feudal institutions or indirectly by way of their increasing hold over the state which offered them the opportunity to dismantle obstructions or alternatives for the market, such as were offered by the guilds or the commons. The interests of the new market elites and the importance of factor markets thus strengthened each other in a feedback loop. At the same time, other social groups—the majority of the people—lost agency and saw their opportunities to shape economic and political life dwindle.

Of the factor markets, the financial market was generally the last to emerge and grow, but it rose very quickly during the last phases of the process. At first, during the initial phases of the rise of factor markets, financial markets met serious objections and only slowly overcame religious and moral norms and opposition to interest and financial dealings, as observed for Iraq, Italy, and the Low Countries, but also for the United States. Still, in the next phase, these normative obstacles were overcome and financial markets started to grow relentlessly once land, lease, and labour markets required the availability of credit and stimulated its rise. Additionally, the rise of financial markets was stimulated by the accumulation of wealth in the hands of elites, who wanted to find a secure outlet for it, whereas ordinary people and public authorities at the same time became more dependent on credit obtained in the market, especially in order to finance their activities in output and factor markets.

At first, the rise of financial markets may have had positive effects, especially on technological innovation and economic growth, since we can assume that they enabled quicker decision making on investments, a better spread of risks and resources, and they helped to pool capital in order to make large investments. The latter became especially vital with the increase in scale and growing costliness of capital goods, as most conspicuously after the Industrial Revolution, although even then most investments in English industries were initially financed in more conventional ways, out of the private funds of elites. As increasing surpluses were accumulated in the further phases of the cycle, the rise of financial markets became unstoppable and inextricable, while at the same time their nature and effects changed, as they became a goal in itself, that is, they became the easiest and most secure way to make accumulated capital profitable. Financial markets in a way started to dominate and suffocate the real economy. Moreover, not only economic actors but also states became ever more dependent on credit and loans, giving the lenders political leverage, as observed for ninth-century Iraq, the fourteenth-century Italian city-states, and the seventeenth-century Dutch Republic.

So, the availability and growth of surpluses invited and stimulated the rise of factor markets, and in turn these markets further stimulated the accumulation of wealth and further strengthened the position of elites benefiting from market exchange. This went hand in hand with the next phase of economic growth, as measured by GDP per capita (see Figure 6.2). As the most recent reconstructions suggest, these cases had already reached relatively high levels of GDP per capita before the rise of factor markets, but now they entered into a next phase of growth which pushed them far ahead of all other, neighbouring societies. At this point, these cases became the absolute economic leaders of their era.

At the same time, this period was characterized by growing social inequality, in income and especially in wealth. Land markets and financial markets enabled elites to accumulate ever more land and capital and offered ways to make their wealth profitable. The distribution of wealth became ever more skewed, as observed for Iraq in the eighth and ninth centuries, Italy in the fourteenth and fifteenth centuries, and the Low Countries in the sixteenth and seventeenth centuries. Towards the end of the periods indicated, wealth distribution reached the highest levels of inequality ever recorded in history, with the Gini coefficients in these cases hitting 0.85, or more. These periods are also the ones in which a long phase of economic growth came to an end, and GDP per capita figures were at their highest point, which probably explains why the same periods feature most conspicuously in the economic-historical literature as examples of florescence.

In the next phase, the high economic inequality observed for these periods was translated into political inequality. The new elites used their economic wealth to acquire political leverage or even outright power, as happened in Iraq in the ninth and tenth centuries, in Italy in the fifteenth century, and in the Dutch Republic in the seventeenth century. The mounting public debts formed a main instrument for the new market elites to get a hold on government, as we saw. Also, in all of these cases, in this phase, the military role of ordinary people dwindled, as their militias or conscript armies were disbanded and replaced by armies of professional soldiers, hired in the labour market, or slaves. The capital and labour markets thus formed crucial elements in the shift from broad participation to the dominance of market elites in the political sphere.

The political leverage acquired by the market elites led to a deterioration of the institutional organization of the markets. Even if factor markets were initially organized in an open way, and favourable to all participants, a century or two after

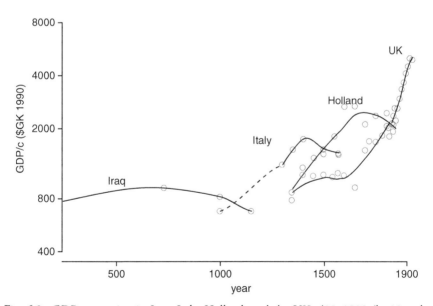

Fig. 6.2. GDP per capita, in Iraq, Italy, Holland, and the UK, 400–1900 (log10 scale, stylized). Data points are from the Maddison Project, <http://www.ggdc.net/maddison/maddison-project/home.htm>, 2013 version.

their rise to dominance there was a tipping point, after which the negative effects came to predominate through the actions of these new economic-cum-political elites who had emerged out of market developments. At that point, the existing institutional organization of exchange, which served the interests of the dominant, successful group, became frozen, because this group increasingly invested in retaining this framework, even if it was no longer conducive to growth when economic conditions were changing. In other instances, the quality of this framework of exchange even deteriorated, with markets becoming distorted towards the interests of the market elites, transaction costs rising, and accessibility of markets declining. As this led to economic stagnation or even decline, as observed in all these cases, the market elites were forced to further pursue this policy in order to protect their absolute levels of income and wealth. This created a lock-in effect, as it further contributed to the relative or even absolute decline of the area in question, that is, the area where factor markets had become dominant, be it a core of an empire, a group of city-states or principalities, or a country. At this point, elites there became tempted, or even forced, to develop more non-economic, coercive instruments, often integrated into the market or linked to it, in order to maintain their position in society, even at the expense of economic growth.

Even if the individuals involved hardly noticed this, because of the slow pace of these long-run protracted changes that spanned several generations, this whole process was a sour one, especially for the category of ordinary people. These people themselves had been the main source of the start of developments, during the positive, first phase. As a result of their revolts, collective action, and self-organization, they had played a major part in doing away with the old, feudal elites and forms of unfreedom. This opened the way for a free market exchange of land, labour, and capital, a process which was even further helped by the actions of these ordinary people, and also through their associations, in organizing the markets, through developing an open, favourable institutional framework. At the same time, after a period of beneficial effects (also on living standards), the rise and functioning of these dynamic markets created inequality and gave rise to a new elite, which increasingly used coercion, also within the markets. At this point, alternative systems of exchange and allocation, and alternative ways of access to resources, had been marginalized or dissolved, leaving many people dependent on the market. Where factor markets at first had offered an additional opportunity, they now became an instrument of coercion, not only economically but to an increasing extent also socially and politically. For ordinary people in the long run the whole process ended in increasing dependency and stagnating or even declining welfare.

The combination of these elements, and especially the increasing distortion of markets, made people, who now saw themselves in a weaker, inferior position vis-à-vis more powerful market actors, retreat from the market if possible. This resulted in a partial return to self-sufficiency, even near large urban centres, as observed for Tuscan country dwellers around Florence in the fifteenth century. Wealthy elites also partially left the market. For them, tying up capital in public debts or investing it in public offices became more profitable. In order to safeguard the accumulated land and capital they tied it up in family foundations, religious foundations, or fiduciary entails. The accumulation of capital in their hands enabled them to become patrons of the fine arts, resulting in the cultural florescence found in Abbasid Iraq, the Italian Renaissance, and the Dutch Golden Age. Rather than signalling economic growth, this florescence can be taken as an indication that a tipping point in the cycle had passed, together with other signals, including a highly skewed distribution of property, the increasing volatility of financial markets, big public indebtedness, the increasing application of non-economic coercion, and the freezing of capital, as will be further discussed in the next section.

In the same period, the market was becoming less dynamic, and its side effects on the economy more negative, leading to further economic stagnation or even decline. In the pre-industrial cases, most notably those of Iraq and Italy, this decline was an absolute one, and in the industrial cases a relative one. The accompanying social polarization made the effect of this absolute or relative decline on the living standards of ordinary people even sharper. In the industrial cases, this decline in living standards was, again, mostly a relative one, but it is more pronounced than the relative decline of GDP per capita, as shown by the case of the United States from the 1960s. In the pre-industrial cases, such as those of the Low Countries, and especially Iraq and Italy, real wages, welfare, and/or average human stature even declined in an absolute sense, as these became lower than they had been at the beginning of this cycle.

6.2. THE CYCLE, ITS SPECIFIC ASPECTS, AND THEORIES OF LONG-RUN DEVELOPMENT

The ideas generated in this book may be compared with the theories formulated on long-run developments in economy and society, and more specifically those on the functioning and effects of market economies, that is, economies that allocate land, labour, and capital predominantly through the market. The latter is an important qualification. The following section, just like the previous one, specifically relates to these market economies, and does not pretend to hold generally for all economies, including those that had factor markets but were not dominated by them. Nor are these sections meant to say something about the relative performance of market economies compared to other economies that were not dominated by factor markets.

With this disclaimer in mind, the evidence assembled in this book, first, seriously qualifies the widely assumed link between (factor) markets and economic growth, a link assumed in both neo-classical economics and the New Institutional Economics, and often based on, or referring to, exactly the cases discussed in the book: the Netherlands, England, and the United States.[1] This book now offers a better and more precise reconstruction of the chronology of the developments in these cases, and this suggests a different causality. Within the favourable settings of

---

[1] For instance North and Thomas, *The rise of the western world*, 132–45; Friedman, *Capitalism and freedom*.

the first phases of the cycle, the rise and growth of factor markets did indeed contribute to economic growth, albeit as the sequel of a growth process having already
started in a situation of non-market systems in combination with thriving product
markets. In the changing social context of the later phases of the cycle, however,
factor markets no longer contributed to economic growth, but rather to stagnation
or even decline.[2] Factor markets are thus not intrinsically good or bad for economic growth, and their effect varies according to their organization and their
social context, both of which change over time.

Market Economies and Inequality

This social context is largely found in, and shaped by, the distribution of property
and power, or the degree of inequality, in the society in question. This is another
issue in which the preceding offers insights. It helps in better understanding the
long-run changes in levels of inequality in market economies. Often, and especially in the older literature, this issue is approached within the framework of the
Kuznets curve, which describes how the first phase of economic growth leads to
rising (income) inequality, but the second phase to a reduction of inequality.[3]
Kuznets suggests that this reduction of inequality is largely the result of the dynamism and ongoing economic growth and the sectoral changes associated with the
growth process. Even though Kuznets focused on a very specific part of history,
that is, developments in the Western world in the nineteenth and first half of the
twentieth century, and he himself was cautious in his interpretation, his curve of
first rising and then declining inequality under economic growth conditions is
sometimes assumed to hold more generally.

It is particularly tempting to apply the idea of a Kuznets curve to the context of
rising markets. These markets are generally assumed to generate economic growth.
Combined, this would mean that rising markets would generate economic growth
and inequality, but in the later phases of market-driven growth this inequality
would decline again. This line of reasoning produces an attractive picture.

Still, two problems exist with this idea of a Kuznets curve: one with respect to
causality and one with respect to chronology. Regarding causality, it has been
remarked that, even if a curve-like development is found in specific cases, the curve
is still more a descriptive than an analytic instrument, and the elements forming
the causal link between economic growth and inequality remain unclear. In uncov-
ering this causality, the focus likely has to be more on social and political factors
than solely economic ones. What Kuznets actually observed in his research is the
decline of inequality in the United States from the First World War, which was not
an automatic result of growth, but rather that of growing self-organization, social
unrest, political reforms, and a resulting rise of state redistribution, as is also suggested by the analysis of this book. Along these lines, we need more specific tests

---

[2] This relationship is further elaborated below for financial markets in particular: 271–4.
[3] Kuznets, 'Economic growth'. See also Korzeniewicz and Moran, 'Theorizing the relationship',
279–85.

in order to unravel the causality of growing and declining inequality.[4] Regarding chronology, there is also a problem with the Kuznets curve. The cases discussed here show, as opposed to an assumed Kuznets curve, that inequality grows most in the phases in which economic growth is most conspicuous, in order to become only further consolidated in the last phases of the cycle, as economic growth is declining. Viewed in a long-term perspective, it is clear that Kuznets merely observed an interlude in the United States, with inequality declining for a short period in the first half of the twentieth century and rising again from the 1960s.

The preceding section, and the book more generally, has hinted at a more important, deeper cause of the rise of inequality within the market economies investigated here, that is, the role of the factor markets themselves. More specifically, a strong link appears to exist between the rise of dominance of factor markets and the growth of wealth inequality. This link is at least suggested by the chronology of the two developments, in which the one (rising inequality) followed the other (dominance of factor markets) in all cases investigated.

For Iraq, the earliest case discussed, the tentative reconstructions showed that in the early tenth century, after three centuries of intense market development, it had become one of the most unequal societies recorded in history.[5] The Gini coefficient for income inequality at that point was around 0.6, while wealth inequality, with a Gini of 0.99, had even reached the highest level for all historical and contemporary cases where estimates are available. Similarly, in Italy around 1400, as factor markets had been dominant for one or two centuries, wealth inequality had risen to great heights. Polarization was most pronounced in the largest market centres. In 1427, in the metropolis of Florence the Gini coefficient for wealth inequality was c. 0.85.[6] While similar figures for earlier periods are not available, it can be surmised that in the twelfth century, before the start of market developments, wealth in Italy was rather evenly spread.

The latter is, thanks to more abundant source material, fully clear for the Low Countries, where wealth traditionally was distributed fairly evenly over people. Factor markets had become dominant here between the fourteenth and sixteenth centuries. Subsequently, and especially in the pinnacle of market development, Holland, inequality rose to extremely high levels.[7] The Amsterdam wealth distribution moved up from a Gini of about 0.74 in 1585 to 0.85 in 1630. In that last year, of the total taxed wealth in Amsterdam, one-third was owned by the top 1 per cent. With regard to income developments were no less marked. In 1732 the Gini coefficient for income inequality in Holland had reached the figure of 0.61, which for income distribution in a comparative perspective is very high.

More specifically, inequality was shown to have increased most in those regions where factor markets were most dominant. The regions in the Low Countries where lease markets were most extended and competitive, such as the Guelders river area and coastal Flanders, where almost all land was leased out for short terms in competitive lease markets and land for prospective users was only accessible

---

[4] An attempt to do so for an earlier period: van Zanden, 'Tracing the beginning'.
[5] Section 2.3, 72–3.   [6] Section 3.3, 128.   [7] Section 4.4, 194–5.

through competition in that market, social differentiation in the countryside was most pronounced.[8] In the fifteenth and sixteenth centuries, the lease land became concentrated in the hands of a small group of successful tenant farmers, who amply relied on labour and credit markets for obtaining labour and capital. That the process of social polarization was strongest exactly in these regions where land was most prominently allocated through the lease market, instead of through inheritance, redistribution, or other allocation mechanisms, forms a clear example that factor markets, exactly in their purest form, acted as drivers of inequality. Likewise, in the towns wealth inequality grew most in those regions where factor markets were most extensive and open, as we observed for the industrial centre of Leiden.[9] More generally, in the period 1500–1650 total capital wealth in Holland, where market development at that point was most conspicuous, came almost fully concentrated in the hands of a small urban elite, whereas it had traditionally been fairly widely distributed over large groups of society.

The causal mechanisms linking dominant factor markets to wealth inequality remain among the least investigated topics in economic literature.[10] Apart from the general neglect of wealth inequality by economists, probably the fact that most mainstream economists assume that markets are self-correcting and lead to equilibrium makes this possible link a non-issue in their eyes.[11] The economic literature that exists on this point is mainly limited to the effects on inequality exerted by the market transition in Eastern Europe after the fall of communism or by the market reforms in China. However, these are *short-run* effects only, they concern mainly *output* markets, and limit themselves to *income* inequality. Here, we will try to make a tentative inventory of possible causes between the rise of factor markets and wealth inequality in the long run, based on the book and some of the scarce literature.

To start with, despite the relative equity characterizing the first phases of the cycle, still some differences in wealth distribution were present. In all of the cases discussed, traditional elites of all kind of denominations were combatted and their power restricted, but some form of social inequality remained. These initial differences in wealth were allowed to grow through the factor markets, as these enabled the profitable investment of wealth. As recently argued by Thomas Piketty, wealth tends to grow at faster rates than GDP, thus leading to inherently growing inequality, especially under conditions in which wealth remains free from disasters or political attacks.[12] When economic growth or population growth, or both, decline, and the rise of GDP thus slows down, as in the later stages of the cycle here, this process even accelerates. A crucial pre-condition for this process to occur, however, is the presence of large factor markets.[13] This is perhaps not sufficiently highlighted

---

[8] Section 4.3, 172–4.   [9] Section 4.4, 194.

[10] As noted by Hodgson, *Conceptualizing capitalism*, chapter 15.

[11] For this assumption: Stiglitz, *Freefall*, 251.

[12] Piketty, *Capital*, 25–7, 52–5, 84, and passim; Milanovic, 'The return of "Patrimonial Capitalism"'. Here, I use the term 'tendency' rather than Piketty's 'law'.

[13] This is the constant drive to inequality in 'capitalist' economies argued for by Korzeniewicz and Moran, 'Theorizing the relationship', 297–300.

by Piketty, who uses the umbrella term 'capitalism', but lists a host of different economies under this term, including ones in which factor markets are weaker and not dominant. This dominance, however, forms a fundamental divide. While non-market systems of allocation can potentially act as powerful brakes on accumulation of land and capital, the dominance of markets for land, labour, and capital helps elites, or nascent elites, to break up restrictions on the accumulation of land and capital, to better gain access to surpluses and to acquire and accumulate more capital and land. It also makes it easier, or even possible at all, to invest surplus capital and to make it more profitable to acquire more land and capital than needed for subsistence. If the tendency of relatively fast wealth growth exists, and wealth growth is likely to outpace GDP growth, it thus mainly does so in *market* economies.

Apart from the fact that market economies do not have restrictions on accumulation, while these are present in most other systems of exchange and allocation, another factor in this is that wealthy elites have more opportunities in factor markets than ordinary participants without wealth do. These opportunities are captured by actions at the micro level, which has not been the central focus of this book, but it still seems useful to list a few of them. First, the wealthy can separate themselves physically from their property, while a worker cannot detach himself from his labour power. The wealthy can collateralize land and capital goods, while ordinary people cannot collateralize labour and therefore are prevented from getting the loans needed to make investments or benefit from economic opportunities.[14] Moreover, the wealthy usually have more access to information or legal expertise. With the growing scale and complexity of markets, the advance this offers them also grows. Profit rates for big wealth are, therefore, substantially higher than those for small wealth.[15] Also, the position of big wealth holders in negotiations is stronger, because of the buffers and backstopping capacity they have, enabling them to wait for the right moment to make a market transaction, especially under difficult circumstances. The effects are demonstrated, for instance, for England around 1300, where the functioning of land markets in a context of rising food prices and growing distress led to forced sales at relatively low prices by the poor, accumulation of landholding, and social polarization.[16] Lastly, in labour and capital markets, because of their complexity and the impossibility of having all relevant actions monitored by a third party or precluded by a contract, power relations always play a role,[17] and this offers leverage to those with more wealth or political influence.

These mechanisms, only briefly indicated here, play out mostly at the micro level, and they are found even in factor markets that can be labelled as nearly fully open and competitive. Considering the fact that no factor market ever is fully open, and also in view of the fact that in all market economies inequality in the

---

[14] Bowles and Gintis, 'Contested exchange', 189 and 193; Hodgson, *Conceptualizing capitalism*, chapter 15.

[15] One of the few empirical tests: Piketty, *Capital*, 447–52.

[16] A simulation by Bekar and Reed, 'Land markets and inequality'.

[17] Bowles and Gintis, 'Contested exchange'. See also section 1.3, 25–9.

long run rose, as demonstrated in this book, there would be reason to investigate this possible link at the micro level more intensively, and empirically test these possible causal links, than done over the past decades in economic research.

We will now leave the micro level and return to the macro level that has been central to this book. Here we can find an additional mechanism that can help to explain the long-run link between factor markets and inequality. This concerns the crucial feedback mechanism in the interaction of markets and inequality by way of the institutional organization of these markets. It was shown how material inequality (that was mostly generated through the dynamics in factor markets or increased through the opportunities these markets offered), in all the cases of market economies discussed, became translated into inequality in political influence and decision-making power, which in its turn was used to adapt the institutional organization of factor markets to the interests of the wealthy.[18] For example, in Florence and Siena in the fourteenth century, as urban market elites had firmly established their dominance, in legal cases between urbanites and countrymen the courts all too often ruled in favour of the urban landowners, creditors, and speculators, thus undermining the security of property rights for the rural population. Also, the costs of litigation and legal aid were raised, making it difficult, or even impossible, for villagers and poorer people to undertake legal action. Also, the institutional organization of the *mezzadria* system, and the way dealings in lease, labour, and credit markets were interlinked in this system, were skewed towards the interests of the urban landowners. Another point in case are the oppressive labour laws enacted after the mid-fourteenth century, laws that froze wages, forced labourers to buy their food at high prices from urban vendors, and restricted their mobility.

This adaptation was also found in the organization of the fiscal system, which taxes levied on the possession of land or capital, on the market income from land, labour, and capital, or on purchases for consumption, and thus often linked to market values or actual market exchange. Often the organization of this system benefited the wealthy. An example is the tax exemption that buyers of state bonds in seventeenth-century Holland received, where the thresholds for tax reduction clearly favoured the large-scale wealth owners over the small-scale owners.[19] More generally, taxes predominantly applied to consumption in the form of excises, and also to visible wealth, most notably houses and land, but much less to movable wealth, shares in trade companies, and the shares in public debts owned by the urban wealthy. In practice it often happened that these forms of movable wealth, held almost solely by the rich, were not even taxed at all.[20] If these taxes were used to pay the interest payments on mounting public debts, as often was the case in the latter phases of the process, and the shares in the public debts were mainly owned by the wealthy, this system thus entailed a redistribution from the poorer to the richer parts of the population.

---

[18] See for the Italian cases in the fourteenth century section 3.2.
[19] Section 4.4, 196–9.
[20] As in Italy in the fourteenth and fifteenth centuries: section 3.3, 125–8.

In all these cases the organization of markets became more skewed towards the interests of the wealthy market elites. This links up with the intuitive claim that the way markets are shaped often makes them result in high inequality, as argued by Joseph Stiglitz.[21] The book, I hope, serves to specify this intuitive notion, to clarify the underlying, causal mechanism and to locate this mechanism more precisely in time, that is, in a specific phase of market development. It also helps to explain why this process proceeds through a feedback loop. The growing skewedness in the organization of factor markets further increases the success and profits of the same group in the market, and thus further contributes to the growth of material inequality, etcetera. This forms an extension of the ideas formulated by Daron Acemoglu and James Robinson, who argue that economic inequality/equality is likely to be translated into political inequality/equality and in turn this political inequality/equality is translated into the quality of institutions and a higher level of economic inequality/equality.[22] It seems, however, that they envisage open market economies as having a virtuous cycle, while other societies are caught in a vicious cycle. They thus endorse a more unilinear view on developments. Here, in contrast, it is argued that mature market economies as a result of this feedback cycle change from being open and equitable to become unequal and distorted.[23]

Possible Counterbalances and the Role of the State

The process of growing economic and political inequality seems to be inevitable in these cases of fully developed market economies, as posited in this book, also because there is no correction mechanism, at least after a point of no return has been reached. Even if we accept the assumption of neo-classical economists that market economies form a dynamic equilibrium and can adjust to changes, the accumulation of changes in power and property as a result of the negative feedback cycle analysed here slowly pushes the system to a tipping point, even if each of these changes in itself is fairly small. From that point onwards, the system loses its self-correcting ability, and a return to the previous situation is no longer possible. There seems to be an analogy with the changes in other complex systems, as those investigated for ecological systems (lakes, forests, coral reefs) that shift into another state, in which the approach of such a tipping point is signalled by a higher volatility of fluctuations.[24] Within the socio-economic systems investigated here, the growing incidence and intensity of the bubbles and bursts in financial markets observed in the last phase of the cycle may form a similar indicator.

In this last phase, the market systems cannot count on more deliberate interventions from within in order to restore the previous situation. In part, this is the result of a fundamental difference between the market and other systems of exchange and allocation such as the family, associations, communities, or cooperatives. These other systems, implicitly or even explicitly, have multiple goals, including societal

---

[21] Stiglitz, *The price of inequality*.   [22] Acemoglu and Robinson, *Why nations fail*, passim.

[23] See for this difference with the work by Acemoglu and Robinson also below, 269.

[24] Scheffer, 'Complex systems', where the author argues that the same may hold for complex social and economic systems.

ones, such as achieving security, long-term continuity, sustainability, equity, and enhancing the welfare of those involved, and they are expected to achieve several of these goals at the same time, and can be held responsible and accountable for the results by their members or associates.[25] Besides organizing exchange, they are also expected to promote the welfare of their members, to organize reciprocity and redistribution, and to dampen the negative externalities of exchange, in order to achieve these multiple goals. In contrast, the market is merely aimed at economic functions, and lacks these multiple, social goals. Even though the market is socially embedded in its formation and organization, as repeatedly argued by Mark Granovetter and many others,[26] the market is not socially embedded in its ends. One could label this the disembedded embeddedness of markets.

Still, even if the market would not have these social goals, many would argue that the rise of markets, or capitalism, at least indirectly brings social benefits. This argument is made along several lines. First, many authors would claim that markets do so through the assumed welfare growth they generate. This book, in contrast, shows that some factor markets indeed do so, but others, or rather, the same markets in a later phase, reduce welfare. Second, some authors, including Deirdre McCloskey, claim that markets foster and stimulate cooperative behaviour and solidarity, but this claim is much more contested. More widely accepted is the position that markets offer more agency and freedom to vulnerable groups, including women, as found by Laurence Fontaine.[27] Here, the book at least qualifies this position. While it may hold for the first phases of development, the preceding shows that the market in the last phases rather serves as an instrument for oppression and coercion by the new market elites. However, all real or assumed benefits brought by markets are at best unintended results, and the market itself cannot be held responsible for their non-delivery. Even though the market is socially embedded in its organization, it is thus not socially embedded in its outcomes. Especially when land, labour, and capital become commodified, and society is increasingly driven by market ends, this disembeddedness grows.[28]

Moreover, the elements that reduce or compensate for negative externalities of market exchange may mainly be supplied by non-market organizations and by norms and values generated outside the market.[29] In the course of time these norms and values, and the associated organizations, are instead eroded, as this book shows, and their roles are usurped or superseded by the market. We have seen in each of the historical cases that the rise of factor markets to dominance went hand in hand with the decline or erosion of family and kinship bonds, guilds, commons, and village communities, especially in the long run. It can be assumed that many of the associated norms about reciprocity, redistribution, personal obligations, and perhaps

[25] The classical account: Streeck and Schmitter, 'Community, market, state—and associations?'.
[26] Sections 1.1, 5, and 1.2, 9. Thanks to Rutger Claassen, who suggested to me the term 'disembedded embeddedness'.
[27] McCloskey, *The bourgeois virtues*, 4, 22–7, 126–38, and 483. Note, however, that she only loosely defines capitalism and may have focused more on commodity than factor markets. See also Fontaine, *Le marché*, 193.
[28] Gemici, 'Karl Polanyi and the antinomies of embeddedness', 9–10.
[29] Gemici, 'Karl Polanyi and the antinomies of embeddedness', 14.

even equity and justice, that existed within the individual group or association, even if not vis-à-vis outsiders, were now eroded in the process.[30] This will have occurred especially as markets became more complex, competitive, abstract, and impersonal, also with the growing scale of exchange, and even more so as in the course of centuries the belief was growing that the outcome of open markets is inherently just and equitable and thus need not, or even should not, be opposed.[31]

Some would argue that the erosion of these external norms and values does not cause a problem for the functioning of markets, since formal institutions, perfect information, and third-party enforcement can replace morality and norms. Either this enforcement and sanctions are offered by networks or associations, as argued for the Middle Ages by Avner Greif, or by way of generalized laws upheld by public authorities, put forward as the main option by Sheilagh Ogilvie.[32] As opposed to this, others argue that markets can only function well with social norms and a sound ethical foundation. This would apply especially to labour and credit markets, much more so than for output markets, since the transaction or exchange is not completed right away, but only in the future, which creates insecurity. Many would thus argue that non-perfect markets with incomplete information for the participants—that is, in practice virtually all labour and credit markets—need morality and a normative foundation.[33] Whether norms and morality are needed or not, however, this discussion only relates to the issue of how to make sure that markets keep on functioning well, especially at the micro level, and it does not relate to the question of how negative externalities and long-run effects of market dominance, especially at the meso and macro levels, can be counterbalanced. Moral considerations in theory would be able to do so, and this is the reason that Adam Smith placed so much weight on morality, but it is unclear where this morality should come from and how it would hold in the face of market competition and pursuit of profit.

To be sure, I do not think the market fosters immorality of individuals and do not want to engage in some cultural or ethical critique on the actions or actors within the market economy. On this single point, at least, I would agree with McCloskey that such a critique would be mistaken.[34] However, this is not because capitalism would improve our ethics, as McCloskey argues, but rather because such a critique misses the crucial mechanism and the essential point. Even if the market itself is not anti-moral, and market behaviour at the *micro level* is not immoral either, the outcome of market dominance at the *macro level* in the longer run will likely be a negative one, as shown in the cases investigated. Here most clearly the divide between actions and behaviour at the micro level and the outcomes at the macro level, as discussed in the introduction,[35] comes to light. This negative outcome is bound to occur particularly within a skewed social context, either in an

---

[30] For the assumed erosion of these norms, an issue that largely remained outside the scope of this book, see the nuanced discussion by Bowles, 'Liberal society'.

[31] See for the latter also below, 268.

[32] Greif, 'History lessons'; Ogilvie and Carus, 'Institutions and economic growth', 407–18.

[33] Bowles, 'Machiavelli's mistake'; Gauthier, *Morals by agreement*, 84–5, 93, and 101–2.

[34] McCloskey, *The bourgeois virtues*, 23.   [35] Section 1.3, 27–8.

initial situation of unevenness,[36] or in a context becoming more skewed over time, as observed in the cycle here. And it will occur even if the actions of individual actors are logical and are not violating morality.

Present-day democracies do not form an exception to this mechanism.[37] Especially if it is assumed or believed that perfect markets in principle produce efficient and economically justifiable outcomes, and they justly match achievement and reward on the basis of voluntary transactions, as seems to be the case among many political strands, opinion leaders, and among the public more generally nowadays, there is hardly an incentive to sustain or develop a moral counterweight to these outcomes. As market outcomes are perceived as objective and just, there is no need for this.

In this sense, Karl Polanyi was right to note that economic considerations will dominate the other ones within a market economy, in contrast to other systems of exchange and allocation which enable society and social considerations and values to predominate in the economy.[38] In addition, as remarked above, the market has no membership, and it cannot be held accountable, in contrast to these other allocation systems, whether guilds, associations, communities, or nation-states, which mostly possess associated organizations with a membership or citizenship. The more general this membership is, the more likely it is that the pressure of the members to counteract the negative effects of exchange will generate a positive outcome for society as a whole.[39] The market, however, does not possess such a mechanism through membership.

Also, in the course of the cycle described here, those groups and organizations in society who would aim for changing the arrangement of the market in order to balance or reduce negative externalities, gradually lost their economic and political power, as we have seen. Their revolts in the later stages of the cycle proved futile. This is also because of the consolidation and entrenchment of the elite in these later stages. If the elite is divided by dissent and conflicts, this opens up opportunities for fundamental changes, as argued by Richard Lachmann.[40] The preceding shows, however, that exactly in the last phases of the cycle the elites instead closed their ranks, also by realigning and combining economic and political interests. Not coincidentally, the historical examples that Lachman provides of the situation in which the elite becomes firmly entrenched, include northern Italy in the Renaissance and the Dutch Republic in the seventeenth and eighteenth centuries, that is, exactly the cases discussed here during their last stages.

The preceding, and the analysis made in the book more generally, also offers material for the discussion about the probability that modern societal institutions can counterbalance the negative effects of dominant factor markets and this would prevent or mitigate the process at least when it concerns modern democracies. Samuel Bowles suggests that liberal civic values are fairly robust against the

---

[36] The 'initial unfairness', described by Gauthier, *Morals by agreement*, 94–6.
[37] See also below, 269.   [38] Polanyi, *The Great Transformation*, 71–5.
[39] Conversely, the more particularistic these groups are, the less likely or smaller this positive effect on society as a whole will be: Ogilvie and Carus, 'Institutions and economic growth', passim.
[40] Lachmann, *Capitalists*, 9, 58–64 (elite divisions), and 70–2 (closure).

corrosive effects of markets.[41] This is based, however, on his assumption that an open law system and a high level of social mobility keep on underpinning these values, while we have seen instead that the organization of the legal system in the course of the process is affected and that social mobility is declining, with the rise of a well-entrenched market elite. The very long-run analysis undertaken here, which Bowles says would be needed to test his hypotheses on this point,[42] thus proves differently.

Others have placed their hope more particularly in the counterbalancing role of democratic governments. Wilhem Röpke, the champion of social market liberalism after the Second World War, for instance, has voiced optimism about the possibility of having a social market economy and of having the negative effects of dominant markets counteracted by democratically controlled governments.[43] The European Union, that has even formally committed to being a social market economy, subscribes to the same idea. In a similar vein, others have suggested that a favourable, inclusive political system would be able to prevent a negative feedback cycle between economic dynamics, inequality, and politics. Acemoglu and Robinson, for instance, argue that inclusive, pluralistic political institutions, a broad distribution of power, and a state that holds a monopoly on violence jointly may provide a check on the concentration of property and production factors.[44] As opposed to this, other scholars, including Wolfgang Streeck, assume a fundamental incompatibility of market-dominated economies, or capitalism, and democracy and material equity.[45]

The findings of this book, which relate exactly to the cases in which factor markets had become dominant, endorse the latter view. None of the different types of states or government systems in the long run was able to sustain or protect the relatively broad distribution of property and power found initially in these societies that became dominated by factor markets, for instance by devising redistributive mechanisms.[46] Rather, in all these cases, the state increasingly came under the influence of those who benefited most from the market system and would resist redistribution. When we look more closely at the role of the state in the process, we can see a clear shift.

In the first phase of the cycle, in each of these cases, the role of the state was not yet very prominent, and it figured next to all kinds of other organizations and associations that fulfilled semi-public roles. These associations did so either directly within their sector or community or indirectly through the local governments they controlled.[47]

---

[41] Bowles, 'Liberal society', 50, 70, and 75–8.

[42] Bowles, 'Liberal society', 49, where he argues particularly for a micro-macro analysis on the very long run; an analysis that is much more difficult to make than the macro analysis undertaken here.

[43] Goldschmidt and Wohlgemuth, 'Social market economy'.

[44] Acemoglu, Johnson, and Robinson, 'Institutions as a fundamental cause', 395–6; Acemoglu and Robinson, *Why nations fail*, 74–81 and passim.

[45] Streeck, 'The crises'.

[46] This leaves open the possibility that such counterforces may prevail in societies that have factor markets but not *dominant* ones.

[47] Except for the case of Iraq, where imperial rule and state bureaucracy were stronger from the outset: section 2.2, 46–52.

In the second phase, states together with local administrations started to act as the guarantor for the protection of property rights to land, labour, and capital, which was vital in reducing insecurity and transaction costs. In this way, states indirectly promoted the rise of factor markets. Also, they increasingly stimulated the rise of markets in more direct ways, induced to do so because of fiscal reasons. These markets, with the associated monetization and the commodification of land and labour, enabled them to tap resources and tax transactions and wealth more easily than with other forms of exchange and allocation, such as barter or communal redistribution. Also, the markets allowed the mobilization of capital and labour to fulfil the state's needs, for instance in infrastructural works and military operations. Especially where states did not have access to resources in a direct way, or by way of coercive means, markets formed an apt road to accessing them.[48] In a yet later stage, the states themselves came under the dominance of the market elites, and still later they even became instruments of coercion by these elites. Through the state, these elites used capital and labour markets, and bent the organization of these markets, in order to exercise control over economy and society. The use of hired soldiers, whose salaries were financed by way of public debts and who were hired in order to crush popular revolts against the market elites or the states dominated by them, forms a telling example.

In the process, factor markets cum market elites and states cum state elites came to overlap and make each other stronger, instead of counterbalancing each other. This is what Braudel labels the 'triumph of capitalism'. At this stage, according to his argument, capitalism became identified with the state, and capitalist elites even became the state, a process he illustrates by pointing to the same cases as discussed here in the book: the Italian city-states, the Dutch Republic, and later England.[49] Factor markets cum market elites and states cum state elites jointly tended to destroy the self-organization of ordinary people. States in the process needed factor markets to strengthen themselves (by way of public debt and hired soldiers) and market elites needed strong states to defend their property rights, even more so in the face of growing inequality and the resulting need for repression of the disadvantaged. Each of the cases discussed saw growing state repression, armed violence, and warfare by states and public authorities, now dominated by market elites, in the last stage of the cycle. It is telling that this was done after the militias of ordinary people were replaced by professional soldiers or slaves, hired or bought in the market and being more dependent on their employers or masters than the independent producers in the former militias were. Here, again, markets were an integral part of the dominance of the market elites, now also acquired in the political-military domain.

These changes in the socio-political constellation in their turn, in a feedback loop, also affected the markets. The new market elites used state power and coercion to maintain or further increase their profits, and were induced to do so ever more clearly in the course of the process, as the economy started stagnating and no

---

[48] See for ancient economies: Garraty, 'Investigating market exchange', 20–4.
[49] Braudel, *Afterthoughts*, 64–5. For his use of the term 'capitalism', see below, 272–4.

longer directly offered growing profits. In the process, by establishing monopolies, by consolidating oligopolistic positions in the market, by skewing the legal framework, by dominating the judiciary, by creating linkages between markets, by introducing coercive elements in the labour market, etcetera, they increasingly hindered the open and free functioning of markets. Reconstructions in this book thus show how they promoted or pushed policies that prevented markets from functioning in an economically efficient and effective way, and even more clearly their influence hindered markets from functioning in a socially optimal way in both the pre-modern and modern cases.[50] The market economy was, as it were, taken hostage by these elites, through their growing economic weight and also their hold on state power. This happened even in a context with strong representative bodies, estates, or a parliament, as they became part of the process instead of being able to counteract it.[51] Thus the state did not offer a check on developments, but instead it became an essential part of them. It is telling that this applies to all three cases of market economies investigated, and also to the modern cases glanced over, even if the type of political organization differed widely between them. The result is an ongoing and virtually unstoppable cycle.

Financial Markets and Capitalism

In the last phases of the cycle, financial markets and public debts played a large and ever more prominent part. At first, secure financial markets in combination with better defined and more absolute property rights may have helped to open up otherwise unused assets, enabling wealth owners to invest them in productive ways and ordinary people to get loans, and thus stimulate growth, along the lines of the argument made by Hernando de Soto, for instance.[52] Some would even argue that financial markets were thus at the basis of economic development and growth. This position is taken by Richard Sylla, who argues that all successful economies in history first had a financial revolution that created sound financial systems, including securities markets, a banking system, and debt and equity markets, before they became successful.[53] In order to underpin his argument he points to exactly the cases discussed in this book: the United States, England, the Netherlands, and, more tentatively, northern Italy. However, the chronology he uses is incorrect. Economic growth in these cases started earlier than Sylla assumes, as he bases his work on the outdated figures provided by Maddison.[54] Also, the financial revolutions he mentions did no more than lay the foundations for a well-functioning financial market, but the actual growth of these markets and their potential role for the economy is found only much later than presented by Sylla. It is striking, rather,

---

[50] See also above, 264–5.

[51] Compare for the Middle Ages: Ogilvie and Carus, 'Institutions and economic growth', 419–26.

[52] De Soto, *The mystery of capital*.

[53] Sylla, 'Financial systems and economic modernization'. This is also the position held by Larry Neal, for instance.

[54] For the more recent assessment of this chronology: section 1.2, 15–16.

that in the first phases of economic growth as reconstructed for each of the cases in this book, as based on the recent GDP per capita estimates, financial markets did not exist yet, or were limited to credit used for trade and consumption, or otherwise played only a negligible role.

So, economic growth started much earlier and the actual growth of the financial market later than Sylla assumed. Using the correct chronology shows that the causality is the reverse of that suggested by Sylla. Rather than promoting economic growth, financial markets are promoted by growth and wealth accumulation. In the later phases of the cycle, more money is invested in them, and especially in public debts, generating a safe return, to be even further increased by monopolistic positions. This induced owners of wealth to shift their investments from production and trade to finance, as happened in Italy in the fourteenth to sixteenth century, in the Dutch Republic in the seventeenth and eighteenth centuries, in England from the late nineteenth century, and in the United States in the second half of the twentieth century. These periods show a preoccupation with financial markets and high levels of private and public debt.[55] In the way they were functioning, these financial markets benefited only a small segment of society, that is, the owners of big wealth and the relatively small number of people employed in high finance. In contrast to sectors such as industry, transport, and trade, they did not offer a broadly based prosperity that could support a larger middle class.

Moreover, the large weight of financial markets in the economy enabled creditors to obtain a hold on the state and to employ the state's instruments of coercion to serve their ends, and partly have them paid for by public revenues and general taxes, as observed in the cases discussed. In the last phase, the financial markets became a goal in themselves, while at the same time the economy stagnated. This simultaneous occurrence of growing financial markets and a stagnating economy in late medieval Italy, and later again in the eighteenth-century Dutch Republic, made Braudel suspect that the innovations and growth in banking and credit each time imploded at a certain point, because they came to exceed the possibilities of pre-industrial economies.[56] It is questionable, however, whether the *pre-industrial* character of the economy really played a role in this. Rather, it is a phenomenon found during the last phase of this cycle in every type of economy, including the industrial and modern ones.

This last phase could perhaps be labelled that of capitalism. The term 'capitalism' is often used in the literature without further elaboration, as if it is immediately clear what is meant. Also, some commentators have given it a negative connotation, using it as a pejorative term, causing again others to abandon using the term altogether, because of the ideological charge associated with it. In the historical sciences, the term disappeared together with the waning interest in the classic 'transition debate', about the so-called transition from feudalism to capitalism, a debate revived in the late 1970s and early 1980s in the articles by Robert Brenner

---

[55] Phillips, *Boiling point*, 193–211. For the second half of the twentieth century: Crouch, 'Privatised Keynesianism'.

[56] Braudel, *Les jeux de l'échange*, 344–8.

and the rebuttals by Michael Postan, Emmanuel le Roy Ladurie, and others.[57] This debate has petered out. Instead of discussing the transition to capitalism or the rise of capitalism, most historians now prefer to use rather vaguer notions, such as 'modernization' and 'rationalization', often portraying these processes as benevolent, almost necessary, lending their histories a teleological flavour, which these studies share, incidentally, with the older studies using the concept of 'the transition' or 'the rise of capitalism'.[58]

Still, all this does not need to force us to abandon the concept of capitalism altogether, since using a sharp concept with a clear definition would help the analysis more than using vague notions of modernization and progress. What does the preceding enable us to say about the concept of capitalism? Capitalism could be defined by the dominance of markets in the exchange and allocation of land, labour, and capital. This is a first element, in which the rise of wage labour is a conspicuous one, found at the beginning of each cycle analysed here. In each of the cases, an accumulation of land, wealth, and capital goods occurred, and an associated division between property-less wage earners and entrepreneurs/investors who privately owned the means of production.[59] In this situation, identified by the loss of ownership of the means of production for many people, and an associated dominance of wage labour, both producers and wage labourers on the one hand and property owners and entrepreneurs on the other became dependent on output and factor markets. This is the next stage in the cycle analysed here. As we have seen, a further stage follows. This stage resembles the way capitalism is defined by Fernand Braudel, who contrasts capitalism with the market economy. The latter, in his words, is down to earth, characterized by daily market exchanges and transparency, and it involves mainly producers and traders, without many intermediate wheels.[60] Capitalism, on the other hand, lacks transparency, is characterized by speculation, by long, sophisticated chains of exchange, a basic inequality of actors, huge profits, accumulation of capital, and the large size of capital enabling the capital possessors to gain a privileged position and monopolies in exchange. This is the stage identified here at the end of the cycle.

Braudel looked mostly at output markets, although, of course, he also mentions land, labour, and capital markets. He did not note, however, how in each of the cases of clear-cut capitalism he presents—that is, northern Italy at the end of the Middle Ages, the Dutch Republic in the seventeenth century, and England in the following period—the rise of *factor* markets to predominance played a crucial role in this process. By including this observation we can combine all elements into a joint approach to the term capitalism, being part of a cycle of market development. In this cycle, the first stage (the dominance of factor markets), which can be labelled 'market economy', was followed by the next one (accumulation and growing

---

[57] Brenner, 'The agrarian roots', and the subsequent debate.
[58] See the ideas on historical progress and transitions shared by those inspired by both Adam Smith and Karl Marx: sections 1.1, 7–8, and 1.3, 22–3.
[59] See also Hilton, 'Capitalism'; van Bavel, 'The transition in the Low Countries'.
[60] Braudel, *Afterthoughts*, 49–65. See also the comments on Braudel by Wallerstein, *Unthinking*, 202–17.

inequality), and yet another one (speculation, monopolies, and a close link between capital and the state), a stage that can be labelled as 'capitalism', that was inescapably following up on it and ended in the decline of the market economy.

Rise and Decline

The findings of this book oppose the idea of a single and unilinear development towards the market economy or a one-way transition to a market economy. This idea is found with many scholars, both with Marxist and neo-classical pedigrees, and with many of those inspired by the New Institutional Economics.[61] Their idea that a unilinear process does exist is understandable, in view of the fact that market economies are more numerous now than before and also cover larger areas and exert a bigger influence on other areas than earlier in history.[62] Moreover, until recently, we did not know a lot about whether factor markets in the distant past existed and how important they were. The material assembled in this book, however, enables us to see that market economies have existed for a long time in history and that they each display a cycle in their development, with the number of these cases increasing over time. What we observe, therefore, is a growing number of cycles, or cyclical chains of transitions, rather than a single transition starting in Western Europe somewhere at the dawn of the modern era. Envisaging this process as composed of separate cycles, and historical development in the very long run as increasingly influenced by these cycles of market growth and decline, would enable us to escape from teleological and Eurocentric thinking that became solidified with the Enlightenment and the Industrial Revolution,[63] and it would enable us to better understand the mechanisms behind change.

Earlier thinkers were more inclined to see socio-economic processes as cycles instead of unilinear developments. The fourteenth-century scholar Ibn Khaldun, for instance, in his 'Introduction to History',[64] describes how cities grow under the protection of stable government, and the inhabitants become wealthy. Next, they become extravagant, to the detriment of business, and eventually lead to downfall and ruin. Machiavelli, knowing the experiences of Renaissance Italy, argues that, after a period of florescence, social inequalities open the way for the wealthy to use their private economic power to dominate political and legal processes, and thus to threaten freedom.[65] There would be corruption, an erosion of civic liberty and virtue, the neglect of the public good, and violent outbursts of poorer people who had lost their interest in preserving civil order. The result would be a cataclysm, from which new, uncorrupted societies would rise again. His view on societies, too, was a cyclical one.

Parts of this cycle have indeed been analysed in economic and economic-historical studies, but not often, and mostly each part is placed there within a larger progressive

---

[61] Section 1.1, 7–8.
[62] See section 6.3, 284–6. See for the reinforcement of the latter idea by recent studies section 1.2, 14–18.
[63] Section 1.3, 22–3.   [64] Khaldun, *The Maqaddimah*, 273–89.
[65] Benner, *Machiavelli's ethics*, 269–79. See also section 3.4, 142.

or teleological framework, not within a cyclical framework. Acemoglu and Robinson, for instance, highlight the part in which regime changes break the power of old elites and create a society with more broadly distributed political rights, which in turn results in more people being able to use economic opportunities and develop a wealthier society.[66] They thus stress the role of people's agency and link broad political participation to economic prosperity, in a historical perspective. They do not make the role of (factor) markets very explicit, however, and they hardly envisage that developments may be reversed, with the quality of the institutional framework declining and worsening again as part of an endogenous development.

Modern studies analysing *the decline* of market economies are very few, even though such a decline is much closer to the thinking of one of the main inspirations of economic thought, Adam Smith, than superficial readers of his work may assume when they propose a teleological view of the road towards the final destination of human society, that of a market economy. Smith himself showed a keen awareness of the possibility of decline of his commercial society. As causes of decline, he mentions land scarcity, military defeat, and the accumulation of debt, but he also identifies a deeper, underlying cause: the tendency of a commercial society to undermine or corrupt the virtues of its citizens, making this society a fragile one.[67] Smith indicates that 200 years is as long as the course of human prosperity within commercial societies usually endures.[68] Although the mechanisms of Smith's decline perhaps differ from the ones proposed here, and I do not think some kind of moral decadence or corruption is a root cause of development, but rather a logical consequence of them,[69] Smith's ideas on the fragility of commercial society and the time path of its rise and decline link up with the evidence presented here.

Parts of the cycle as reconstructed here can also be found in the work by Jack Goldstone, especially in his discussion of the efflorescences of pre-modern economies.[70] The economies he discusses, including the early modern Netherlands, each experienced a pulsation of economic growth and growing complexity, often later characterized as a 'golden age', but then declined again, in his view as a result of population pressure, social unrest, and crisis. Goldstone, however, fails to notice that all of these cases were characterized by dynamic factor markets, and thus the effects of the market and mounting inequality do not play a role in his description of these cases. There are also similarities with other studies on the rise and fall of societies and shifts in economic hegemony. Already mentioned is Braudel, who investigates the way dominant cities replace each other, from the northern Italian ones to those in the Low Countries (first Antwerp and next Amsterdam), to London, and to New York. He describes how each of these leaders was capitalist and views the successive shifts as revealing the fragility of each of these situations

---

[66] Acemoglu and Robinson, *Why nations fail*, 3–4 and 79–87. See also above, 265.
[67] Smith, *Wealth of nations*, 781–8. See also Alvey, 'Adam Smith's three strikes', 1431–3.
[68] Smith, *Wealth of nations*, 425–7; Heilbroner, 'The paradox of progress'.
[69] See section 6.2, 267–8 (against a moral critique of the market economy) and section 6.3, 278–9.
[70] Goldstone, 'Efflorescences and economic growth'.

of capitalist leadership.[71] It is not fully clear, however, what mechanism he sees behind this process of rise and decline, and his work seems more intuitive and descriptive than analytical.[72]

More emphasis is placed on the period of decline by Kevin Phillips, describing the processes of financialization, social polarization, and economic stagnation for the cases of the Dutch Republic, England, and the United States.[73] Most akin to the present book, however, is perhaps Giovanni Arrighi's investigation of how capital accumulation, financial markets, public debts, and state formation interact. In *The long twentieth century* he reconstructs this process for several successive cases of hegemonic powers, from medieval Genoa to the modern United States. However valuable and inspirational his analysis is, also for me when writing this book, Arrighi only deals with one phase in this cycle—a final phase— and he refrains from investigating the underlying structures of the market economy.[74] Above I have tried to do this, and also to analyse the whole of the cycle, which made it possible to sketch a wider perspective and to show how this phase is only part of a much longer, endogenous process.

6.3. THE CYCLE IN TIME AND SPACE

In the cases in which this process started, and in which factor markets assumed a dominant position, this cycle unrolled in an inevitable process. We have discussed three conspicuous, successive cases from the pre-industrial period and, more succinctly, three modern periods. These six cases can be rather clearly identified, thanks to the sources and studies available, but comparable cases can probably be found in other, less-documented parts of the world and in earlier times. In Chapter 1 we pointed to China in the Song period, Roman Italy, or, earlier in time, classical Athens/Attica and Iraq in the neo-Babylonian period. These are early examples of market economies, or at least economies which were highly monetized and commercialized and in which markets for land, labour, and capital played a major role.[75]

Early Market Economies and Their Decline

Just like the cases discussed more extensively in this book, these very early cases of (possible) market economies after one or two centuries of growing markets and rising wealth witnessed growing inequality, declining welfare, and factor markets disappearing again. For instance, Babylonia in the long sixth century BC, in a period of growing factor markets, witnessed economic growth, but at the same time food prices rose sharply, resulting in the longer run in declining welfare, even followed by food crises and famine, which became structural phenomena in the

---

[71] Braudel, *Le temps du monde*, 21–4.
[72] As remarked by Lachmann, *Capitalists*, 44. See for Braudel also above, 270, 272–3, 275.
[73] Phillips, *Boiling point*.
[74] As Arrighi, *The long twentieth century*, 355, himself explicitly states.
[75] Section 1.4, 31–3.

fifth century BC.[76] In the same period, markets lost importance again as allocation systems for land, labour, and capital.

Likewise, in the first and second centuries AD, after a period of dynamic factor markets and unprecedented expansion which had started at the beginning of the second century BC, Roman Italy saw the accumulation of land, the rise of large latifundia, the building of fortified villas with watch towers and guards, and more violent social relations. An ever smaller elite exercised an increasing control over ever larger shares of the economic surpluses.[77] At the same time, after a peak in labour productivity and incomes had been reached in the first century AD, economic decline set in during the late second century. The severest decline in all of the Roman Empire was found in its political and economic core, Italy, where average income declined to a level barely above subsistence.[78] Living standards dramatically declined, as shown by the decline of human stature. Both men and women in the Roman period were substantially shorter on average than in the preceding period, with the figures declining especially from the late second century.[79] In the next two centuries, ever more people were pushed towards subsistence level, whereas the accumulation of property and power in the hands of an ever tinier elite proceeded. In the fourth century, senatorial estates got even larger, and wealth was further concentrated into the hands of a small imperial elite,[80] while at the same time average incomes declined further.

For China in the late Middle Ages, the picture is less clear. We do know, however, that after the florescence of markets in the Song era, the following period, between the late thirteenth century and the fifteenth, saw decreasing urbanization, political upheaval and wars, famines, imperial policies turning against foreign trade, and a decline of interregional trade.[81] At the end of the period, many peasants had become heavily indebted and had to sell themselves and their family members as slaves. Unfree labour became more important again.

Even if the picture for these early societies is still hazy, it is clear that these were all cases of florescence, or 'golden ages', which came to an end after two or three centuries.[82] Many causes for the decline of these thriving economies have been put forward in the literature, and among these the exogenous factors such as plagues, barbarian invasions, warfare, or climatic deterioration figure prominently. Similar explanations have sometimes also been proposed for the decline of the three medieval and early modern cases investigated more extensively in this book, but the more precise chronology the book offers allows us to discard these exogenous events as explanation. As we have seen, the greatest shocks are either too early to be

---

[76] Kleber, 'Famine in Babylonia', 235–8; Jursa, *Aspects of the economic history*, 745–53.

[77] Jongman, 'The early Roman empire', 615–17. See also the short, rough sketch by Jongman, 'Rise and fall of the Roman economy'.

[78] Milanovic, 'Income level'.

[79] Gianecchini and Moggi-Cecchi, 'Stature in archeological samples'; Jongman, 'The early Roman empire', 607–9.

[80] Milanovic, 'Income level'.

[81] Liu, *The Chinese market economy*, chapter 7. A more positive account for rural Jiangnan: Bozhong, 'Was there a "fourteenth-century turning point"?'.

[82] For the concept of florescence, see section 6.2, 275.

blamed for decline, or too late, as they strike an economy that already was struggling or declining. For Iraq, for instance, the Mongol invasion and the sack of Baghdad are often blamed for its downfall.[83] This shock, however, took place only in the thirteenth century, long after the economic decline had set in. Likewise, the Black Death in Italy rather accelerated the downfall that had already started there, instead of being its cause. Moreover, the same Black Death, despite the dramatic population decline, could also have beneficial economic effects, as shown by the contemporary developments in the Low Countries, where the favourable social and institutional setting of factor markets allowed the growing capital per capita ratio to be translated into productive investments and growing welfare, and the Black Death did not prevent economic growth to occur at all.

The three cases extensively investigated in this book suggest that the endogenous cycle found here played a much more crucial role than exogenous events in the stagnation or downfall of these market economies. The same arguably holds for the more ancient cases. Although the data are often too scarce to establish exactly what kind of factors were underlying the process in the early market economies, we can deduce from the medieval and modern cases analysed here that this cycle weakened the resilience of these societies, making them more vulnerable to bad climate, epidemics, or barbarian attacks. These exogenous shocks mainly stand out because they are more visible and were better observed in the ancient sources, especially the literary ones, and perhaps also because they appeal more to a wider audience, because of their dramatic nature, but the vulnerability of these societies was caused by an endogenous, structural process.

To illustrate this, we can again point, as an example, to the divergent developments after the shock of the Black Death. In Italy, the response to the ensuing scarcity of labour was the enactment of tight labour laws and coercion, while in the Low Countries labour mobility and freedom instead increased in the wake of the same population decline, which in turn allowed labour to benefit from its scarcity through rising real wages.[84] This observation links up with the growing awareness in disaster studies that disasters are social occurrences, with hazards of a similar nature and force having very different consequences, especially in the long run, depending on the social and institutional organization that acts as a kind of prism, allowing a society to buffer a shock, or not, and bend the effects into a positive or negative direction.[85]

The reconstruction of this cycle also enables us to place another factor brought forward for the decline of these ancient cases, but also for the decline of Iraq, Italy, and the Low Countries, into another perspective. This is the traditional story of moral decadence or the so-called 'treason of the bourgeoisie'. Many authors have empirically or intuitively argued for a process in which merchants and entrepreneurs after some generations start to lose their interest in economic activities, reduce their investments in trade and especially industries, and shift their attention

[83] Especially in the older and more general overviews: Lewis, *The Middle East*, 97–9.

[84] See for the Italian labour restrictions: section 3.2, 119–24, and for labour in the Low Countries in the same period: section 4.2, 159–64.

[85] Tierney, 'From the margins'.

more to political offices, state debts, rent seeking, and conspicuous consumption. At the same time, they became part of the patriciate or even the nobility, or in merchant towns they closed themselves off to become a patriciate. Fernand Braudel told this story, for instance, for the Medici family and other Italian elites around 1500.[86] An ancient case of decline assumed to be caused by decadence is the Roman economy in the late imperial era, the third to fifth century, as Roman citizens presumably lost their virtues and became decadent rentiers, as in the famous rendering by Edward Gibbon, in his *Decline and Fall of the Roman Empire*. The persons thus 'betraying' their economic roles all lived in a period of economic decline of their societies, and they are often blamed for this decline, exactly because of their alleged addiction to consumption, laziness, or moral decadence.

This picture has been nuanced or criticized. Indeed, not all merchant or entrepreneur families display this addiction or decay, and sometimes they combine the acquisition of social status and political offices with a continuation of their economic activities.[87] More fundamentally, however, the evocation of a supposed moral decline or sinfulness, or speculations about the absence of a certain mentality, mainly seem to have been inspired by the absence of an understanding of the mechanism behind the supposed decay.[88] Placing the shifting focus of these merchants and entrepreneurs into the more general cycle analysed here, however, makes clear what this mechanism was. This obviates the necessity to evoke all kinds of mental or moral elements. We have observed how, in the last phases of the cycle, the market framework becomes less favourable, leading to the economic decline of the area. Elites thus become tempted to develop more non-economic, coercive instruments, and to 'invest' the capital they have accumulated in public debts, in family foundations, or in acquiring public offices, or to spend it on the fine arts, which generates social capital and prestige. What they do is logical in this phase of the cycle, and there is no need to invoke any moral decadence.

The preceding also opposes ideas about a 'feudal mentality' that in earlier eras supposedly prevented a shift to a real, sustained market economy, up to the moment that a 'capitalist mentality' arose. Rather than belonging to a fundamentally different mentality, the decisions and changing preferences of merchants and entrepreneurs becoming rentiers were part of the market cycle. Their turn towards becoming non-economic elites did not obstruct a shift to mature capitalism but was instead the result of the maturity of the market economy and its effects, and it can be found both in the pre-industrial and in industrial, contemporary cases.

Urban Centres and Rural Hinterlands

The rest of this section will look particularly at the spatial dimension of the cycle and its constituent developments. Relevant aspects to be discussed are the geographical scale in which developments played out, the geographical variations

---

[86] Braudel, *Les jeux de l'échange*, 426–9. See also Pinto, '"Honour" and "profit"', for late medieval Siena.

[87] Soly, 'The betrayal of the sixteenth-century bourgeoisie'.

[88] See for the issue of immorality, from another perspective, section 6.2, 267–8.

within the cases discussed, and the growing interaction between these cases. Another spatial aspect, and the one I would like to start with, is the relationship between urban centres and rural hinterlands, or between town and countryside. The cycle of market economies analysed in the book has not been restricted to the towns, but played out in town and countryside, which were in mutual interaction through the markets for land, labour, capital, and output. Sometimes, these markets between town and countryside were even fully linked within one system, as in the *mezzadria* in late medieval Italy, where urban capital, rural landed property owned by urban burghers, rural labour, and rural products were integrated within a single system of lease, labour, credit, and output markets.

In the process of the rise of factor markets the countryside was not lagging behind, as a place of traditionalism, untouched by markets. On the contrary: developments here often proceeded further than in the towns. This is shown especially by developments in the Low Countries, where the oldest and largest towns, as those found in Flanders, were long dominated by guilds and saw the fierce protection of small-scale commodity production by independent producers, who mostly owned their means of production, and thus kept factor markets at a distance, while at the same time a number of rural areas in Flanders became characterized by agrarian capitalism, with large-scale farmers intensively using lease and capital markets and employing large numbers of wage labourers. In these cases, the countryside was not backward at all but moved fastest to becoming a market economy, as illustrated particularly by the importance of the labour market and the share of wage labour in the total labour input, which in many regions was larger in the countryside than in the towns.

The negative social effects of the cycle analysed here also came to light earliest in the countryside, as country dwellers lost their land through the land market, often to urbanites, and became dependent on urban capital, as observed in Iraq, Italy, and the Low Countries, where the countryside in each of these cases was slowly sucked dry of cash. As, moreover, urban elites were able to use the towns as a political instrument, and via these towns or their dominant position in financial markets, or both, acquired a hold over state power, they were often able to adapt and skew factor markets, and especially rural factor markets, to better serve their goals. As a result, and combined with the growing economic imbalance between urbanites and country dwellers, the position of most rural inhabitants in the factor markets further deteriorated. In the next stage, investments in the countryside declined, as country dwellers no longer had the means to invest and resources were increasingly drained to the towns, where urban elites spent them on luxuries, financial speculation, the development of coercive means, and the acquisition of prestige and political power.

As a result, agricultural productivity declined, the rural society became more vulnerable to hazards and famines grew in number. The negative social and later also the economic effects of this cycle were thus observed first in the countryside, not in the towns where production and retailing of luxuries, financial markets, and political power were concentrated; sectors that sustained some of the economic florescence longer there. This process and the associated skewedness between the fortune of towns and countryside can be observed in Iraq in the ninth and tenth centuries, and in Italy in the fourteenth and fifteenth centuries. In the Dutch Republic in the seventeenth and eighteenth centuries and in England in the nineteenth century this difference between town and countryside was less pronounced, also because many of the negative effects were now found in rural areas further away. The rural areas were found, for instance, in Poland, where serfs worked on latifundia to produce grain for Dutch markets, or in colonies overseas, where slaves worked on plantations to produce cash-crops for the market cores, and which were dependent on these market cores, by economic ties or military coercion.[89]

Regional Differences

Also, more needs to be said about the geographical scale of the cycle discussed. The book has focused on a cycle occurring within areas of about 50,000–150,000 km^2 in size, where the core of market developments was found and they interacted most clearly with political power at the state level. The size of these core areas was gradually increasing over time, especially within the modern cases. In their turn, these cores in the course of history extended their influence over ever wider areas, associated with the growth of technology, transport opportunities, and mobility of capital, labour, and output, leading to the situation nowadays in which the influence of these cores even spans large parts of the globe.[90]

One could, however, also investigate and analyse these developments at other, smaller geographical levels than the ones highlighted in this book. Especially in the Middle Ages, in Europe, as larger empires were absent or weak, and national states had not emerged yet, developments were perhaps even more remarkable at this smaller level. One could label this the regional level. Examples in late medieval Italy are the regions or city-states of Tuscany, Lombardy, and the Veneto, with the cities of Florence, Milan, and Venice as their main centres. Each of these regions possessed its own geographical and socio-economic characteristics and had its own chronology in the rise of factor markets. Tuscany underwent this development earliest, while Lombardy was some one or two centuries later, but developing furthest in a capitalist, market-dominated direction.[91] They thus formed separate cores in this northern Italian market development, interacting with each other and with the surrounding regions where factor markets sometimes developed to a lesser extent.

These regional differences were even more pronounced, and perhaps they are also better charted, within the Low Countries. Here, the rise of factor markets and the development of a market-dominated economy was found first and foremost in coastal Flanders, Zeeland, and the Guelders river area from the fourteenth century, while regions such as Holland underwent these developments some two centuries later, and regions such as the Campine and Drenthe almost fully retained their

---

[89] See also this section, 284–6.
[90] See more extensively this section, 284–7, and section 5.3.
[91] Section 3.4, 138–40.

peasant character and observed hardly any rise of factor markets up to the nineteenth century.[92] The rise of factor markets was thus concentrated in specific regions. These interacted with each other, and also with the surrounding regions where factor markets remained more limited, especially through an intense exchange of output. Also, there was some exchange of labour, through immigration and migrant labour, and of capital. Further, entrepreneurs from the market cores bought up some land in other regions, as Holland entrepreneurs did in Drenthe, and Flemish investors in the northwest of Brabant.

It is striking to see, however, that this interaction did not lead to the convergence of regions through land, labour, or capital markets. The regions outside the market cores did not in any way become seamlessly incorporated in the market-dominated economy. Rather, the interaction sharpened the regional differences. The extent to which regions responded to growing markets varied according to the social context. Small-scale peasant producers, such as those in Drenthe and also in inland Flanders, were often less inclined to enter the output and factor markets, or did so in such a way that these markets were only complementary to a non-market socio-economic system,[93] whereas tenant farmers in regions dominated by leased large landholdings, including the Guelders river area, were compelled to do so, because they needed to maximize profits to compete in the lease market. The extent of involvement in the market also depended on the availability and viability of alternative systems of exchange, such as associations and families. Where associations were strong, as in Drenthe (villages, commons) or inland Flanders (guilds), and property was fairly equally distributed, further market-driven development was slowed, preventing markets from becoming fully dominant in the exchange of land, labour, and capital. The Guelders river area, on the other hand, experienced a swift and early transition to becoming a market economy, as a result of the dominance of large landed property and the easy availability of lease land, and the fact that horizontal associations were fairly weak there. Alternatives to market exchange were less easily available, and independent small-scale producers had fewer opportunities to shield themselves from the influence and (negative) effects of dominant markets and the ensuing market competition.

This regional diversity points to the fact that the rise of factor markets to dominance was not an automatic, self-evident process or one that attracted all people and areas right away, leading to a swift absorption of neighbouring regions into this market system, but a protracted and highly contested one, intrinsically linked to the interests of social groups and power balances. Within late medieval Europe, only northern Italy and the Low Countries saw a number of these regions grow into forming a larger area. The formation of this larger area, dominated by the market, was furthered in the Low Countries by the political unification process starting in the later Middle Ages. In the fifteenth and sixteenth centuries, the Burgundian-Habsburg regime was extending its power over the whole of the Low

---

[92] Van Bavel, *Manors and markets*, 378–406.
[93] Thoen, 'A "commercial survival economy"'. For the different use and effect of credit markets, for instance: Thoen and Soens, 'Appauvrissement et endettement'.

Countries and central authorities increased their influence at regional and local levels through legislation and the administration of justice, dismantling where possible the political influence exercised by associations at the local or regional level and thus—at least indirectly—promoting the rise of factor markets. Still, even in the Habsburg period, the position of the state was not strong enough to overrule all other interest groups and eradicate regional differences. A next step in this process was only taken with the Dutch Revolt, as the political regime of the Dutch Republic came to overlap more with the interests of the Holland merchant entrepreneurs and the link between the new market elites and political power thus became consolidated. Thus, the scale and scope of the process is determined not only by economic factors, but also by social and political factors, with the outcome becoming crystallized most clearly at the level of the state.

In England a somewhat similar development can be observed, including the regional differences. In a region such as Norfolk, the rural economy became commercialized in the Middle Ages, with the rise of intensive husbandry, and in the early modern period it saw the early rise of a market-dominated rural economy and an increase in scale in agriculture, while other regions, for instance in the Midlands, retained more of a peasant character or saw the rise of proto-industries.[94] However, some regional convergence occurred earlier in the cycle in England, also because the role of central government and central, nationwide legislation was stronger than in the Low Countries. Examples are the Poor Law and its effect on labour markets and the enclosure acts and their effects on land markets, thus promoting the convergence of regional developments. In this case, too, the cycle assumed a spatial character in relation to the dominant form of state organization, just as with the regions/principalities in the Low Countries and the city-states in Italy.

Industrialization also contributed to this convergence between regions, as trade and the importance of capital investments grew, and so, too, did spatial mobility and flexibility, compared to agriculture that by nature is more bound to the soil. Nevertheless, it is striking how long industrial development remained a regional phenomenon. This can be observed most clearly in the process of early modern proto-industrialization, which was tied in with the formulation and distribution of rights to land, and with the effect of rights to land on household formation and labour supply, and thus directly linked to regional structures. Even the Industrial Revolution was mainly a regional phenomenon, especially because many of the relevant social and institutional factors, including demographic ones, were linked to the use and possession of the land.[95] This may have changed after the Industrial Revolution and its immense leap forward in the scale and scope of capital goods, making regional structures linked to the land less important and reducing the region specificity of developments. Even though regional trajectories are still quite clearly discernible,[96] the convergence and uniformity within these cycles is now larger than ever before.

---

[94] Whittle, *The development of agrarian capitalism*, passim; Hudson, 'The regional perspective'.

[95] See the classic paper by Hudson, 'The regional perspective'.

[96] The regional dimension thus remains important in the analysis of present-day economic developments: Henning, Stam, and Wenting, 'Path dependence research in regional economic development'.

The Growing Scale and Influence of Market Cores

Together with this process, and further driven by technological development and growing mobility, there is another spatial effect, that is, the growing influence of the market cores over ever larger areas outside these cores, as noted above. The influence of market economies and their markets for land, labour, and capital over wider geographical areas increases over time. Roman Italy and early medieval Iraq still had fairly small cores of market economies, while their influence over larger areas was rather the result of the military power over their empires (the Roman and the Umayyad/Abbasid empire), and also of their output markets, than of factor markets. When labour from outside was needed by these market cores, it took the form of slaves or dependent labour rather than of wage labour hired through the labour market.

First with medieval Italy, where the cities and their surrounding countryside were joined through factor markets, and later in the case of the Low Countries and England, where larger regions were joined to each other through factor markets, and with the market cores affecting ever larger areas outside the cores, the influence of the capital and labour markets of these market economies increased. This process reached the most recent peak in the case of the United States, a market core that affects large parts of the globe. There is now a big, almost global influence of the market cores in labour markets, with the mobility of labour over large areas, and especially the hiring of wage labourers all over the world by companies from the cores, and even more in financial markets. Even in land markets this effect exists, with foreign capital finding an outlet in land and resource markets in Latin America and Africa. Further, the market cores acquire ever more direct military and diplomatic power, also through the international political, economic, and financial organizations they control or dominate, and thus are able to influence the organization and functioning of factor markets worldwide.[97] So, both economic and political-institutional developments affect ever larger areas.

The influence of the market core over other areas could, and can, also display more acute manifestations. Two of these are settlement and coercion or colonization. In the case of settlement, the social and institutional framework of the market core area in that particular phase of the cycle is likely to be transported to another, new area.[98] An example is the two main types of settlement originating from the northern parts of the Low Countries. One was from the beginning of its cycle, in the eleventh to thirteenth century, as settlers from those areas brought personal freedom, relative material equity, and broad political participation to the marshes of northern Germany which they reclaimed and inhabited.[99] The other was from the end of its cycle, in the seventeenth century, as the settlers from the northern parts of the Low Countries created a society on the southern tip of Africa which

---

[97] Arrighi, *The long twentieth century*, 14, 44–5, 300, and passim.
[98] A somewhat related argument for law: La Porta, Lopez-de-Silanes, and Shleifer, 'The economic consequences of legal origins'. See also Acemoglu, Johnson, and Robinson, 'The colonial origins', who additionally stress the role of settlement conditions.
[99] Van der Linden, *De cope*, 173–82.

was characterized by inequality, unfreedom, slavery, privileges, and monopolies.[100] English settlement in the American colonies in the seventeenth and eighteenth centuries is another, positive example, as the settlers brought with them the market institutions, and also their resentment of lordly arbitrariness and privileges, and their desire for freedom and equity, that all had been developing in England in the first phase of its cycle.

Colonization, or other forms of coercion through force, is a second type of influence exercised by the core over other areas. This type is predominantly found in the penultimate or ultimate phase of the cycle of the core, as capital was amply available, a new elite had emerged, this elite had become accustomed to using coercion, non-coercive outlets for accumulated capital lost their profitability, and there were plenty of mercenary wage labourers. All this is reflected in the process of colonization by the market cores, in which inequality, violence, coercion, and markets played a key role, be it in Cyprus colonized by Venice in the fourteenth and fifteenth centuries, the East Indies colonized by the Dutch Republic from the seventeenth century on, India colonized by Britain in the nineteenth century, and the United States 'colonizing', or at least coercing, Chile, Iraq, and a host of other areas from the late twentieth century. Some of the elements found there can also be found with non-market colonizers, but not the link to factor markets, the scope of financial organization, and the huge amounts of capital that can be mobilized by the colonizing market cores.

The effects are found in areas that are much weaker than the core, with the market core either settling or coercing or colonizing them. Another type of effect is found when the core is interacting with other market economies that are in another phase of their cycle. In the course of history, the interaction of such areas became ever more intense and, as a result, this interaction sometimes sped up the cycle. More advanced technology, infrastructure, and transport caused the interaction of new leading cases with the older ones to become more intense and the force of this interaction stronger. As a result, the old leaders which were in the last phase of the cycle sped up the pace of the cycle in the new ones, especially through the flows of accumulated capital.

The intensity of this process grew in the course of history. In the main cases investigated in the book, this kind of influence was still small. Developments in eleventh- and twelfth-century Italy were not influenced by the area where accumulation and coercion were most developed, Iraq, which was in the last phase of its cycle at that point. The only link was some market exchange of luxuries between the two areas, which may have sped up the process of commercialization in Italy a little, but this was all. Nor were the developments in the Low Countries during the fourteenth to sixteenth century much influenced by Italy, although some influence existed there, as with the Italian long-distance merchants and most notably the Lombards, who became active in the capital market in the Low Countries in the thirteenth century.[101] Through the capital they brought they sped up the rise of financial markets and gave princes opportunities for enhancing their central power.

---

[100] See section 4.4, 200.   [101] Section 4.2.

Developments in seventeenth-century England, being the next case, were even more sped up by influence from the Dutch Republic, which was in the last phase of its cycle at that point, through the Dutch invasion of 1688, the Dutch investments made in England, and the institutional innovations borrowed from the Dutch. While money from Venice and other Italian cities in their decadence had financed businesses in the Low Countries, in the eighteenth century financiers from Holland—having lost its commercial and industrial lead—lent large amounts of money to English entrepreneurs, as noted already by Karl Marx.[102] Even more clearly, developments in the eighteenth- and nineteenth-century United States were sped up by English influence, most notably through the flows of English capital to the United States in the second half of the nineteenth century. Likewise, the influence of the United States in the second half of the twentieth century has intensively influenced developments in northwest European countries.

Technology was, and is, a major factor behind this growth of scale. Technological innovation also pushed up the levels of GDP per capita and real wages, especially after the Industrial Revolution. However, although the technologies used became more advanced, the scale of developments bigger, and the economic level on which the cycle enacts higher, the essence of the cycle remains the same. At most, its intensity may be increasing with its scale. At a small scale, for instance within a local community where people meet each other face to face, moral sentiments, cooperative behaviour, and solidarity will likely play a more substantial role within market interaction than with more anonymous, impersonal exchanges on a global level.

As a result of this almost inevitable feedback cycle, factor markets may have a positive effect on economic growth in the short run, but in the longer run they do not have an outstanding track record in promoting economic growth and they have an outright negative effect on welfare. This process, and its chronology, also suggest that free markets, market dominance, equity, freedom, and material prosperity are not as closely or naturally connected as sometimes assumed. Rather, they are linked in very specific historical contexts, as most conspicuously in Italy, the Netherlands, England, and the United States in a particular, early phase of the cycle, but not generally. Moreover, the preceding suggests that freedom and equity come first in time, before free markets. The idea that free markets can be introduced, and that freedom and equity follow automatically, seems to be misguided. Instead, the dominance of factor markets is at the base of the erosion of equity and freedom in a later stage.

All this has implications for our understanding of the Great Divergence between 'the West and the rest' in economic development and the causes of the differences between rich and poor in the world today. The success of the West is perhaps not the result of the rise and functioning of factor markets per se, but rather of other factors found in some parts of the West, such as the social balance offered by many countervailing powers within society, the diversity of exchange and allocation

---

[102] Marx, *Capital* I, 755–6. See also section 5.1, 214; and for British capital in the United States: section 5.2, 227–8.

systems, the high degree of self-organization of ordinary people, and the bravery, and success, of people in revolt against arbitrariness and elite power. It is not factor markets that are the main point, but the social context surrounding these factor markets and determining their exact organization and their effects on economy and society.

This insight may have policy implications. The introduction or promotion of factor markets in developing countries, and a concomitant reduction of alternative mechanisms of exchange and allocation, such as the state, kinship systems, and communities, without having the right social context and a wide distribution of property and power, is bound to have mixed effects on the economy, at best, and negative effects on welfare. More generally, the above undermines any assumptions about the beneficial long-term effects of the rise of factor markets, especially since there is no correction mechanism to the negative feedback cycle analysed here—an insight which is equally instructive to the developed, Western world. None of the market economies in history has ever been able to produce such a mechanism. Accepting market developments and their effects as objective and natural, and the rise and influence of a market elite as logical or at most a kind of collateral damage, is unlikely to help us to generate such a mechanism now.

Bibliography

Note: names beginning with 'van' and 'de' are listed under the last name. Thus 'van Bavel' is listed under 'Bavel', etc.

Acemoglu, D., and Robinson, J. A., *Why nations fail: The origins of power, prosperity, and poverty* (New York, 2012).

Acemoglu, D., Johnson, S., and Robinson, J. A., 'The colonial origins of comparative development: An empirical investigation', *American Economic Review* 91 (2001), 1369–401.

Acemoglu, D., Johnson, S., and Robinson, J. A., 'Institutions as a fundamental cause of long-run growth', in P. Aghion and S. N. Durlauf (eds), *Handbook of Economic Growth* 1A (2005), 386–472.

Ackerberg, D. A., and Botticini, M., 'The choice of agrarian contracts in early-Renaissance Tuscany: Risk sharing, moral hazard, or capital market imperfections?', *Explorations in Economic History* 37 (2000), 241–57.

Adams, J., *The familial state: Ruling families and merchant capitalism in early modern Europe* (New York, 2005).

Adams, R. McC., *Land behind Baghdad: A history of settlement on the Diyala Plains* (Chicago, 1965).

Adams, R. McC., *Heartland of cities: Surveys of ancient settlement and land use on the central floodplain of the Euphrates* (Chicago/London, 1981).

Adams, R. McC., and Nissen, H. J., *The Uruk countryside: The natural setting of urban societies* (Chicago, 1972).

Adriaenssen, L. F. W., *Staatsvormend geweld: Overleven aan de frontlinies in de meierij van Den Bosch, 1572–1629* (Tilburg, 2007).

Ahsan, M. M., *Social life under the Abbasids, 170–289 AH, 786–902 AD* (London/New York, 1979).

Al-Hassan, A. Y., and Hill, D. R., *Islamic technology: An illustrated history* (Cambridge/Paris, 1986).

Al-Muqaddasi, *The best divisions for knowledge of the regions: A translation of Ahsan Al-Taqasim Fi Ma'Rifat Al-Aqalim*, tr. B. A. Collins (Reading, 1994).

Al-Qādī, W., 'Population census and land surveys under the Umayyads', *Der Islam* 83 (2006), 341–416.

Alfani, G., 'Population dynamics, Malthusian crises and Boserupian innovation in pre-industrial societies: The case study of northern Italy (ca. 1450–1800) in the light of Lee's "dynamic synthesis"', *Rivista di politica economica: Selected papers* 100 (2010), 23–57.

Alfani, G., 'Wealth, inequalities and population dynamics in early modern northern Italy', *Journal of Interdisciplinary History* 40 (2010), 513–49.

Alfani, G., 'The famine of the 1590s in northern Italy: An analysis of the greatest "system shock" of the sixteenth century', *Histoire and Mesure* 26 (2011), 17–50.

Alfani, G., and Ammannati, F., 'Economic inequality and poverty in the very long run: The case of the Florentine state', Dondena working paper 70 (2014).

Allen, R. C., *Enclosure and the yeoman: The agricultural development of the South Midlands, 1450–1850* (Oxford, 1992).

Allen, R. C., 'Economic structure and agricultural productivity in Europe, 1300–1800', *European Review of Economic History* 4 (2000), 1–25.

Allen, R. C., 'The great divergence in European wages and prices from the Middle Ages to the First World War', *Explorations in Economic History* 38 (2001), 411–47.

Altheim, F., and Stiehl, R., *Ein asiatischer Staat: Feudalismus unter den Sasaniden und ihren Nachbarn* (Wiesbaden, 1954).

Alvey, J. E., 'Adam Smith's three strikes against commercial society', *International Journal of Social Economics* 25 (1998), 1425–41.

Andreolli, B., *Contadini su terre di signori: Studi sulla contrattualistica agraria dell'Italia medievale* (Bologna, 1999).

Aperghis, G. G., *The Seleukid royal economy: The finances and financial administration of the Seleukid Empire* (Cambridge, 2004).

Appleby, J., 'Commercial farming and the "agrarian myth" in the early republic', *Journal of American History* 68 (1982), 833–49.

Appleby, J. O., *Economic thought and ideology in seventeenth-century England* (Princeton, 1978).

Arrighi, G., *The long twentieth century: Money, power, and the origins of our times* (London, 1996).

Arsenault, A., and Castells, M., 'Switching power: Rupert Murdoch and the global business of media politics: A sociological analysis', *International Sociology* 23 (2008), 488–513.

Ashtor, E., *A social and economic history of the Near East in the Middle Ages* (London, 1976).

Atack, J., 'America', in L. Neal and J. G. Williamson (eds), *The Cambridge history of capitalism* (Cambridge, 2014).

Avant, D., 'Private security companies', *New Political Economy* 10 (2005), 121–31.

Aylmer, G. E. (ed.), *The Levellers in the English Revolution* (London, 1975).

Aymard, M., 'From feudalism to capitalism in Italy: The case that doesn't fit', *Review: A Journal of the Fernand Braudel Center for the Study of Economies, Historical Systems and Civilizations* 6 (1982), 131–208.

Baerten, J., *De munten van de graven van Loon, 12de–14de eeuw* (Sint-Truiden, 1981).

Balestracci, D., 'Lavoro e povertà in Toscana alla fine del Medioevo', *Studi Storici: Rivista Trimestrale dell'Istituto Gramsci* 23 (1982), 565–82.

Balleisen, E., 'Vulture capitalism in Antebellum America: The 1841 federal bankruptcy act and the exploitation of financial distress', *Business History Review* 70 (1996), 473–516.

Banaji, J., *Agrarian change in late antiquity: Gold, labour and aristocratic dominance* (Oxford, 2007).

Banaji, J., 'Aristocracies, peasantries and the framing of the early Middle Ages', *Journal of Agrarian Change* 9 (2009), 59–91.

Bangs, J. D., 'Holland's civic lijfrente loans (XVth century): Some recurrent problems', *Publications du Centre Européen d'Études Burgondo Médianes* 23 (1983), 75–82.

Barbero, A., *Un'oligarchia urbana: Politica ed economia a Torino fra Tre e Quattrocento* (Viella, 1995).

Baron, H., 'Civic wealth and the new values of the Renaissance: The spirit of the Quattrocento', in H. Baron (ed.), *In search of Florentine civic humanism* I (1988), 226–57.

Bautier, A. M., 'Les plus anciennes mentions de moulins hydrauliques industriels et de moulins a vent', *Bulletin Philologique et Historique (Jusqu'a 1610) du Comité des Travaux Historiques et Scientifiques* 2 (1960), 567–626.

Bavel, B. J. P. van, 'Land, lease and agriculture: The transition of the rural economy in the Dutch river area from the fourteenth to the sixteenth century', *Past and Present* 172 (2001), 3–43.

Bavel, B. J. P. van, 'People and land: Rural population developments and property struc-tures in the Low Countries, c. 1300–c. 1600', *Continuity and Change* 17 (2002), 9–38.

Bavel, B. J. P. van, 'Early proto-industrialization in the Low Countries? The importance and nature of market-oriented non-agricultural activities in the countryside in Flanders and Holland, c. 1250–1570', *Revue Belge de Philologie et d'Histoire* 81 (2003), 1109–65.

Bavel, B. J. P. van, 'The land market in the North Sea area in a comparative perspective, 13th–18th centuries', in S. Cavaciocchi (ed.), *Il mercato della terra secc. XIII–XVIII: Atti delle 'Settimane di Studi' e altri convegni* 35 (Prato, 2003), 119–45.

Bavel, B. J. P. van, 'Rural wage labour in the sixteenth-century Low Countries: An assess-ment of the importance and nature of wage labour in the countryside of Holland, Guelders and Flanders', *Continuity and Change* 21 (2006), 37–72.

Bavel, B. J. P. van, 'The transition in the Low Countries: Wage labour as an indicator of the rise of capitalism in the countryside, 1300–1700', *Past and Present* 195 (2007), 286–303.

Bavel, B. J. P. van, 'The emergence and growth of short-term leasing in the Netherlands and other parts of northwestern Europe (eleventh-seventeenth centuries): A chronology and a tentative investigation into its causes', in B. J. P. van Bavel and P. Schofield (eds), *The development of leasehold in northwestern Europe, c. 1200–1600* (Turnhout, 2008), 179–213.

Bavel, B. J. P. van, 'The organization and rise of land and lease markets in northwestern Europe and Italy, c. 1000–1800', *Continuity and Change* 23 (2008), 13–53.

Bavel, B. J. P. van, 'Rural development and landownership in Holland, c. 1400–1650', in O. Gelderblom (ed.), *The political economy of the Dutch Republic* (Aldershot, 2009), 167–96.

Bavel, B. J. P. van, 'Rural revolts and structural change in the Low Countries, 13th–14th centuries', in R. Goddard, J. L. Langdon, and M. Müller (eds), *Survival and discord in medieval society: Essays in honour of Chris Dyer* (Turnhout, 2009).

Bavel, B. J. P. van, *Manors and markets: Economy and society in the Low Countries, 500–1600* (Oxford, 2010).

Bavel, B. J. P. van, 'The medieval origins of capitalism in the Netherlands', *Bijdrage en Mededelingen betreffende de Geschiedenis der Nederlanden* 125 (2010), 45–80.

Bavel, B. J. P. van, 'Markets for land, labor, and capital in northern Italy and the Low Countries, twelfth to seventeenth centuries', *Journal of Interdisciplinary History* 41 (2011), 503–31.

Bavel, B. J. P. van, 'New perspectives on factor markets and ancient Middle Eastern econo-mies: A survey', *Journal of the Economic and Social History of the Orient* 57 (2014), 145–72.

Bavel, B. J. P. van, 'History as a laboratory to better understand the formation of institu-tions', *Journal of Institutional Economics* 11 (2015), 69–91.

Bavel, B. J. P. van, and Frankema, E., 'Low income inequality, high wealth inequality: The puzzle of the Rhineland welfare states', CGEH working paper series 50 (2013).

Bavel, B. J. P. van, and Hoppenbrouwers, P. C. M., 'Landholding and land transfer in the North Sea area (late Middle Ages–19th century)', in B. J. P. van Bavel and P. C. M. Hoppenbrouwers (eds), *Landholding and land transfer in the North Sea area (late Middle Ages–19th century)* (Turnhout, 2004), 13–43.

Bavel, B. J. P. van, and Rijpma, A., 'How important were formalized charity and social spending before the rise of the welfare state? A long-run analysis of selected western European cases, 1400–1850', *Economic History Review* 69 (2016), 159–87.

Bavel, B. J. P. van, and Schofield, P. (eds), *The development of leasehold in northwestern Europe, c. 1200–1600* (Turnhout, 2008).

Bavel, B. J. P. van, and Zanden, J. L. van, 'The jump-start of the Holland economy during the late-medieval crisis, c. 1350–c. 1500', *Economic History Review* 57 (2004), 503–32.

Bavel, B. J. P. van, Campopiano, M., and Dijkman, J. E. C., 'Factor markets in early Islamic Iraq, c. 600–1100 AD', *Journal of the Economic and Social History of the Orient* 57 (2014), 262–89.

Bavel, B. J. P. van, Dijkman, J. E. C., Kuijpers, E., and Zuijderduijn, J., 'The organisation of markets as a key factor in the rise of Holland from the fourteenth to the sixteenth century: A test case for an institutional approach', *Continuity and Change* 27 (2012), 347–78.

Bavel, B. J. P. van, Moor, T. de, and Zanden, J. L. van, 'Introduction: Factor markets in global economic history', *Continuity and Change* 24 (2009), 9–21.

Béaur, G., and Schofield, P. (eds), *Property rights, land markets and economic growth* (Turnhout, 2012).

Beg, M. A. J., 'Agricultural and irrigation labourers in social and economic life of Iraq during the Umayyad and Abbasid caliphates', *Islamic Culture* 47 (1973), 15–30.

Beg, M. A. J., 'The "serfs" of Islamic society under the Abbasid regime', *Islamic Culture* 49 (1975), 107–18.

Bekar, C., and Reed, C., 'Land markets and inequality: Evidence from medieval England', *European Review of Economic History* 17 (2013), 294–317.

Belfanti, C. M., 'Rural manufactures and rural proto-industries in the "Italy of the cities" from the sixteenth through the eighteenth centuries', *Continuity and Change* 8 (1993), 253–80.

Belfanti, C. M., 'Town and country in central and northern Italy, 1400–1800', in S. R. Epstein (ed.), *Town and country* (Cambridge, 2001), 292–314.

Belich, J., *Replenishing the earth: The settler revolution and the rise of the Anglo-World, 1783–1939* (Oxford, 2008).

Ben Abdallah, H., *De l'iqta' étatique à l'iqta' militaire: Transition économique et changements sociaux à Baghdad, 247–447 de l'Hégire/861–1055 ap. J.* (Uppsala, 1986).

Benner, E., *Machiavelli's ethics* (Princeton, 2009).

Bentmann, R., and Müller, M., *Die Villa als Herrschaftsarchitektur: Versuch einer kunst- und sozialgeschichtlichen Analyse* (Frankfurt am Main, 1979).

Berents, D. A., 'Gegoede burgerij in Utrecht in de 15e eeuw', *Jaarboek Oud-Utrecht* (1972), 78–92.

Berkel, M. van, *Accountants and men of letters: Status and position of civil servants in early tenth century Baghdad* (Amsterdam, 2003).

Berkel, M. van, 'Embezzlement and reimbursement: Disciplining officials in Abbasid Baghdad (8th–10th centuries AD)', *International Journal of Public Administration* 34 (2010), 712–19.

Bertocchi, G., 'The vanishing bequest tax: The comparative evolution of bequest taxation in historical perspective', *Economics and Politics* 23 (2011), 107–31.

Bhaduri, A., 'Cropsharing as a labour process, size of farm and supervision cost', *Journal of Peasant Studies* 10 (1983), 88–93.

Bhandari, R., 'Slavery and wage labor in history', *Rethinking Marxism* 19 (2007), 396–408.

Bieleman, G. J. H., *Boeren op het Drentse zand, 1600–1910: Een nieuwe visie op de 'oude' landbouw* (Wageningen, 1987).

Bigwood, G., 'Les financiers d'Arras', *Revue Belge de Philologie et d'Histoire* 3 (1924), 465–508 and 769–819.

Bijsterveld, A. J. A., *Do ut des: Gift giving, memoria, and conflict management in the medieval Low Countries* (Hilversum, 2007).

Bijsterveld, A. J. A., and Trio, P., 'Van gebedsverbroedering naar broederschap: De evolutie van het fraternitas-begrip in de zuidelijke Nederlanden in de volle Middeleeuwen', *Jaarboek voor Middeleeuwse Geschiedenis* 6 (2003), 7–48.

Bimber, B., 'Three faces of technological determinism', in M. Roe Smith and L. Marx (eds), *Does technology drive history?* (1994), 79–100.

Blanshei, S. R., 'Perugia, 1260–1340: Conflict and change in a medieval Italian urban society', *Transactions of the American Philosophical Society, new series* 66 (1976).

Blickle, P., *Kommunalismus: Skizzen einer gesellschaftlichen Organisationsform* 2: *Europa* (Munich, 2000).

Blockmans, W. P., 'Nieuwe gegevens over de gegoede burgerij van Brugge in de 13e en vooral in de 14e eeuw', in W. P. Blockmans (ed.), *Studiën betreffende de sociale strukturen te Brugge, Kortrijk en Gent in de 14e en 15e eeuw* I (reprint *Standen en Landen* 54) (Heule, 1971), 133–54.

Blockmans, W. P., 'The Low Countries in the Middle Ages', in R. Bonney (ed.), *The rise of the fiscal state in Europe, c. 1200–1815* (Oxford, 1999), 281–308.

Blockmans, W. P., *Metropolen aan de Noordzee: De geschiedenis van Nederland, 1100–1560* (Amsterdam, 2010).

Blockmans, W. P., Pieters, G., and Prevenier, W., 'Het sociaal-economische leven 1300–1482: Tussen crisis en welvaart: Sociale veranderingen 1300–1500', in D. P. Blok and A. G. Weiler (eds), *Algemene geschiedenis der Nederlanden* IV (Haarlem, 1980), 42–86.

Blok, D. P., 'Beke's bron voor de Kennemer opstand', in G. N. M. Vis (ed.), *Egmond tussen kerk en wereld* (Hilversum, 1993), 225–8.

Blok, D. P., 'Drie boerenopstanden uit de dertiende eeuw', *Academiae Analecta* 56 (1994), 77–96.

Blondé, B., and Hanus, J., 'Beyond building craftsmen: Economic growth and living standards in the sixteenth-century Low Countries: The case of 's-Hertogenbosch (1500–1560)', *European Review of Economic History* 14 (2010), 179–208.

Bodenhorn, H., Guinnane, T. W., and Mroz, T. A., 'Problems of sample-selection bias in the historical heights literature: A theoretical and econometric analysis', Yale Economics Department working paper 114 (2013).

Bonner, M., 'Definitions of poverty and the rise of the Muslim urban poor', *Journal of the Royal Asiatic Society* 6 (1996), 335–44.

Boogaart, T. A., 'Reflections on the Moerlemaye: Revolt and reform in late medieval Bruges', *Revue Belge de Philologie et d'Histoire* 79 (2001), 1133–57.

Boone, M. H., and Brand, H., 'Vollersoproeren en collectieve actie in Gent en Leiden in de 14e en 15e eeuw', *Tijdschrift voor Sociale Geschiedenis* 19 (1993), 168–92.

Boone, M. H., and Prak, M., 'Rulers, patricians and burghers: The great and little traditions of urban revolt in the Low Countries', in C. A. Davids and J. M. W. G. Lucassen (eds), *A miracle mirrored: The Dutch Republic in European perspective* (Cambridge, 1995), 99–134.

Bos-Rops, J. A. M. Y., *Graven op zoek naar geld: De inkomsten van de graven van Holland en Zeeland, 1389–1433* (Haarlem, 1993).

Bosker, M., Buringh, E., and Zanden, J. L. van, 'From Baghdad to London: The dynamics of urban growth in Europe and the Arab world, 800–1800', CEPR discussion papers 6833 (2008).

Botticini, M., 'A tale of "benevolent" governments: Private credit markets, public finance, and the role of Jewish lenders in medieval and Renaissance Italy', *Journal of Economic History* 60 (2000), 164–89.

Botzem, S., and Quack, S., 'Contested rules and shifting boundaries', in M. L. Djelic and K. Sahlin (eds), *Transnational governance* (2006), 266–86.

Bowles, S., 'Machiavelli's mistake: Why good laws are no substitute for good citizens', Castle lectures, Yale University (2010).

Bowles, S., 'Is liberal society a parasite on tradition?', *Philosophy and Public Affairs* 39 (2011), 46–82.

Bowles, S., and Gintis, H., 'Contested exchange: Political economy and modern economic theory', *American Economic Review* 78 (1988), 145–50.

Bozhong, L., 'Was there a "fourteenth-century turning point"? Population, land, technology, and farm management', in P. Smith and J. von Glahn (eds), *The Song-Yuan-Ming transition in Chinese history* (Cambridge, 2003), 134–75.

Brandon, P., 'Marxism and the "Dutch miracle": The Dutch Republic and the transition-debate', *Historical Materialism* 19 (2011), 106–46.

Braudel, F., *Afterthoughts on material civilization and capitalism*, tr. P. M. Ranum (Baltimore, 1977).

Braudel, F., *Civilisation matérielle, économie et capitalisme, XVe– XVIIIe siècle* 2: *Les jeux de l'échange* (Paris, 1979).

Braudel, F., *Civilisation matérielle, économie et capitalisme, XVe– XVIIIe siècle* 3: *Le temps du monde* (Paris, 1979).

Brenner, R. P., 'The agrarian roots of European capitalism', *Past and Present* 97 (1982), 16–113.

Brenner, R. P., *The economics of global turbulence: The advanced capitalist economies from long boom to long downturn, 1945–2005* (London, 2006).

Brenner, R. P., 'Property and progress: Where Adam Smith went wrong', in C. Wickham (ed.), *Marxist history-writing for the twenty-first century* (Oxford, 2007), 49–111.

Bresson, A., *L'économie de la Grèce (fin VIe-Ier siècle a. C.)* 1: *Les structures et la production* (Paris, 2007).

Brezis, E. S., 'Foreign capital flows in the century of Britain's industrial revolution: New estimates, controlled conjectures', *Economic History Review* 48 (1995), 46–69.

Britnell, R. H., 'Commerce and capitalism in late medieval England: Problems of description and theory', *Journal of Historical Sociology* 6 (1993), 359–76.

Britnell, R. H., and Campbell, B. M. S. (eds), *A commercialising economy* (Manchester, 1995).

Broadberry, S., Campbell, B. M. S., Klein, A., Overton, M., and Leeuwen, B. van, *British economic growth, 1270–1870* (Cambridge, 2015).

Brusse, P., *Overleven door ondernemen: De agrarische geschiedenis van de Over-Betuwe, 1650–1850* (Wageningen, 1999).

Bulliet, R. W., *Cotton, climate, and camels in early Islamic Iran* (New York, 2009).

Caferro, W., 'City and countryside in Siena in the second half of the fourteenth century', *Journal of Economic History* 54 (1994), 85–103.

Caferro, W., *Mercenary companies and the decline of Siena* (Baltimore, 1998).

Caferro, W. P., 'Warfare and economy in Renaissance Italy, 1350–1450', *Journal of Interdisciplinary History* 39 (2008), 167–210.

Cahen, C., 'Le service de l'irrigation en Irak au début du XIe siècle', *Bulletin d'Études Orientales* 13 (1949), 117–43.

Cahen, C., 'L'évolution de l'iqta' du IXe au XIIIe siècle: Contribution à une histoire comparée des sociétés médiévales', *Annales: Économies, Sociétés, Civilisations* 8 (1953), 25–52.

Cahen, C., 'Fiscalité, propriété, antagonismes sociaux en Haute-Mésopotamie au temps des premiers 'Abbasides, d'après Denys de Tell-Mahré', *Arabica* 1 (1954), 136–52.

Cahen, C., 'Réflexions sur le waqf ancien', *Studia Islamica* 14 (1961), 37–56.

Cain, L. P., 'Entrepreneurship in the Antebellum United States', in D. S. Landes, J. Mokyr, and W. J. Baumol (eds), *The invention of enterprise: Entrepreneurship from ancient Mesopotamia to modern times* (Princeton, 2008), 331–66.

Campbell, B. M. S., 'Factor markets in England before the Black Death', *Continuity and Change* 24 (2009), 79–106.

Campopiano, M., 'Land tax alā l-misāa and muqasama: Legal theory and the balance of social forces in early medieval Iraq (6th–8th centuries C.E.)', *Journal of the Economic and Social History of the Orient* 54 (2011), 239–70.

Campopiano, M., 'Land tenure, land tax and social conflictuality in Iraq from the late Sasanian to the early Islamic period (fifth to ninth centuries)', in P. Sijpesteijn (ed.), *Authority and control in the countryside: Late antiquity and early Islam: Continuity and change in the Mediterranean 6th–10th century* (Leiden, 2012), 75–89.

Campopiano, M., 'State, land tax and agriculture in Iraq from the Arab conquest to the crisis of the Abbasid caliphate (seventh–tenth centuries)', *Studia Islamica* 3 (2012), 5–50.

Capasso, S., and Malanima, P., 'Economy and population in Italy', *SIDeS: Popolazione e Storia* 2 (2007), 15–40.

Carwardine, R. J., ' "Antinomians" and "Arminians": Methodists and the market revolution', in M. Stokes and S. Conway (eds), *The Market Revolution in America: Social, political and religious expressions, 1800–1880* (Charlottesville, VA, 1996), 282–307.

Casari, M., 'Emergence of endogenous legal institutions: Property rights and community governance in the Italian Alps', *Journal of Economic History* 67 (2007), 192–226.

Cavaciocchi, S. (ed.), *Il mercato della terra secc. XIII–XVIII* (Prato, 2003).

Chaci, A., 'Origin and development of commercial and Islamic banking institutions', *Journal of King Abdulaziz University: Islamic Economics* 18 (2005), 3–25.

Chandler, A. D., *The visible hand: The managerial revolution in American business* (Cambridge, 1977).

Chase, M., *Early trade unionism: Fraternity, skill, and the politics of labour* (Aldershot, 2000).

Chatterjee, P., *Halliburton's army: How a well-connected Texas oil company revolutionised the way Americans make war* (New York, 2009).

Cherubini, G., *Signori, contadini, borghesi: Ricerche sulla società italiana del basso Medioevo* (Florence, 1974).

Chittolini, G., 'Notes sur la politique fiscale de Charles Quint dans le duché de Milan: Le "nuovo catasto" et les rapports entre ville et campagne', in W. P. Blockmans and N. Mout (eds), *The world of Emperor Charles V* (Amsterdam, 2004), 143–60.

Clark, C., 'The agrarian context of American capitalist development', in M. Zakim and G. J. Kornblith, *Capitalism takes command: The social transformation of nineteenth-century America* (Chicago, 2012), 13–38.

Clark, E., 'Medieval labor law and English local courts', *American Journal of Legal History* 27 (1983), 330–53.

Clark, G., 'The political foundations of modern economic growth: England, 1540–1800', *Journal of Interdisciplinary History* 26 (1996), 563–88.

Clark, G., 'Debts, deficits and crowding out', *European Review of Economic History* 5 (2001).

Clark, G., 'The condition of the working class in England, 1209–2004', *Journal of Political Economy* 113 (2005), 1307–40.

Clarke, S., 'Marx and the market', paper presented at Centre for Social Theory, University of California (1995).

Cluse, C., *Studien zur Geschichte der Juden in den mittelalterlichen Niederlanden* (Hannover, 2000).

Cohen, A. C., *Athenian economy and society: A banking perspective* (Princeton, 1992).

Cohen, G. A., *Karl Marx's theory of history: A defence* (Princeton, 2000).

Cohen, H. J., 'The economic background and the secular occupations of Muslim jurisprudents and traditionalists in the Classical Period of Islam (until the middle of the eleventh century)', *Journal of the Economic and Social History of the Orient* 13 (1970), 16–59.

Cohen, J. N., '"Economic freedom" and economic growth: Questioning the claim that freer markets make societies more prosperous', MPRA paper 33758 (2011).

Cohn, S. K., 'The character of protest in Mid-Quattrocento', in *Il tumulto dei Ciompi: Un momento di storia fiorentina ed europea* (Florence, 1981), 199–221.

Cohn, S. K., *Creating the Florentine state: Peasants and rebellion, 1348–1434* (New York, 1999).

Cohn, S. K., Lust for liberty: The politics of social revolt in Medieval Europe, 1200–1425: Italy, France, and Flanders (Cambridge, 2006).

Cohn, S. K., 'After the Black Death: Labour legislation and attitudes towards labour in late-medieval western Europe', *Economic History Review* 60 (2007), 457–85.

Cohn, S. K., 'Revolts of the late Middle Ages and the peculiarities of the English', in R. Goddard, J. Langdon, and M. Müller (eds), *Survival and discord: Essays in honour of Christopher Dyer* (Turnhout, 2010), 269–85.

Collavini, S. M., 'La condizione giuridica', in *La signoria rurale* (Pisa, 2006), 331–84.

Conti, E., *La formazione della struttura agraria moderna nel contado Fiorentino* (Rome, 1965).

Cooper, J. P., 'Patterns of inheritance and settlement by great landowners from the fifteenth to the eighteenth centuries', in J. Goody, J. Thirsk, and E. P. Thompson (eds), *Family and inheritance: Rural society in western Europe, 1200–1800* (Cambridge, 1976), 192–327.

Crone, P., 'Zoroastrian communism', *Comparative Studies in Society and History* 36 (1994), 447–62.

Crouch, C., 'Privatised Keynesianism: An unacknowledged policy regime', *British Journal of Politics and International Relations* 11 (2009), 382–99.

Cull, R., Davis, L. E., Lamoreaux, N. R., and Rosenthal, J., 'Historical financing of small- and medium-sized enterprises', *Journal of Banking and Finance* 30 (2006), 3017–42.

Cumming, D., Siegel, D. S., Wright, W., 'Private equity, leveraged buyouts and governance', *Journal of Corporate Finance* 13 (2007), 439–60.

Curtis, D., 'Florence and its hinterlands in the late Middle Ages: Contrasting fortunes in the Tuscan countryside, 1300–1500', *Journal of Medieval History* 38 (2012), 472–99.

Curtis, D., *Coping with crisis: The resilience and vulnerability of pre-industrial settlements* (Farnham, 2014).

Curtis, D., and Campopiano, M., 'Medieval land reclamation and the creation of new societies: Comparing Holland and the Po Valley c. 800–c. 1500', *Journal of Historical Geography* 44 (2014), 93–108.

Dam, P. J. E. M., van, 'Digging for a dike: Holland's labor market ca. 1510', in P. Hoppenbrouwers and J. L. van Zanden (eds), *Peasants into farmers?* (Brepols, 2001), 220–55.

Dambruyne, J., *Corporatieve middengroepen: Aspiraties, relaties en transformaties in de 16de-eeuwse Gentse ambachtswereld* (Gent, 2002).

Dameron, G., 'Episcopal lordship in the Diocese of Florence and the Origins of the Commune of San Casciano Val di Pesa, 1230–1247', *Journal of Medieval History* 1 (1986), 135–54.

Daniel, E. L., 'Arabs, Persians, and the advent of the Abbasids reconsidered', *Journal of the Marican Oriental Society* 117 (1997), 542–8.

Daryaee, T., *Sasanian Persia: The rise and fall of an empire* (London, 2009).

Daunton, M., *Progress and poverty: An economic and social history of Britain, 1700–1850* (Oxford, 1995).

Daunton, M. J., *Trusting Leviathan: The politics of taxation in Britain, 1799–1914* (Cambridge, 2001).

Davids, C. A., *The rise and decline of Dutch technological leadership: Technology, economy and culture in the Netherlands, 1350–1800* (Leiden, 2008).

Davies, J. B., Sandström, S., Shorrocks, A. B., and Wolff, E. N., 'The level and distribution of global household wealth', NBER working papers 15508 (2009).

Day, J., *The medieval market economy* (Oxford, 1987).

Deligne, C., *Bruxelles et sa rivière: Genèse d'un territoire urbain (12e–18e siècle)* (Turnhout, 2003).

DeLong, J. B., 'Did J. P. Morgan's men add value? An economist's perspective on financial capitalism', in P. Temin (ed.), *Inside the business enterprise: Historical perspectives on the use of information* (Chicago, 1991), 205–36.

Demsetz, H., 'Toward a theory of property rights', *American Economic Review* 57 (1967), 347–59.

Derville, A., 'Les draperies flamandes et artésiennes vers 1250–1350: Quelques considerations critiques et problématiques', *Revue du Nord* 54 (1972), 353–70.

Derville, A., 'La finance Arragoise: Usure et banque', in M. M. Castellini and J. P. Martin (eds), *Arras au Moyen Âge: Histoire et littérature* (Paris, 1994), 37–52.

Derycke, L., 'The public annuity market in Bruges at the end of the fifteenth century', in M. Boone, K. Davids, and P. Janssens (eds), *Urban public debts: Urban government and the market for annuities in western Europe (14th–18th centuries)* (Turnhout, 2003), 165–82.

Devereux, M. P., Griffith, R., and Klemm, A., 'Corporate income tax reforms and international tax competition', *Economic Policy* 17 (2002), 449–95.

Devroey, J. P., *Le polyptyque et les listes de biens de l'abbaye Saint-Pierre de Lobbes (IXe–XIe siècles)* (Brussels, 1986).

Dhondt, J., 'Les "solidarités" médiévales: Une société en transition, la Flandre en 1127–1128', *Annales. Économies, Sociétés, Civilisations* 12 (1957), 529–60.

Didry, C., and Vincensini, C., 'Beyond the market-institutions dichotomy: The institutionalism of Douglass C. North in response to Karl Polanyi's challenge', HAL working papers halshs-00601544 (2011).

Dijkman, J. E. C., 'The fabric of society: The organization of textile manufacturing in the Middle East and Europe, c. 700–c. 1500', unpublished paper, Utrecht University (2011).

Dijkman, J. E. C., *Shaping medieval markets: The organisation of commodity markets in Holland, c. 1200–c. 1450* (Leiden, 2011).

Dokkum, H. W., and Dijkhof, E. C., 'Oude Dordtse lijfrenten', in L. M. Verloren van Themaat (ed.), *Oude Dordtse lijfrenten: Stedelijke financiering in de vijftiende eeuw* (Amsterdam, 1983), 37–90.

Dols, M. W., 'Plague in early Islamic history', *Journal of the American Oriental Society* 94 (1974), 371–83.

Donner, F. M., *The early Islamic conquests* (Princeton, 1981).

Dowd, D. F., 'The economic expansion of Lombardy, 1300–1500: A study in political stimuli to economic change', *Journal of Economic History* 21 (1961), 143–60.

Driel, G. van, 'Agricultural entrepreneurs in Mesopotamia', in H. Klengel and J. Renger, *Landwirtschaft im Alten Orient* (Berlin, 1999), 213–23.

Dumolyn, J., 'The legal repression of revolts in late medieval Flanders', *Tijdschrift voor Rechtsgeschiedenis* 68 (2000), 479–521.

Dumolyn, J., 'Dominante klassen en elites', *Jaarboek voor Middeleeuwse Geschiedenis* 5 (2002), 69–107.

Dumolyn, J., and Haemers, J., 'Patterns of urban rebellion in medieval Flanders', *Journal of Medieval History* 31 (2005), 369–93.

Dunaway, W. A., *The first American frontier: Transition to capitalism in southern Appalachia, 1700–1860* (Chapel Hill, NC, 1996).

DuPlessis, R. S., and Howell, M. C., 'Reconsidering the early modern economy: The cases of Leiden and Lille', *Past and Present* 94 (1982), 49–84.

Duri, A. A., *Arabische wirtschaftsgeschichte* (Zürich, 1979).

Duri, A. A., 'Baghdad', in C. E. Bosworth (ed.), *Historic cities of the Islamic world* (Leiden/Boston, 2007), 30–46.

Dyer, C., 'A redistribution of incomes in fifteenth-century England?', *Past and Present* 39 (1968), 11–33.

Dyer, C., *Standards of living in the later Middle Ages: Social change in England, c.1200–1520* (Cambridge, 1989).

Dyer, C., 'A note on calculation of GDP for 1086 and c. 1300', in R. H. Britnell and B. M. S. Campbell (eds), A *commercialising* economy: *England 1086* to c. *1300* (Manchester, 1995), 196–8.

Edwards, J., and Ogilvie, S., 'Contract enforcement, institutions, and social capital: The Maghribi traders reappraised', *Economic History Review* 65 (2012), 421–44.

Ehbrecht, W., 'Gemeinschaft, Land und Bund im Friesland des 12. bis 14. Jahrhunderts', in H. van Lengen (ed.), *Die Friesische Freiheit des Mittelalters—Leben und Legende* (Aurich, 2003), 135–93.

Ehrenkreutz, A. S., 'Studies in the monetary history of the Near East in the Middle Ages', *Journal of the Economic and Social History of the Orient* 2 (1959), 128–61.

Eichengreen, B., and Mitchener, K. J., 'The Great Depression as a credit boom gone wrong', *Research in Economic History* 22 (2004), 183–238.

Elbaum, B., and Lazonick, W., 'The decline of the British economy: An institutional perspective', *Journal of Economic History* 44 (1984), 567–83.

Elvin, M., *The pattern of the Chinese past* (Stanford, 1973).

Emigh, R. J., 'Loans and livestock: Comparing landlords' and tenants' declarations from the Catasto of 1427', *Journal of European Economic History* 25 (1996), 705–23.

Emigh, R. J., 'The spread of sharecropping: The political economy of transaction costs', *American Sociological Review* 62 (1997), 423–42.

Emigh, R. J., *The undevelopment of capitalism: Sectors and markets in fifteenth-century Tuscany* (Philadelphia, 2008).

Epperlein, C. S., *Bauernbedrückung und Bauernwiderstand im hohen Mittelalter* (Berlin, 1960).

Epstein, S. A., *Genoa and the Genoese, 958–1528* (Chapel Hill, 1996).

Epstein, S. R., 'Town and country: Economy and institutions in late-medieval Italy', *Economic History Review* 46 (1993), 453–77.

Epstein, S. R., 'The peasantries of Italy', in T. Scott (ed.), *The peasantries of Europe from the fourteenth to the eighteenth centuries* (London, 1998), 75–109.

Epstein, S. R., *Freedom and growth: The rise of states and markets in Europe, 1300–1750* (London, 2000).

Espinas, G., Jehan Boine Broke: Bourgeois et drapier Douaisien (?–1310 env.) (Leipzig, 1904).

Fasano-Guarini, A., 'Politique et population dans l'histoire des villes italiennes aux XVIe et XVIIe siècles', *Annales de Démographie Historique* (1982), 77–90.

Federico, G., and Malanima, P., 'Progress, decline, growth: Product and productivity in Italian agriculture, 1000–2000', *Economic History Review* 57 (2004), 437–64.

Feinman, G. M., and Garraty, C. P., 'Preindustrial markets and marketing: Archaeological perspectives', *Annual Review of Anthropology* 39 (2010), 167–91.

Feinstein, C., 'Pessimism perpetuated: Real wages and the standard of living in Britain during and after the Industrial Revolution', *Journal of Economic History* 58 (1998), 625–58.

Feller, L., 'Quelques problèmes liés à l'étude du marché de la terre durant le Moyen Âge', in S. Cavaciocchi (ed.), *Il mercato della terra secc. XIII–XVIII* (Prato, 2003), 21–45.

Feller, L., and Wickham, C., *Marché de la terre au Moyen Âge* (Rome, 2005).

Finley, M. I., *The ancient economy* (Berkeley/Los Angeles, 1973).

Fischel, W. J., 'The origin of banking in medieval Islam: A contribution to the economic history of the Jew of Baghdad in the tenth century', *Journal of the Royal Asiatic Society* (1933), 339–52 and 569–603.

Fischel, W. J., 'Neue Beiträge zur Geschichte der Juden Baghdads im islamischen Mittelalter', *Monatsschrift für Geschichte und Wissenschaft des Judentums* 5 (1937), 416–22.

Fischel, W. J., *Jews in the economic and political life of medieval Islam* (New York, 1969).

Fligstein, N., and Dauter, L., 'The sociology of markets', *Annual Review of Sociology* 33 (2007), 105–28.

Foldvari, P., and Leeuwen, B. van, 'Comparing per capita income in the Hellenistic world: The case of Mesopotamia', *Review of Income and Wealth* 58 (2012), 550–68.

Fontaine, L., *Le marché: Histoire et usages d'une conquête sociale* (Paris, 2014).

Forand, P. G., 'The status of the land and the inhabitants of the Sawad during the first two centuries of Islam', *Journal of the Economic and Social History of the Orient* 14 (1971), 25–37.

Formsma, W. J., 'Beklemrecht en landbouw: Een agronomisch-historische studie over het beklemrecht in Groningen in vergijking met ontwikkelingen elders', *Historia Agriculturae* 13 (1981), 7–135.

Forstner, M., *Das Kalifat des Abbasiden al-Musta'in* (Mains, 1968).

Francescoli, F., *Oltre il 'tumulto': I lavoratori fiorentini dell'Arte della Lana fra Tre e Quattrocento* (Florence, 1993).

French, H. R., and Hoyle, R. W., 'The land market of a Pennine manor: Slaidburn, 1650–1780', *Continuity and Change* 14 (1999), 349–83.

French, H. R., and Hoyle, R. W., 'English individualism refuted—and reasserted: The land market of Earls Colne (Essex), 1550–1750', *Economic History Review* 56 (2004), 595–622.

Frick, J. R., and Grabka, M. M., 'Wealth inequality on the rise in Germany', *German Institute for Economic Research* 10 (2009), 62–73.

Friedman, M., *Capitalism and freedom* (Chicago, 1962).

Fukuyama, F., *The end of history and the last man* (New York, 1992).

Fumagalli, V., 'L'evoluzione dell'economia agraria e dei patti colonici dall'alto al basso Medioevo: Osservazioni su alcune zone dell'Italia settentrionale', in B. Andreolli, V. Fumagalli, and M. Montanari (eds), *Le campagne italiane prima e dopo il Mille: Una società in trasformazione* (Bolgna, 1985), 95–132.

Garraty, C. P., 'Investigating market exchange in ancient societies: A theoretical review', in C. P. Garraty and B. L. Stark (eds), *Archaeological approaches to market exchange in ancient societies* (Boulder, CO, 2010), 3–32.

Gauthier, D., *Morals by agreement* (Oxford, 1986).

Gelderblom, O. C., *Zuid-Nederlandse kooplieden en de opkomst van de Amsterdamse stapel-markt (1578–1630)* (Hilversum, 2000).

Gelderblom, O. C., 'The Golden Age of the Dutch Republic', in D. S. Landes, J. Mokyr, and W. J. Baumol (eds), *The invention of enterprise: Entrepreneurship from ancient Mesopotamia to modern times* (Princeton, 2012), 156–82.

Gelderblom, O. C., and Jonker, J., 'Completing a financial revolution, the finance of the Dutch East India trade and the rise of the Amsterdam capital market, 1595–1612', *Journal of Economic History* 64 (2004), 641–72.

Gelderblom, O. C., and Jonker, J. P. B., 'Public finance and economic growth: The case of Holland in the seventeenth century', *Journal of Economic History* 71 (2011), 1–39.

Gelderblom, O. C., de Jong, A., and Jonker, J., 'An admiralty for Asia: Isaac le Maire and conflicting conceptions about the corporate governance of the VOC', ERIM report series research in management ERS-2010-026-F&A (2010).

Gemici, K., 'Karl Polanyi and the antinomies of embeddedness', *Socio-economic Review* 6 (2008), 5–33.

Genicot, L, *L'économie rurale Namuroise au bas moyen âge* (Louvain-la-Neuve/Brussels, 1982).

Ghazi, M. F., 'Un groupe social: "les raffinés" (zurafa')', *Studia Islamica* 9 (1957), 39–71.

Gianecchini, M., and Moggi-Cecchi, J., 'Stature in archeological samples', *American Journal of Physical Anthropology* 135 (2008), 284–92.

Ginatempo, M., *Prima del debito: Finanziamento della spesa pubblica e gestione del déficit nelle grandi città toscane* (Florence, 2000).

Glennie, P., 'In search of agrarian capitalism: Manorial land markets and the acquisition of land in the Lea Valley c. 1450–c. 1560', *Continuity and Change* 3 (1988), 11–40.

Godding, P., *Le droit foncier a Bruxelles au moyen âge* (Brussels, 1960).

Godding, P., and Pycke, J., 'La paix de Valenciennes de 1114', *Bulletin de la commission royale pour la publication des anciennes lois et ordonnances de Belgique* 29 (1979), 1–142.

Goldschmidt, N., and Wohlgemuth, M., 'Social market economy: Origins, meanings and interpretations', *Constitutional Political Economy* 19 (2008), 261–76.

Goldsmith, R. W., *Premodern financial systems: A historical comparative study* (New York, 1987).

Goldstone, J. A., 'Efflorescences and economic growth in world history: Rethinking the "rise of the west" and the Industrial Revolution', *Journal of World History* 13 (2002).

Goldthwaite, R., *Private wealth in Renaissance Florence: A study of four families* (Princeton, 1968).

Goldthwaite, R., *Wealth and the demand for art in Italy 1300–1600* (Baltimore, 1993).

Gordon, M. S., *The breaking of a thousand swords: A history of the Turkish military of Samarra (AH 200–275/815–889 CE)* (Albany, 2001).

Granovetter, M., 'Economic action and social structure: The problem of embeddedness', in R. Swedberg and M. Granovetter (eds), *The Sociology of Economic Life* (Boulder, 2001), 51–76.

Grapperhaus, F., *Alva en de tiende penning* (Zutphen, 1982).

Green, D. R., and Ownes, A., 'Gentlewomanly capitalism? Spinsters, widows, and wealth holding in England and Wales, c. 1800–1860', *Economic History Review* 56 (2003), 510–36.

Greif, A., 'Contract enforceability and economic institutions in early trade: The Maghribi traders' coalition', *American Economic Review* 83 (1993), 525–48.

Greif, A., 'On the political foundations of the late medieval commercial revolution: Genoa during the twelfth and thirteenth centuries', *Journal of Economic History* 54 (1994), 271–87.

Greif, A., 'The fundamental problem of exchange: A research agenda in historical institutional analysis', *European Review of Economic History* 4 (2000), 251–84.

Greif, A., 'History lessons: The birth of impersonal exchange: The community responsibility system and impartial justice', *Journal of Economic Perspectives* 20 (2006), 221–36.

Grotzfeld, H., Klimageschichte des Vorderen Orients 800–1800 A.D. nach arabischen Quellen, in R. Glaser, and R. Walsh (eds), *Historische Klimatologie in verschiedenen Klimazonen* (Würzburg, 1991), 21–43.

Guenzi, A., 'L'immigration urbain au XVe siècle: Bologne', *Annales de Démographie Historique* (1982), 33–42.

Hager, S. B., 'What happened to the bondholding class? Public debt, power and the top one per cent', *New Political Economy* 19 (2014), 155–82.

Halkos, G. E., and Kyriazis, N. C., 'The Athenian economy in the age of Demosthenes: Path dependence and change', *European Journal of Law and Economics* 29 (2010), 255–77.

Hall, P. A., and Soskice, D., 'An introduction to varieties of capitalism', in P. A. Hall and D. Soskice (eds), *Varieties of capitalism: The institutional foundations of comparative advantage* (Oxford, 2001), 1–69.

Hallaq, W. B., *Sharī'a: Theory, practice, transformations* (Cambridge, 2012).

Hanus, J., *Tussen stad en eigen gewin, Stadsfinanciën, renteniers en kredietmarkten in 's-Hertogenbosch (begin zestiende eeuw)* (Amsterdam, 2007).

Hart, M. C. 't, *The making of a bourgeois state: War, politics and finance during the Dutch revolt* (Manchester, 1993).

Hart, M. C. 't, 'The merits of a financial revolution: Public finance 1550–1700', in M. C. 't Hart, J. Jonker, and J. L. van Zanden (eds), *A financial history of the Netherlands 1550–1990* (Cambridge, 1997), 11–36.

Harvey, P. D. A. (ed.), *The peasant land market in medieval England* (Oxford, 1984).

Hayek, F. A., *The road to serfdom* (London, 1944).

Heidemann, S., 'Der Kleingeldumlauf in der Ghazīra in früh'abbāsidischer Zeit und die Münzemissionen aus al Kūfa', in S. Heidemann, and A. Becker (eds), *Raqqa* II: *Die islamische Stadt* (Mainz, 2003), 141–60.

Heidemann, S., 'The Agricultural Hinterland of Baghdad, al-Raqqa and Samarra: Settlement Patterns in the Diyar Mudar', in A. Borrut, M. Debié, A. Papaconstantinou, D. Pieri, and J. P. Sodini (eds), *Le Proche-Orient de Justinien aux Abbasides: Peuplement et dynamiques spatiales* (Turnhout, 2007), 43–58.

Heidemann, S., 'Die Renaissance der Städte im Vorderen Orient zur Zeit der Kreuzfahrer', in M. Pfaffenbichler (ed.), *Kreuzritter: Pilger, Krieger, Abenteurer* (Sankt Pölten, 2007), 34–43.

Heidemann, S., 'Numismatics', in C. F. Robinson (ed.), *New Cambridge History of Islam* I (2010), 648–63.

Heilbroner, R., 'Technological determinism revisited', in M. Roe Smith and L. Marx (eds), *Does technology drive history?* (1994), 67–78.

Heilbroner, R. L., 'The paradox of progress: Decline and decay in the wealth of nations', *Journal of the History of Ideas* 34 (1973), 243–62.

Henderson, J., *Piety and charity in medieval Florence* (Oxford, 1994).

Henning, M., Stam, E., and Wenting, R., 'Path dependence research in regional economic development: Cacophony or knowledge accumulation?', *Regional Studies* 47 (2013), 1348–62.

Herlihy, D., 'The agrarian revolution in southern France and Italy, 801–1150', *Speculum* 33 (1958), 23–41.

Herlihy, D., *Pisa in the early Renaissance: A study of urban growth* (New Haven, 1958).

Herlihy, D., 'Population, plague and social change in rural Pistoia, 1201–1430', *Economic History Review* 18 (1965), 225–44.

Herlihy, D., *Medieval and Renaissance Pistoia: The social history of a medieval town, 1200–1430* (New Haven, 1967).

Herlihy, D., and Klapisch-Zuber, C., *Les Toscans et leurs familles: Une étude du catasto florentin de 1427* (Paris, 1978).

Hill, C., *The world turned upside down* (London, 1972).

Hilton, R. H., 'Capitalism—what's in a name?', *Past and Present* 1 (1952), 32–43.

Hipkin, S., 'Tenant farming and short-term leasing on Romney Marsh 1587–1705', *Economic History Review* 53 (2000), 646–76.

Hodgson, G. M., 'Markets', in J. B. Davis and W. Dolfsma (ed.), *The Elgar companion to social economics* (2008), 251–66.

Hodgson, G. M., 'The great crash of 2008 and the reform of economics', *Cambridge Journal of Economics* 33 (2009), 1205–21.

Hodgson, G. M., *Conceptualizing capitalism: Institutions, evolution, future* (Chicago, 2015).

Hoffman, P. T., Postel-Vinay, G., and Rosenthal, J. L., *Priceless markets: The political economy of credit in Paris, 1660–1870* (Chicago, 2000).

Hoffmann, G., 'Al-Amin, al-Ma'mun und der "Pöbel" von Bagdad in den Jahren 812/813', *Zeitschrift der Deutschen Morgenländischen Gesellschaft* 143 (1993), 27–44.

Hopcroft, R. L., and Emigh, R. J., 'Divergent paths of agrarian change: Eastern England and Tuscany compared', *Journal of European Economic History* 29 (2000), 9–51.

Hoppenbrouwers, P. C. M., 'Rebels with a cause: The peasant movement of northern Holland in the later Middle Ages', in W. Blockmans and A. Janse (eds), *Showing status: Representation of social positions in the late Middle Ages* (Turnhout, 1999), 445–82.

Hoppenbrouwers, P. C. M., 'Town and country in Holland, 1300–1550', in S. R. Epstein (ed.), *Town and country in Europe, 1300–1800* (Cambridge, 2001), 54–79.

Hoppenbrouwers, P. C. M., 'The use and management of commons in the Netherlands: An overview', in M. de Moor, P. Sharpe, and L. Shaw-Taylor (eds), *The management of common land in northwest Europe, c. 1500–1850* (Turnhout, 2002), 87–112.

Horn, R. van, and Mirowski, P., 'The rise of the Chicago School', in P. Mirowski and D. Plehwe (eds), *The road from Mount Pèlerin* (Harvard, 2009).

Houtte, J. A. van, and Uytven, R. van, 'Wirtschaftspolitik und Arbeitsmarkt in den Niederlanden vom Spätmittelalter bis zur Schwelle des Industriezeitalters', in H. Kellenbenz (ed.), *Wirtschaftspolitik und Arbeitsmarkt* (Munich, 1974), 47–68.

Houtzager, D., *Hollands lijf- en losrenteleningen vóór 1672* (Schiedam, 1950).

Huang, P. C. C., *The peasant family and rural development in the Yangzi Delta, 1350–1988* (Stanford, 1990).

Hudson, P., 'The regional perspective', in P. Hudson (ed.), *Regions and industries: A perspective on the Industrial Revolution in Britain* (Cambridge, 1989).

Huertas, E., 'Between law and economy: "Divided property" and land rent market in Tuscany, twelfth–thirteenth centuries', in P. Schofield and G. Béaur (eds), *Property rights, land market and economic growth* (Turnhout, 2012).

Hunt, E. S., *The medieval super-companies: A study of the Peruzzi company of Florence* (Cambridge, 1994).

Ingham, G., *Capitalism divided? City and industry in British social development* (Basingstoke, 1984).

Innes, S. C., *Labor in a new land: Economy and society in seventeenth-century Springfield* (Princeton, NJ, 1983).

Isaacs, A., 'Le campagne senesi fra Quattro e Cinquecento: Regime fondiario e governo signorile', in G. Giorgetti (ed.), *Contadini e proprietari nella Toscana moderna: Atti del Convegno di Studi in Onore di Giorgio Giorgetti 1: Dal Medioevo all'età moderna* (Florence, 1979), 377–403.

Israel, J. I., *Dutch primacy in world trade, 1585–1740* (Oxford, 1990).

Issar, A. S., and Zohar, M., *Climate change; Environment and civilization in the Middle East* (Berlin, 2004).

Izdebski, A., 'Why did agriculture flourish in the late antique East?', *Millennium* 8 (2011), 291–312.

Jacks, D. S., 'Market integration in the North and Baltic Seas, 1500–1800', *Journal of European Economic History* 33 (2004), 285–329.

Jansen, H. P. H., *Landbouwpacht in Brabant in de 14e en 15e eeuw* (Assen, 1955).

Johansen, B., *The Islamic law on land tax and rent: The peasants' loss of property rights as interpreted in the Hanafite legal literature of the Mamluk and Ottoman periods* (London, 1988).

Johansen, B., 'Le contrat salam: Droit et formation du capital dans l'Empire abbasside (XIe–XIIe siècle)', *Annales: Histoire, Sciences Sociales* 61 (2006), 863–99.

Jones, P. J., 'From manor to mezzadria: A Tuscan case-study in the medieval origins of modern agrarian society', in N. Rubinstein (ed.), *Florentine studies* (London, 1968), 193–241.

Jones, P. J., *The Italian city-state: From commune to signoria* (Oxford, 1997).

Jong, A. de, Röell, A., and Westerhuis, G., 'Changing national business systems: Corporate governance and financing in the Netherlands, 1945–2005', *Business History Review* 84 (2010), 773–98.

Jongman, W., 'Rise and fall of the Roman economy', in P. Bang, M. Ikeguchi, and H. Ziche (eds), *Ancient economies—modern methodologies: Archaeology, comparative history, models and institutions* (Bari, 2007).

Jongman, W., 'The early Roman empire: Consumption', in W. Scheidel, I. Morris, and R. Saller (eds), *The Cambridge economic history of the Greco-Roman world* (Cambridge, 2008), 592–618.

Jursa, M., *Aspects of the economic history of Babylonia in the first millennium BC: Economic geography, economic mentalities, agriculture, the use of money and the problem of economic growth* (Münster, 2010).

Jursa, M., 'Factor markets in Babylonia from the late seventh to the third century BCE', *Journal of the Economic and Social History of the Orient* 57 (2014), 173–202.

Kabir, M., *The Buwayhid dynasty of Baghdad (334/946–447/1055)* (Calcutta, 1964).

Kalveen, C. A. van, 'Bijdrage tot de geschiedenis der gildenbewegingen te Utrecht, mei-augustus 1525', *Jaarboek Oud-Utrecht* 3 (1979), 54–86.

Katz-Nelson, J., *The patron's payoff: Conspicuous consumption* (Princeton, 2008).

Kennedy, H., *The early Abbasid caliphate: A political history* (London, 1981).

Kennedy, H., *The armies of the Caliphs: Military and society in the early Islamic State* (London/New York, 2001).

Ketelaar, F. C. J., 'Van pertinent register en ordentelijk protocol: Overdracht van onroerend goed in de tijd van de Republiek', *Ars notariatus* 32: *De levering van onroerend goed: Vijf opstellen over de overdracht van onroerend goed vanaf het Romeinse Recht tot het Nieuw Burgerlijk Wetboek* (Deventer, 1985), 39–56.

Khaldun, I., and Dawood, N. J. (ed.), *The Maqaddimah: An introduction to history*, tr. F. Rosenthal (London, 1978).

Kim, K., 'Adam Smith's theory of economic development', *European Journal of the History of Economic Thought* 16 (2009), 41–64.

Kirby, M.W., 'Institutional rigidities and economic decline: Reflections on the British experience', *Economic History Review* 45 (1992), 637–60.

Kirshner, J., and Molho, A., 'The dowry fund and the marriage market in early quattrocento Florence', *Journal of Modern History* 50 (1978), 403–38.

Kishimoto, M., 'Property rights, land, and law', in D. Ma and J. L. van Zanden (eds), *Law and long-term economic change: A Eurasian perspective* (Stanford, 2011), 68–90.

Klassen, P. J., *The economics of Anabaptism, 1525–1560* (The Hague, 1964).

Kleber, K., 'Famine in Babylonia: A microhistorical approach to an agricultural crisis in 528–526 BC', *Zeitschrift für Assyriologie* 102 (2012), 219–44.

Klein, N., *The shock doctrine: The rise of disaster capitalism* (New York, 2007).

Klein, P. W., *De Trippen in de 17e eeuw: Een studie over het ondernemersgedrag op de Hollandse stapelmarkt* (Assen, 1965).

Komlos, J., 'Shrinking in a growing economy? The mystery of physical stature during the Industrial Revolution', *Journal of Economic History* 58 (1998), 779–95.

Konig, D. T., *Law and society in Puritan Massachusetts: Essex County, 1629–1692* (Chapel Hill, 1979).

Korzeniewicz, R. P., and Moran, T. P., 'Theorizing the relationship', *Theory and Society* 34 (2005), 277–316.

Kovalev, R. K., and Kaelin, A. C., 'Circulation of Arab silver in medieval Afro-Eurasia: Preliminary observations', *History Compass* 5 (2007), 560–80.

Krader, L., *The Asiatic mode of production: Sources, development and critique in the writings of Karl Marx* (Assen, 1975).

Krippner, G. R., 'The financialization of the American economy', *Socio-Economic Review* 3 (2005), 173–208.

Kuchenbuch, L., *Bäuerliche Gesellschaft und Klosterherrschaft im 9. Jahrhundert: Studien zur Sozialstruktur der Familia der Abtei Prüm* (Wiesbaden, 1978).

Kulikoff, A., *The agrarian origins of American capitalism* (Charlottesville, 1992).

Kuran, T., 'The provision of public goods under Islamic law: Origins, impact, and limitations of the waqf system', *Law and Society Review* 35 (2001), 841–97.

Kuran, T., 'Islamic redistribution through zakat', in M. Bonner, M. Ener, and A. Singer (eds), *Poverty and charity in Middle Eastern contexts* (New York, 2008), 275–93.

Kuran, T., *The long divergence: How Islamic law held back the Middle East* (Princeton, 2010).

Kuran, T., 'Legal Roots of Authoritarian Rule in the Middle East: Civic Legacies of the Islamic Waqf', *American Journal of Comparative Law* 63 (in press).

Kussmaul, A., *Servants in husbandry in early modern England* (Cambridge, 1981).

Kuttner, E., *Het hongerjaar 1566* (Amsterdam, 1949).

Kuys, J. A. E., and Schoenmakers, J. T., *Landpachten in Holland, 1500–1650* (Amsterdam, 1981).

Kuznets, S., 'Economic growth and income inequality', *American Economic Review* 45 (1955), 1–28.

La Porta, R., Lopez-de-Silanes, F., and Shleifer, A., 'The economic consequences of legal origins', *Journal of Economic Literature* 46 (2008), 285–332.

Labib, S. Y., 'Capitalism in medieval Islam', *Journal of Economic History* 29 (1969), 79–96.

Lachmann, R., *Capitalists in spite of themselves: Elite conflict and economic transitions in early modern Europe* (Oxford, 2000).

Lamoreaux, N., 'Entrepreneurship in the United States, 1865–1920', in D. S. Landes, J. Mokyr, and W. J. Baumol (eds), *The invention of enterprise: Entrepreneurship from ancient Mesopotamia to modern times* (Princeton/Oxford, 2010), 401–42.

Landes, D. S., *The wealth and poverty of nations: Why some are so rich and some so poor* (London, 1998).

Lane, F. C., *Venice: A maritime republic* (Baltimore/London, 1973).

Lane, F. C., and Mueller, R., *Money and banking in medieval and renaissance Venice* (Baltimore, 1985).

Larson, J. L., *The market revolution in America: Liberty, ambition, and the eclipse of the common good* (Cambridge, 2010).

Lazonick, W., and O'Sullivan, M., 'Maximizing shareholder value: A new ideology for corporate governance', *Economy and Society* 29 (2000), 13–35.

Leemans, W. F., 'The role of land lease in Mesopotamia in the early second millennium BC', *Journal of the Economic and Social History of the Orient* 18 (1975), 134–45.

Leeuwen, M. H. D. van, 'Guilds and middle-class welfare, 1550–1800: Provisions for burial, sickness, old age, and widowhood', *Economic History Review* 65 (2012), 61–91.

Levi, G., *Le pouvoir au village: Histoire d'un exorciste dans le Pièmont du XVIIe siècle* (Paris, 1989).

Lewis, B., 'Sources for the economic history of the Middle East', in M. A. Cook, *Studies in the economic history of the Middle East: From the rise of Islam to the present day* (London, 1970).

Lewis, B., *The Middle East: A brief history of the last 2000 years* (New York, 1995).

Lillie, A., *Florentine villas in the fifteenth century: An architectural and social history* (New York, 2005).

Limberger, M., *Sixteenth-century Antwerp and its rural surroundings: Social and economic changes in the hinterland of a commercial metropolis, ca. 1450–ca. 1570* (Turnhout, 2008).

Linden, H. van der, *De cope: Bijdrage tot de rechtsgeschiedenis van de openlegging der Hollands-Utrechtse laagvlakte* (Alphen aan den Rijn, 1956).

Linden, H. van der, *Recht en territoir: Een rechtshistorisch-sociografische verkenning* (Assen, 1972).

Linden, H., van der, 'Het platteland in het noordwesten met nadruk op de occupatie circa 1000–1300', in D. P. Blok (ed.), *Nieuwe Algemene Geschiedenis der Nederlanden* II (Haarlem, 1982), 48–82.

Lindert, P. H., 'Poor relief before the welfare state: Britain versus the Continent, 1780–1880', *European Review of Economic History* 2 (1998), 101–41.

Lindert, P. H., *Growing public: Social spending and economic growth since the eighteenth century* 1: *The Story* (New York, 2004).

Lindert, P. H., and Williamson, J. G., 'American incomes before and after the revolution', *Journal of Economic History* 69 (2013), 725–65.

Lis, C., and Soly, H., *Poverty and capitalism in pre-industrial Europe* (Hassocks, 1979).

Lis, C., and Soly, H., 'Different paths of development: Capitalism in the northern and southern Netherlands during the late Middle Ages and the early modern period', *Review: A Journal of the Fernand Braudel Center for the Study of Economies, Historical Systems, and Civilizations* 20 (1997), 211–42.

Liu, W. G., *The Chinese market economy, 1000–1500* (New York, 2015).

Lo Cascio, E., and Malanima, P., 'GDP in pre-modern agrarian economies (1–1820 AD): A revision of the estimates', *Revista di Storia Economica* 25 (2009), 391–419.

Løkkegaard, F., *Islamic taxation in the classic period: With special reference to circumstances in Iraq* (Lahore, 1979).

Lottum, J. van, and Lucassen, J., 'Six cross-sections of the Dutch maritime labour market: A preliminary reconstruction and its implications (1607–1850)', in Richard Gorski (ed.), *Maritime labour: Contributions to the history of work at sea, 1500–2000* (Amsterdam, 2007), 13–42.

Löwith, K., *Weltgeschichte und Heilsgeschehen: Zur Kritik der Geschichtsphilosophie* (Stuttgart, 1983).

Lucassen, J., *Naar de kusten van de Noordzee: Trekarbeid in Europees perspektief, 1600–1900* (Gouda, 1984).

Lucassen, J., 'Deep monetisation: The case of the Netherlands', *Tijdschrift voor sociale en economische geschiedenis* 11(2014), 73–121.

Luzzati, M., 'Firenze e le origini della banca moderna', *Studi Storici* 28 (1987), 423–34.

Maat, G., 'Two millennia of male stature development and population health and wealth in the Low Countries', *International Journal of Osteoarchaeology* 15 (2005), 276–90.

Macfarlane, A., *The origins of English individualism: The family, property and social transition* (Oxford, 1979).

Macpherson, C. B., *The political theory of possessive individualism: Hobbes to Locke* (Oxford, 1964).

Maddison, A., *The world economy: A millennial perspective* (Paris, 2006).

Malanima, P., 'Industrie cittadine e industrie rurali nell'eta moderna', *Rivista Storica Italiana* 94 (1982), 247–81.

Malanima, P., 'Urbanisation and the Italian economy during the last millennium', *European Review of Economic History* 9 (2005), 97–122.

Malanima, P., 'Economy and population in Italy, 1300–1913', *Popolazione e Storia* 2 (2007), 15–40.

Malanima, P., 'Wages, productivity and working time in Italy, 1270–1913', *Journal of European Economic History* 36 (2007), 127–71.

Malanima, P., 'The long decline of a leading economy: GDP in central and northern Italy, 1300–1913', *European Review of Economic History* 15 (2011), 169–219.

Mancall, P. C., and Weiss, T., 'Was economic growth likely in colonial British North America?', *Journal of Economic History* 59 (1999), 17–40.

Margoliouth, D. S., *The table-talk of a Mesopotamian judge* (London, 1922).

Marlow, L., *Hierarchy and egalitarianism in Islamic thought* (Cambridge, 2002).

Marnef, G., *Antwerpen in de tijd van de Reformatie* (Amsterdam/Antwerpen, 1996).

Mårtensson, U., ' "It's the economy, stupid!" Al-Tabari's analysis of the freerider problem in the Abbasid caliphate', *Journal of the Economic and Social History of the Orient* 54 (2011), 203–38.

Martines, L., *Power and imagination: City-states in Renaissance Italy* (Baltimore, 1988).

Marx, K., *Capital* I: *An analysis of capitalist production* (Moscow, 1959).

Marx, K., and Engels, F., *Economic and philosophic manuscripts of 1844 and the Communist Manifesto* (Buffalo, 1988).

Mate, M., 'The economic and social roots of medieval popular rebellion: Sussex in 1450 to 1451', *Economic History Review* 45 (1992), 661–76.

Mauer, G., *Das Formular der altbabylonischen Bodenpachtverträge* (Munich, 1979).

Mayhew, N. J., 'The circulation and imitation of sterlings in the Low Countries', in N. J. Mayhew (ed.), *Coinage in the Low Countries (800–1500): The third Oxford symposium on coinage and monetary history* (Oxford, 1979), 54–68.

McArdle, F., *Altopascio: A study in Tuscan rural society, 1587–1784* (New York, 1978).

McCloskey, D. N., 'Other things equal: Polanyi was right and wrong', *Eastern Economic Journal* 23 (1997), 483–7.

McCloskey, D. N., *The bourgeois virtues: Ethics for an age of commerce* (Chicago, 2006).

McFarlane, A., *The British in the Americas 1480–1815* (London, 1994).

McNeill, W. H., *The pursuit of power: Technology, armed force, and society since AD 1000* (Chicago, 1982).

Meek, C., *Lucca 1369–1400: Politics and society in an early Renaissance state* (Oxford, 1978).

Melles, J., *Bisschoppen en bankiers: De eerste lombardiers in de lage landen, ±1260* (Rotterdam, 1962).

Mez, A. (ed.), *Abulâsim, ein bagdâder Sittenbild* (Heidelberg, 1902).

Mez, A., *Die Renaissance des Islam* (Heidelberg, 1922).

Micheau, F., 'Baghdad in the Abbasid era: A cosmopolitan and multi-confessional capital', in S. K. Jayyusi, R. Holod, A. Petruccioli, and A. Raymond (eds), *The city in the Islamic World* I (Leiden/Boston, 2008), 219–46.

Milanovic, B., 'Income level and income inequality in the Euro-Mediterranean region: From the Principate to the Islamic conquest', MPRA paper 46640 (2013).

Milanovic, B., 'The return of "Patrimonial Capitalism": A review of Thomas Piketty's Capital in the Twenty-First Century', *Journal of Economic Literature* 52 (2014), 519–34.

Milanovic, B., Lindert, P. H., and Williamson, J. G., 'Measuring ancient inequality', NBER working papers 13550, National Bureau of Economic Research (2007).

Moberg, L., 'The political economy of special economic zones', *Journal of Institutional Economics* 11 (2015), 167–90.

Mokyr, J., *The lever of riches: Technological creativity and economic progress* (New York, 1990).

Mokyr, J., 'Entrepreneurship and the Industrial Revolution in Britain', in D. S. Landes, J. Mokyr, and W. J. Baumol (eds), *The invention of enterprise: Entrepreneurship from ancient Mesopotamia to modern times* (Princeton, 2008), 183–210.

Mol, J. A., 'Hoofdelingen en huurlingen: Militaire innovatie en de aanloop tot 1498', in J. A. Frieswijk, A. H. Huussen, Jr., and Y. B. Kuiper (eds), *Fryslân, staat en macht 1450–1650: Bijdragen aan het historisch congres te Leeuwarden van 3 tot 5 juni 1998* (Hilversum/Leeuwarden, 1999), 65–84.

Molho, A., *Florentine public finance in the early Renaissance, 1400–1433* (Cambridge, 1971).

Molho, A., 'The state and public finance: A hypothesis based on the history of late medieval Florence', *Journal of Modern History* 67 (1995), 97–135.

Montanari, M., 'Mutamenti economico-sociali e trasformazione del paesaggio dall'alto al pieno Medioevo: Considerazioni sull'Italia Padana', in V. Fumagalli and G. Rossetti (eds), *Medioevo rurale: Sulle tracce della civiltà contadina* (Bologna, 1980), 79–97.

Moor, M. de, 'Common land and common rights in Flanders', in M. de Moor, L. Shaw-Taylor, and P. Warde (eds), *The management of common land in northwest Europe c.1500–1850* (Turnhout, 2002), 113–41.

Moor, T. de, 'The silent revolution: A new perspective on the emergence of commons, guilds, and other forms of corporate collective action in western Europe', *International Review of Social History* 53 (2008), 175–208.

Moor, T. de, Zanden, J. L. van, and Zuijderduijn, J., 'Micro-credit in late medieval Waterland: Households and the efficiency of capital markets in Edam en De Zeevang (1462–1563)', in S. Cavaciocchi (ed.), *La famiglia nell'economia europea. Secc. XIII–XVIII* (Florence 2009), 651–68.

Morony, M. G., 'Landholding in seventh-century Iraq: Late Sasanian and early Islamic patterns', in A. L. Udovitch (ed.), *The Islamic Middle East, 700–1900* (Princeton, 1981), 135–75.

Morony, M. G., *Iraq after the Muslim conquest* (Princeton, 1984).

Morony, M. G., 'Grundeigentum im frühislamischen Irak', in B. Brentjes (ed.), *Jahrbuch für Wirtschaftsgeschichte: Sonderband 1987: Das Grundeigentum in Mesopotamien* (Berlin, 1988), 135–47.

Muldrew, C., 'Credit and the courts: Debt litigation in a seventeenth-century urban community', *Economic History Review* 46 (1993), 23–38.

Muldrew, C., *The economy of obligation: The culture of credit and social relations in early modern England* (Basingstoke, 1998).

Muldrew, C., 'Interpreting the market: The ethics of credit and community relations in early modern England', *Social History* 18 (1993), 163–83.

Müller-Jentsch, W., 'Gewerkschaften und Korporatismus. Vom Klassenkampf zur Konfliktpartnerschaft', in K. C. Führer, J. Mittag, A. Schildt, and K. Tenfelde (eds), *Revolution und Arbeiterbewegung in Deutschland 1918–1920* (Essen, 2013), 81–96.

Munck, B. de, 'One counter and your own account: Redefining illicit labour in early modern Antwerp', *Urban History* 37 (2010), 26–44.

Munck, B. de, Lourens, P., and Lucassen, J., 'The establishment and distribution of craft guilds in the Low Countries, 1000–1800', in M. Prak, C. Lis, J. Lucassen, and H. Soly (eds), *Craft guilds in the early modern Low Countries: Work, power, and representation* (Aldershot, 2006), 32–73.

Munro, J. H., 'The medieval origins of the Financial Revolution: Usury, rentes, and negotiability', *International History Review* 25 (2003), 505–62.

Munro, J. H., 'Wage-stickiness, monetary changes, and real incomes in late-medieval England and the Low Countries, 1300–1500: Did money matter?', *Research in Economic History* 21 (2003), 185–297.

Munro, J. H., 'The usury doctrine and urban public finances in late-medieval Flanders (1220–1550): Rentes (annuities), excise taxes, and income transfers from the poor to the rich', in *La fiscalità nell'economia Europea, secc. XIII–XVIII, Fondazione Istituto Internazionale di Storia Economica* (2008), 973–1026.

Murphy, A. L., *The origins of English financial markets: Investment and speculation before the South Sea bubble* (Cambridge, 2009).

Murray, J. M., *Bruges: Cradle of capitalism, 1280–1390* (Cambridge, 2005).

Nee, V., and Ingram, P., 'Embeddedness and beyond', in M. Brinton and V. Nee (eds), *The new institutionalism in sociology* (1998), 19–45.

Neri, M., 'Perugia e il suo contado nei secoli XIII e XIV, interventi urbanistici e legislazione statuaria', *Storia della Città* 3 (1977), 28–37.

Nicholas, D., *Town and countryside: Social, economic, and political tensions in fourteenth-century Flanders* (Bruges, 1971).

Nicholas, D., 'Economic reorientation and social change in fourteenth century Flanders', *Past and Present* 70 (1976), 3–29.

Nicholas, D., *Medieval Flanders* (London, 1992).

Nicholas, D., 'Commercial credit and central place functions in thirteenth-century Ypres', in *Money, markets and trade in late medieval Europe: Essays in honour of John H. A. Munro* (Leiden, 2007), 310–48.

North, D. C., 'Markets and other allocation systems in history: The challenge of Karl Polanyi', *Journal of European Economic History* 6 (1977), 703–16.

North, D. C., *Structure and change in economic history* (New York, 1981).

North, D. C., *Institutions, institutional change and economic performance* (Cambridge, 1990).

North, D. C., and Thomas, R. P., *The rise of the western world: A new economic history* (Cambridge, 1973).

North, D. C., and Weingast, B. R., 'Constitutions and commitment: The evolution of institutions governing public choice in seventeenth-century England', *Journal of Economic History* 49 (1989), 803–32.

North, D. C., Wallis, J. J., and Weingast, B. R., *Violence and social orders: A conceptual framework for interpreting recorded human history* (Cambridge, 2009).

O'Brien, P. K., 'The costs and benefits of British imperialism 1846–1914', *Past and Present* 120 (1988), 163–200.

Oexle, O. G., 'Gilden als soziale Gruppen in der Karolingerzeit', in H. Jankuhn, W. Janssen, R. Schmidt-wiegand, and H. Tiefenbach (eds), *Das Handwerk in vor- und frühgeschichtlicher Zeit* 1: *Historische und rechtshistorische Beiträge und Untersuchungen zur Frühgeschichte der Gilde* (Göttingen, 1981), 284–354.

Oexle, O. G., 'Gilde und Kommune: Über die Entstehung von "Einung" und "Gemeinde" als Grundform des Zusammenlebens in Europa', in P. Blickle (ed.), *Theorien kommunaler Ordnung in Europa* (Munich, 1996), 75–97.

Offer, A., *Property and politics, 1870–1914: Landownership, law, ideology, and urban development in England* (Cambridge, 1981).

Ogilvie, S., ' "Whatever is, is right"? Economic institutions in pre-industrial Europe', *Economic History Review* 60 (2007), 649–84.

Ogilvie, S., and Carus, A. W., 'Institutions and economic growth in historical perspective', in P. Aghion and S. Durlauf (eds), *Handbook of economic growth* 2A (2014), 403–86.

Ogilvie, S., Küpker, M., and Maegraith, J., 'Household debt in early modern Germany: Evidence from personal inventories', *Journal of Economic History* 72 (2012), 134–67.

Olson, M., *The rise and decline of nations: Economic growth, stagflation, and social rigidities* (Yale, 1982).

Onacker, E. van, *Leaders of the pack? Village elites and social structures in the fifteenth- and sixteenth-century Campine area* (Turnhout, 2015).

Orhangazi, Ö., 'Financialisation and capital accumulation in the non-financial corporate sector: A theoretical and empirical investigation on the US economy: 1973–2003', *Cambridge Journal of Economics* 32 (2008), 863–86.

Origo, I., 'The domestic enemy: The Eastern slaves in Tuscany in the fourteenth and fifteenth centuries', *Speculum* 30 (1955), 321–66.

Osheim, D. J., 'Countrymen and the law in late-medieval Tuscany', *Speculum* 64 (1989), 317–37.

Ouerfelli, M., *Le sucre: Production, commercialisation et usages dans la Méditerranée médiévale* (Leiden/Boston, 2008).

Overton, M., *Agricultural revolution: The transformation of the agrarian economy 1500–1850* (Cambridge, 1996).

Pamuk, S., 'Changes in factor markets in the Ottoman Empire, 1500–1800', *Continuity and Change* 24 (2009), 1–30.

Pamuk, S., and Shatzmiller, M., 'Plagues, wages, and economic change in the Islamic Middle East, 700–1500', *Journal of Economic History* 74 (2014), 196–229.

Panero, F., *Terre in concessione e mobilità contadina: Le campagne fra Po, Sesia e Dora Baltea (secoli XII e XIII)* (Bologna, 1984).

Panero, F., 'Il lavoro salariato nelle campagne dell'Italia centro-settentrionale dal secolo XII all'inizio del Quattrocento', in A. Cortonesi, A. Nelli, and M. Montanari (eds), *Contratti agrari e rapporti di lavoro nell'Europa medievale: Atti del convegno internazionale di studi, Montalcino, 20–22 settembre* (Bologna, 2006), 1–24.

Peers Brewer, H., 'Eastern money and western mortgages in the 1870s', *Business History Review* 50 (1976), 356–80.

Pellat, C., *Le livre des avares de Gahiz* (Paris, 1951).

Perikhanian, A., 'Iranian society and law', in E. Yarshater (ed.), *The Cambridge History of Iran* III (Cambridge, 1983), 627–80.

Perol, C., *Cortona pouvoirs et sociétés aux confins de la Toscane* (XVe–XVIe siècle) (Rome, 2004).

Persson, K. G., *Grain markets in Europe, 1500–1900: Integration and deregulation* (Cambridge, 1999).

Phillips, K. P., *Boiling point: Democrats, republicans, and the decline of middle-class prosperity* (New York, 1993).

Pigulevskaja, N., *Les villes de l'etat ironien aux epoques parthe et sassanide* (Paris, 1963).

Piketty, T., *Capital in the twenty-first century* (Cambridge, 2014).

Pincus, S. C. A., *1688: The first modern revolution* (New Haven, 2009).

Pinto, G., 'I mercanti e la terra', in F. Cardini, M. Cassandro, G. Cherubini, G. Pinto, and M. Tangheroni (eds), *Banchieri e Mercanti di Siena* (Rome, 1987), 221–90.

Pinto, G., '"Honour" and "profit": Landed property and trade in medieval Siena', in T. Dean and C. Wickham (eds), *City and Countryside* (London, 1990), 81–91.

Pocock, J. G. A., *The Machiavellian moment: Florentine political thought and the Atlantic tradition* (Princeton, 1975).

Polanyi, K., *The great transformation: The political and economic origins of our time* (Boston, 2001).

Polanyi, K., and Pearson, H. W. (ed.), *The livelihood of man* (New York, 1977).

Pollard, S., 'Fixed capital in the Industrial Revolution in Britain', *Journal of Economic History* 24 (1964), 299–314.

Pomeranz, K., *The great divergence: China, Europe, and the making of the modern world economy* (Princeton, 2000).

Pomeranz, K., 'Land markets in late imperial and republican China', *Continuity and Change* 23 (2008), 101–50.

Pontusson, J., *Inequality and prosperity: Social Europe vs. liberal America* (New York, 2006).

Popovic, A., *The revolt of African slaves in Iraq in the 3rd/9th century* (Princeton, 1999).

Posthumus, N. W., *De geschiedenis van de Leidsche lakenindustrie* I (The Hague, 1908).

Prak, M., *Gezeten burgers: De elite in een Hollandse stad, Leiden 1700–1780* (Amsterdam, 1985).

Prak, M., *The Dutch Republic in the seventeenth century: The Golden Age* (Cambridge, 2005).

Pullan, B. S., *Rich and poor in Renaissance Venice: The social institutions of a catholic state, to 1620* (Oxford, 1971).

Rahman, F., 'Ribā and interest', *Islamic Studies* 3 (1964), 1–43.

Rao, R., 'I villaggi abbandonati nel Vercellese: Due crisi a confronto (secoli XIV–XVII)', *Popolazione e storia* 10 (2009), 39–56.

Ray, N. D., 'The medieval Islamic system of credit and banking: Legal and historical considerations', *Arab Law Quarterly* 12 (1997), 43–90.

Redan, O., 'Seigneurs et communautés rurales', *Mélanges de l'Ecole francaise de Rome* 91 (1979), 149–96 and 619–57.

Reichert, W., 'Lombarden zwischen Rhein und Maas: Versuch einer Zwischenbelanz', *Rheinische Vierteljahrsblatter* 51 (1987), 188–223.

Rezakhani, K., and Morony, M. G., 'Markets for land, labour and capital in late antique Iraq, AD 200–700', *Journal of Economic and Social History of the Orient* 57 (2014), 231–61.

Rigby, S. H., *Marxism and history: A critical introduction* (Manchester, 1999).

Robinson, C. F., *Empire and elites after the Muslim conquest: The transformation of northern Mesopotamia* (Cambridge, 2000).

Rodinson, M., *Islam and capitalism* (London, 1974).

Roine, J., and Waldenström, D., 'Common trends and shocks to top incomes: A structural breaks approach', *Review of Economics and Statistics* 93 (2011), 832–46.

Rossini, A., *Le campagne Bresciane nel cinquecento: Territorio, fisco, società* (Milan, 1994).

Rothenberg, W. B., 'The emergence of a capital market in rural Massachusetts, 1730–1838', *Journal of Economic History* 45 (1985), 781–801.

Rothenberg, W. B., 'The emergence of farm labor markets and the transformation of the rural economy: Massachusetts, 1750–1855', *Journal of Economic History* 48 (1988), 537–66.

Rubin, J., 'Institutions, the rise of commerce and the persistence of laws: Interest restrictions in Islam and Christianity', *Economic Journal* 121 (2011), 1310–39.

Sabari, S., *Mouvements populaires à Baghdad à l'époque 'Abbasside, IXe–XIe siècles* (Paris, 1981).

Sabbe, J., *Vlaanderen in opstand 1323–1328: Nikolaas Zannekin, Zeger Janszone en Willem de Deken* (Bruges, 1992).

Sabelberg, E., *Der Zerfall der Mezzadria in der Toskana Urbana: Entstehung, Bedeutung und gegenwärtige Auflösung eines agraren Betriebssystems in Mittelitalien* (Cologne, 1975).

Saito, O., 'Land, labour and market forces in Tokugawa Japan', *Continuity and Change* 24 (2009), 169–96.

Saker, V. A., 'Creating an agricultural trust: Law and cooperation in California, 1898–1912', *Law and History Review* 10 (1992), 93–129.

Savage, E., *A gateway to hell, a gateway to paradise: The North African response to the Arab conquest* (Princeton, 1997).

Scheffer, M., 'Complex systems: Foreseeing tipping points', *Nature* 467 (2010), 411–12.

Scheidel, W., 'The monetary systems of the Han and Roman empires', in W. Scheidel (ed.), *Rome and China: Comparative perspectives on ancient world empires* (New York, 2009), 137–207.

Schenk, G. J., ' "… prima ci fu la cagione de la mala provedenza de' Fiorentini …" Disaster and "life world": Reactions in the commune of Florence to the Flood of November 1333', *Medieval History Journal* 10 (2007), 86–355.

Scherman, M., 'La distribuzione della ricchezza in una città: Treviso e i suoi estimi del quattrocento (1434–1499)', in G. Alfani and M. Barbot (eds), *Ricchezza, valore, proprietà in età preindustriale, 1450–1800* (Venice, 2009), 169–84.

Schmidt, H., 'Hochmittelalterliche "Bauernaufstände" im südlichen Nordseeküstengebiet', in W. Rösener (ed.), *Grundherrschaft und bäuerliche Gesellschaft im Hochmittelalter* (Göttingen, 1995), 413–42.

Schofield, P. R., 'Access to credit in the early fourteenth century', in P. R. Schofield and N. J. Mayhew (eds), *Credit and debt in medieval England, c.1180–c.1350* (Oxford, 2002), 89–105.

Schofield, P. R., and Lambrecht, T. (eds), *Credit and the rural economy in northwestern Europe, c. 1200–c. 1850* (Turnhout, 2009).

Schulte, P., *Scripturae publicae creditur: Das Vertrauen in Notariatsurkunden im kommunalen Italien des 12. und 13. Jahrhunderts* (Tübingen, 2003).

Scott, J., *England's troubles: Seventeenth-century English political instability in European context* (Cambridge, 1999).

Sella, D., 'Household, land tenure and occupation in north Italy in the late sixteenth century', *Journal of European Economic History* 16 (1987), 487–509.

Sellers, C., *The market revolution: Jacksonian America, 1815–1846* (New York, 1991).

Sen, A., *Poverty and famines: An essay on entitlement and deprivation* (Oxford, 1988).

Sen, A., 'Uses and abuses of Adam Smith', *History of Political Economy* 43 (2011), 257–71.

Shatzmiller, M., *Labour in the medieval Islamic world* (Leiden, 1994).

Shatzmiller, M., 'Economic performance and economic growth in the early Islamic World', *Journal of the Economic and Social History of the Orient* 54 (2011), 132–84.

Shemesh, B., *Taxation in Islam* I (Leiden, 1958).

Shemesh, B., *Taxation in Islam* II (Leiden, 1965).

Shemesh, B., *Taxation in Islam* III (Leiden, 1969).

Shimizu, M., 'Les finances publiques de l'Etat "abbāsside"', *Der Islam* 42 (1965), 1–24.

Shiller, R. J., *Irrational exuberance* (Princeton, NJ, 2000).

Silva, P., 'Technocrats and politics in Chile: From the Chicago Boys to the CIEPLAN monks', *Journal of Latin American Studies* 23 (1991), 385–410.

Silver, M., 'Karl Polanyi and markets in the ancient Near East: The challenge of the evidence', *Journal of Economic History* 43 (1983), 795–829.

Sivéry, G., *Structures agraires et vie rurale dans le Hainaut à la fin du Moyen-Âge* (Lille, 1977).

Skopek, N., Buchholz, S., and Blossfeld, H. P., 'Wealth inequality in Europe and the delusive egalitarianism of Scandinavian countries', MPRA paper 35307 (2011).

Smith, A., *An inquiry into the nature and causes of the wealth of nations*, R. H. Campbell and A. S. Skinner (eds) (Oxford, 1976).

Smith, A., *An inquiry into the nature and causes of the wealth of nations*, W. B. Todd (ed.) (Oxford, 1979).

Smith, A. E., 'The indentured servant and land speculation in seventeenth century Mary-land', *American Historical Review* 40 (1935), 467–72.

Snooks, G. D., 'The dynamic role of the market in the Anglo-Norman economy and beyond, 1086–1300', in R. H. Britnell and B. M. S. Campbell (eds), *A commercialising economy* (Manchester, 1995), 27–54.

Soens, T., 'Polders zonder poldermodel? Een onderzoek naar de rol van inspraak en overleg in de waterstaat van de laatmiddeleeuwse Vlaamse kustvlakte (1250–1600)', *Tijdschrift voor Sociale en Economische Geschiedenis* 3 (2006), 3–36.

Soens, T., 'Floods and money: Funding drainage and flood control in coastal Flanders (13th–16th centuries)', *Continuity and Change* 26 (2011), 333–65.

Soens, T., 'Flood security in the medieval and early modern North Sea area: A question of entitlement?', *Environment and History* 19 (2013), 209–32.

Soens, T., and Thoen, E, 'The origins of leasehold in the former county of Flanders', in B. J. P. van Bavel and P. Schofield (eds), *The development of leasehold in northwestern Europe, c. 1200–1600* (Turnhout, 2008), 31–56.

Sokoloff, K. L., and Engerman, S. T., 'History lessons: Institutions, factor endowments, and paths of development in the New World', *Journal of Economic Perspectives* 14 (2000), 217–32.

Solar, P. M, 'Poor relief and English economic development before the Industrial Revolution', *Economic History Review* 48 (1995), 1–22.

Soltow, L., 'Annual inequality through four centuries: Conjectures for Amsterdam', in L. Soltow and J. L. van Zanden (eds), *Income and wealth: Inequality in the Netherlands 1500–1990* (Amsterdam, 1998), 77–110.

Sołtysiak, A., 'Preliminary report on human remains from Tell Ashara-Terqa: Seasons 2003–2004', *Athenaeum: Studi di Letteratura e Storia dell'Antichità* 95 (2007), 435–9.

Soly, H., 'The betrayal of the sixteenth-century bourgeoisie: A myth? Some considerations of the behaviour pattern of the merchants of Antwerp in the sixteenth century', *Acta Historae Neerlandicae* 8 (1975), 31–49.

Soly, H., *Urbanisme en kapitalisme te Antwerpen in de 16e eeuw: De stedebouwkundige en industriële ondernemingen van Gilbert van Schoonbeke* (Brussels, 1977).

Sosson, J. P., *Les travaux publics de la ville de Bruges XIVe–XVe siècles: Les matériaux: Les hommes* (Brussels, 1977).

Soto, H. de, *The mystery of capital: Why capitalism triumphs in the West and fails everywhere else* (New York, 2000).

Speet, B. M. J., 'Joden in het hertogdom Gelre', in J. Stinner, K. H. Tekath, and D. M. Oudesluijs (eds), *Gelre, Geldern, Gelderland, geschiedenis en cultuur van het hertogdom Gelre* (Utrecht, 2001), 337–42.

Spierenburg, P. C., 'Early modern prisons and the dye trade: The fate of convict rasping as proof for the insufficiency of the economic approach to prison history', *Economic and Social History in the Netherlands* III (1991), 1–17.

Spinelli, F., *I Lombardi in Europa* (Milano, 2006).

Spufford, P., *Money and its use in medieval Europe* (Cambridge, 1988).

Stabel, P., *De kleine stad in Vlaanderen: Bevolkingsdynamiek en economische functies van de kleine en secundaire stedelijke centra in het Gentse kwartier (14de–16de eeuw)* (Brussels, 1995).

Stabel, P., 'Guilds in late Medieval Flanders: Myths and realities of guild life in an export oriented environment', *Journal of Medieval History* 30 (2004), 187–212.

Stahl, A. M., *Zecca: The Mint of Venice in the Middle Ages* (Baltimore, 2000).

Steckel, R. H., 'Strategic ideas in the rise of the new anthropometric history and their implications for interdisciplinary research', *Journal of Economic History* 58 (1998), 803–21.

Steensgaard, N., *The Asian trade revolution of the seventeenth century: The East India Companies and the decline of the caravan trade* (Chicago/London, 1974).

Stegl, M., and Baten, J., 'Tall and shrinking Muslims, short and growing Europeans: The long-run welfare development of the Middle East, 1850–1980', *Explorations in Economic History* 46 (2009), 132–48.

Steinfeld, R. J., *The invention of free labor: The employment relation in English and American law and culture, 1350–1870* (Chapel Hill, 1991).

Steinkeller, P., 'The renting of fields in early Mesopotamia and the development of the concept of interest in Sumerina', *Journal of the Economic and Social History of the Orient* 24 (1981), 113–45.

Stella, A., *La révolte des Ciompi: Les hommes, les lieux, le travail* (Paris, 1993).

Steurs, W., 'Les franchises du duché de Brabant au Moyen Age', *Bulletin de la Commission Royale des Anciennes Lois et Ordonnances de Belgique* 25 (1972), 139–295.

Stiglitz, J. E., *Freefall: America, free markets, and the sinking of the world economy* (New York, 2010).

Stiglitz, J. E., *The price of inequality* (New York, 2012).

Stiglitz, J. E., Sen, A., and Fitoussi, J. P., *Report by the commission on the measurement of economic performance and social progress* (Paris, 2009).

Stol, T., *De veenkolonie Veenendaal: Turfwinning en waterstaat in het zuiden van de Gelderse Vallei, 1546–1653* (Zutphen, 1992).

Streeck, W., 'The crises of democratic capitalism', *New Left Review* 71 (2011), 5–29.

Streeck, W., and Schmitter, P. C., 'Community, market, state—and associations?', *European sociological review* 1 (1985), 119–38.

Swart, K. W., 'Holland's bourgeoisie and the retarded industrialization of the Netherlands', in F. Krantz and P. M. Hohenberg (eds), *Failed transitions to modern industrial society: Renaissance Italy and seventeenth century Holland* (Montreal, 1975), 44–8.

Sylla, R., 'Financial systems and economic modernization', *Journal of Economic History* 2 (2002), 279–92.

Taggart, R. A., Jr., 'The growth of the "junk" bond market and its role in financing take-overs', in A. Auerbach (ed.), *Mergers and acquisitions* (Chicago, 1987), 5–24.

Talhami, G. H., 'The Zanj rebellion reconsidered', *International Journal of African Historical Studies* 10 (1977), 443–61.

TeBrake, W. H., *A plague of insurrection: Popular politics and peasant revolt in Flanders, 1323–1328* (Philadelphia, 1993).

Temin, P., 'The labor market of the early Roman Empire', *Journal of Interdisciplinary History* 34 (2004), 513–38.

Terpstra, N., *Lay confraternities and civic religion in Renaissance Bologna* (Cambridge, 1995).

Thoen, E., *Landbouwekonomie en bevolking in Vlaanderen gedurende de late Middeleeuwen en het begin van de moderne tijden. Testregio: De kasselrijen van Oudenaarde en Aalst (eind 13de—eerste helft van de 16de eeuw)* (Gent, 1988).

Thoen, E., 'Le demarrage économique de la flandre au moyen age', in A. Verhulst and Y. Morimoto (eds), *Economie rurale et économie urbaine au Moyen Age: Landwirtschaft und Stadtwirtschaft im Mittelalter* (Gent, 1994).

Thoen, E., 'A "commercial survival economy" in evolution: The Flemish countryside and the transition to capitalism (Middle Ages–19th century)', in P. C. M. Hoppenbrouwers and J. L. van Zanden (eds), *Peasants into farmers? The transformation of rural economy and society in the Low Countries (Middle Ages–19th century) in light of the Brenner debate* (Turnhout, 2001), 102–57.

Thoen, E., and Soens, T., 'Appauvrissement et endettement dans le monde rural. Etude comparative du crédit dans les différents systèmes agraires en Flandre au bas Moyen Age et au début de l'Epoque Moderne', in S. Cavaciocchi (ed.), *Il mercato della Terra secc. XIII–XVIII* (Prato, 2004), 703–20.

Thompson, E. P., *The making of the English working class* (London, 1963).

Tierney, K. J., 'From the margins to the mainstream? Disaster research at the crossroads', *Annual Review of Sociology* 33 (2007), 503–26.

Tits-Dieuaide, M. J., *La formation des prix céréaliers en Brabant et en Flandre au XVe siècle* (Brussels, 1975).

Toch, M., 'Lords and peasants: A reappraisal of medieval economic relationships', *Journal of European Economic History* 15 (1986), 163–82.

Tomlins, L., *The state and the unions: Labour relations, law and the organized labor movement 1880–1960* (Cambridge, 1985).

Toubert, P., 'L'Italie rurale aux VIIIe–IXe siècles: Essai de typologie domaniale', in G. Arnaldi (ed.), *I problemi dell'Occidente nel secolo VIII* I (Spoleto, 1973), 95–132.

Tracy, J. D., *A financial revolution in the Habsburg Netherlands: Renten and renteniers in the county of Holland, 1515–1565* (Berkeley, 1985).

Tracy, J. D., 'On the dual origins of long-term debt in medieval Europe', in M. H. Boone, C. A. Davids, and P. Janssens (eds), *Urban public debts, Urban government and the market for annuities in western Europe (14th–18th centuries)* (Turnhout, 2003), 13–24.

Tucker, W. F., *Mahdis and Millenarians: Shiite extremists in early Muslim Iraq* (Cambridge, 2008).

Udovitch, A. L., 'Credit as a means of investment in medieval Islamic trade', *Journal of the American Oriental Society* 87 (1967), 260–4.

Udovitch, A. L., 'Labour partnerships in early Islamic law', *Journal of the Economic and Social History of the Orient* 10 (1967), 64–80.

Udovitch, A. L., *Partnership and profit in medieval Islam* (Princeton, 1970).

Udovitch, A. L., 'Reflections on the institutions of credit and banking in the medieval: Islamic Near East', *Studia Islamica* 41 (1975), 5–21.

Udovitch, A. L., *Bankers without banks: Commerce, banking and society in the Islamic world of the Middle Ages* (Princeton, NJ, 1981).

Unger, R. W., *A history of brewing in Holland, 900–1900: Economy, technology and the state* (Leiden, 2001).

Unger, R. W., 'Prices, consumption patterns and consumer welfare in the Low Countries at the end of the Middle Ages', *Jaarboek voor Middeleeuwse Geschiedenis* 8 (2005), 252–82.

Uytven, R. van, 'Plutokratie in de "oude demokratieën der Nederlanden"', *Koninklijke Zuidnederlandse Maatschappij voor Taal- en Letterkunde en Geschiedenis* 16 (1962), 373–409.

Uytven, R. van, 'Die ländliche Industrie während des Spätmittelalters in den südlichen Niederlanden', in H. Kellenbenz (ed.), *Agrarisches Nebengewerbe und Formen der Reagrarisierung im Spätmittelalter und 19./20. Jahrhundert* (Stuttgart, 1975), 57–77.

Vallance, E., *A radical history of Britain: Visionaries, rebels and revolutionaries: The men and women who fought for our freedoms* (London, 2009).

Vanhaute, E., 'From famine to food crisis: What history can teach us about local and global subsistence crises', *Journal of Peasant Studies* 38 (2011), 47–65.

Vercauteren, F., 'Note sur l'origine et l'évolution du contrat de mort-gage en Lotharingie du XIe au XIIIe siècle', in *Miscellanea historica in honorem Leonis van der Essen Universitatis tholicae in oppido Lovaniensi iamannos XXXV professoris* (Brussels, 1947), 217–27.

Violante, C., *La società Milanese nell'età precomunale* (Bari, 1953).

Violante, C., 'Quelques caractéristiques des structures familiales en Lombardie, Emilie et Toscane aux XIe et XIIe siècles', in G. Duby and J. le Goff (eds), *Famille et parenté dans l'occident médiéval* (Rome, 1977), 87–147.

Vogt, S., Glaser, R., Luterbacher, J., Riemann, D., Al Dyab, Gh., Schoenbein J., and Garcia-Bustamante, E., 'Assessing the medieval climate anomaly in the Middle East: The potential of Arabic documentary sources', *PAGES news* 19 (2011), 28–9.

Vries, S. de, 'Rederijkersspelen als historische dokumenten', *Tijdschrift voor Geschiedenis* 57 (1942), 185–98.

Vries, J. de, *The Dutch rural economy in the Golden Age: 1500–1700* (New Haven, 1974).

Vries, J. de, *European urbanization 1500–1800* (London, 1984).

Vries, J. de, 'The labour market', in K. Davids and L. Noordegraaf (eds), *The Dutch economy in the Golden Age: Nine studies* (Amsterdam, 1993), 55–78.

Vries, J. de, and Woude, A. M. van der, *The first modern economy, Success, failure, and perseverance of the Dutch economy, 1500–1815* (Cambridge, 1997).

Waines, D., 'The third century of internal crisis of the Abbasids', *Journal of the Economic and Social History of the Orient* 20 (1977), 282–306.

Waines, D., 'Cereals, bread and society: An essay on the staff of life in medieval Iraq', *Journal of the Economic and Social History of the Orient* 30 (1987), 255–85.

Waley, D., *The Italian city-republics* (London/New York, 1988).

Wallerstein, I., *Unthinking social science: The limits of nineteenth-century paradigms* (Cambridge, 1991).

Wallis, J. J., 'American government finance in the long run: 1790 to 1990', *Journal of Economic Perspectives* 14 (2000), 61–82.

Wang, H., 'Official salaries and local wages in Juyan, northwest China, first century BCE to first century CE', in J. Lucassen (ed.), *Wages and currency: Global comparisons from antiquity to the twentieth century* (Bern, 2007), 59–76.

Watson, A. M., 'The Arab agricultural revolution and its diffusion, 700–1100', *Journal of Economic History* 34 (1974), 8–35.

Weaver, J. C., *The great land rush and the making of the modern world, 1650–1900* (Montreal, 2003).

Wee, H. van der, *The growth of the Antwerp market and the European economy (fourteenth–sixteenth centuries)* (The Hague, 1963).

Wee, H. van der, 'Structural changes and specialization in the industry of the southern Netherlands, 1100–1600', *Economic History Review* 28 (1975), 203–21.

Wee, H. van der, 'Antwerp and the new financial methods', in H. van der Wee (ed.), *The Low Countries in the early modern world* (London, 1993), 145–66.

Wee, H. van der, 'Nutrition and diet in the ancient régime', in H. van der Wee (ed.), *The Low Countries in the early modern world* (London, 1993), 223–41.

Wells, R. V., 'The population of England's colonies in America: Old English or new Americans?', *Population Studies* 46 (1992), 85–102.

Werveke, H. van, 'Currency manipulation in the Middle Ages: The case of Louis de Male, count of Flanders', *Transactions of the Royal Historical Society* 4 (1949), 115–27.

Whittle, J. C., *The development of agrarian capitalism: Land and labour in Norfolk 1440–1580* (Oxford, 2000).

Whittle, J. C., 'Leasehold tenure in England c. 1300–c. 1600: Its form and incidence', in B. J. P. van Bavel and P. Schofield (eds), *The development of leasehold in northwestern Europe, c. 1200–1600* (Turnhout, 2008), 138–54.

Wichard, J. C., *Zwischen Markt und Moschee: Wirtschaftliche Bedürfnisse und religiöse Anforderungen im frühen islamischen Vertragsrecht* (Paderborn, 1995).

Wickham, C., *The mountains and the city: The Tuscan Apennines in the early Middle Ages* (Oxford, 1988).

Wickham, C., 'Rural communes and the city of Lucca at the beginning of the thirteenth century', in T. Dean and C. Wickham (eds), *City and countryside in late medieval and Renaissance Italy: Essays presented to Philip Jones* (London, 1990).

Wickham, C., 'Land sales and land market in the eleventh century', in C. Wickham, *Land and power: Studies in Italian and European social history, 400–1200* (London, 1994), 257–74.

Wickham, C., *Framing the early Middle Ages: Europe and the Mediterranean, 400–800* (Oxford, 2004).

Wiesehöfer, J., *Ancient Persia from 550 BC to 650 AD* (London/New York, 1996).

Williamson, C., *American suffrage from property to democracy, 1760–1860* (Princeton, 1986).

Williamson, J. G., *Did British capitalism breed inequality?* (London/NewYork, 2006).

Williamson, O. E., 'The new institutional economics: Taking stock, looking ahead', *Journal of Economic Literature* 38 (2000), 595–613.

Wood, A., *The 1549 rebellions and the making of early modern England* (Cambridge, 2007).

Wright, R. E., 'The first phase of the Empire State's "triple transition": Bank's influence on the market, democracy, and federalism in New York', *Social Science History* 21 (1997), 521–58.

Wyffels, C., 'L'usure en Flandre au XIIIe siècle', *Revue Belge de Philologie et d'Histoire* 69 (1991), 853–71.

Yanagihashi, H., *A history of the early Islamic law of property: Reconstructing the legal development, 7th–9th centuries* (Leiden/New York/Cologne, 2004).

Zamperetti, S., ' "Sinedri dolosi": La formazione e lo sviluppo dei corpi territoriali nello stato regionale Veneto tra '500 e '600', *Rivista Storica Italiana* 99 (1987), 269–320.

Zanden, J. L., *The long road to the Industrial Revolution: The European economy in a global perspective, 1000–1800* (Leiden/Boston, 2009).

Zanden, J. L. van, 'Economic growth in the Golden Age: The development of the economy of Holland, 1500–1650', in *The Dutch economy in the Golden Age: Nine studies* (Amsterdam, 1993).

Zanden, J. L. van, *The rise and decline of Holland's economy: Merchant capitalism and the labour market* (Manchester, 1993).

Zanden, J. L. van, 'Tracing the beginning of the "Kuznets curve", Western Europe during the early modern period', *Economic History Review* 48 (1995), 643–64.

Zanden, J. L. van, 'The paradox of the marks: The exploitation of commons in the eastern Netherlands, 1250–1850', *Agricultural History Review* 47 (1999), 125–44.

Zanden, J. L. van, 'Wages and the standard of living in Europe, 1500–1800', *European Review of Economic History* 3 (1999), 175–98.

Zanden, J. L. van, 'A third road to capitalism: Proto-industrialisation and the moderate nature of the late medieval crisis in Flanders and Holland, 1350–1550', in J. L. van Zanden and P. C. M. Hoppenbrouwers (eds), *Peasants into farmers? The transformation of rural economy and society in the Low Countries (Middle Ages–19th century) in the light of the Brenner debate* (Turnhout, 2001), 85–101.

Zanden, J. L. van, 'Taking the measure of the early modern economy: Historical national accounts for Holland in 1510/14', *European Review of Economic History* 6 (2002), 131–63.

Zanden, J. L. van, and Leeuwen, B. van, 'Persistent but not consistent: The growth of national income in Holland, 1347–1807', *Explorations in Economic History* 49 (2012), 119–30.

Zanden, J. L. van, and Riel, A. van, *The strictures of inheritance: The Dutch economy in the nineteenth century* (Princeton, NJ, 2004).

Zucman, G., 'Taxing across borders: Tracking personal wealth and corporate profits', *Journal of Economic Perspectives* 28 (2014), 121–48.

Zuijderduijn, C. J., 'Assessing the rural economy: Household wealth, economic traffic and the domestic market in Holland and Tuscany, 15th and 16th centuries', unpublished paper, Utrecht University (2007).

Zuijderduijn, C. J., 'Assets frozen in time: Intergenerational transfers, mobility of capital within families and economic growth in Italy and the Low Countries, 1000–1800', unpublished paper, Utrecht University (2009).

Zuijderduijn, C. J., *Medieval capital markets: Markets for renten, state formation and private investment in Holland (1300–1550)* (Leiden, 2009).

Index Locorum

Note: all page references relating to figures or tables are cited with the letter '*f*' or '*t*', respectively.

Index of Names

Note: all page references relating to figures or tables are cited with the letter '*f*' or '*t*', respectively.

General Index

Note: all page references relating to figures or tables are cited with the letter 'f' or 't', respectively

Printed in the USA/Agawam, MA
January 12, 2021

768207.056